THE HISTORY OF AL-ṬABARĪ

AN ANNOTATED TRANSLATION

VOLUME VIII

The Victory of Islam

MUḤAMMAD AT MEDINA

A.D. 626–630/A.H. 5–8

The History of al-Ṭabarī

Editorial Board

Ihsan Abbas, University of Jordan, Amman

C. E. Bosworth, The University of Manchester

Franz Rosenthal, Yale University

Everett K. Rowson, The University of Pennsylvania

Ehsan Yar-Shater, Columbia University (*General Editor*)

Estelle Whelan, *Editorial Coordinator*

Center for Iranian Studies
Columbia University

SUNY

SERIES IN NEAR EASTERN STUDIES

Said Amir Arjomand, Editor

The preparation of this volume was made possible in part by a grant from the National Endowment for the Humanities, an independent federal agency.

Bibliotheca Persica
Edited by Ehsan Yar-Shater

The History of al-Ṭabarī

(Ta'rīkh al-rusul wa'l-mulūk)

VOLUME VIII

The Victory of Islam

translated and annotated
by

Michael Fishbein

University of California, Los Angeles

State University of New York Press

Published by
State University of New York Press, Albany

Printed in the United States of America

For information, contact State University of New York Press, Albany, NY
www.sunypress.edu

Library of Congress Cataloging-in-Publication Data

Ṭabarī, 838?–923.
[Tārīkh al-rusul wa-al-mulūk. English. Selections]
The victory of Islam / translated and annotated by Michael Fishbein.
p. cm. — (SUNY series in Near Eastern studies) (The History of al-Ṭabarī = Ta'rīkh al-rusul wa'l-mulūk ; v. 8) (Bibliotheca Persica)
Includes bibliographical references (p.) and index.
ISBN 0-7914-3149-5 (alk. paper). — ISBN 0-7914-3150-9 (pbk. : alk. paper)
1. Islam—History. 2. Islamic Empire—History—622–661. 3. Muḥammad, Prophet, d. 632. I. Fishbein, Michael. II. Title. III. Series. IV. Series: Ṭabarī, 838–923. Tārīkh al-rusul wa-al-mulūk. English ; v. 8. V. Series: Bibliotheca Persica (Albany, N.Y.)
DS38.2.T313 1985 vol. 8
[BP55]
909'.097671—dc20 96-30872
CIP

10 9 8 7 6 5 4 3 2 1

Preface

The History of Prophets and Kings (*Ta'rīkh al-rusul wa'l-mulūk*) by Abū Ja'far Muḥammad b. Jarīr al-Ṭabarī (839–923), here rendered as *The History of al-Ṭabarī*, is by common consent the most important universal history produced in the world of Islam. It has been translated here in its entirety for the first time for the benefit of non-Arabists, with historical and philological notes for those interested in the particulars of the text.

In his monumental work al-Ṭabarī explores the history of the ancient nations, with special emphasis on biblical peoples and prophets, the legendary and factual history of ancient Iran, and, in great detail, the rise of Islam, the life of the Prophet Muḥammad, and the history of the Islamic world down to the year 915. The first volume of this translation contains a biography of al-Ṭabarī and a discussion of the method, scope, and value of his work. It also provides information on some of the technical considerations that have guided the work of the translators. The thirty-ninth volume is a compendium of biographies of early members of the Muslim community, compiled by al-Ṭabarī; although not strictly a part of his *History*, it complements it.

The *History* has been divided here into thirty-nine volumes, each of which covers about 200 pages of the original Arabic text in the Leiden edition. An attempt has been made to draw the dividing lines between the individual volumes in such a way that each is to some degree independent and can be read as such. The page numbers of the Leiden edition appear in the margins of the translated volumes.

Al-Ṭabarī very often quotes his sources verbatim and traces the chain of transmission (*isnād*) to an original source. The chains of transmitters are, for the sake of brevity, rendered by only a dash (—) between the individual links in the chain. Thus, "According to Ibn Ḥumayd—Salamah—Ibn Isḥāq" means that al-Ṭabarī received the report from Ibn Ḥumayd, who said that he was told by Salamah, who said that he was told by Ibn Isḥāq, and so on. The numerous subtle and important differences in the original Arabic wording have been disregarded.

The table of contents at the beginning of each volume gives a brief survey of the topics dealt with in that particular volume. It also includes the headings and subheadings as they appear in al-Ṭabarī's text, as well as those occasionally introduced by the translator.

Well-known place names, like Mecca, Baghdad, Jerusalem, Damascus, and the Yemen, are given in their English spellings. Less common place names, which are the vast majority, are transliterated. Biblical figures appear in the accepted English spelling. Iranian names are usually transcribed according to their Arabic forms, and the presumed Iranian forms are often discussed in the footnotes.

Technical terms have been translated wherever possible, but some, such as "dirham," and "imām," have been retained in Arabic forms. Others that cannot be translated with sufficient precision have been retained and italicized, as well as footnoted.

The annotation is aimed chiefly at clarifying difficult passages, identifying individuals and place names, and discussing textual difficulties. Much leeway has been left to the translators to include in the footnotes whatever they consider necessary and helpful.

The bibliographies list all the sources mentioned in the annotation.

The index in each volume contains all the names of persons and places referred to in the text, as well as those mentioned in the notes as far as they refer to the medieval period. It does not include the names of modern scholars. A general index, it is hoped, will appear after all the volumes have been published.

For further details concerning the series and acknowledgments, see Preface to Volume 1.

Ehsan Yar-Shater

Contents

Preface / v

Abbreviations / ix

Translator's Foreword / xi

The Events of the Year 5 (626/627) / 1

Muḥammad's Marriage to Zaynab bt. Jaḥsh / 1
The Expedition to Dūmat al-Jandal and Other Events / 4
The Battle of the Trench / 5
The Expedition against the Banū Qurayẓah / 27

The Events of the Year 6 (627/628) / 42

The Expedition against the Banū Liḥyān / 42
The Expedition to Dhū Qarad / 43
The Expedition against the Banū al-Muṣṭaliq / 51
An Account of the Lie / 57
The Prophet's Lesser Pilgrimage from Which the Polytheists Turned Him Back: The Story of al-Ḥudaybiyah / 67
A Report That Khālid b. al-Walīd Was Already a Muslim / 71
The Missions to Foreign Rulers / 98

The Events of the Year 7 (628/629) / 116

The Expedition to Khaybar / 116
The Expedition of the Messenger of God to Wādī al-Qurā / 124
The Affair of al-Ḥajjāj b. ʿIlāṭ al-Sulamī / 126
The Division of the Spoils of Khaybar / 128
Various Notices / 131
The Lesser Pilgrimage of Fulfillment / 133

The Events of the Year 8 (629/630) / 139

The Expedition against the Banū al-Mulawwiḥ / 139
Other Notices / 142
ʿAmr b. al-ʿĀṣ and Khālid b. al-Walīd Go to Medina as Muslims / 143
Other Events of the Year 8 of the Hijrah / 146
The Expedition of Dhāt al-Salāsil / 146
The Expedition Known as al-Khabaṭ / 147
Expeditions Involving Ibn Abī Ḥadrad and Abū Qatādah / 149
The Expedition to Mu'tah / 152
The Conquest of Mecca / 160
The Destruction of Idolatrous Shrines / 187
The Expedition against the Banū Jadhīmah / 188

Bibliography of Cited Works / 193

Index / 197

Index of Qur'ānic Passages / 215

Abbreviations

BSOAS: *Bulletin of the School of Oriental and African Studies*
EI[1]: *Encyclopaedia of Islam*, 1st edition. Leiden, 1913–42
EI[2]: *Encyclopaedia of Islam*, 2nd edition. Leiden, 1960–
GAS: F. Sezgin, *Geschichte des arabischen Schrifttums*, Leiden, 1967–
IH: Ibn Hishām, *Sīrat Rasūl Allāh*, ed. M. al-Saqqā et al., Cairo, 1936
W: al-Wāqidī, *Kitāb al-maghāzī*, ed. Marsden Jones, London, 1966

Translator's Foreword

This volume deals with the history of the Muslim community from A.H. 5 to the first part of A.H. 8, roughly the middle of A.D. 626 to the beginning of 630. During this time, the position of Muḥammad and of the community acknowledging his prophethood and following the religion embodied in the Qur'ān changed dramatically. At the beginning of the period the Meccan pagans with their allies mounted a direct attack against Medina; by the end of the period Mecca itself had capitulated, and most of its influential leaders had become at least nominal Muslims. Medina itself had become a purely Muslim polity. The last remaining Jewish tribe, the Banu Qurayẓah, had been defeated and annihilated, and the internal Arab opposition (the so-called "hypocrites" led by 'Abdallāh b. Ubayy) had disintegrated. There were signs that Muḥammad had begun to think about the future of Islam within and beyond the Arabian peninsula. Although the factual basis of the stories of Muḥammad's letters to the rulers of the Byzantine, Persian, and Ethiopian empires and their satellites in the Arabian peninsula during this period cannot be determined, Muslim military expeditions to destinations in northern Arabia (Dūmat al-Jandal and Khaybar) and the penetration into Byzantine territory that ended with the battle of Mu'tah give evidence of expanding political horizons. In short, although Muḥammad and Islam at the beginning of the period could still be seen as a local phenomenon, by the end of the period Muḥammad was, as one of his former opponents put it, "the king of the Ḥijāz."

Although the political developments of the period are well-documented in al-Ṭabarī's account, there is less material about the doctrinal development of Islam. Some incidents may have become part of the traditional biography of Muḥammad because of their ramifications for Islamic law. Muḥammad's marriage to the divorced wife of his adoptive son Zayd and the punishment meted out to those involved in spreading false rumors about the chastity of Muḥammad's young wife 'Ā'ishah had legal ramifications and as such merited inclusion, despite the sensitivity of the subject. The arrangements made concerning the conquered lands of Khaybar became important precedents for the treatment of conquered agricultural land in the early years of the caliphate and beyond. As for the letters to foreign rulers, one can say that they document the direction in which later Muslims believed Muḥammad's sense of universal mission developed during this period. Finally, the text of Muḥammad's speech after the conquest of Mecca contains interesting theological, as well as legal, material.

Muḥammad's Marriages

The marriage to Zaynab bt. Jaḥsh, with which al-Ṭabarī's account of the events A.H. 5 begins, was unlike Muḥammad's previous marriages. These had either cemented friendships with leading Muslims (such were the marriages to 'Ā'ishah bt. Abī Bakr in A.H. 1 and to Ḥafṣah bt. 'Umar in A.H. 3) or involved Muslim widows in need of support and protection (such were the marriages to Sawdah bt. Zam'ah, whom Muḥammad married while still at Mecca, Umm Salamah bt. al-Mughīrah in A.H. 4, and Zaynab bt. Khuzaymah in A.H. 4). At the time of his marriage to Zaynab bt. Jaḥsh, Muḥammad was married probably to four women (there is question about the date of his marriage to Juwayriyah, who was captured in a raid dated by al-Wāqidī in A.H. 5, but which al-Ṭabarī, following Ibn Isḥāq, places in A.H. 6). The account given by al-Ṭabarī, drawn from al-Wāqidī (who uses material from 'Ā'ishah) and the Egyptian scholar Yūnus b. 'Abd al-A'lā, but not from Ibn Isḥāq, portrays the marriage as growing out of strong physical attraction. Zaynab, who was Muḥammad's cousin, had been married by Muḥammad's arrangement to Muḥammad's freed slave Zayd b. Ḥārithah, who lived in Muḥammad's household and came to be regarded as his adoptive son—so that he was regularly addressed as Zayd, son of Muḥammad. Whether the marriage between Zayd and Zaynab was a *mésalliance* from the beginning is speculation, though the account maintains that Zayd was not reluctant to divorce his wife and allow her to marry Muḥammad. Muḥammad is portrayed as reluctant to proceed with the marriage because of scruples about whether marrying one's adopted son's former wife violated the prohibited degrees of marriage. Arab customary practice recognized kinship relations not based on blood ties: fosterage (having nursed from the same woman) was one such relationship; the question whether adoption fell into this category must have been unclear among Muslims. The marriage did not take place until after a Qur'ānic revelation was received, giving permission for believers to marry the divorced wives of their adopted sons. One can see this as part of the development of Islamic family law—a rejection of the legal fiction that a stepparent has a blood relationship with his ward that could affect the physical relationship of marriage. The account presented by al-Ṭabarī is forthright about the strength of the attraction and its role in the marriage. Similar frankness appears in the account in A.H. 6 of Muḥammad's marriage to Juwayriyah, "a sweet, beautiful woman, who captivated anyone who looked at her" (the words are 'Ā'ishah's). She had been captured during a raid on the Banū al-Muṣṭaliq and, in accordance with custom, became the slave of one of her captors. The latter agreed to free her in exchange for a sum of money. Juwayriyah approached Muḥammad for help, and the latter, captivated by her beauty, offered her "something better" than payment of the price of her freedom—namely, marriage with himself. Other marriages during this period were to Rayḥānah bt. 'Amr, captured in the attack on the Banū Qurayẓah in A.H. 5 (she apparently remained a concubine, rather than a full wife); Māriyah the Copt in A.H. 6 or 7 (she was a gift from the ruler of Egypt); Umm Ḥabībah bt. Abī Sufyān in A.H. 6 or 7 (she was the widow of a Muslim emigrant to Ethiopia); Ṣafiyyah bt. Ḥuyayy in A.H. 7 (she was captured in the conquest of Khaybar); and Maymūnah bt. al-Ḥārith in A.H. 7 (she was a widow and the sister-in-law of Muḥammad's uncle al-'Abbās; the marriage, contracted while Muḥammad was in a state of ritual consecration in connection with the lesser pilgrimage, had legal ramifications).

The Battle of the Trench (al-Khandaq)

The previous major engagement between the Muslims and the Meccan pagans, the battle of Uḥud, had ended inconclusively in Shawwāl of A.H. 3 (March 625). The Muslims had suffered heavier casualties than in any previous engagement (the figure seventy is given), but the Meccans also had suffered casualties and had returned home without pressing for a more decisive conclusion. Muslim morale had been badly shaken. The next major assault by the Meccans on Medina—it was to be the last—took place two years later, in Shawwāl of A.H. 5 (February 627). According to the composite account in al-Ṭabarī, the initial stimulus came from a group of Jews from the expelled Medinan tribe of Banū al-Naḍīr. They went to Mecca and promised to aid Quraysh against their common enemy, and they also enlisted the help of the north Arabian tribe of Ghaṭafān. Because the attack included these Jewish and north Arabian allies of the Meccans, it came to be known as the attack of "the Allied Parties" (*al-aḥzāb*). The Meccans and their allies considerably outnumbered the Muslims (the figure of 10,000 attackers against 3,000 Muslim defenders is given), and the Meccans had come with horses. The Meccan position, however, was less commanding than it might appear. The remaining Jews of Medina (the Banū Qurayẓah) sided only reluctantly with the attackers; Muḥammad thus was able to trick the Meccans into believing that the Medinan Jews intended to betray them. The allies from Ghaṭafān proved ready to be bought off by an offer of a third of the year's date harvest. Finally, employing a strategy suggested by a Persian convert, Salmān, the Muslims had constructed a defensive trench along the northern approaches to Medina (the southern approach, being mountainous, needed no fortification), and this trench could not be jumped by the Meccan horsemen. After nearly a month of standing in position, their provisions low and the weather taking its toll, the Meccans retreated, their morale broken. They never again attempted an assault on Medina.

The Attack on the Banū Qurayẓah

An immediate consequence of the failure of the Meccan attack was the extermination of the Jewish tribe of Banū Qurayẓah for their support of the Meccans, however lukewarm it had been.

Several motives for Muḥammad's behavior can be seen. There was strategic fear that the Banū Qurayẓah might continue to be open to the blandishments of their coreligionists. There was a religious element too. Although the Banū Qurayẓah were clients of the Arab tribe of al-Aws, the leader of al-Aws deputed to pass judgment on them (Sa'd b. Mu'ādh) decided to reject the claims of the Banū Qurayẓah as his clients and to act "for the sake of God." This seems to indicate a feeling that the continued religious opposition of the Jews made coexistence with them within Medina impossible. The brutality of the punishment (extermination of all adult males, rather than expulsion or enslavement) points to darker motives of ethnic hatred and vengeance, and this dark side can be seen in the fury with which the attack was launched. According to the account from Ibn Isḥāq, the Angel Gabriel himself came to Muḥammad immediately after the withdrawal of Quraysh and forbade him to lay down his arms: he was to hasten immediately to attack the Banū Qurayẓah, and the angels would fight also. This supernatural element indicates something beyond political calculation. It also points to the fact that the treatment of the Banū Qurayẓah was unique and did not become a precedent for subsequent Muslim treatment of the Jews, which, as demonstrated by the fate of the Jews of Khaybar in A.H. 7, was more lenient. Although the Jews of Khaybar had been involved in compromising relations with the Meccan pagans, they were allowed to remain on their land and work it as sharecroppers for their new Muslim overlords. Only in the caliphate of 'Umar were they forced to leave, and then as free men.

The Slander against 'Ā'ishah

The events of A.H. 6 included a number of expeditions. The expedition against the Banū Liḥyān, allies of Quraysh, involved a considerable force of men sent to avenge the murder of a number of Muslims. The expedition to Dhū Qarad was in reprisal for a raid by Ghaṭafān. The expedition to al-Muraysī' against the Banū al-Muṣṭaliq can be seen as a demonstration of Muslim control of the coastal caravan route to Syria. The military and political aspects of the raid were, however, overshadowed by an incident involving Muḥammad's young wife 'Ā'ishah. The first-person narrative by

'Ā'ishah of how she accidentally was left behind by the returning Muslim caravan, her rescue by a young Muslim rider, the rumors that this generated, and her eventual vindication in a Qur'ānic revelation forms one of the most interesting narratives of this section of al-Ṭabarī. 'Ā'ishah, who must have told the story to a scholar years later (note her asides about how little she weighed at the time, how insignificant she felt herself to be, and the primitive toilet arrangements in Medina), comes across as a talented *raconteuse*, with a good deal of psychological finesse and a sense of time's changes. The narrative deserves careful literary, as well as historical, attention.

Relations with Mecca from al-Ḥudaybiyah to the Conquest

In Dhū al-Qa'dah of A.H. 6 (March-April 628), about a year after the Meccan retreat from Medina after the battle of the Trench, Muḥammad decided to set out with a body of his followers to perform the rites of the lesser pilgrimage (*'umrah*) in Mecca. The framework of al-Ṭabarī's account of the episode is drawn from Ibn Isḥāq, with added details from a variety of other sources. For all its richness, it says almost nothing about Muḥammad's motives or the political calculations involved. Al-Wāqidī's account (W, II, 572) attributes the initial inspiration to a dream, but al-Ṭabarī does not include this detail. Under customary Arab religious practice the Meccans should have allowed the pilgrimage. The months of Dhū al-Qa'dah and Dhū al-Ḥijjah were sacred months in which fighting was banned, and Mecca itself was sacred territory throughout the year. However, the Muslims had been known to violate the sacred months, and the attitude of the new religion toward the Meccan sanctuary, bound up as it was with the old pagan dispensation, must have been a matter of question to the Meccans. On the other hand, such a pilgrimage implied that Islam did not intend to do away with Mecca's religious significance and that a modus vivendi might even be reached between Mecca and the Muslim community. The extent to which Muḥammad expected the Meccans to come round to his side, now that they had apparently despaired of conquering Medina, cannot be determined from the account. He traveled in pilgrim garb and brought animals for sacrifice to demonstrate his peaceful intentions, but he also traveled with a large party of men, which, according to one account, was armed. The Meccans put up a show of force and blocked the main road. Muḥammad managed to evade them, cross a difficult pass, and encamp on the border of the Meccan sacred territory, at al-Ḥudaybiyah, but he did not attempt to enter. Messengers came and went between the two sides, and eventually a compromise was reached, although there were tense moments when rumors of Meccan treachery against the Muslim negotiators spread and it seemed that the negotiations would break down. At one such moment, Muḥammad summoned his followers to renew their allegiance to him in what came to be known as "the Pledge of Good Pleasure" (*bayʿat al-riḍwān*). The agreement finally reached at al-Ḥudaybiyah between Muḥammad and the Meccans contained something for each side. Muḥammad agreed to a ten-year halt to hostilities against Mecca. The Meccans could therefore resume the caravan trade to Syria on which their economy was based but were bound not to attack the Muslims. In return, they agreed to allow Muḥammad to make the pilgrimage the following year, provided that he came unarmed and stayed only three nights. Muḥammad, for his part, agreed not to accept converts who came from Mecca without the permission of their guardians. In return for this concession, the Meccans agreed to allow any Arab tribes who desired to ally themselves with Muḥammad to do so, even if by implication this meant abandoning a previous alliance with Quraysh. In effect, Muḥammad had extracted recognition as an equal from Quraysh. Although some members of the community showed their disappointment at turning back without entering Mecca, the disappointment gave rise to no organized opposition. The days of the "hypocrites" were over. In any case, a series of expeditions, climaxing in the conquest of the oasis of Khaybar to the north, diverted the attention of the community. In the following year, Muḥammad made the lesser pilgrimage unopposed.

According to the sources used by al-Ṭabarī, within a month after the conclusion of the Treaty of al-Ḥudaybiyah Muḥammad dispatched letters to six foreign rulers, inviting them to become

Muslims. The implication is that the Treaty of al-Ḥudaybiyah was the beginning of a period of Muslim diplomatic activity. The historical basis of this assumption is unclear. While there is much to suggest that Muḥammad was interested in expanding his sphere of influence northward, which would place him in contact with the Byzantine and Persian spheres of influence; that he received reports of the Byzantine-Persian war then drawing to its conclusion, just as Byzantine intelligence received reports of events in the Arabian peninsula; and that he knew of the usefulness of Arab tributary states to these empires, the actual letters are clearly literary fictions. They are comprehensible from the point of view of Islamic law, in terms of the obligation to summon non-Muslims to Islam before invading their territory, but in their laconic wording they would have been incomprehensible to their recipients. Only one of the letters, that to the Ethiopian negus, contains significant individuating material; however, that material (of a christological nature) uses Qur'ānic language that would have been readily available to later Muslims. The reply by the negus (the only reply quoted), with its offer to come personally, is clearly apocryphal.

Another example of Muḥammad's interest in the north is the expedition that set out for Syria and was defeated by Byzantine troops and their Arab allies at Mu'tah in Jordan during the month of Jumādā I, A.H. 8 (August-September 629). Al-Ṭabarī's account, which relies almost entirely on Ibn Isḥāq, says nothing about the causes of the expedition. Al-Wāqidī (W, II, 755) indicates that the immediate occasion was the killing by Shuraḥbīl b. 'Amr al-Ghassānī (the Banū Ghassān were allies of the Byzantines) of a messenger whom Muḥammad had sent to the ruler of Buṣrā in Syria. Thus, although the motive for this mission to Buṣrā remains a mystery, the immediate motive for the expedition was retaliation. The deaths of Muḥammad's adoptive son Zayd b. Ḥārithah, his cousin Ja'far b. Abī Ṭālib, and 'Abdallāh b. Rawāḥah were a blow, but the total Muslim casualties were extremely light. Al-Ṭabarī gives no figures, but al-Wāqidī lists only eight men.

Shortly after the return of the unsuccessful expedition to Mu'tah, the truce of al-Ḥudaybiyah broke down when violence erupted between the Banū Bakr, allies of Quraysh, and the Banū

Khuzā'ah, allies of Muḥammad. A group of Quraysh armed and supported the Banū Bakr, who killed several of the Banū Khuzā'ah. A tribesman of the Khuzā'ah then made his way to Medina and called on the Muslims for aid. He was favorably received. Realizing the gravity of the situation, Abū Sufyān himself made his way to Medina to attempt to repair the treaty. He was unsuccessful. Soon Muḥammad had set out with an army for Mecca. Further negotiations took place near Mecca between Abū Sufyān and Muḥammad, who was poised to enter Mecca by force. In the end, it was Abū Sufyān who, by accepting Islam and Muḥammad's terms, made it possible for Muḥammad to enter Mecca with a minimum of fighting. The internal politics of Mecca that led Abū Sufyān to make such a volte-face must be pieced together from other historical accounts. Muḥammad did not demand that the Meccans convert to Islam. He promised safety to anyone who entered the area around the Ka'bah, anyone who stayed within the doors of his house, and anyone who took refuge in Abū Sufyān's house. A few diehards fought, a few fled the city, but most of the Meccans accepted the inevitable. Muḥammad entered the city and pronounced a general amnesty, with the exception of six men and four women who were guilty of particular crimes. After a sermon delivered by the door of the Ka'bah, he declared the Meccans "free" (by convention they were legally his slaves as prisoners of war). This was followed by a ceremony in which the Meccans swore allegiance to Muḥammad as Muslims.

Thus, in a period of four years, Muḥammad had gone from being besieged in Medina by the Meccans and their allies to being the master of Mecca. It was a tremendous change of fortune, though one should not exaggerate the extent of his success. Islam had not yet made significant inroads into the tribes of central Arabia, which could pose a threat even to the combined forces of Medina and Mecca, as they did later in A.H. 8 at the battle of Ḥunayn. Muḥammad's religious policy was quite cautious at first. There was no attempt at this date to make the Meccan pilgrimage an exclusively Islamic rite. Pagans were allowed to make the pilgrimage this year and the following year. But the victory of Islam in Arabia, an object of faith alone in A.H. 5, had become a realistic possibility in A.H. 8.

Al-Ṭabarī: His Sources and Methods

As in the earlier sections of his *History* dealing with the life of the Prophet, al-Ṭabarī in this section relies mainly on the biography of the Prophet composed by Ibn Isḥāq (d. 150/767).[1] Al-Ṭabarī, who was born in A.H. 224 or 225 (winter of A.D. 839), studied the bulk of this material early in his life, when he was a student of Abū 'Abdallāh Muḥammad b. Ḥumayd in Rayy (near modern Tehran). Ibn Ḥumayd had studied the work with Salamah b. al-Faḍl, also of Rayy, who in turn had studied it with the author, Ibn Isḥāq. This means that al-Ṭabarī had access to the work in a version antedating the version that has survived to modern times, the abridgment and recension made by 'Abd al-Malik b. Hishām (d. 218/834). The typical *isnād* for al-Ṭabarī's citations therefore runs "Ibn Ḥumayd—Salamah—Ibn Isḥāq," to which al-Ṭabarī frequently appends the *isnād* found in Ibn Isḥāq. Al-Ṭabarī also studied other recensions of Ibn Isḥāq's work. For example, at page 1630 of the *History* we find the *isnād*, "Abū Kurayb—Yūnus b. Bukayr—Muḥammad b. Isḥāq." This refers to al-Ṭabarī's study of Ibn Isḥāq's book under the Kūfan scholar Abū Kurayb (d. 248/862), who transmitted the recension made by Yūnus b. Bukayr (d. 199/815). Al-Ṭabarī's citations from Ibn Isḥāq are extensive and preserve virtually all the significant material of the original, as comparison with the surviving text of the *Sīrah* will show.

The main other work cited by al-Ṭabarī in this section is the *Kitāb al-maghāzī* by the Medinan historian Muḥammad b. 'Umar al-Wāqidī (d. 207/823 in Baghdād). His attitude toward this work was very different from his attitude toward Ibn Isḥāq's. In a notice preserved in Yāqūt's biographical encyclopedia, *Irshād al-arīb*,[2] al-Ṭabarī is quoted as saying that he considered al-Wāqidī unreliable as a transmitter of *ḥadīth* and therefore quoted him in his work on Qur'ānic exegesis only when he referred to "history, biography, or Arab stories" and only when the material could be found only in his work; he quoted no legal traditions from al-Wāqidī. A

1. The work is commonly known by the title *Sīrah* or *Sīrat Rasūl Allāh*, which is the title of the recension of the work prepared by Ibn Hishām. Ibn Isḥāq's original three-volume work was entitled *Kitāb al-maghāzī* and consisted of three parts: *al-Mubtada'*, *al-Mab'ath*, and *al-Maghāzī*. See *EI*², s.v. Ibn Isḥāḳ.

2. Translated in Rosenthal, "General Introduction," p. 110.

comparison between the material from al-Wāqidī quoted in the *History* and the text of the *Kitāb al-maghāzī* demonstrates al-Ṭabarī's cautious use of al-Wāqidī. Al-Ṭabari rarely quotes al-Wāqidī fully. Many details, sometimes crucial ones, are omitted. I have therefore drawn attention to parallels to al-Wāqidī in the footnotes of my translation. Unfortunately, no English translation of this text exists at the present time.

To the material derived from these two main sources al-Ṭabarī added material derived from his studies with many leading scholars of his time. Franz Rosenthal's "General Introduction" to the first volume of this series is the most convenient place for the English reader to gain an idea of the scope of this material. The work of Fuat Sezgin in the first volume of his *Geschichte des arabischen Schrifttums* should also be consulted for its thorough presentation of the Islamic scholarship on which al-Ṭabarī drew.

A Note on the Text

The translation follows the text of the Leiden edition, which appeared in installments between 1879 and 1898 under the general editorship of M. J. de Goeje. The section here translated (A.H. 5–8) appears in Volume I/3, pages 1460–1654, which was edited by the Dutch scholar Pieter de Jong of Utrecht, after the death in 1881 of Professor Otto Loth of Leipzig, to whom the section was originally assigned. De Jong edited I, 1083–2015. The following manuscripts were available for pages 1460–1654: Istanbul, Köprülü 1042 (siglum C in the *apparatus*), part of a three-volume set copied in Cairo in 651 A.H., covering the entire section; Codex Muir (siglum M) in the British India Office library, covering the section to page 1480; and Codex Spitta (siglum S) in the Deutsche Morgenländische Gesellschaft, covering the entire section. Thus de Jong had at least two manuscripts for this section, and for the first twenty pages he had three with which to work. In addition, he carefully collated the text with parallel passages in the standard collections of *ḥadīth*, Ibn Hishām, al-Ṭabarī's *Tafsīr*, the *Kitāb al-Aghānī* of Abū al-Faraj al-Iṣfahānī, and later historians such as Ibn al-Athīr. The result is a text with few real problems.

Al-Ṭabarī's *History* was reedited in Egypt by Muḥammad Abū al-Faḍl Ibrāhīm (1960), who used the printed Leiden text as a basis but consulted a few additional manuscripts, none of which contained the text for the section translated here. Nevertheless, I have consulted the Cairo edition for its useful explanatory notes and have noted where its text differs from that of ed. Leiden because of editorial decision or possible misprint.

I have indicated parallel passages, especially in the works of Ibn Hishām and al-Wāqidī, occasionally in other works. I do not pretend that this is a complete list of parallels. Given the selective nature of al-Ṭabarī's work for this period, the historian must supplement it with readings in other surviving Arabic works. In addition to Ibn Hishām and al-Wāqidī, the material on the life of the Prophet in Ibn Sa'd's *Ṭabaqāt* and in al-Balādhurī's *Ansāb al-ashrāf* is particularly rich.

For the conversion of Islamic dates I have used the standard tables of F. Wüstenfeld and E. Mahler. These follow the later Arabic convention of assuming that the present purely lunar Islamic calendar with no intercalated months was in force from the first year of Muḥammad's residence in Medina, almost certainly a false assumption. The custom of intercalating extra months to keep the lunar months in phase with the seasons was followed by the pre-Islamic Arabs, as by the Jews, and was forbidden only in the tenth year of the Hijrah. It is therefore likely that three or four of the Islamic years from 1 to 10 contained an extra month. As we do not know in what years such months were added, we have no way of working out exact correspondences. Furthermore, as the introduction of dating by the Islamic era occurred during the caliphate of 'Umar, the dating of events of the Prophet's lifetime was often a matter on which there was disagreement. This was frequently the case with some of the minor expeditions, which are mentioned by Ibn Hishām without dates in a separate section at the end of the *Sīrah*.

I wish to express my appreciation to four previous translators in this series who blazed a well-marked trail. To use Arabic terminology, I have used their works through *wijādah* (finding them) but without *ijāzah* (license to transmit personally bestowed by a master on a pupil). To Franz Rosenthal of Yale University, the translator of Volume I of this series, all English-speaking students of al-Ṭabarī owe a great debt of gratitude, especially for his masterful "General Introduction." M. V. McDonald and W. Montgomery

Watt, who translated and annotated Volume VII, have done much to clarify the complicated tribal politics of the period. Ismail K. Poonawala, my colleague at the University of California at Los Angeles and the translator of Volume IX, helped especially with the *isnāds*. For the inevitable errors and shortcomings, I alone bear responsibility.

Michael Fishbein

The Events of the Year

5

(June 2, 626–May 22, 627)

Muḥammad's Marriage to Zaynab bt. Jaḥsh

In this year the Messenger of God married Zaynab bt. Jaḥsh.[1] [1460]
According to Muḥammad b. ʿUmar [al-Wāqidī][2]—ʿAbdallāh b. ʿĀmir al-Aslamī[3]—Muḥammad b. Yaḥyā b. Ḥabbān,[4] who said:

---

1. Zaynab was the daughter of Muḥammad's paternal aunt Umaymah bt. ʿAbd al-Muṭṭalib and Jaḥsh b. Riʾāb, a member of the tribe of Asad b. Khuzaymah, who had settled in Mecca and become a confederate of the Banū Umayyah of the ʿAbd Shams clan of Quraysh. Muḥammad had arranged her marriage to his freedman and adopted son, Zayd b. Ḥārithah. Cf. *EI*[1], s.v. Zainab bint Dj̲aḥsh; Lings, *Muhammad,* 40; Stowasser, *Women in the Qur'an, Traditions, and Interpretation,* 87–89.

2. Muḥammad b. ʿUmar al-Wāqidī (b. 130/747 in Medina, d. 207/823 in Baghdād) was a major historian and author of *Kitāb al-maghāzī* on the military campaigns of the Prophet. See *GAS,* I, 294–97.

3. ʿAbdallāh b. ʿĀmir al-Aslamī Abū ʿĀmir al-Madanī was a traditionist who died in Medina in 150/767–68 or 151/768. As a transmitter of *ḥadīth* he was considered "weak." See Ibn Ḥajar, *Tahdhīb,* V, 275–76.

4. Muḥammad b. Yaḥyā b. Ḥabbān al-Anṣārī al-Māzinī was a scholar who taught in Medina. He died in 121/738–39 at the age of seventy-four. See Ibn Ḥajar, *Tahdhīb,* IX, 507–8.

The Messenger of God came to the house of Zayd b. Ḥārithah.[5] (Zayd was always called Zayd b. Muḥammad.) Perhaps the Messenger of God missed him at that moment, so as to ask, "Where is Zayd?" He came to his residence to look for him but did not find him. Zaynab bt. Jaḥsh, Zayd's wife, rose to meet him. Because she was dressed only in a shift, the Messenger of God turned away
[1461] from her. She said: "He is not here, Messenger of God. Come in, you who are as dear to me as my father and mother!" The Messenger of God refused to enter. Zaynab had dressed in haste when she was told "the Messenger of God is at the door." She jumped up in haste and excited the admiration of the Messenger of God, so that he turned away murmuring something that could scarcely be understood. However, he did say overtly: "Glory be to God the Almighty! Glory be to God, who causes hearts to turn!"

When Zayd came home, his wife told him that the Messenger of God had come to his house. Zayd said, "Why didn't you ask him to come in?" She replied, "I asked him, but he refused." "Did you hear him say anything?" he asked. She replied, "As he turned away, I heard him say: 'Glory be to God the Almighty! Glory be to God, who causes hearts to turn!'"

So Zayd left, and, having come to the Messenger of God, he said: "Messenger of God, I have heard that you came to my house. Why didn't you go in, you who are as dear to me as my father and mother? Messenger of God, perhaps Zaynab has excited your admiration, and so I will separate myself from her." The Messenger of God said, "Keep your wife to yourself." Zayd could find no possible way to [approach] her after that day. He would come to the Messenger of God and tell him so, but the Messenger of God

5. Zayd b. Ḥārithah was brought to Mecca as a slave by a nephew of Muḥammad's first wife, Khadījah. The nephew sold Zayd to Khadījah, who gave him to Muḥammad before the beginning of his calling as a prophet. Although Zayd's father later came to Mecca to free his son, Zayd refused to leave Muḥammad, who subsequently freed him and adopted him. Zayd came to be known thereafter as Zayd b. Muḥammad. He was a very early convert to Islam and emigrant to Medina; fought at Badr, Uḥud, and the Trench; was present at al-Ḥudaybiyah; and commanded several expeditions. He died as one of the commanders of the expedition to Mu'tah in A.H. 8. See *EI*[1], s.v. Zayd b. Ḥārit͟hah.

would say to him, "Keep your wife." Zayd separated from her and left her, and she became free.[6]

While the Messenger of God was talking with 'Ā'ishah,[7] a fainting[8] overcame him. When he was released from it, he smiled and said, "Who will go to Zaynab to tell her the good news, saying that [1462]
God has married her to me?" Then the Messenger of God recited: "And when you said unto him on whom God has conferred favor and you have conferred favor, 'Keep your wife to yourself . . .'"—and the entire passage.[9]

According to 'Ā'ishah, who said: "I became very uneasy because of what we heard about her beauty and another thing, the greatest and loftiest of matters—what God had done for her by giving her in marriage. I said that she would boast of it over us."

According to 'Ā'ishah, who said: "Salmā, the maidservant of the Messenger of God, went out to inform Zaynab of this, and [Zaynab] gave [Salmā] some anklets that she was wearing."[10]

---

6. Sc. from any impediment to marriage. Ordinarily this implied abstinence from conjugal relations with the former husband for a time (*'iddah*) long enough to establish that the woman was not pregnant by him, thereby removing any uncertainty about the paternity of any future children. The passage implies that Zayd divorced Zaynab.

7. The marriage of Muḥammad to Abū Bakr's daughter 'Ā'ishah was arranged after the death of Khadījah and three years before the emigration to Medina. 'Ā'ishah was only six years old at the time, and the marriage was not consummated until seven or eight months after the Hijrah, when 'Ā'ishah was about ten years old (v. al-Ṭabarī, I, 1261). She was very beautiful and remained Muḥammad's favorite wife. See *EI*[2], s.v. 'Ā'ishah bt. Abī Bakr; Abbott, *Aishah the Beloved of Muhammad*; and Spellberg, *Politics, Gender, and the Islamic Past.*

8. Arabic *ghashyah,* a swoon or fainting spell; literally "a covering": here signifying an episode of revelation (*waḥy*). See *EI*[1], s.v. *waḥy,* for a description of such episodes.

9. Qur'ān 33:37. The verse continues: "'. . . and fear God.' And you did hide in your mind that which God was to bring to light, and you did fear mankind whereas God had a better right that you should fear Him. So when Zayd had performed the necessary formality [of divorce] from her, We gave her unto you in marriage, so that [henceforth] there may be no sin for believers in respect of wives of their adopted sons, when the latter have performed the necessary formality [of release] from them. The commandment of God must be fulfilled." Cf. the commentary on the passage in al-Ṭabarī, *Jāmi' al-bayān,* XXII, 10–11.

10. The pronouns in the Arabic are ambiguous regarding who gave whom the anklets. My translation is suggested by a similar incident at p. 109, below, where another prospective bride of the Prophet gives the bearer of the good news a gift out of joy.

According to Yūnus b. 'Abd al-A'lā[11]—Ibn Wahb[12]—Ibn Zayd,[13] who said: The Messenger of God had married Zayd b. Ḥārithah to Zaynab bt. Jaḥsh, his paternal aunt's daughter. One day the Messenger of God went out looking for Zayd. Now there was a covering of haircloth over the doorway, but the wind had lifted the covering so that the doorway was uncovered. Zaynab was in her chamber, undressed, and admiration for her entered the heart of the Prophet. After that happened, she was made unattractive to the other man.[14] So he came and said, "Messenger of God, I want to separate myself from my companion." Muḥammad asked: "What is wrong? Has anything on her part disquieted you?" "No, by God," replied Zayd, "nothing she has done has disquieted me, Messenger of God, nor have I seen anything but good." The Messenger of God said to him, "Keep your wife to yourself, and fear God." That is [the meaning of] the Word of God:[15] "And when you said unto him on whom God has conferred favor and you have conferred favor, 'Keep your wife to yourself, and fear God.' And you did hide in your mind that which God was to bring to light." *You did hide in your mind* [the thought] that "if he separates himself from her, I will marry her."

The Expedition to Dūmat al-Jandal and Other Events

According to al-Wāqidī: In this year he mounted an expedition
[1463] against Dūmat al-Jandal[16] in the month of Rabī' I.[17] The reason for

11. Yūnus b. 'Abd al-A'lā was born in 170/787 and died in 264/877. He was Egypt's leading scholar in the fields of *ḥadīth* and Qur'ān reading. Al-Ṭabarī studied with him in Egypt. See *GAS*, I, 38 (which identifies this *isnād* as pointing to a Qur'ān commentary by 'Abd al-Raḥmān b. Zayd b. Aslam); and F. Rosenthal, in "General Introduction," 27.

12. 'Abdallāh b. Wahb b. Muslim al-Fihrī al-Qurashī was born in Egypt in 125/743 and died in 197/812. He was a traditionist, Qur'ān commentator, and jurist, and was a student of Mālik b. Anas. See *GAS*, I, 466.

13. 'Abd al-Raḥmān b. Zayd b. Aslam al-'Adawī of Medina (d. 182/798) was known primarily as a Qur'ān commentator. See Ibn Ḥajar, *Tahdhīb*, VI, 177–78; *GAS*, I, 38.

14. I.e., God caused her to become unattractive to her husband Zayd. Cf. Stowasser, *Women in the Qur'an, Traditions, and Interpretation*, 88.

15. Qur'ān 33:37.

16. Dūmat al-Jandal is an oasis in northern Arabia at the head of Wādī Sirḥān. It was inhabited by the Banū Kinānah subtribe of the Banū Kalb, plus some Christian Arabs. The present town of al-Jawf is on the site. See *EI*², s.v. Dūmat al-D̲jandal.

17. Rabī' I of A.H. 5 began on 31 July 626. Parallels: IH, III, 213 (tr. Guillaume, 449); W, I, 402–4 (fuller version).

it was that word reached the Messenger of God that a host had assembled there and had approached his territories; so the Messenger of God mounted an expedition against them and reached Dūmat al-Jandal, but he had no clash with the enemy. He left Sibāʿ b. ʿUrfuṭah al-Ghifārī in charge of Medina.

According to Abū Jaʿfar [al-Ṭabarī]: In this year the Messenger of God made a truce with ʿUyaynah b. Ḥiṣn[18] that the latter might pasture his herds in Taghlamān and its vicinity.

According to Muḥammad b. ʿUmar [al-Wāqidī]—Ibrāhīm b. Jaʿfar—his father [Jaʿfar b. Maḥmūd]:[19] This was because ʿUyaynah's lands became affected by drought. The Messenger of God therefore made a truce, so that ʿUyaynah might pasture his herds in Taghlamān as far as al-Marāḍ.[20] The land there had become lush with pasturage because of a rain cloud that had arrived. The Messenger of God made a truce with him that he might pasture his herds there.

According to al-Wāqidī: In this year the mother of Saʿd b. ʿUbādah[21] died while Saʿd was journeying with the Messenger of God to Dūmat al-Jandal.

The Battle of the Trench

In this year the battle of the Messenger of God at the trench took place in the month of Shawwāl,[22] according to Ibn Ḥumayd[23]—

18. ʿUyaynah b. Ḥiṣn b. Ḥudhayfah was leader of the Banū Fazārah subdivision of the tribe of Dhubyān (itself part of Ghaṭafān). See Watt, *Muhammad at Medina*, 91–92; and *EI²*, s.v. Fazāra.

19. Parallel: W, II, 552. Ibrāhīm b. Jaʿfar b. Maḥmūd b. Muḥammad b. Maslamah al-Anṣārī al-Ḥārithī was a frequent informant of al-Wāqidī, providing information from his father. See Ibn Ḥajar, *Tahdhīb*, II, 106.

20. Al-Marāḍ was about 36 Arab miles from Medina, in the area of al-Ṭaraf (present-day al-Ṣuwaydirah) on the road to Iraq, according to al-Samhūdī, *Khulāṣat al-wafāʾ*, 578–79, 604.

21. Saʿd b. ʿUbādah of the Banū Sāʿidah clan was a leader of the tribe of al-Khazraj of Medina. See also Ibn Ḥajar, *Tahdhīb*, III, 475–76.

22. Shawwāl of A.H. 5 began on 23 February 627. For general background, the article Khandaḳ in *EI²* by W. Montgomery Watt may be consulted, as well as Hamidullah, *The Battlefields of the Prophet Muhammad*, 29–36.

23. Muḥammad b. Ḥumayd b. Ḥayyān al-Rāzī al-Tamīmī died in al-Rayy in 248/862. See Ibn Ḥajar, *Tahdhīb*, IX, 127–31; al-Khaṭīb al-Baghdādī, *Taʾrīkh Baghdād*, II, 259–64.

Salamah[24]—Ibn Isḥāq.[25] What brought on the battle of the Messenger of God at the trench, according to what has been reported, was what happened because of the expulsion of the Banū al-Naḍīr from their settlements by the Messenger of God.[26]

According to Ibn Ḥumayd—Salamah—Muḥammad b. Isḥāq—Yazīd b. Rūmān[27] (a *mawlā* of the family of al-Zubayr)—'Urwah b. al-Zubayr;[28] and [according to] someone whom I do not doubt—'Ubaydallāh b. Ka'b b. Mālik,[29] al-Zuhrī,[30] 'Āṣim b. 'Umar b. Qatā-
[1464] dah,[31] 'Abdallāh b. Abī Bakr b. Muḥammad b. 'Amr b. Ḥazm,[32] Muḥammad b. Ka'b al-Quraẓī,[33] and others of our learned men

24. Salamah b. al-Faḍl al-Anṣārī died in 191/806. See Ibn Ḥajar, *Tahdhīb*, IV, 153–54.

25. Muḥammad b. Isḥāq b. Yasār, born in Medina ca. 85/207, died in Baghdād in 150/767, was the most influential of the early biographers of the Prophet. His *Kitāb al-maghāzī*, in its recension by Ibn Hishām, d. 218/834, generally known as *Sīrat Rasūl Allāh*, or simply the *Sīrah*, became the standard treatment of the events of the Prophet's life. See *EI*², s.v. Ibn Isḥāḳ; Guillaume, *The Life of Muhammad* (tr. of Ibn Hishām's *Sīrah*), pp. xiii-xli; *GAS*, I, 288–90.

26. For the expulsion of the Jewish tribe of Banū al-Naḍīr in the previous year, see al-Ṭabarī, I, 1448–53. The tribe had left for Khaybar and Syria to the north, forfeiting their property in Medina. See *EI*², s.v. Naḍīr, Banū 'l-.

27. Yazīd b. Rūmān al-Asadī (d. 130/747) was a *mawlā* (a client, i.e., a freed slave or a person of non-Arab origin) of the al-Zubayr family and author of a book about the Prophet's campaigns. See Ibn Ḥajar, *Tahdhīb*, XI, 325; *GAS*, I, 284.

28. 'Urwah b. al-Zubayr b. al-'Awwām al-Asadī (b. between 23/643 and 29/649, d. 94/712–13) was the son of a prominent companion of the Prophet and the younger brother of 'Abdallāh b. al-Zubayr, whose challenge to the caliphate of the Umayyads ended with his death in 73/692. He became one of the most respected authorities of Medina on traditions and early Islamic history. See Ibn Ḥajar, *Tahdhīb*, VII, 180–85; *GAS*, I, 278–79; Duri, *Rise of Historical Writing*, 76–95.

29. Abū Faḍālah 'Ubaydallāh b. Ka'b b. Mālik al-Anṣārī (d. 97/715 or 98) is identified by al-Ṭabarī (I, 1364) as "one of the most learned of the Anṣār." See Ibn Ḥajar, *Tahdhīb*, VII, 44–45; *GAS*, I, 276–77.

30. Muḥammad b. Muslim b. 'Ubaydallāh b. 'Abdallāh b. Shihāb al-Zuhrī (b. 50/670 or 51, d. 124/742) was a celebrated traditionist and historian. See Ibn Ḥajar, *Tahdhīb*, IX, 445–51; *EI*¹, s.v. al-Zuhrī; *GAS*, I, 280–83; Duri, *Rise of Historical Writing*, 95–121.

31. 'Āṣim b. 'Umar b. Qatādah al-Anṣārī (d. 120/737) was known as an authority on the campaigns of the Prophet. See Ibn Ḥajar, *Tahdhīb*, V, 53–54; *GAS*, I, 279–80.

32. 'Abdallāh b. Abī Bakr b. Muḥammad b. 'Amr b. Ḥazm al-Madanī was born in 60/679 (or in 56) in Medina and died in 130/747 (or 135). He was a transmitter of historical reports and traditions, which he received from his father (died 120/737) and from Anas b. Mālik. See Ibn Ḥajar, *Tahdhīb*, V, 164–65; *GAS*, I, 284.

33. Muḥammad b. Ka'b b. Sulaym al-Quraẓī (d. 118/736), the son or grandson of a convert to Islam from the Banū Qurayẓah, was known primarily as a commentator on the Qur'ān. See Ibn Sa'd, *Tabaqāt*, V, 272–73; VII/2, 193; Ibn Ḥajar, *Tahdhīb*, IX, 420–22; *GAS*, I, 32.

(the report of each has been combined in this account of the Trench, some of them relating what others do not relate):[34] The account of the trench is as follows. A group of Jews, including Salām b. Abī al-Ḥuqayq al-Naḍarī,[35] Ḥuyayy b. Akhṭab al-Naḍarī, Kinānah b. al-Rabī' b. Abī al-Ḥuqayq al-Naḍarī, Hawdhah b. Qays al-Wā'ilī, and Abū 'Ammār al-Wā'ilī, along with a group of men from the Banū al-Naḍīr and a group from the Banū Wā'il,[36] were the ones who assembled parties of men against the Messenger of God. They went to the Quraysh in Mecca and invited them to make war on the Messenger of God. They said, "We will be with you against him until we root him out." The Quraysh said to them: "People of the Jews, you are the people of the first scripture,[37] and you have knowledge about the subject on which we and Muḥammad have come to differ. Is our religion better or his?" "Your religion is better," they said, "and you are closer to the truth than he."

They are the ones concerning whom God revealed: "Have you not seen those to whom a portion of the scripture has been given, how they believe in idols and false deities, and how they say of those who disbelieve, 'These are more rightly guided than those who believe'?"—until the words, "Hell is sufficient for [their] burning."[38]

When they said this to Quraysh, the latter were pleased by what they said and embarked enthusiastically on what they invited them to do, namely, make war on the Messenger of God. They determined to do it and decided on a time for it.[39] Then the same

---

34. Parallel: IH, III, 214 ff.; tr. Guillaume, 450 ff.

35. I.e., of the Jewish tribe of Banū al-Naḍīr.

36. The Banū Wā'il were a clan of the Aws Manāt of Medina. They seem to have lived among the Jews; here they are treated as if they were Jews. See Watt, *Muhammad at Medina*, 154, 164.

37. I.e., the Torah.

38. Qur'ān 4:51–55. For "idols and false deities" the Arabic reads *al-jibt* and *al-ṭāghūt.*" Commentators disagreed on the exact meaning. Al-Sha'bī said that the words meant "they believe in enchantment and the devil." Ibn 'Abbās thought the words referred specifically to Ḥuyayy b. Akhṭab and Ka'b b. al-Ashraf or that these two Jews prostrated themselves before the gods of Quraysh in order to induce Quraysh to join with them in a league against Muḥammad. See Lane, *Lexicon*, I, 373, s.v. *jibt*.

39. For *itta'adū* "decided on a time," Ms. S reads *ista'addū* "prepared themselves."

group of Jews set out and came to [the tribe of] Ghaṭafān,[40] a division of Qays 'Aylān, and called on them to make war on the
[1465] Messenger of God. The Jews told them that they would be with them against him and that Quraysh had followed them and had decided on the matter. So they responded favorably. Quraysh set out under the leadership of Abū Sufyān b. Ḥarb;[41] Ghaṭafān set out under the leadership of 'Uyaynah b. Ḥiṣn b. Ḥudhayfah b. Badr with the Banū Fazārah, al-Ḥārith b. 'Awf b. Abī Ḥārithah al-Murrī with the Banū Murrah, and Mas'ūd b. Rukhaylah b. Nuwayrah b. Ṭarīf b. Suḥmah b. 'Abdallāh b. Hilāl b. Khalāwah b. Ashja' b. Rayth b. Ghaṭafān with those of his fellow tribesmen from Ashja' who followed him. When the Messenger of God received word of them and what they had determined to do, he laid out a trench to protect Medina.

According to Muḥammad b. 'Umar [al-Wāqidī], who said:[42] The person who advised the Messenger of God about the trench was Salmān.[43] It was the first combat that Salmān saw with the Messenger of God. He was a free man at this time. He said, "Messenger of God, in Persia, whenever we were surrounded, we would dig a trench to protect ourselves."

Resumption of the account of Ibn Isḥāq: The Messenger of God worked [at building the trench] in order to inspire the Muslims with hope of reward, and they set to work on it. He toiled at it, and
[1466] they toiled. Certain men of the hypocrites[44] hung back from the

---

40. Ghaṭafān was a group of North Arabian tribes to the east of Medina and Mecca in the land between the Ḥijāz and the Shammar Mountains. Among its divisions were 'Abs, Ashja', and Dhubyān—the latter with its divisions Fazārah (the tribe of 'Uyaynah b. Ḥiṣn), Murrah, and Tha'labah. See Watt, *Muhammad at Medina*, 91–95; *EI²*, s.v. Ghaṭafān.

41. Abū Sufyān b. Ḥarb b. Umayyah, of the clan of 'Abd Shams of Quraysh, was a prominent Meccan merchant. See *EI²*, s.v. Abū Sufyān.

42. Parallel: W, 445.

43. For the religious quest and conversion to Islam of Salmān, a Persian landowner's son who had gone to Syria to learn about Christianity and then to Arabia to investigate prophecies of a new religion, see IH, I, 214–22; tr. Guillaume, 95–98; *EI¹*, s.v. Salmān al-Fārisī.

44. The *munāfiqūn* "hypocrites, waverers"—Brockett in *EI²*, s.v., prefers the rendering "dissenters"—were nominal Muslims who secretly opposed many of Muḥammad's policies. 'Abdallāh b. Ubayy was said to be their leader. See also Watt, *Muhammad at Medina*, 180–91.

Messenger of God and from the Muslims in their work. They began pretending to be too weak to work and slipping away to their families without the knowledge or permission of the Messenger of God. As for the Muslims, whenever some matter of unavoidable necessity befell any of them, he would mention it to the Messenger of God and ask leave to attend to his need, and the Messenger of God would grant him leave. Having attended to his need, the person would return to the work he had been doing—this from a desire for good and because he reckoned on a reward for his work. Concerning this, God revealed: "They only are the true believers who believe in God and His Messenger and, when they are with him on some common enterprise, go not away until they have asked leave of him"—until the words "and ask for them forgiveness of God. Lo! God is forgiving, merciful."[45] This verse was revealed about all those believers who were people who reckoned [on a reward in the world to come], desired good, and obeyed God and His Messenger. God then said, referring to the hypocrites who would slip away from work and depart without leave from the Messenger of God: "Make not the calling of the Messenger among you as your calling one of another"—until the words "He knows your condition."[46] (That is, He knows your condition with regard to truthfulness or lying.) The Muslims worked at the trench until they had finished it solidly. As they were working, they improvised a work song[47] about a Muslim who used to be called Ju'ayl but whom the Messenger of God had named 'Amr. They said:

After he had been Ju'ayl, he named him 'Amr;
    and to the once needy man he was backing.

Whenever they came to the word "'Amr," the Messenger of God [1467]
would say "'Amr"; whenever they said "backing," the Messenger of God would say "backing."

45. Qur'ān, 24:62.
46. Qur'ān, 24:63–64.
47. Arabic: "they recited a verse in *rajaz*" (the meter used for extemporized poems). See Goldziher, *Abhandlungen zur arabischen Philologie*, I, 80. The name change to which the verse alludes may have been made to improve Ju'ayl's morale, as his name appears to be a diminutive of *ju'al* "dung beetle." In W, 447, Ju'ayl is said to have been "pious but ugly." Cf. Ibn Ḥajar, *Iṣābah*, I, 49.

According to Muḥammad b. Bashshār[48]—Muḥammad b. Khālid Ibn 'Athmah[49]—Kathīr b. 'Abdallāh b. 'Amr b. 'Awf al-Muzanī[50]—his father ['Abdallāh b. 'Amr][51]—his father ['Amr b. 'Awf],[52] who said: The Messenger of God laid out the trench in the Year of the Parties,[53] from the Fortress of the Two Shaykhs (*ujum al-shaykhayn*) on the side of the Banū Ḥārithah[54] until it reached al-Madhād.[55] He divided it up forty cubits between each ten [men].[56] The Emigrants[57] and the Anṣār[58] disputed over Salmān the Persian, who was a strong man. The Anṣār said, "Salmān is one of us." The Emigrants said, "Salmān is one of us." So the Messenger of God said, "Salmān is one of us, the People of the Household."[59]

According to 'Amr b. 'Awf: I, along with Salmān, Ḥudhayfah b. al-Yamān, al-Nu'mān b. Muqarrin al-Muzanī, and six of the Anṣār, was in a 40-cubit [section of the trench]. We dug beneath

48. Abū Bakr Muḥammad b. Bashshār b. 'Uthmān b. Dāwūd al-'Abdī (b. 167/783 in al-Baṣrah, died 252/866) was considered a reliable transmitter of traditions. See Ibn Ḥajar, *Tahdhīb*, IX, 70–71; *GAS*, I, 113–14.

49. For Muḥammad b. Khālid, who was called Ibn 'Athmah after his mother 'Athmah, see Ibn Ḥajar, *Tahdhīb*, IX, 142–43.

50. Kathīr b. 'Abdallāh b. 'Amr b. 'Awf al-Yashkurī al-Muzanī (died between 150/767 and 160/777 in Medina) was generally considered a weak transmitter of *ḥadīth*. See Ibn Ḥajar, *Tahdhīb*, VIII, 421–23.

51. 'Abdallāh b. 'Amr b. 'Awf b. Zayd al-Muzanī was a transmitter of *ḥadīth* generally considered sound. See Ibn Ḥajar, *Tahdhīb*, V, 339–40.

52. 'Amr b. 'Awf al-Anṣārī was present at the Battle of Badr and died during the caliphate of 'Umar. See Ibn Ḥajar, *Tahdhīb*, VIII, 85–86.

53. Years were named after their most prominent events: hence Year of the Hijrah and Year of the *Aḥzāb* (the parties, confederates, or allied clans that attacked Medina in this year). Sūra 33 of the Qur'ān, *Sūrat al-Aḥzāb*, is named for them.

54. The Banū Ḥārithah, a clan of the al-Aws, had land on the northeast side of Medina. See Watt, *Muhammad at Medina*, 152 (map); Hamidullah, *Battlefields*, 26, 32 (photograph of a mosque on the site).

55. Al-Madhād was a stronghold belonging to the Banū Ḥaram of the Banū Salimah clan of al-Khazraj (see al-Samhūdī, *Khulāṣat al-wafā'*, 603). It lay to the west of Mt. Sal' (see map in Hamidullah, *Battlefields*, 31).

56. I.e., he divided the work so that ten men were responsible for digging each 40-cubit section (approximately 60 feet).

57. The Emigrants (*al-muhājirūn*) were the followers of Muḥammad who had migrated from Mecca to Medina with him. See *EI*², s.v. Muhādjirūn.

58. The Anṣār ("helpers") were Muslims from Medina, primarily from the tribes of al-Aws and al-Khazraj. See *EI*², s.v. Anṣār.

59. Arabic *ahl al-bayt* designates the Prophet's household.

Dhūbāb[60] until we reached al-Nadā.[61] Then God caused a white rock to emerge from the bottom of the trench, a flint that broke our iron implements and exhausted us. So we said, "Salmān, go up to the Messenger of God and inform him about this rock—either [1468] that we may turn aside from it, for the place to turn aside is near, or that he may give us his order about it—for we do not wish to deviate from his plan."

Salmān climbed out and went to the Messenger of God, who was pitching a Turkish-style round tent[62] nearby, and said: "O Messenger of God, who are as dear to us as father and mother, a white rock came out of the trench, a flint that broke our iron implements and exhausted us, so that we can make no impression small or great on it. Give us your order concerning it, for we do not wish to deviate from your plan." The Messenger of God went down into the trench with Salmān, and we nine climbed up onto its side. The Messenger of God took the pickaxe from Salmān and struck the rock a blow that cracked it, and a flash of lightning shot out, illuminating everything between the two tracts of black stones—that is, Medina's two tracts of black stones[63]—like a lamp inside a dark room. The Messenger of God shouted, "God is greatest!"—a shout of victory—and the Muslims, too, shouted, "God is greatest!" Then the Messenger of God struck it again and cracked it, and a flash of lightning shot out, illuminating everything between Medina's two tracts of black stones—like a lamp inside a dark room. The Messenger of God shouted, "God is greatest!"—a shout of victory—and the Muslims, too, shouted, "God is greatest!" Then the Messenger of God struck it a third time and broke it, and a flash of lightning shot out, illuminating

---

60. Dhūbāb (or Dhubāb) was located to the north of Mt. Sal'. According to al-Samhūdī, *Khulāṣat al-wafā'*, 552, it became the site of the Mosque of the Banner. See Hamidullah, *Battlefields*, 32, for a photograph of the site.

61. The reading al-Nadā is uncertain; see the apparatus of ed. Leiden.

62. As noted in ed. Leiden, *Glossarium*, p. CL, "Turkish-style round tent" (*qubbah turkiyyah*) is an apparent anachronism, at least as regards the adjective "Turkish." Note, however, that the Prophet's tent at the time of the conquest of Mecca (p. 177, below) is called a *qubbah*, which normally implies a round tent. In any case, that this is not a very great anachronism is shown by a report from A.H. 16 (al-Ṭabarī, I, 2444) indicating that the Arab conquerers of al-Madā'in found *qibāb turkiyyah* "Turkish round tents" containing baskets of treasure.

63. Medina is surrounded by black lava flows called *ḥarrah* or *lābah*.

everything between Medina's two tracts of black stones—like a lamp inside a dark room. The Messenger of God shouted, "God is greatest!"—a shout of victory—and the Muslims, too, shouted,
[1469] "God is greatest!" Then he took Salmān's hand and climbed out. Salmān said: "You are as dear to me as father and mother, Messenger of God! I have seen something I never saw before." The Messenger of God turned to the men and asked, "Did you see what Salmān says?" They said: "Yes, Messenger of God, you who are as dear to us as father and mother; we saw you strike and lightning come out like waves. We saw you shout 'God is greatest,' and so we shouted 'God is greatest.' We saw nothing else." "You have spoken truly," he said. "I struck my first blow, and what you saw flashed out, so that the palaces of al-Ḥīrah[64] and al-Madā'in[65] of Kisrā lit up for me from it as if they were dogs' teeth, and Gabriel informed me that my nation would be victorious over them. Then I struck my second blow, and what you saw flashed out, so that the palaces of the pale men in the land of the Byzantines lit up for me from it as if they were dogs' teeth, and Gabriel informed me that my nation would be victorious over them. Then I struck my third blow, and what you saw flashed out, so that the palaces of Ṣan'ā'[66] lit up for me from it as if they were dogs' teeth, and Gabriel informed me that my nation would be victorious over them, [saying]: "Rejoice; victory shall come to them! Rejoice; victory shall come to them! Rejoice; victory shall come to them!" So the Muslims rejoiced and said: "Praise be to God! The promise of One who is true and faithful! He has promised us victory after tribulation." So when the allied clans came up, the believers said: "This is what God and His Messenger promised us. God and His Messenger have spoken truly." And it only increased them in faith and surrender.[67] But the hypocrites said: "Do you not wonder? He

---

64. Al-Ḥīrah, on the west bank of the Euphrates, southeast of the present Najaf in Iraq, was the capital of the pre-Islamic Arab vassal state of the Sasanian empire governed by the Banū Lakhm (Lakhmids). See *EI*², s.v. al-Ḥīra.

65. Al-Madā'in (Ctesiphon), on the Tigris about 20 miles south of the site of later Baghdād, was the winter capital of the Sasanian emperors, who in Arabic are normally given the title Kisrā (from Persian Khusraw, the name of several rulers in the dynasty). See *EI*², s.v. al-Madā'in.

66. At this time Ṣan'ā' in Yemen was ruled by a Persian governor. One of the palaces was presumably the famous Ghumdān, said to have been twenty stories tall. See *EI*¹, s.v. Ṣan'ā.

67. Cf. Qur'ān 33:22.

discourses to you, raises your hopes, and promises you false things. He tells you that from Yathrib[68] he can see the palaces of al-Ḥīrah and al-Madā'in of Kisrā and that they will be conquered by you—and this while you are digging the trench and cannot go forth!" So the following [verse of the] Qur'ān was revealed: "And [1470] when the hypocrites and those in whose hearts is sickness were saying, 'God and His Messenger promised us naught but delusion.'"[69]

According to Ibn Ḥumayd—Salamah—Muḥammad b. Isḥāq—someone not to be doubted—Abū Hurayrah:[70] When these cities were conquered in the time of 'Umar,[71] 'Uthmān,[72] and afterward, [Abū Hurayrah] used to say, "Conquer for yourselves whatever seems good to you; for, by the One who holds Abū Hurayrah's soul in His hand, you have conquered no city, neither shall you conquer any until the Day of Resurrection, but that Muḥammad was given its keys beforehand."

According to Ibn Ḥumayd—Salamah—Ibn Isḥāq, who said: The people of the trench were 3,000.

When the Messenger of God had finished the trench, Quraysh came and encamped where the stream beds meet at Rūmah, between al-Juruf and al-Ghābah,[73] with 10,000 of their Aḥābīsh[74] and those of the Banū Kinānah and people of Tihāmah[75]

---

68. Yathrib was the old name of Medina.

69. Qur'ān 33:12.

70. Abū Hurayrah, a companion of the Prophet, is said to have acquired his nickname ("the man with the kitten") because he kept a kitten to play with while he herded his goats. He came to Medina in A.H. 7. Later he became noted as a prolific narrator of traditions. See *EI*², s.v. Abū Hurayra.

71. 'Umar b. al-Khaṭṭāb ruled as caliph from 13/634 to 23/644.

72. 'Uthmān b. 'Affān ruled as caliph from 23/644 to 35/656.

73. IH, III, 219 reads "Zaghābah," for al-Ghābah. Al-Ṭabarī's reading of al-Ghābah is noted by Yāqūt, *Mu'jam al-buldān*, s.v. Zaghābah. Yāqūt implies that al-Ṭabarī chose his reading because he believed a place called "Zaghābah" was unknown; Yāqūt then cites *ḥadīth* to show that such a place was known. Al-Ghābah was eight miles north of Medina. See Yāqūt, *Mu'jam al-buldān*, s.v.; Hamidullah, *Battlefields*, 31 (map).

74. Aḥābīsh (plural of *uḥbūsh* or *uḥbūshah*) means "companies or bodies of men not all of one tribe." They consisted of a number of small clans or subtribes allied with Quraysh. The most important was Banū al-Ḥārith b. 'Abd Manāt b. Kinānah; others were al-Muṣṭaliq (of Khuzā'ah) and al-Hūn (of Khuzaymah, with subdivisions 'Aḍal and al-Qārah). The thesis of Henri Lammens that they were Abyssinian slave mercenaries is mistaken. Cf. *EI*², s.v. Ḥabash; W. Montgomery Watt, *Muhammad at Mecca*, 153–56; *Muhammad at Medina*, 81–83.

75. Tihāmah is the Red Sea coastal plain of the Arabian peninsula.

who followed them. Ghaṭafān and the people of Najd who followed them came and encamped at Dhanab Naqamā, beside Uḥud.[76] The Messenger of God and the Muslims went out and set their backs toward Sal'[77] with 3,000 of the Muslims. There he pitched his camp, with the trench between him and the enemy. He commanded that the children and women should be taken up into the strongholds.[78]

[1471] The enemy of God, Ḥuyayy b. Akhṭab, went out and came to Ka'b b. Asad al-Quraẓī, who was the possessor of the treaty and covenant of the Banū Qurayẓah.[79] Ka'b had made a truce with the Messenger of God for his people, making a contract and covenanting with him on it. When Ka'b heard Ḥuyayy b. Akhṭab, he shut his fortress in his face. Ḥuyayy asked to be allowed in, but Ka'b refused to open to him. Ḥuyayy called to him, "Ka'b, open to me!" "Woe to you, Ḥuyayy," answered Ka'b, "you are a man who brings bad luck! I have made a treaty with Muḥammad and will not break the pact that exists between me and him. I have seen nothing but faithfulness and truth on his part." Ḥuyayy said: "Woe to you! Open to me, and I will speak to you!" "I will not do it," said Ka'b. Ḥuyayy said, "By God, you have shut me out only on account of your gruel,[80] lest I should eat any of it with you." This angered the man, so that he opened to him. Ḥuyayy said: "Woe to you, Ka'b! I have brought you everlasting might and an overflowing sea. I have brought you Quraysh, with their leaders and chiefs, and have caused them to encamp where the stream beds meet at Rūmah;

---

76. Uḥud, where a battle between the Muslims and Meccans had taken place in Shawwāl 3 A.H. (March 625), is about a mile north of Medina. See Yāqūt, *Mu'jam al-buldān*, s.v.; Hamidullah, *Battlefields*, 22, 31 (maps).

77. Sal' was a hill in the central area of Medina. See Yāqūt, *Mu'jam al-buldān*, s.v.; Hamidullah, *Battlefields*, 31 (map).

78. "Medina was at first not a compact town, but a collection of scattered settlements, surrounded by groves of date palms and cultivated fields. For defense, therefore, a large number of forts or strongholds (*āṭām*, sing. *uṭum*; also *ājām*, sing. *ujum*) had been constructed, perhaps 200 in all. In these the local inhabitants took refuge in times of danger." M. Watt in *EI*², s.v. al-Madīna, p. 994.

79. The Banū Qurayẓah were one of the three main Jewish tribes of Medina, with lands toward the southeast of the oasis; see *EI*², s.v. Ḳurayẓa. On this treaty, cf. W, 454–56, which implies that it was a document written by Muḥammad and that Ḥuyayy, having persuaded Ka'b to go over to his side, tore it up.

80. *Jashīshah* was a gruel of coarsely ground wheat or barley, sometimes with the addition of dates and meat. See Lane, *Lexicon*, II, 425.

and Ghaṭafān, with their leaders and chiefs, and have caused them to encamp at Dhanab Naqamā beside Uḥud. They have made a treaty and covenant with me not to withdraw until they root out Muḥammad and those who are with him." Ka'b b. Asad said to him: "By God, you have brought me everlasting humiliation—a cloud that has already shed its water, that thunders and lightens but has nothing in it. Woe to you! Leave me to continue with Muḥammad as I am now, for I have seen nothing from Muḥammad except truth and faithfulness." But Ḥuyayy kept wheedling[81] Ka'b until he yielded to him, Ḥuyayy having given him a promise [1472] and oath by God that "if Quraysh and Ghaṭafān retreat without having killed Muḥammad, I will enter your fortress with you, so that whatever happens to you shall happen to me." So Ka'b b. Asad broke his treaty and renounced the bond that had existed between him and the Messenger of God.

When the news reached the Messenger of God and the Muslims, the Messenger of God sent out Sa'd b. Mu'ādh b. al-Nu'mān b. Imru' al-Qays (one of the Banū 'Abd al-Ashhal who at that time was the chief of al-Aws), Sa'd b. 'Ubādah b. Dulaym (one of the Banū Sā'idah b. Ka'b b. al-Khazraj who at that time was the chief of al-Khazraj[82]), and with them 'Abdallāh b. Rawāḥah[83] (a member of the Banū al-Ḥārith b. al-Khazraj) and Khawwāt b. Jubayr (a member of the Banū 'Amr b. 'Awf), and said: "Go and see whether what has reached us about these men is true or not. If it is true, speak to me in words that we can understand but that will be unintelligible to others, and do not break the strength of the people. But, if these men remain loyal to the pact between us and them, announce it to the people."

So they went out and came to them. They found them engaged in the worst of what had been reported about them. They slan-

---

81. Literally, "kept twisting [the fur of] the upper part and the fore part of the hump"; the metaphor is of a refractory camel that must be massaged and coaxed before it will allow the nose rein to be attached. See Lane, *Lexicon*, VI, s.v. *ghārib*.

82. Al-Aws and al-Khazraj were the two most important Arab tribes of Medina (as opposed to the Jews); see Watt, *Muhammad at Medina*, 151 ff. (genealogical table, p. 154); and *EI*[1], s. vv. Sa'd b. Mu'ādh, Sa'd b. 'Ubāda.

83. 'Abdallāh b. Rawāḥah was a leader of his clan and a poet. He was one of the Medinans who pledged allegiance to Muḥammad at the Second Pledge of 'Aqabah, a year before the Hijrah. He fought at Badr, Uḥud, and the Trench and was killed at Mu'tah in A.H. 8. See *EI*[2], s.v. 'Abd Allāh b. Rawāḥa; *GAS*, II, 292–93.

dered the Messenger of God and said, "There is no treaty between us and Muḥammad and no covenant." Sa'd b. 'Ubādah reviled them, and they reviled him—Sa'd was a man with a sharp temper.
[1473] So Sa'd b. Mu'ādh said to him, "Stop reviling them, for the disagreement between us and them is too serious for an exchange of taunts." The two Sa'ds and the men with them went back to the Messenger of God and, having greeted him, said, "'Aḍal and al-Qārah!" [They meant that it was] like the treachery of 'Aḍal and al-Qārah to the companions of the Messenger of God who were [betrayed] at al-Rajī', Khubayb b. 'Adī and his companions.[84] The Messenger of God said: "God is greatest! Rejoice, people of the Muslims!"

Soon the trial became great, and fear intensified. Their foe came at them from above them and below them, so that the believers were beset with fears of all kinds.[85] The hypocrisy of some of the hypocrites became evident. Mu'attib b. Qushayr, a member of the Banū 'Amr b. 'Awf, said, "Muḥammad was promising us that we should eat up the treasures of Kisrā and Caesar, and now none of us can go out to relieve himself!" Aws b. Qayẓī, one of the Banū Ḥārithah b. al-Ḥārith, said, "Messenger of God, our houses lie exposed to the enemy"[86]—he had been put up to this by certain

---

84. For the story of how a group of men from the clans of 'Aḍal and al-Qārah came to Muḥammad in Medina in A.H. 4 and asked for men to instruct them in Islam and how, after Muḥammad had sent six men back with them (including Khubayb b. 'Adī), they betrayed the six to the pro-Meccan Liḥyān subtribe of Hudhayl (which had a vendetta against the Muslims) at the watering place of al-Rajī', see al-Tabarī, I, 1431–37; Watt, *Muhammad at Medina,* 33–34; and *EI*[2], s.v. Liḥyān. For an account of Muḥammad's eventual retaliation, see p. 42 [I, 1501], below.

85. The sentence is virtually a paraphrase of Qur'ān 33:10. According to al-Ṭabarī, *Jāmi' al-bayān,* ad loc. (XXI, 71), those who came "from above" refers to 'Uyaynah b. Ḥiṣn, who came from the highlands of Najd, and those who came "from below" refers to Quraysh from Mecca. The final phrase in al-Ṭabarī, *ḥatta ẓanna al-mu'minūna kulla ẓannin,* parallels the Qur'ānic *wa-taẓunnūna billāhi al-ẓunūna,* generally translated as if the verb *ẓanna* meant "thinking unsubstantiated thoughts, making vain suppositions." But with the omission of *billāhi,* "concerning God," it seems more natural to translate according to another meaning of the idiom *ẓann al-ẓunūn.* Cf. Dozy, *Supplément,* II, 86: "*s'abandonner aux pensées les plus douloureuses,* se dit en parlant de celui qui est rempli de crainte."

86. Cf. Qur'ān 33:13.

chiefs of his tribe—"therefore give us leave, and let us return to our dwelling place, for it lies outside Medina."

The Messenger of God and the polytheists[87] stayed in their positions for over twenty nights—nearly a month—with no warfare between the troops, except for the shooting of arrows and the siege.

According to Ibn Ḥumayd—Salamah—Muḥammad b. Isḥāq—'Āṣim b. 'Umar b. Qatādah and Muḥammad b. Muslim b. Shihāb al-Zuhrī:[88] When the trial became great for the people, the Messenger of God sent to 'Uyaynah b. Ḥiṣn and al-Ḥārith b. 'Awf b. [1474]
Abī Ḥārithah al-Murrī, the two leaders of Ghaṭafān, and offered them a third of the date harvest of Medina on condition that they and their followers go back, leaving the Messenger of God and his companions. The truce between the two sides progressed to the point of drawing up a written document, but there was no witnessing or firm determination to make peace; it was only a matter of maneuvering. So the two of them acted as they did. When the Messenger of God was about to act, he sent to Sa'd b. Mu'ādh and Sa'd b. 'Ubādah, gave them an account, and asked their advice. The two said, "Messenger of God, is it something you would like us to do, or is it something God has commanded you to do that we must do, or is it something you are doing for us?" He answered: "Indeed, it is for you. By God, I am doing it only because I saw that the Arabs had shot at you from a single bow[89] and had dogged you from every side; so I wanted somehow to avert their furor from you for a time." Sa'd b. Mu'ādh said: "Messenger of God, we and these people used to be polytheists, associating [other divinities] with God and worshiping idols, and we neither worshiped God nor knew him; and they did not hope to eat a single date of ours except in hospitality or by buying. Now that God has conferred Islam on us, guided us to it, and strengthened us with your presence, shall we give them our wealth? We have no need for this! By God, we

---

87. *Mushrikūn,* those who associate other divinities with Allāh, is the regular Qur'ānic term for pagans.

88. Parallel with more details: W, 477–80.

89. I.e., were unanimous against you. See Lane, *Lexicon,* VII, 2575, for the proverb.

will offer them only the sword, until God judge between us and them." "As you wish," said the Messenger of God. So Sa'd took the sheet and erased the writing on it. Then he said, "Let them do their utmost against us."

[1475] The Messenger of God and the Muslims remained besieged by their enemy. There was no fighting between them, except that some horsemen of Quraysh—among them were 'Amr b. 'Abd Wudd b. Abī Qays (a member of the Banū 'Āmir b. Lu'ayy), 'Ikrimah b. Abī Jahl and Hubayrah b. Abī Wahb (both from Makhzūm), Nawfal b. 'Abdallāh, and Ḍirār b. al-Khaṭṭāb b. Mirdās (a member of the Banū Muḥārib b. Fihr) clad themselves for battle.[90] They rode out on their horses and passed by the Banū Kinānah and said: "Get ready for warfare, Banū Kinānah. Today you shall know who are the real horsemen." Then they advanced toward the trench and halted by it. When they saw it, they said, "By God, this is a stratagem that the Arabs have never employed." They headed to a place where the trench was narrow and struck their horses, so that they rushed through it and carried them round onto the marshy ground between the trench and Sal'. 'Alī b. Abī Ṭālib went out with a band of Muslims and blocked the gap through which they had driven their horses. The horsemen rode at a fast pace toward them. 'Amr b. 'Abd Wudd had fought at the Battle of Badr[91] until he was immobilized by wounds, and therefore he had not been present at Uḥud. When the Battle of the Trench took place, he went forth wearing a mark, so that his position would be visible. When he and his horsemen drew to a halt,[92] 'Alī said to him, "'Amr, you used to swear to God that if a man of Quraysh ever summoned you to one of two alternatives, you would accept one of them from him." "Yes," he replied. 'Alī b. Abī Ṭālib said, "I summon you to God, to His Messenger, and to Islam." He replied, "I have no need of this." So 'Alī said, "Then I
[1476] summon you to fight." 'Amr said: "Why, O son of my brother? By God, I do not want to kill you." 'Alī said, "But I, by God, want to kill you." 'Amr then became very angry. He jumped from his

90. Parallel with many more details: W, 470–72.

91. At the Battle of Badr in 2/642, a Muslim force from Medina defeated a large Meccan force; see al-Ṭabarī, I, 1282–338.

92. IH, III, 225, adds: "He said, 'Who will come out for single combat?' 'Alī b. Abī Ṭālib came out to him."

horse, hamstrung it[93] (or he struck it on its face), and advanced toward 'Alī. The two fought in single combat with each other, and 'Alī killed 'Amr. His horsemen went away in a rout and rushed through the trench in flight. Two men were killed along with 'Amr: Munabbih b. 'Uthmān b. 'Ubayd b. al-Sabbāq b. 'Abd al-Dār (he was hit by an arrow and died of it in Mecca) and Nawfal b. 'Abdallāh b. al-Mughīrah of the Banū Makhzūm. Nawfal plunged into the trench and became trapped in it. They pelted him with stones. He said, "People of the Arabs, a slaying better than this!" So 'Alī went down and killed him. The Muslims took his body. They asked the Messenger of God to sell them his body. The Messenger of God said: "We have no need for his body or its price. Do with it as you like." So he left them to do as they pleased with it.

According to Ibn Ḥumayd—Salamah—Muḥammad b. Isḥāq—Abū Laylā 'Abdallāh b. Sahl b. 'Abd al-Raḥmān b. Sahl al-Anṣārī[94] (a member of the Banū Ḥārithah): At the time of the Battle of the Trench, 'Ā'ishah, the Mother of the Faithful,[95] was in the fortress of the Banū Ḥārithah, one of Medina's strongest fortresses, and the mother of Sa'd b. Mu'ādh was there with her.

According to 'Ā'ishah: That was before the curtain[96] was imposed on us. Sa'd [b. Mu'ādh] passed by wearing a coat of mail

---

93. A horse was hamstrung when its rider resolved not to attempt escape but to fight to the death.

94. His exact dates are unknown. His name is also given as Abū Laylā b. 'Abdallāh b. 'Abd al-Raḥmān b. Sahl al-Anṣārī, and he is said to have been a reliable transmitter. See Ibn Ḥajar, *Tahdhīb*, XII, 215.

95. On the title "Mother of the Faithful" conferred on Muḥammad's wives, see Watt, *Muhammad at Medina*, 286–87.

96. Arabic: *ḥijāb*, "anything that veils, conceals, hides, covers, or protects" (Lane, *Lexicon*, II, 516). Originally, the word designated the curtain that was set up in Muḥammad's house to separate his wives from the view of unrelated male visitors; in later usage it was applied to a veil or article of clothing concealing any Muslim woman's features and thereby protecting her from the desire of men. The institution of such a curtain in Muḥammad's house is usually dated to this year, A.H. 5, and sometimes connected with the behavior of certain guests at the wedding of the Prophet and Zaynab bt. Jaḥsh. Qur'ān 33:53 enunciates the injunction: "O believers, enter not the houses of the Prophet, except leave is given you for a meal, without watching for its hour. But when you are invited, then enter; and when you have had the meal, disperse, neither lingering for idle talk; that is hurtful to the Prophet, and he is ashamed before you; but God is not ashamed before the truth. And when you ask his wives for any object, ask them from behind a curtain (*ḥijāb*); that is cleaner for your hearts and theirs." 'Ā'ishah's account of the so-

tucked up so that his entire forearm was exposed, with his lance in
[1477] his hand. He was running about with it and reciting:

Wait a little, and Ḥamal shall be present at the fray:
There is no harm in death when one's time is come.[97]

His mother said to him, "Hurry up, son; by God, you are late!"

According to 'Ā'ishah: I said to her, "Umm Sa'd,[98] I wish Sa'd's coat of mail were ampler than it is." I feared for him where the arrow struck him. Sa'd b. Mu'ādh was shot with an arrow, and the median vein of his arm was cut.

According to Ibn Ḥumayd—Salamah—Muḥammad b. Isḥāq—'Āṣim b. 'Umar b. Qatādah: The arrow was shot by Ḥibbān b. Qays b. al-'Ariqah (one of the Banū 'Āmir b. Lu'ayy). When he hit Sa'd, Ḥibbān said: "Take that! I am Ibn al-'Ariqah." Sa'd replied: "God make your face sweat[99] in hellfire! O God, if Thou hast saved any portion of the warfare with Quraysh, save me for it; for there are no men against whom I would rather strive than men who hurt Thy Messenger, called him a liar, and cast him out. O God, if Thou hast set warfare between us and them, grant me martyrdom, and do not let me die until Thou make my eye see its desire upon the Banū Qurayẓah."

According to Sufyān b. Wakī'[100]—Muḥammad b. Bishr[101]—Muḥammad b. 'Amr[102]—his father ['Amr b. 'Alqamah][103]—

called "Affair of the Lie" in A.H. 6 (p. 59, below) implies that by that date seclusion of the Prophet's wives was in force. On the development of regulations concerning the modest behavior expected from Muḥammad's wives, see Watt, *Muhammad at Medina*, 284–87; *EI*[2], s.v. Ḥidjāb; and Stowasser, *Women in the Qur'an, Traditions, and Interpretation*, 90–94, 127–31.

97. The verse was proverbial. Commentators give various identifications for Ḥamal (whose name sometimes appears as Jamal).

98. I.e., "Mother (*umm*) of Sa'd," using the form of address (*kunyah*) that names a person after his or her first son.

99. *'Arraqa* ("make sweat") is a pun on the name al-'Ariqah.

100. Sufyān b. Wakī' b. al-Jarrāḥ al-Kūfī died in 247/861; see Ibn Ḥajar, *Tahdhīb*, IV, 123–24.

101. Muḥammad b. Bishr b. al-Farāfiṣah b. al-Mukhtār, a Kūfan scholar, died in 203/818. See Ibn Ḥajar, *Tahdhīb*, IX, 73–74.

102. Muḥammad b. 'Amr b. 'Alqamah b. Waqqāṣ al-Laythī died in 144/761–62 or 145/762–63. See Ibn Ḥajar, *Tahdhīb*, IX, 375–77.

103. For 'Amr b. 'Alqamah b. Waqqāṣ al-Laythī of Medina (exact dates not known), see Ibn Ḥajar, *Tahdhīb*, VIII, 79–80.

'Alqamah[104]—'Ā'ishah, who said: I went out at the time of the Battle of the Trench following the footsteps of the people. Suddenly, as I was walking, I heard footsteps on the ground behind me. Turning around, I saw Sa'd; so I sat down on the ground. With him, carrying his shield, was his brother's son, al-Ḥārith b. Aws (who, according to Muḥammad b. 'Amr, had been present at Badr with the Messenger of God). Sa'd was wearing an iron coat of mail, but the extremities of his limbs stuck out of it—he was one of the biggest and tallest of men. I feared for Sa'd's limbs. He passed by me reciting:[105] [1478]

Wait a little, and Ḥamal shall reach the fray:
How fair is death when one's time is come!

After he passed me I stood up and hurried into a walled garden where there were a group of Muslims. Among them were 'Umar b. al-Khaṭṭāb and a man wearing his *tasbighah* (according to Muḥammad [b. Hishām], a *tasbighah* is a *mighfar*[106]), so that only his eyes could be seen. 'Umar said: "You are very brave! Why have you come? How can you tell?—perhaps there may be a retreat or trouble." By God, he kept scolding me until I wished the earth would split open for me to enter it. Then the man threw back the *tasbighah* and revealed his face. It was Ṭalḥah,[107] and he said [to 'Umar]: "You have talked too much! What flight and what retreat, except to God?" Sa'd b. Mu'ādh was shot with an arrow that day by [1479] a man named Ibn al-'Ariqah, who said: "Take that! I am Ibn al-'Ariqah." Sa'd said, "God make your face sweat in hellfire![108] He had hit his median vein and cut it. (According to Muḥammad b. 'Amr: Some have said that whenever a person's median vein is

---

104. Ed. Cairo, index, identifies him as 'Alqamah b. Qays al-Nakha'ī. He was supposedly ninety years old when he died sometime between 61/680 and 63/683. See Ibn Ḥajar, *Tahdhīb*, 276–78. However, the rest of the *isnād* points to 'Alqamah b. Waqqāṣ al-Laythī. See note 153, below.

105. Literally, "reciting verse in *rajaz* meter."

106. I.e., "a portion of the mail of the coat of mail, that is conjoined to the helmet, and protects the neck"—Lane, *Lexicon*, IV, 1299.

107. For a biography of Ṭalḥah b. 'Ubaydallāh, a member of the Quraysh clan of Banū Taym b. Murrah, who accompanied Muḥammad on the Hijrah and distinguished himself at the Battle of Uḥud, see *EI*[1], s.v. Ṭalḥa. The incident reveals Ṭalḥah's coolness toward 'Umar and his closeness to 'Ā'ishah, elements that would be important in his subsequent career.

108. See note 99, above.

cut, it keeps oozing blood until the person dies.) Sa'd said, "O God, do not let me die until Thou make my eye see its desire upon the Banū Qurayẓah"—in the Time of Ignorance[109] they had been his confederates and clients.

According to Ibn Ḥumayd—Salamah—Muḥammad b. Isḥāq—someone not to be doubted—'Ubaydallāh b. Ka'b b. Mālik, who used to say: No one hit Sa'd with an arrow that day but Abū Usāmah al-Jushamī, a confederate of the Banū Makhzūm. God knows best what actually happened.

According to Ibn Ḥumayd—Salamah—Muḥammad b. Isḥāq—Yaḥyā b. 'Abbād b. 'Abdallāh b. al-Zubayr[110]—his father, 'Abbād, who said:[111] Ṣafiyyah[112] bt. 'Abd al-Muṭṭalib was in Fāri', the fortress of Ḥassān b. Thābit.[113]

According to Ṣafiyyah, who said: Ḥassān was with us there with the women and children. A man from the Jews passed by us and began to circle the fortress. The Banū Qurayẓah had gone to war and had broken their pact with the Messenger of God. There was no one between us and them to defend us—the Messenger of God and the Muslims, being face to face with the enemy, could not leave them to come back to us when anyone came at us. So I said:
[1480] "Ḥassān, this Jew, as you see, is circling the fortress. By God, I fear he will point out our exposed places to the Jews who are to our rear while the Messenger of God and his companions are too busy to attend to us. So go down to him and kill him." He replied: "God forgive you, daughter of 'Abd al-Muṭṭalib! You know I am not the man to do it." When he said that to me and I saw that nothing could be expected from him, I girded myself, took a club, and, having gone down from the fortress to the man, I struck him with

109. Arabic, "in the *jāhiliyyah*," the "time of ignorance" before Islam. See *EI*², s.v. Djāhiliyya.

110. Yaḥyā b. 'Abbād b. 'Abdallāh b. al-Zubayr b. al-'Awwām is said to have died at the age of thirty-six, but no exact date is given. See Ibn Ḥajar, *Tahdhīb*, XI, 234–35.

111. On 'Abbād b. 'Abdallāh b. al-Zubayr b. al-'Awwām, see Ibn Ḥajar, *Tahdhīb*, V, 98. Parallels: IH, III, 228 (tr. Guillaume, 458); *Aghānī*, IV, 15 (ed. Cairo, IV, 1378).

112. Muḥammad's paternal aunt; the daughter of 'Abd al-Muṭṭalib's last marriage, she was slightly younger than Muḥammad.

113. Ḥassān b. Thābit of the tribe of al-Khazraj in Medina was the most prominent of the poets supporting Muḥammad. See *EI*², s.v. Ḥassān b. Thābit; *GAS*, II, 289–92.

the club until I killed him. When I had finished with him, I returned to the fortress and said: "Ḥassān, go down to him and strip him"—only his being a man kept me from stripping him. Ḥassān replied, "I have no need for his spoils, daughter of ʿAbd al-Muṭṭalib."[114]

According to Ibn Isḥāq: The Messenger of God and his companions continued in the fear and distress that God has described [in the Qurʾān], because their enemies had leagued together against them and had come at them "from above them and below them."[115] Then Nuʿaym b. Masʿūd b. ʿĀmir b. Unayf b. Thaʿlabah b. Qunfudh b. Hilāl b. Khalāwah b. Ashjaʿ b. Rayth b. Ghaṭafān came to the Messenger of God and said, "I have become a Muslim, but my tribesmen do not know of my Islam; so command me whatever you will." The Messenger of God said to him: "You are only one man among us. Make them abandon [each other], if you can, so that they leave us; for war is deception."

Nuʿaym b. Masʿūd therefore set out and came to the Banū Qurayẓah—he had been their drinking companion in the Time of Ignorance—and said to them, "Banū Qurayẓah, you know my affection for you and the special tie between myself and you." "Yes," they said, "you are not a person whom we doubt." He said to them: "Quraysh and Ghaṭafān have come to make war on [1481] Muḥammad, and you have backed them against him. The position of Quraysh and Ghaṭafān is not like yours. The land is your land. Your wealth, your children, and your women are in it; you cannot move from it to another. The wealth, children, women, and land of Quraysh and Ghaṭafān are elsewhere; so they are not in a position like yours. If they see an opportunity and booty, they will take it; if it turns out otherwise, they will return to their lands and

114. The editor of ed. Cairo adds the following note: "According to al-Suhaylī, people infer from this tradition that Ḥassān was very cowardly. One scholar disputes this and denies it on the ground that the tradition has a broken chain of transmission. He says that if it were true, Ḥassān would have been mocked for it: for he used to compose satirical verses against such poets as Ḍirār and Ibn al-Zibaʿrā, and they would engage in polemics and reply to him; yet no one ever berated him for cowardice or branded him a coward. This indicates the weakness of Ibn Isḥāq's tradition. If the tradition is true, perhaps he was sick that day with an illness that prevented him from being present at the fighting."

115. See note 85, above.

leave you exposed to this man in your land, and you will have no strength to deal with him if he is left to deal with you alone. So do not fight on the side of the men [of Quraysh and Ghaṭafān], until you take from them hostages from their nobles, to be in your hands as surety for you that they will fight Muḥammad with you until you have fought it out with him." They said, "You have given good counsel and advice."

Nu'aym then set out and came to Quraysh. He said to Abū Sufyān b. Ḥarb and the men of Quraysh who were with him: "People of Quraysh, you know my affection for you and how I have separated from Muḥammad. Word has come to me of something that I consider it my duty to pass on to you as a matter of sincere advice; but keep to yourselves what I say." "We will," they said. "Then know," he said, "that the Jews have regretted what they did regarding relations between them and Muḥammad. They have sent to him, saying: 'We regret what we have done. Will you be satisfied with us if we take nobles from the tribes of Quraysh and Ghaṭafān and give them to you, so that you can behead them? Then we will be on your side against any of them that remain.' He has sent them word saying yes. So if the Jews send to you asking for hostages from your men, do not give them a single one of your men."

[1482] Then Nu'aym set out and came to Ghaṭafān. He said: "People of Ghaṭafān, you are my stock and my kin, the dearest of people to me. I think you have no doubts about me." "Truly spoken," they said. He said, "Keep to yourselves what I say." "We will," they said. Then he spoke to them as he had spoken to Quraysh, warning them as he had warned Quraysh.

Thus, on a Sabbath eve in the month of Shawwāl of the year 5, by the favor of God toward His Messenger, Abū Sufyān and the chiefs of Ghaṭafān sent to the Banū Qurayẓah 'Ikrimah b. Abī Jahl with a group of men from Quraysh and Ghaṭafān. They said to the Banū Qurayẓah: "We are not in a place where one can stay. Our camels and horses have perished. Come out to do battle tomorrow morning, so that we can fight it out with Muḥammad and finish matters between us and him." The Banū Qurayẓah sent back word to Quraysh, saying: "Today is the Sabbath, a day on which we do no labor. One of us violated it once, and you know what befell him.[116] Moreover, we will not fight on your side until you give us some of your men as hostages to be in our hands as surety to us until we fight it out with Muḥammad; for we fear that if the warfare tests your mettle and the fighting becomes difficult for you, you will hurry back to your lands, leaving us with the man in our land, and then we shall have no strength to deal with Muḥammad."

When the messengers brought back to them what the Banū Qurayẓah had said, Quraysh and Ghaṭafān said, "You know, by God, that what Nu'aym b. Mas'ūd told you is indeed true." So they sent to the Banū Qurayẓah, saying: "By God, we will not give you a single one of our men. If you want to fight, come out and fight." When the messengers reached them with this message, the Banū Qurayẓah said [to each other]: "What Nu'aym b. Mas'ūd told you is indeed true! The men [of Quraysh and Ghaṭafān] only want to fight. If they find an opportunity, they will take it; if not, they will [1483] hurry back to their lands and leave you exposed to this man in your lands." So they sent to Quraysh and Ghaṭafān, saying, "By God, we will not fight on your side until you give us hostages." Quraysh and Ghaṭafān refused. God caused them to abandon each other. Then God sent against them in the bitter cold winter nights a wind that began overturning their cooking pots and blowing away their tents. When word of their disagreement and how God had disrupted their unity reached the Messenger of God, he called Ḥudhayfah b. al-Yamān and sent him to them by night to see what the enemy was doing.

According to Ibn Ḥumayd—Salamah—Muḥammad b. Isḥāq—Yazīd b. Ziyād[117]—Muḥammad b. Ka'b al-Quraẓī, who said: A young man of al-Kūfah[118] asked Ḥudhayfah b. al-Yamān, "Abū

---

116. See note 127, below.

117. Yazīd b. Ziyād (dates unknown; the name is also given as Yazīd b. Abī Ziyād, or Yazīd b. Ziyād b. Abī Ziyād) of Medina was a *mawlā* of 'Abdallāh b. 'Ayyāsh b. Abī Rabī'ah al-Makhzūmī. See Ibn Ḥajar, *Tahdhīb*, XI, 328.

118. The Muslim garrison city of al-Kūfah was founded ca. 17/638 in the caliphate of 'Umar on the Euphrates near the older city of al-Ḥīrah; see *EI*², s.v. This report portrays Ḥudhayfah as being asked many years later, after the conquest of Iraq and the settlement of al-Kūfah, by a young Kūfan (*fatā* implies a man who has recently reached military age) to recall the events of the battle.

'Abdallāh,[119] you saw the Messenger of God and accompanied him?" "Yes, nephew," he replied. The young man asked, "How did things go with you?" "By God we toiled!" said Ḥudhayfah. The young man said, "By God, had we lived in his time, we would not have left him to walk on the ground; we would have carried him on our necks." Ḥudhayfah said: "Nephew, by God, I can see us with the Messenger of God at the trench. He prayed part of the night, then turned to us and said, 'Who is a man who will go up and see for us how the enemy is doing?'—the Messenger of God stipulated for him that he should come back—'and God shall cause him to enter paradise.'[120] Not a man stood up. Again the Messenger of God prayed part of the night and turned to us and said the same words, but not one of us stood up. Again the Messenger of God prayed part of the night and turned to us and said, 'Who is a man who will go up and see for us how the enemy is doing and then come back?'—the Messenger of God stipulated
[1484] that he should return—'and I will ask God that he may be my companion in paradise.' But none of the men stood up, so intense were the fear, the hunger, and the cold. When no one stood up, the Messenger of God called me. I had no choice but to stand up when he called me. He said, 'Ḥudhayfah, go and enter among the enemy, and see what they are doing; make no disturbance, and come back to us.'

"So I went and entered among the enemy. The wind and God's hosts[121] were taking their toll on them, allowing not a cooking pot, fire, or tent of theirs to stay put. Abū Sufyān b. Ḥarb stood up and said, 'People of Quraysh, let every man see who is sitting next to him.' So I took hold of the hand of the man who was beside me. I asked who he was, and he gave his name. Then Abū Sufyān said: 'People of Quraysh, by God you are not in a place where one can stay. Horses and camels have perished. The Banū Qurayẓah have

---

119. Abū 'Abdallāh is Ḥudhayfah's *kunyah* (nickname). Since the verbs in the question are in the second person plural, the young man must have meant something like, "Did you *and the people of your generation* see the Messenger of God?"

120. I.e., he would be assured of paradise even though he had not died a martyr's death.

121. God's hosts (*junūd Allāh*) apparently refers to angels (so according to al-Ṭabarī, *Jāmi' al-bayān*, XXII, 81). Cf. Qur'ān 33:9, "O you who believe! Remember God's favor to you when there came against you hosts, and We sent against them a great wind and hosts (*junūdan*) you could not see."

broken their promise to us. Words hateful to us have come to us from them, and you can see what we have suffered from this wind. By God, no pot of ours stays put, no fire of ours keeps burning, and no tent of ours holds together. So saddle up, for I am leaving!' Then he went over to his camel, which was hobbled, seated himself on it, and struck it. It jumped up with him, standing on three legs, for its hobble was untied only after it stood up. Had it not been for the injunction of the Messenger of God to me that I should not cause any disturbance until I came to him—and I wanted to—I would have killed him with an arrow."

Ḥudhayfah continued: "I went back to the Messenger of God. He was standing, praying in a woolen wrapper woven with a camel-saddle pattern that belonged to one of his wives. When he saw me, he sat me at his feet and threw the edge of the wrapper over me. Then he bowed down and prostrated himself, but I disturbed him. After he pronounced a greeting,[122] I told him the [1485] news. Ghaṭafān heard what Quraysh had done, and they hastened back to their lands."

According to Ibn Ḥumayd—Salamah—Muḥammad b. Isḥāq, who said: The next morning, the Prophet of God left the trench and went back to Medina with the Muslims, and they laid down their weapons.

The Expedition against the Banū Qurayẓah[123]

According to Ibn Ḥumayd—Salamah—Muḥammad b. Isḥāq—Ibn Shihāb al-Zuhrī: At noontime Gabriel,[124] wearing a cloth-of-gold turban, came to the Messenger of God on a mule with a brocade-covered saddle. He said, "Have you laid down your arms, Messenger of God?" "Yes," he replied. Gabriel said: "The angels have not laid down their arms! I have just returned from pursuing the enemy. God commands you, Muḥammad, to march to the Banū Qurayẓah. I, too, will betake myself to the Banū Qurayẓah."[125]

122. I.e., either after he pronounced the salutation to the guardian angels with which Islamic prayers end or after he greeted Ḥudhayfah.

123. Parallels: IH, III, 233–54 (tr. Guillaume, 461–69); W, II, 496–531.

124. Gabriel (Jibrīl) was the angel who brought revelations to Muḥammad (cf. Qur'ān 2:97). See *EI*², s.v. Djabrā'īl.

125. IH, III, 233, and W, II, 497, add "and will shake them."

The Messenger of God commanded a crier to announce to the people that whoever would heed and obey should not pray the afternoon prayer until they were in [the territory of] the Banū Qurayẓah. The Messenger of God sent 'Alī b. Abī Ṭālib ahead with his banner to the Banū Qurayẓah, and the people hastened to it. 'Alī b. Abī Ṭālib marched and, having approached the fortresses, heard foul words from them about the Messenger of God. He went back and met the Messenger of God on the way and said, "Messenger of God, it would be better for you not to go near these most wicked men." "Why?" he asked, "I think you have heard them insult me." He said, "Yes, Messenger of God." He said,[126] "If they had seen me, they would not have said anything of the sort."

When the Messenger of God had approached their fortresses, he
[1486] said: "You brothers of apes![127] Has God shamed you and sent down his retribution on you?" They said, "Abū al-Qāsim,[128] you have never been one to act impetuously."[129]

Before reaching the Banū Qurayẓah, the Messenger of God passed his companions at al-Ṣawrān.[130] "Has anyone passed you?" he asked. "Yes, Messenger of God," they replied. "Diḥyah b. Khalīfah al-Kalbī[131] passed us on a white mule with a brocade-covered saddle." The Messenger of God said, "That was Gabriel, sent to the Banū Qurayẓah to shake their fortresses and cast terror into their hearts."

When the Messenger of God came to the Banū Qurayẓah, he halted at one of their wells in a part of their territory called Bi'r

---

126. Ed. Cairo omits "He said," making the next sentence a continuation of 'Alī's words.

127. The Qur'ān contains references to how God punished a group of Jews who violated the Sabbath by changing them into apes; cf. Qur'ān 2:65, 5:60, and 7:166. See pp. 24, above, and 30, below, where the Jews themselves allude to the legend.

128. Abū al-Qāsim (father of al-Qāsim) was Muḥammad's *kunyah* (a familiar name usually derived from the name of the bearer's first male child).

129. Arabic: *mā kunta jahūlan*. On the meanings of the root *j-h-l*, which includes both the ideas of ignorance and of violent, blind, or impulsive action, see Goldziher, *Muslim Studies*, I, 201–8; and Blachère et al., *Dictionnaire arabe-français-anglais*, I, 1845–46.

130. According to al-Samhūdī, *Khulāṣat al-wafā'*, 575–76, the place was located at the farther end of al-Baqī', alongside the road to the Banū Qurayẓah.

131. Diḥyah b. Khalīfah al-Kalbī was traditionally represented as a rich merchant of such beauty that the Angel Gabriel assumed his features. When he arrived in Medina, all the women were said to have come out to see him. See *EI*², s.v. Diḥya.

Annā,[132] and the men joined up with him. Some men came to him after the last evening prayer. They had not prayed the afternoon prayer because of what the Messenger of God had said—that no one should pray the afternoon prayer until in [the territory of] the Banū Qurayẓah because of the warfare against them that was incumbent on them. They refused to pray because the Prophet had said "until they reach the Banū Qurayẓah"; so they prayed the afternoon prayer there after the last evening prayer. God did not find fault with them in His Book, nor did the Messenger of God reprimand them for it. (This report is according to Muḥammad b. Isḥāq—his father [Isḥāq b. Yasār][133]—Maʻbad b. Kaʻb b. Mālik al-Anṣārī.[134])

According to [Sufyān] b. Wakīʻ—Muḥammad b. Bishr—Muḥammad b. ʻAmr—his father [ʻAmr b. ʻAlqamah]—ʻAlqamah—ʻĀʼishah, who said: The Messenger of God pitched a round tent over Saʻd in the mosque.[135] He laid down his arms—that is, when he had come back from [the Battle of] the Trench—and the Muslims, too, laid down their arms. Then Gabriel came to [1487] him and said: "Have you laid down your arms? By God, the angels have not yet laid down their arms! Go out to them, and fight them!" The Messenger of God called for his breastplate and put it on. Then he went out, and the Muslims went out too. When he passed by the Banū Ghanm,[136] he said, "Who passed by you?" They replied, "Diḥyah al-Kalbī passed by us." (His demeanor, beard, and face were likened to Gabriel's.) Then he encamped by [the Banū Qurayẓah]. (Saʻd was in his tent that the Messenger of God had pitched over him in the mosque.) He besieged them for a month or for twenty-five nights. When the siege became too severe for them, they were told to submit to the judgment of the Messenger of God. Abū Lubābah b. ʻAbd al-Mundhir gave a sign that it would mean slaughter. So they said, "We will submit to the judgment of Saʻd b. Muʻādh." The Messenger of God said, "Submit

---

132. Also vocalized Unā.

133. Isḥāq b. Yasār, the father of Muḥammad b. Isḥāq, was a *mawlā* of Qays b. Makhramah. He was considered a very reliable transmitter. His exact dates are not known. See Ibn Ḥajar, *Tahdhīb*, I, 257.

134. The brother of ʻUbaydallāh b. Kaʻb b. Mālik al-Anṣārī. See *GAS*, I, 276–77.

135. To shelter Saʻd b. Muʻādh while he was recuperating from his wound.

136. A clan of the al-Aws; see Watt, *Muhammad at Medina*, 154.

to his judgment." So they submitted. The Messenger of God sent to him a donkey with a saddle padded with palm fiber, and he was mounted on it.

According to 'Ā'ishah: His wound had healed, so that nothing of it was visible except what looked like a ring.

Resumption of the account of Ibn Isḥāq: The Messenger of God besieged them twenty-five nights, until the siege exhausted them and God cast terror into their hearts. Ḥuyayy b. Akhṭab had entered among the Banū Qurayẓah in their fortress when Quraysh and Ghaṭafān had gone back leaving them; this he did in fulfillment of his compact with Ka'b b. Asad. When they became certain that the Messenger of God would not depart from them until he
[1488] had fought it out with them, Ka'b b. Asad said to them: "People of the Jews, you see what has befallen you. I shall propose three alternatives to you. Take whichever one you will." "What are they?" they asked. He said: "That we follow[137] this man and believe him; for, by God, it has become clear to you that he is indeed a prophet sent [from God] and that it is he whom you used to find [mentioned] in your book. Then you will be secure in your lives, your property, your children, and your wives." They said, "We will never depart from the law of the Torah or exchange it for another." "Since you reject this proposal of mine," he said, "come let us kill our children and wives and go out to Muḥammad and his companions as men who brandish swords, leaving behind us no impediments to worry us, until God judges between us and Muḥammad. If we die, we shall die having left nothing behind us for which we fear; if we win victory, by my life we shall find women and children." They said: "Kill these poor ones? What would be the good of living after them?" He said: "Since you have rejected these proposals of mine, tonight is the night of the Sabbath. Perhaps Muḥammad and his companions feel themselves safe in it. Go down; perhaps we can take Muḥammad and his companions by surprise." They said, "Profane our Sabbath and do on it what none of our predecessors has ever done, except those you know about—and they were transformed in a way that you surely know?" He said, "No man among you has ever for a single night shown sound judgment since his mother bore him!"

137. Variant, "swear allegiance to."

Then they sent to the Messenger of God, saying, "Send us Abū Lubābah b. 'Abd al-Mundhir, one of the Banū 'Amr b. 'Awf"[138]— [1489] they[139] were confederates of al-Aws—"so that we can ask his advice in this affair." The Messenger of God sent him to them. When they saw him, the men rose to meet him, and the women and children rushed to grab hold of him, weeping before him, so that he felt pity for them. They said to him, "Abū Lubābah, do you think we should submit to Muḥammad's judgment?" "Yes," he said, but he pointed with his hand to his throat, that it would be slaughter. (Abū Lubābah [later] said, "By God, as soon as my feet moved, I knew that I had betrayed God and His Messenger.") Abū Lubābah rushed away at a loss. Before coming to the Messenger of God, he tied himself to one of the pillars in the mosque, saying, "I will not leave this spot until God forgives me for what I have done." He promised God that he would never set foot on the territory of the Banū Qurayẓah. "Never," he said, "shall God see me in a land where I betrayed God and His Messenger." When news of him reached the Messenger of God—Abū Lubābah was slow in coming to him, and the Messenger of God deemed him late—he said, "Had he come to me, I would have sought forgiveness for him; but, since he has done what he did, I cannot release him from his place, until God forgives him."

According to Ibn Ḥumayd—Salamah b. al-Faḍl—Muḥammad b. Isḥāq—Yazīd b. 'Abdallāh b. Qusayṭ:[140] The forgiving of Abū Lubābah was revealed to the Messenger of God while he was in the apartment of Umm Salamah.[141] Umm Salamah said, "I heard the Messenger of God laughing at daybreak; so I said, 'Why are you laughing, Messenger of God?—may God make you laugh heart-

---

138. 'Amr b. 'Awf was a clan of al-Aws.

139. I.e., the Banū Qurayẓah; on the alliance between the Banū Qurayẓah and al-Aws, see Watt, *Muhammad at Medina*, 214.

140. Yazīd b. 'Abdallāh b. Qusayṭ died in 122/740 at the age of ninety. See Ibn Ḥajar, *Tahdhīb*, XI, 342–43.

141. Muḥammad married Umm Salamah Hind bt. al-Mughīrah, whose husband, Abū Salamah, had died of wounds after the Battle of Uḥud, in 4/626; see Poonawala, *Last Years*, 132, [I, 1771]. Muḥammad's wives lived in separate apartments of his residence, which was adjacent to the mosque in Medina. He is said to have spent a night with each of them in turn; cf. Watt, *Muhammad at Medina*, 284, 396.

ily!'[142] He replied, 'Abū Lubābah has been forgiven.' I said, 'Shall I not announce the good news to him?' 'Yes,' he said, 'if you will.'" So Umm Salamah stood at the door of her chamber (it was before
[1490] the curtain was imposed on them) and said: "Abū Lubābah, rejoice! God has forgiven you." The people swarmed toward him to release him, but he said: "No, by God! Not until the Messenger of God is the one who releases me with his own hand!" And so, when he went out for the morning prayer, he released him.

According to Ibn Isḥāq: Tha'labah b. Sa'yah,[143] Usayd[144] b. Sa'yah, and Asad b. 'Ubayd—a group of men from the Banū Hadl,[145] not from the Banū Qurayẓah or al-Naḍīr (their genealogy was superior to that), but cousins of the men in question—became Muslims the night that Qurayẓah submitted to the judgment of the Messenger of God. During that night, 'Amr b. Su'dā al-Quraẓī went out and passed by the guards of the Messenger of God—Muḥammad b. Maslamah al-Anṣārī was in charge of them that night. When the latter saw 'Amr, he said, "Who is it?" "'Amr b. Su'dā," he replied. 'Amr had refused to go along with the Banū Qurayẓah in their treachery toward the Messenger of God. "Never," he had said, "will I act treacherously toward Muḥammad." Having recognized him, Muḥammad b. Maslamah said, "O God, do not deprive me of [forgiveness for][146] the lapses of the noble"—and he let him pass. 'Amr went his way and spent that night in the mosque of the Messenger of God in Medina. Then he went away, and no one knows to this day into which of God's lands he went. His story was mentioned to the Messenger of God,
[1491] who said, "He was a man whom God rescued for his loyalty."

142. *Aḍḥaka Allāhu sinnaka*—literally, "may God make your tooth laugh"; i.e., may He make you laugh or smile heartily, so that you reveal your side teeth. The teeth immediately behind the four eyeteeth were called *ḍawāḥik* ("laughers") because they became visible in laughter or smiling; see *Lisan*, IV, 2558.

143. So vocalized by ed. Leiden; perhaps to be vocalized "Sa'iyyah," as by the editor of W, II, 503.

144. So vocalized by IH and ed. Cairo. Ed. Leiden prefers the vocalization "Asīd" on the basis of al-Dhahabī, *Mushtabih*, 299.

145. On the clan of Hadl, which had become closely connected to the Banū Qurayẓah, see Watt, *Muhammad at Medina*, 193–94.

146. Understanding *iqālah*, as in W, 504; IH, III, 238; cf. ed. Leiden, *Glossarium*, p. CCCL.

According to Ibn Isḥāq: Some men allege that he was bound with an old frayed rope along with the Banū Qurayẓah who were bound when they submitted to the judgment of the Messenger of God. In the morning his rope was cast aside, and no one knew where he had gone. Then the Messenger of God said this saying about him. But God knows best [what really happened].

According to Ibn Isḥāq: In the morning, they submitted to the judgment of the Messenger of God. The al-Aws jumped up and said: "Messenger of God, they are our clients (*mawālī*), not clients of al-Khazraj. You know what you did the other day with the clients of al-Khazraj!" (Before besieging the Banū Qurayẓah, the Messenger of God had besieged the Banū Qaynuqā', who were confederates of al-Khazraj.[147] They had submitted to his judgment. 'Abdallāh b. Ubayy b. Salūl[148] had asked him for them, and he had given them to him.) Therefore, when the al-Aws spoke to him, the Messenger of God said, "People of al-Aws, will you not be satisfied if one of your own men passes judgment on them?" "Yes," they said. So he said, "It shall be entrusted to Sa'd b. Mu'ādh." The Messenger of God had placed Sa'd b. Mu'ādh in the tent of a Muslim[149] woman named Rufaydah in his mosque. She used to nurse the wounded and earn merit for herself by serving Muslims who were impoverished. When Sa'd was struck by the arrow in the ditch, the Messenger of God said to his tribesmen, "Put him in Rufaydah's tent, so that I can visit him from nearby."[150] When the Messenger of God appointed him judge over the Banū Qurayẓah, his tribesmen came to him and lifted him onto a donkey on which they had put a leather cushion, for he was a stout man. They brought him to the Messenger of God, saying, [1492]
"Abū 'Amr,[151] treat your clients well; for the Messenger of God has put you in charge of the matter only that you may treat them well." After they had plied him with many such requests, he said,

147. For the campaign in 2/624 against the Jewish tribe of Banū Qaynuqā' and their expulsion, see Watt and McDonald, *Foundation*, 85–87 [I, 1359–62].

148. 'Abdallāh b. Ubayy, a leader of al-Khazraj and one of the leading men of Medina, had become a Muslim but was usually deemed to be a "hypocrite" (*munāfiq*) because of his opposition to some of Muḥammad's decisions; see *EI*², s.v. 'Abd Allāh b. Ubayy.

149. IH and ed. Cairo: "a woman of Aslam."

150. Muḥammad's house adjoined the mosque.

151. Addressing Sa'd by his *kunyah*.

"The time has come for Sa'd for the sake of God not to be influenced by anyone's reproach." Then one of his tribesmen who was with him went back to the dwelling place of the Banū 'Abd al-Ashhal and announced to them the death of the men of the Banū Qurayẓah before Sa'd b. Mu'ādh reached them because of the words he had heard from him.

According to Abū Ja'far [al-Ṭabarī]: When Sa'd reached the Messenger of God and the Muslims, the Messenger of God said (according to Ibn Wakī'—Muḥammad b. Bishr—Muḥammad b. 'Amr—his father—'Alqamah, in a report that he attributed to Abū Sa'īd al-Khudrī,[152] who said: When he—that is, Sa'd—came into sight, the Messenger of God said), "Arise and go to your master (*sayyid*)" (or he said "to the best of you"), "and help him dismount." The Messenger of God said [to Sa'd], "Pass judgment on them." He replied, "I pass judgment on them that their fighters shall be killed and their children made captives and that their property shall be divided." The Messenger of God said, "You have passed judgment on them with the judgment of God and the judgment of His Messenger."

Resumption of the account of Ibn Isḥāq: As for Ibn Isḥāq, he said in his report: When Sa'd reached the Messenger of God and the Muslims, the Messenger of God said, "Arise and go to your master." So they arose and went to him and said, "Abū 'Amr, the Messenger of God has entrusted you with your clients (*mawālī*), so that you may pass judgment on them." Sa'd said, "God's oath and covenant be upon you in this matter, that the judgment on them shall be what I judge!" "Yes," they replied. He said, "And
[1493] upon the one who is here"—[this he said] in the direction of the Messenger of God, while turning away from the Messenger of God out of respect for him. The Messenger of God said, "Yes." Sa'd said, "I pass judgment on them that the men shall be killed, the property divided, and the children and women made captives."

According to Ibn Ḥumayd—Salamah—Muḥammad b. Isḥāq—'Āṣim b. 'Umar b. Qatādah—'Abd al-Raḥmān b. 'Amr b. Sa'd b.

152. Abū Sa'īd Sa'd b. Mālik b. Sinān al-Khudrī al-Anṣārī (the Banū Khudrah were a small group in the Banū al-Ḥārith clan of al-Khazraj; cf. Watt, *Muhammad at Medina*, 167), a companion of the Prophet, used to give legal opinions in Medina. He died ca. 63/682–83. See Ibn Sa'd, *Ṭabaqāt*, II/2, 124, 127; Ibn Ḥajar, *Iṣābah*, III, 78–80.

Mu'ādh—'Alqamah b. Waqqāṣ al-Laythī,[153] who said: The Messenger of God said to Sa'd, "You have passed judgment on them with the judgment of God from above seven heavens."[154]

According to Ibn Isḥāq: Then they were made to come down, and the Messenger of God imprisoned them in the dwelling of al-Ḥārith's daughter, a woman of the Banū al-Najjār.[155] The Messenger of God went out into the marketplace of Medina (it is still its marketplace today) and had trenches dug in it; then he sent for them and had them beheaded in those trenches. They were brought out to him in groups. Among them were the enemy of God, Ḥuyayy b. Akhṭab, and Ka'b b. Asad. the head of the tribe. They numbered 600 or 700—the largest estimate says they were between 800 and 900. As they were being taken in groups to the Messenger of God, they said to Ka'b b. Asad, "Ka'b, what do you think will be done to us?" Ka'b said: "On each occasion you do not understand. Do you not see that the summoner does not discharge [anyone] and that those of you who are taken away do not come [1494] back? By God, it is death!" The affair continued until the Messenger of God had finished with them.

Ḥuyayy b. Akhṭab, the enemy of God, was brought. He was wearing a rose-colored[156] suit of clothes that he had torn all over with fingertip-sized holes so that it would not be taken as booty from him, and his hands were bound to his neck with a rope. When he looked at the Messenger of God, he said, "By God, I do not blame myself for being hostile to you, but whomever God forsakes is forsaken."[157] Then he turned to the people and said:

---

153. 'Alqamah b. Waqqāṣ al-Laythī was born during the lifetime of the Prophet. See Ibn Ḥajar, *Tahdhīb*, VII, 280–81.

154. The phrase, which uses the Hebrew loanword *raqī'* for "heaven," is usually taken to mean, "You have judged with the judgment of God [written on the preserved tablet] above the seven heavens"; cf. Lane, *Lexicon*, III, 1137.

155. The Banū al-Najjār were the most numerous clan or clan group among al-Khazraj; see Watt, *Muhammad at Medina*, 165–66.

156. Arabic *fuqqāḥiyyah* refers either to the color of the garments (that of the desert flower called *fuqqāḥ*; Lane, *Lexicon*, VI, 2424), or to a kind of embroidery (IH, III, 241).

157. Here and in the verses that follow I read *man yakhdhuli llāhu*, rather than *man yakhdhuli llāha*, the voweling of edd. Leiden and Cairo, which would mean "whoever forsakes God." Ḥuyayy, who remained a Jew to the end, certainly would not have considered hostility to Muḥammad to be a forsaking of God. Furthermore, *khadhala* (fail to aid, forsake) and its opposite *naṣara* (aid) are normally

"People, there is no injury in God's command. It is the book of God, His decree, and a battlefield of great slaughter ordained against the Children of Israel." Then he sat down and was beheaded. Jabal b. Jawwāl al-Tha'labī said:

By your life, Ibn Akhṭab did not censure himself [for his action];
but whomever God forsakes is forsaken.
He fought until he made his soul attain its vindication,
and he strove to the utmost seeking glory.

According to Ibn Ḥumayd—Salamah—Muḥammad b. Isḥāq—Muḥammad b. Ja'far b. al-Zubayr[158]—'Urwah b. al-Zubayr—'Ā'ishah, who said: Only one of their women was killed. By God, she was by me, talking with me and laughing unrestrainedly while the Messenger of God was killing their men in the marketplace, when suddenly a mysterious voice[159] called out her name, saying, "Where is so and so?" She said, "Here I am, by God." I asked, "Alas, what is wrong?" She said, "I shall be killed." "Why?" I
[1495] asked. She said, "A misdeed[160] that I committed." She was taken away and beheaded. ('Ā'ishah used to say: I shall never forget my wonder at her cheerfulness and much laughter, even when she knew that she would be killed.)

According to Ibn Ḥumayd—Salamah—Muḥammad b. Isḥāq—Ibn Shihāb al-Zuhrī: Thābit b. Qays b. Shammās came to al-Zabīr b. Bāṭā al-Quraẓī, whose familiar name was Abū 'Abd al-Raḥmān. Al-Zabīr had done Thābit b. Qays b. Shammās a favor in the Time of Ignorance [before Islam]. (According to Muḥammad [b. Isḥāq]: One of al-Zabīr's descendants told me that he had done him this favor at the battle of Bu'āth.[161] He had captured him but had cut off his forelock and released him.) Thābit came to al-Zabīr, now an

---

predicated of God. Cf. Qur'ān 3:154: "If God helps you, none can overcome you; but if He forsakes you, who then can help you after Him?"

158. Muḥammad b. Ja'far b. al-Zubayr died between 110/728–29 and 120/738. See Ibn Ḥajar, *Tahdhīb*, IX, 93.

159. Arabic *hātif*, a voice from an unseen source, often with supernatural overtones.

160. Arabic *ḥadathun aḥdathtuhū* (literally, "a happening or a novelty that I caused to happen") usually has a negative sense; see Lane, *Lexicon*, II, 528.

161. The battle of Bu'āth, the climax of the war of Ḥāṭib between Medina's two Arab tribes, al-Aws and al-Khazraj, took place ca. A.D. 617, shortly before the Hijrah and was fought in the territory of the Banū Qurayẓah. See Watt, *Muhammad at Medina*, 155–58; *EI*², s.v. Bu'āth.

old man, and said, "Abū 'Abd al-Raḥmān, do you recognize me?" Al-Zabīr replied, "Can someone like me fail to recognize someone like you?" Thābit said, "I want to repay you for your favor to me." Al-Zabīr said, "Truly the noble man repays the noble!" Thābit then went to the Messenger of God and said: "Messenger of God, al-Zabīr did me a favor and I owe him a debt of gratitude. I wish to repay him for it. Grant me his life." The Messenger of God said, "It is yours." So Thābit went to him and said: "The Messenger of God has granted me your life. It is yours." He replied, "An old man with no family and no children—what will he do with life?" So Thābit went to the Messenger of God and said, "Messenger of God, his family and children?" "They are yours," he said. So Thābit went to him and said: "The Messenger of God has given me your wife and your children. They are yours." He replied, "A household in the Ḥijāz with no wealth—how can they survive?" So Thābit went to the Messenger of God and said, "His wealth?" "It is yours," he said. So Thābit went to him and said: "The Messenger of God has given me your wealth. It is yours." He replied, "O Thābit, how fares it with the one whose face was like a Chinese mirror in which the virgins of the tribe viewed [1496] themselves—Ka'b b. Asad?" Thābit said, "He has been killed." "And how fares it," he said, "with the chief of the settled folk and the nomads, Ḥuyayy b. Akhṭab?" Thābit said, "He has been killed." "And how fares it," he said, "with our vanguard when we attacked and our defense when we wheeled round,[162] 'Azzāl b. Shamwīl?" Thābit said, "He has been killed." "And how fares it," he said, "with the two assemblies?" (He meant the Banū Ka'b b. Qurayẓah and the Banū 'Amr b. Qurayẓah.) Thābit said, "They have gone to their death." He said: "Then I ask you for the sake of the favor I once did for you to join me to my kinsmen, for by God there is no good in living after them. I will not wait patiently for God, not even [the time needed] to take the bucket of a watering trough, until I meet my dear ones." So Thābit brought him forward, and he was beheaded. When what he said—"until I meet my dear ones"—was reported to Abū Bakr, he said, "He will meet them, by God, in the fire of Gehenna, there to dwell forever and

162. Arabic *kararnā*; IH, III, 243, reads *fararnā*, "we fled"; W, II, 519, reads *wallaw* "they turned back." Al-Wāqidī gives the name as Ghazzāl b. Samaw'al.

forever." Concerning this, Thābit b. Qays b. al-Shammās said, mentioning al-Zabīr b. Bāṭā:

My obligation has been acquitted: I was generous and was
patient, when the folk turned away from patience.
Zabīr of all men had the greatest claim to gratitude
on me; therefore, when his wrists were tied with a thong,
I came to the Messenger of God, that I might untie him;
and the Messenger of God to us was a flowing sea.[163]

The Messenger of God had commanded that all of them who had reached puberty should be killed.

According to Ibn Ḥumayd—Salamah—Muḥammad b. Isḥāq—
[1497] Ayyūb b. 'Abd al-Raḥmān b. 'Abdallāh b. Abī Ṣa'ṣa'ah[164] (a member of the Banū 'Adī b. al-Najjār): Salmā bt. Qays, the mother of al-Mundhir and sister of Salīṭ b. Qays, was one of the maternal aunts of the Messenger of God. She had prayed with him facing both of the *qiblah*s[165] and had sworn allegiance to him after the manner of women.[166] She asked him for [the life of] Rifā'ah b. Shamwīl al-Quraẓī, who had come of age. He had taken refuge with her and had previously been one of their acquaintances. She said: "Prophet of God, you are as dear to me as my father and mother! Give me Rifā'ah b. Shamwīl, for he has said that he will pray and eat camel meat.[167] He gave him to her, and thus she saved his life.

According to Ibn Isḥāq: Then the Messenger of God divided the wealth, wives, and children of the Banū Qurayẓah among the Muslims. On that day he made known the shares of horsemen and shares of foot soldiers, and he deducted from these shares the fifth

---

163. I.e., granted the request. The sea is a metaphor for generosity.

164. His name is also given as Ayyūb b. 'Abd al-Raḥmān b. Ṣa'ṣa'ah. His exact dates are not known. See Ibn Ḥajar, *Tahdhīb*, I, 408.

165. The *qiblah* is the direction that Muslims face in prayer. Originally Muḥammad followed the practice of the Jews in facing Jerusalem, but changed the *qiblah* to the direction of the Ka'bah in Mecca during A.H. 2 (see Watt and McDonald, *Foundation*, 24–25 [I, 1279–81]; the change is alluded to in Qur'ān 2:136 ff.). In other words, Salmā's conversion to Islam took place before the change in the *qiblah*. See *EI*², s.v. Ḳibla.

166. Arabic: *bāya'athu bay'ata al-nisā'i*—this was the term for a pledge of allegiance in which no obligation to fight was involved.

167. Camel meat is permitted under Islamic dietary regulations but prohibited under Jewish regulations.

(*khums*).[168] A horseman received three shares: two shares for the horse and one share for its rider. A foot soldier who had no horse received one share. The cavalry at the battle with the Banū Qurayẓah numbered thirty-six horses. It was the first booty (*fay'*)[169] in which shares were allotted and from which the *khums* was deducted; and according to its precedent (*sunnah*) and the procedure of the Messenger of God in it divisions of booty took place and precedent was followed in [succeeding] expeditions. However, if a man had horses with him, he appointed shares only for two horses.

Then the Messenger of God sent Sa'd b. Zayd al-Anṣārī (a member of the Banū 'Abd al-Ashhal) with some of the captives from the Banū Qurayẓah to Najd, and in exchange for them he purchased horses and arms. The Messenger of God selected for himself from their women Rayḥānah bt. 'Amr b. Khunāfah, a woman from the [1498] Banū 'Amr b. Qurayẓah, and she remained his concubine; when he predeceased her, she was still in his possession.[170] The Messenger of God offered to marry her and impose the curtain (*ḥijāb*) on her, but she said, "Messenger of God, rather leave me in your possession [as a concubine], for it is easier for me and for you." So he did so. When the Messenger of God took her captive, she showed herself averse to Islam and insisted on Judaism. So the Messenger of God put her aside, and he was grieved because of her. Then, while he was with his companions, he heard the sound of shoes behind him and said, "This must be Tha'labah b. Sa'yah coming to bring me tidings of Rayḥānah's acceptance of Islam." He came to him and said, "Messenger of God, Rayḥānah has become a Muslim"—and it gave the Messenger of God joy.

After the affair of the Banū Qurayẓah had ended, the wound of Sa'd b. Mu'ādh broke open. The account of this is as follows, according to Ibn Wakī'—Ibn Bishr—Muḥammad b. 'Amr—his father—'Alqamah (in a report that he attributed to 'Ā'ishah): After Sa'd b. Mu'ādh had passed judgment as he did on the Banū Qurayẓah, he prayed, saying: "O God, Thou knowest that there

---

168. The *khums* was the one-fifth of booty reserved to Muḥammad under Qur'ān 8:14 (said to have been revealed after the battle of Badr) to be used for communal purposes; see Watt, *Muhammad at Medina*, 232, 255.

169. On the development of the term *fay'* ("chattels taken as booty") see *EI*², s.v.

170. I.e, she never became a full wife. See Ibn Sa'd, *Ṭabaqāt*, VIII, 92–94.

are no men against whom I would rather fight and strive than men who called Thy Messenger a liar. O God, if Thou hast saved any portion of warfare with Quraysh for Thy Messenger, save me for it; but if Thou hast cut off the warfare between him and them, take me to Thee." So his wound broke open. The Messenger of
[1499] God returned him to the tent he had pitched over him in the mosque.

'Ā'ishah said: The Messenger of God, Abū Bakr, and 'Umar came to him. By the One holds the soul of Muḥammad in His hand, I could tell Abū Bakr's weeping from 'Umar's even while I was in my chamber. They were, as God has said, "merciful among themselves."[171]

'Alqamah asked ['Ā'ishah], "Mother [of the Faithful],[172] how did the Messenger of God behave?" She replied: "His eye did not weep for anyone. When his grief for someone became intense or when he was upset, he would only take hold of his beard."

According to Ibn Ḥumayd—Salamah—Ibn Isḥāq, who said: At the Battle of the Trench only six Muslims and three polytheists were killed. At the battle with the Banū Qurayẓah, Khallād b. Suwayd b. Tha'labah b. 'Amr b. Balḥārith b. al-Khazraj was killed: a millstone was thrown onto him and badly crushed him. Abū Sinān b. Miḥṣan b. Ḥurthān, a member of the Banū Asad b. Khuzaymah, died while the Messenger of God was besieging the Banū Qurayẓah and was buried in the cemetery of the Banū Qurayẓah. After the Messenger of God returned from the trench, he said, "Now we shall attack them"—meaning Quraysh—"and they will not attack us"—and thus it was, until God granted His Messenger the conquest of Mecca.

According to Ibn Isḥāq, the conquest of the Banū Qurayẓah took place in the month of Dhū al-Qa'dah or in the beginning of Dhū al-Ḥijjah.[173] Al-Wāqidī, however, has said that the Messenger of God attacked them a few days before the end of Dhū al-Qa'dah. He asserted that the Messenger of God commanded that furrows should be dug in the ground for the Banū Qurayẓah. Then he sat

---

171. Qur'ān 48:29.
172. See note 95, above.
173. Dhū al-Qa'dah of A.H. 5 began on 24 March 627; Dhū al-Ḥijjah began on 23 April.

down, and 'Alī and al-Zubayr began cutting off their heads in his [1500]
presence. He asserts that the woman whom the Prophet killed that day was named Bunānah, the wife of al-Ḥakam al-Quraẓī—it was she who had killed Khallād b. Suwayd by throwing a millstone on him. The Messenger of God called for her[174] and beheaded her in retaliation for Khallād b. Suwayd.

There is disagreement over the date of the Prophet's expedition against the Banū al-Muṣṭaliq. This was the expedition called the expedition of al-Muraysī'—al-Muraysī' being the name of a watering place belonging to [the tribe of] Khuzā'ah, near Qudayd toward the coast.[175] According to Ibn Isḥāq (as transmitted to us by Ibn Ḥumayd—Salamah—Ibn Isḥāq), the Messenger of God attacked the Banū al-Muṣṭaliq [clan] of Khuzā'ah in Sha'bān of the year 6 of the Hijrah.[176] Al-Wāqidī has said that the Messenger of God attacked al-Muraysī' in Sha'bān of the year 5 of the Hijrah.[177] He asserted that the Battle of the Trench and the battle with the Banū Qurayẓah took place after al-Muraysī'—referring to the warfare with the Banū al-Muṣṭaliq of Khuzā'ah. Ibn Isḥāq (as transmitted to us by Ibn Ḥumayd—Salamah—Ibn Isḥāq) asserted that the Messenger of God returned after concluding the affair of the Banū Qurayẓah at the end of Dhū al-Qa'dah or at the beginning of Dhū al-Ḥijjah. He remained in Medina during Dhū al-Ḥijjah, Muḥarram, Ṣafar, and the two months of Rabī'.[178] During the year 5, the polytheists were in charge of the pilgrimage.

---

174. For ed. Leiden's *da'ā bihā* ("called for her"), ed. Cairo reads *da'ā lahū* ("prayed for him"—i.e., for Khallād).

175. The place, about 15 kilometers from Medina, was the site of the shrine to Manāt at al-Mushallal. See the article by T. Fahd in *EI²*, s.v. Manāt.

176. Sha'bān of A.H. 6 began on 16 December 627.

177. Sha'bān of A.H. 5 began on 26 December 626. For al-Wāqidī's account, see W, I, 404 ff. Cf. al-Ṭabarī's account p. 51, below. Cf. also Hamidullah, *Battlefields*, 29–30, who argues for the earlier dating.

178. Roughly from 23 April 627 (the beginning of Dhū al-Ḥijjah, 5) to 17 September 627 (the end of Rabī' II, 6).

The Events of the Year 6

(May 23, 627–May 10, 628)

The Expedition against the Banū Liḥyān[179]

According to Abū Ja'far [al-Ṭabarī]: The Messenger of God set out
[1501] during Jumādā I[180] at the end of six months from the conquest of the Banū Qurayẓah to the Banū Liḥyān, seeking [vengeance] for the men [who were betrayed] at al-Rajī', Khubayb b. 'Adī and his companions.[181] To take the enemy by surprise, he pretended to be setting out for the north.[182] He left Medina and traveled by Ghurāb, a mountain near Medina, on his way north, then by Makhīḍ[183] and al-Batrā'.[184] Then he veered to the left and, having passed Yayn and Ṣukhayrāt al-Yamām,[185] his route led him directly by the main road to Mecca. He traveled quickly and halted at Ghurān, where there were settlements of the Banū

179. Parallels: W, II, 535–37; IH, III, 279–81 (tr. Guillaume, 484–86).
180. Jumādā I of A.H. 6 began on 18 September 627.
181. See note 84, above.
182. Arabic *al-sha'm* means both "north" and "Syria."
183. IH, III, 279: al-Maḥīṣ; but Yāqūt, *Mu'jam al-buldān*, VII, 411, records Makhīḍ with reference to this passage and gives Maḥīṣ as a place within Medina (VII, 401).
184. Al-Batrā' is a mountain about 150 miles northwest of Medina, about midway between Medina and Tabūk; it is not to be confused with the ancient Nabatean city of Petra, which has the same name in Arabic.
185. In W, II, 536, the names are given as Bīn and Ṣukhayrāt al-Thumām, respectively.

Liḥyān. (Ghurān is a valley between Amaj and 'Usfān[186] extending toward a village called Sāyah.) He found that they were on the alert and had taken secure positions on the mountain tops. After the Messenger of God had halted there and failed to take them by surprise as he intended, he said, "If we went down to 'Usfān, the Meccans would think that we had come for Mecca." So he set out with two hundred riders of his companions and halted at 'Usfān. He sent out two horsemen of his companions. They reached Kurā' al-Ghamīm[187] and then returned, and he turned back.

According to Ibn Ḥumayd—Salamah—Ibn Isḥāq (who transmitted the report about the expedition against the Banū Liḥyān from 'Āṣim b. 'Umar b. Qatādah and 'Abdallāh b. Abī Bakr, who transmitted it from 'Ubaydallāh b. Ka'b): Then the Messenger of God returned to Medina. He had stayed only a few nights before 'Uyaynah b. Ḥiṣn b. Ḥudhayfah b. Badr al-Fazārī with horsemen of [1502]
Ghaṭafān raided the milch camels of the Messenger of God at al-Ghābah.[188] Tending them were a man of the Banū Ghifār[189] and his wife. They killed the man and carried off the woman with the camels.

The Expedition to Dhū Qarad

According to Ibn Ḥumayd—Salamah—Muḥammad b. Isḥāq—'Āṣim b. 'Umar b. Qatādah, 'Abdallāh b. Abī Bakr, and someone whom I do not doubt—'Ubaydallāh b. Ka'b b. Mālik (each of whom transmitted part of the report about the expedition to Dhū Qarad): The first person to know about them[190] was Salamah b.

186. Yāqūt, *Mu'jam al-buldān*, VI, 173–74, locates 'Usfān at two stages or 33 Arab miles from Mecca on the road to Medina. The name is preserved by a modern town about 50 miles northwest of Mecca.

187. Kurā' al-Ghamīm was a mountain on the edge of a lava field eight miles from 'Usfān; see Yāqūt, *Mu'jam al-buldān*, VII, 226.

188. For al-Ghābah, see note 73, above. Parallels: W, II, 537–49; IH, III, 281–89 (tr. Guillaume, 486–90).

189. The Banū Ghifār, a subdivision of the Banū Ḍamrah b. Bakr b. 'Abd Manāt b. Kinānah, lived in the Ḥijāz between Mecca and Medina. They became allies of the Muslims and eventually embraced Islam. Some of them must have settled within Medina. Cf. p. 5, above, where Muḥammad is said to have left Sibā' b. 'Urfuṭah al-Ghifārī in charge of Medina during his absence. See *EI*², s.v. Ghifār.

190. I.e., the raiding party from Ghaṭafān mentioned in the previous paragraph.

'Amr b. al-Akwa' al-Aslamī.[191] He set out for al-Ghābah early in the morning, with his bow and arrows suspended from his shoulder, accompanied by a slave of Ṭalḥah b. 'Ubaydallāh.[192]

However, the account of this expedition of the Messenger of God from Salamah b. al-Akwa' [himself dates it] after his return to Medina from Mecca in the Year of al-Ḥudaybiyah.[193] If that is correct, the events narrated on the authority of Salamah b. al-Akwa' must have taken place either in Dhū al-Ḥijjah of A.H. 6 or in the beginning of A.H. 7, because the return of the Messenger of God from Mecca to Medina in the Year of al-Ḥudaybiyah took place in Dhū al-Ḥijjah of A.H. 6. Thus, nearly six months separate the date given by Ibn Isḥāq for the expedition to Dhū al-Qarad and the date transmitted from Salamah b. al-Akwa'.

The account of Salamah b. al-Akwa' [is as follows]. According to al-Ḥasan b. Yaḥyā[194]—Abū 'Āmir al-'Aqadī[195]—'Ikrimah b. 'Ammār al-Yamāmī[196]—Iyās b. Salamah[197]—his father [Salamah b. al-Akwa'], who said: We returned to Medina with the Messenger of God—that is, after the peace of al-Ḥudaybiyah. The Mes-
[1503] senger of God sent out his camels with Rabāḥ, the slave of the Messenger of God, and I went out with him with a horse belonging to Ṭalḥah b. 'Ubaydallāh. When we woke up in the morning, we saw that 'Abd al-Raḥmān b. 'Uyaynah had raided the camels of the Messenger of God, driving off all of them and killing their herdsman. I said: "Rabāḥ, take this horse and get to Ṭalḥah. Tell the

---

191. Salamah is more frequently called "Ibn al-Akwa'," after his grandfather's nickname ("having a prominent or deformed wrist"). Known for his bravery, Salamah died in 74/693–94 when he was about eighty. See Ibn Ḥajar, *Tahdhīb*, IV, 150–52.

192. The reading of ed. Cairo, "Ṭalḥah b. 'Abdallāh," is probably a misprint. At I, 1507, ed. Cairo agrees with ed. Leiden in reading "Ṭalḥah b. 'Ubaydallāh."

193. In accordance with the custom of naming years after their most important event, A.H. 6 came to be known as the Year of al-Ḥudaybiyah, after the episode narrated at pp. 67 ff., below.

194. Al-Ḥasan b. Yaḥyā al-Jurjānī died in 263/876 in his eighties. See Ibn Ḥajar, *Tahdhīb*, II, 324–25.

195. Abū 'Āmir 'Abd al-Malik b. 'Amr al-'Aqadī died in 204 or 205/819–21. See Ibn Ḥajar, *Tahdhīb*, VI, 409–10.

196. 'Ikrimah b. 'Ammār al-'Ijlī Abū 'Ammār al-Yamāmī was born in al-Baṣrah and died in 159/775–76. See Ibn Ḥajar, *Tahdhīb*, VII, 261–63.

197. Iyās b. Salamah b. al-Akwa' al-Aslamī Abū Salamah was born in Medina and died there in 119/737 at the age of seventy-seven. See Ibn Ḥajar, *Tahdhīb*, I, 388–89.

Messenger of God that the polytheists have raided his camels." Standing on a hill, I faced Medina and shouted, "A raid!"[198] three times. Then I set out after the enemy, shooting arrows at them and saying these *rajaz* verses:

I am Ibn al-Akwaʿ!
Today is the day for the mean [to receive destruction].[199]

By God, I kept shooting at them and hitting their riding animals. Whenever one of their horsemen came back toward me, I would go to a tree, sit beneath it, and shoot at him and hit his mount. Whenever the mountain [track] narrowed and they went into a narrow place, I would climb the mountain and pelt them with stones. I kept doing this, by God, until I had set behind me every one of the Messenger of God's camels that God had created and they had left me free to do as I pleased with them. They had cast off more than thirty spears and thirty cloaks to lighten themselves, and I placed stones to mark everything they cast off so that the Messenger of God and his companions would notice it. Finally they came to a narrow place on a pass, and ʿUyaynah b. Ḥiṣn b. [1504] Badr came to them bringing help. They sat down for a midmorning meal, and I sat down on a ridge above them. ʿUyaynah looked and said, "What is it I see?" They said: "This fellow has given us trouble. By God, he never left us since dawn, shooting at us until he rescued everything that was in our hands." ʿUyaynah said, "Four of you get up and attack him." Four of them made for me. When they came within speaking range, I said, "Do you recognize me?" "Who are you?" they asked. I said: "Salamah b. al-Akwaʿ! By Him who has honored Muḥammad, I will overtake every one of you that I pursue, but none shall pursue me and overtake me." One of them said, "I don't think so!"

They went back, and I did not leave my place until I saw the horsemen of the Messenger of God coming through the trees. The

198. Arabic: *yā ṣabāḥāh*, literally, "O my morning!" or "O what a morning!" See Lane, *Lexicon*, IV, 1642, for the idiom.

199. Arabic: *al-yawmu yawmu l-ruḍḍaʿi*, literally, "today is the day of the ones who suck." In pre-Islamic Arab folklore one sign of stinginess (one of the lowest of vices in Bedouin society) was for a man to suck the teats of his milch camel rather than milk it, so that the sound of milk streaming into the bucket would not attract guests. See Lane, *Lexicon*, III, 1098.

first of them was al-Akhram al-Asadī; following him came Abū Qatādah al-Anṣārī, and after him was al-Miqdād b. al-Aswad al-Kindī.[200] I took hold of the rein of al-Akhram's horse and said: "Akhram, the men are few. Be on guard against them; don't let them cut you off before the Messenger of God reaches us with his companions." Al-Akhram said, "Salamah, if you believe in God and the Last Day and know that Paradise is real and that the Fire is real, do not stand between me and martyrdom!"

I let him go. He and 'Abd al-Raḥmān b. 'Uyaynah met. Al-Akhram hamstrung 'Abd al-Raḥmān's horse, but 'Abd al-Raḥmān
[1505] thrust at him with a spear and killed him. 'Abd al-Raḥmān then shifted onto his horse. Abū Qatādah overtook 'Abd al-Raḥmān and thrust at him and killed him. 'Abd al-Raḥmān had hamstrung Abū Qatādah's horse, so Abū Qatādah shifted onto al-Akhram's horse. They left in flight.

According to Salamah: By Him who honored Muḥammad, I followed them, running on foot until I could not see any of Muḥammad's companions behind me, or even their dust. Before sunset they turned aside into a canyon called Dhū Qarad where there was water to drink, for they were thirsty. They saw me running after them, and I drove them away so that they tasted not a drop of it. Then they went up into the mountain trail of Dhū Athīr. One of them turned back to attack me, and I shot him with an arrow that landed in his shoulder blade. I said, "Take that!":[201]

I am Ibn al-Akwa'!
Today is the day for the mean [to receive destruction].

He said, "My al-Akwa' of early this morning?" "Yes," I said, "you enemy of your own soul!" Then I saw two horses on the trail, and I led them back toward the Messenger of God. My uncle 'Āmir met me after dark with a skin of watered milk and one of water. I made my ablutions, prayed, and drank; then I came to the Messenger of

---

200. He was also called al-Miqdād b. 'Amr; cf. IH, III, 282 (tr. Guillaume, 487). See *EI*[2], s.v. al-Miḳdād b. 'Amr.

[illegible]e should follow ed. Cairo in reading the words "Take that!" as part of the verse, which would then form a complete hemistich of *rajaz* meter: *khudhhā wa_na_bnu_l-'akwa'ī*. However, on p. 48, below, the same verse is introduced with the words "Take that from me" (*khudhhā minnī*), which could not form part of the verse metrically.

God, who was at the watering place from which I had driven them at Dhū Qarad. Behold, the Messenger of God had taken the camels [1506] I had rescued from the enemy and each spear and cloak. Bilāl[202] had slaughtered a female camel from the ones I had rescued from the foe and was roasting some of its liver and hump for the Messenger of God. I said, "Messenger of God, let me choose a hundred men and follow the enemy, so that not one of them shall remain." The Messenger of God laughed until his back teeth became visible and could be clearly seen [in the light of the fire];[203] then he said, "Would you do it?" I said, "Yes, by Him who has honored you!" The next morning the Messenger of God said, "Now they are being received as guests in the country of Ghaṭafān."

A man then came from Ghaṭafān and said that so and so "slaughtered a camel for them. When they had stripped off its skin, they saw dust; so they said, 'The enemy is upon you,' and left fleeing."

The next morning the Messenger of God said, "Our best horseman today has been Abū Qatādah, and our best foot soldier has been Salamah b. al-Akwaʿ." The Messenger of God gave me the share of a horseman and the share of a footman. Then the Messenger of God mounted me behind him on al-ʿAḍbāʾ.[204] While we were traveling, a footman of the Anṣār who was unbeatable at running began saying, "Is there no one who will race?" He said this several times. When I heard him, I said, "Do you not honor a generous man and fear a noble man?" He said, "No, unless he be the Messenger of God." So I said: "Messenger of God, you are as dear to me as my father and mother! Permit me to race the man." "If you wish," he said. So I leaped down and ran. I held back for one

---

202. Bilāl, an Ethiopian slave, tortured by his pagan master for accepting Islam, was rescued by Abū Bakr and became the first muezzin of the Muslim community. See *EI*², s.v. Bilāl b. Rabāḥ.

203. Arabic *nawājidh* could be used for the wisdom teeth, all the molars, or the teeth next to the eye teeth. The lexicographers were concerned about the possibility of Muḥammad's laughing immoderately. See the discussion in Lane, *Lexicon*, VIII, 2769. Instead of ed. Leiden's (*badā aw bānat nawājidhuhū*) "his back teeth became visible or could be clearly seen," I translate ed. Cairo (*badā wa-qad bānat nawājidhuhā* [*fī ḍawʾi al-nār*]). The bracketed words are from the parallel text in the *Ṣaḥīḥ* of Muslim (3:1433–41).

204. Al-ʿAḍbāʾ ("slit-eared," or "short in the foreleg") was Muḥammad's she-camel; see Lane, *Lexicon*, V, 2071.

or two hills,[205] then I caught up with him and slapped him be-
[1507] tween the shoulders. "I've beaten you, by God," I said. "I don't think so!" he said.[206] So I beat him back to Medina. We stayed there only three nights before setting out for Khaybar.[207]

Resumption of the account of Ibn Isḥāq:[208] Salamah b. al-Akwaʿ was accompanied by a slave of Ṭalḥah b. ʿUbaydallāh, and with the slave was a horse of Ṭalḥah's that he was leading. When Salamah went up into al-Wadāʿ Pass,[209] he saw some of [the raiders'] horsemen; so he looked in the direction of Salʿ and shouted, "A raid!" Then he set out at full speed after the enemy—he was like a beast of prey. Having overtaken them, he began to turn them away with arrows. When he shot, he would say, "Take that from me"—

I am Ibn al-Akwaʿ!
 Today is the day for the mean [to receive destruction].

Whenever the horses came toward him, he fled and attacked them from the side. Whenever he could shoot, he would shoot and say, "Take that"—

I am Ibn al-Akwaʿ!
 Today is the day for the mean [to receive destruction].

One of their men said, "Our little al-Akwaʿ it is at the beginning of the day!"[210]

When a report of Ibn al-Akwaʿ's shout reached the Messenger of God, he sounded the alarm in Medina. The horsemen all came following one another to the Messenger of God. The first of the

---

205. The text in the *Ṣaḥīḥ* of Muslim is fuller: "I held myself back from him for one hill or two to save my breath; then I ran on his heels. I held back from him for one hill or two; then I sprinted and overtook him"; see ed. Leiden, *Glossarium*, p. CCLVI.

206. Following ed. Leiden (*in aẓunnu*); ed. Cairo reads *innī aẓunnu*, "I think so."

207. See pp. 116–24, below, for an account of the expedition to Khaybar in A.H. 7.

208. This continues the report begun at al-Ṭabarī, I, 1502, above.

209. *Thaniyyat al-Wadāʿ* ("Farewell Pass") was the pass over which the road to Mecca left Medina. See Yāqūt, *Muʿjam al-buldān*, III, 25; photograph in Hamidullah, *Battlefields*, 10.

210. The text is uncertain. Ed. Leiden reads, *ukayyiʿunā huwwa awwala l-nahāri*, which is what I have translated. This seems to be a contemptuous rejoinder, using the diminutive form of the name *al-Akwaʿ*. Ed. Cairo has a different reading, which also puns on the name: *a-wa-yakiʿunā huwwa* . . . (and will he sting, or butt, us . . .).

horsemen to reach him was al-Miqdād b. 'Amr. The first horseman to stand by the Messenger of God after al-Miqdād from the Anṣār was 'Abbād b. Bishr b. Waqsh b. Zughbah b. Za'ūrā (a member of the Banū 'Abd al-Ashhal); then came Sa'd b. Zayd (one of the Banū Ka'b b. 'Abd al-Ashhal), Usayd b. Ẓuhayr (a member of the [1508] Banū Ḥārithah b. al-Ḥārith, but there is uncertainty about him), 'Ukkāshah b. Miḥṣan (a member of the Banū Asad b. Khuzaymah), Muḥriz b. Naḍlah (a member of the Banū Asad b. Khuzaymah), Abū Qatādah al-Ḥārith b. Rib'ī (a member of the Banū Salimah), and Abū 'Ayyāsh (that is, 'Ubayd b. Zayd b. Ṣāmit, a member of the Banū Zurayq). When they had gathered round the Messenger of God, he appointed Sa'd b. Zayd as their commander and said, "Set out in pursuit of the enemy until I catch up to you with men."

According to a report that has come to me from members of the Banū Zurayq, the Messenger of God said to Abū 'Ayyāsh, "Abū 'Ayyāsh, why don't you give this horse to a man who rides better than you, so that he can overtake the enemy?"

According to Abū 'Ayyāsh, who said: I replied, "Messenger of God, I am the best rider among the people!" Then I struck the horse, but I swear to God that before it had run fifty cubits it threw me. So I marveled about how the Messenger of God had said, 'Why don't you give it to someone who rides better than you?' and about how I had said that I was the best rider among the people."

Some of the Banū Zurayq asserted that the Messenger of God gave Abū 'Ayyāsh's horse to Mu'ādh b. Mā'iṣ (or 'Ā'idh b. Mā'iṣ) b. Qays b. Khaldah, who was an eighth man. Some people count Salamah b. 'Amr b. al-Akwa' as one of the eight and reject Usayd b. Ẓuhayr of the Banū Ḥārithah; however, Salamah on that day was not a horsemen: he was the first to overtake the enemy on foot. So the horsemen set forth in pursuit of the enemy and met them.

According to Ibn Ḥumayd—Salamah—Muḥammad b. Isḥāq— [1509] 'Āṣim b. 'Umar b. Qatādah: The first horseman to overtake the enemy was Muḥriz b. Naḍlah of the Banū Asad b. Khuzaymah (Muḥriz was called al-Akhram and was also called Qumayr). When the alarm was sounded, a horse belonging to Maḥmūd b. Maslamah started running around in its enclosure when it heard the neighing of the horses—it was a specially tended, well-rested horse. Some of the women of the Banū 'Abd al-Ashhal said [to him] when he saw the horse running around in the enclosure, dragging the trunk of the palm tree to which it had been tied, "Qumayr, would you like to ride this horse—you see how it is—and catch up with the Messenger of God and with the Muslims?" He said yes; so they gave it to him, and he set out on it. The horse being rested, it did not cease to outstrip the [other] horses until it reached the enemy. Muḥriz stopped before them and said, "Halt, you sons of vile slave women, until the Emigrants and Anṣār riding after you catch up with you!" One of them attacked him and killed him. The horse wheeled round, and they could not stop it until it stood by its pen among the Banū 'Abd al-Ashhal. No other Muslims were killed. The name of Maḥmūd's horse was Dhū al-Limmah.[211]

According to Ibn Ḥumayd—Salamah—Muḥammad b. Isḥāq—someone whom people do not doubt—'Ubaydallāh b. Ka'b b. Mālik al-Anṣārī: Muḥriz in fact was riding a horse called al-
[1510] Janāḥ[212] belonging to 'Ukkāshah b. Miḥṣan. When Muḥriz was killed, al-Janāḥ was taken as booty. When the horsemen met, Abū Qatādah al-Ḥārith b. Rib'ī of the Banū Salimah killed Ḥabīb b. 'Uyaynah b. Ḥiṣn, covered him with his cloak, and rejoined the men. When the Messenger of God approached with the Muslims, there was Ḥabīb covered with Abū Qatādah's cloak. The people exclaimed, "Surely we belong to God, and to Him we return!"[213] and said that Abū Qatādah had been killed; but the Messenger of God said, "It is not Abū Qatādah, but someone killed by Abū Qatādah; he has put his cloak on him so that you will know that he did it." 'Ukkāshah b. Miḥṣan overtook Awbār and his son 'Amr b. Awbār, who were riding on one camel, and ran them through with a spear, killing both of them. They rescued some of the camels. The Messenger of God traveled until he halted at the mountain of Dhū Qarad, and the people came to him in groups. The Messenger of God made camp and stayed there a day and a night. Salamah b. al-Akwa' said to him, "Messenger of God, if you sent me out with a hundred men, I would rescue the remaining animals and seize the enemy by their necks." The Messenger of God said, as I have been informed, "They are now being given

211. *Dhū al-limmah* means "having a long lock of hair."
212. *Al-janāḥ* means "wing."
213. Qur'ān 2:156, traditionally said in times of misfortune.

their evening drink in [the territory of] Ghaṭafān." The Messenger of God divided the meat of one camel among each hundred of his companions. They stayed there, and then the Messenger of God returned to Medina. He stayed there part of Jumādā II and Rajab; then he raided the Banū al-Muṣṭaliq[214] [clan] of Khuzā'ah in Sha'bān of the year 6.[215]

The Expedition against the Banū al-Muṣṭaliq[216] [1511]

According to Ibn Ḥumayd—Salamah b. al-Faḍl and 'Alī b. Mujāhid[217]—Muḥammad b. Isḥāq—'Āṣim b. 'Umar b. Qatādah, 'Abdallāh b. Abī Bakr, and Muḥammad b. Yaḥyā b. Ḥabbān. [Ibn Isḥāq] said, "Each transmitted to me part of the report on the Banū al-Muṣṭaliq." They said: Word reached the Messenger of God that the Banū al-Muṣṭaliq were gathering against him under the leadership of al-Ḥārith b. Abī Ḍirār. (Al-Ḥārith was the father of Juwayriyah bt. al-Ḥārith, [who subsequently became] the wife of the Messenger of God.) When the Messenger of God heard about them, he set out toward them and met them at one of their watering places called al-Muraysī', near Qudayd toward the coast. The people advanced toward each other and fought fiercely. God put the Banū al-Muṣṭaliq to flight and killed some of them. He gave their children, women, and property to the Messenger of God as booty—God gave them to him as spoil. A Muslim named Hishām b. Ṣubābah from the Banū Kalb b. 'Awf b. 'Āmir b. Layth b. Bakr was wounded by one of the Anṣār who was a close kinsman of 'Ubādah b. al-Ṣāmit; he mortally wounded him by mistake, thinking he was one of the enemy.

While the people were at that watering place, they brought their animals down to drink. With 'Umar b. al-Khaṭṭāb was a hired man of his from the Banū Ghifār named Jahjāh b. Sa'īd, leading his

---

214. The name is given sometimes in its full form of Banū al-Muṣṭaliq and sometimes in the abbreviated form of Balmuṣṭaliq. I have normalized to the longer form throughout.

215. Sha'bān of A.H. 6 began on 16 December 627.

216. Parallels: W, I, 404–II, 426 (dated A.H. 5, see p. 41, above); IH, III, 289–96 (tr. Guillaume, 490–93).

217. 'Alī b. Mujāhid b. Muslim al-Rāzī, a historian and traditionist, was born in 100/718 in Rayy and died in 182/798. See Ibn Ḥajar, *Tahdhīb*, VII, 377–78; *GAS*, I, 312.

horse. Jahjāh and Sinān al-Juhanī (a confederate of the Banū 'Awf
[1512] b. al-Khazraj) began crowding each other at the watering place and fought. Al-Juhanī shouted, "People of the Anṣār!" and Jahjāh shouted, "People of the Emigrants!" 'Abdallāh b. Ubayy b. Salūl, who had with him a band of his fellow tribesmen including the young lad Zayd b. Arqam,[218] became angry and said: "Have they really done it? They have tried to outrank us and outnumber us in our own lands. By God, the proverb, 'Fatten your dog and he will eat you up!' fits us and [the wearers of] the *jilbāb*[219] of Quraysh to a tee. By God, if we go back to Medina, those who are stronger will drive out the weaker from it."[220] Then he turned to his tribesmen who were with him and said: "This is what you have done to yourselves! You allowed them to settle in your lands and divided your wealth with them. Had you kept from them what you had, by God they would have moved to lands other than yours."

Zayd b. Arqam heard this and took it to the Messenger of God—this when the Messenger of God had finished with his enemies—and he gave him a report. 'Umar b. al-Khaṭṭāb, who was with him, said, "Messenger of God, order 'Abbād b. Bishr b. Waqsh to kill him." The Messenger of God said: "'Umar, how will it be if people start saying that Muḥammad kills his companions? No, announce our departure instead." (It was at an hour when the Messenger of God usually did not break camp.) So the people departed.

---

218. Zayd b. Arqam b. Zayd b. Qays b. al-Nu'mān b. Mālik b. al-Agharr b. Tha'labah b. Ka'b b. al-Khazraj al-Anṣārī participated in seventeen expeditions with the Prophet. He later emigrated to al-Kūfah and fought on 'Alī's side at Ṣiffin. He died between 65/784 and 68/688. See Ibn Ḥajar, *Tahdhīb*, 394–95.

219. Arabic: *jalābīb Quraysh* "the shirts (or coarse waist wrappers) of Quraysh." The origin of this apparently derogatory epithet for the Emigrants remains obscure; none of the older Arabic dictionaries explains it. Abū Dharr's note printed in most editions of IH, reads: "An epithet that the polytheists applied to the Emigrants who had become Muslims. *Jalālīb* (plural of *jilbāb*) originally means 'coarse waist wrappers.' They used to wrap themselves in them, and so they acquired this nickname." One may see it as a reference to poverty or simply to distinctive dress. At p. 59, below, 'Ā'ishah uses the word to designate the outer garment in which she wrapped herself and lay down while waiting for the departed caravan to notice her absence. See ed. Leiden, *Glossarium*, p. CLXVII. W. Arafat has argued that the word may be derived from the verb *jalaba* (to import) and may therefore mean "the imported ones." See the note in his article, "A Controversial Incident in the Life of Ḥassān b. Thābit," p. 197 n. 4.

220. Qur'ān 63:8 quotes these words.

Now when ʿAbdallāh b. Ubayy b. Salūl heard that Zayd b. Arqam had informed the Messenger of God of what he had heard him say, he went to the Messenger of God and swore, "By God, I did not say what he said, neither did I speak of it." ʿAbdallāh b. Ubayy was a great noble among his people; so those who were present with the Messenger of God—companions of his from the Anṣār—said, "Messenger of God, perhaps the lad was mistaken in his [1513] report and did not remember exactly what the man said." They said this out of affection for ʿAbdallāh b. Ubayy and to defend him.

After the Messenger of God had mounted and set out, Usayd b. Ḥuḍayr met him and, having greeted him as a prophet and wished him peace, said, "Messenger of God, you have set out at an unheard-of hour at which you usually do not set out." The Messenger of God said to him, "Have you not heard what your companion has said?" "Which companion, Messenger of God?" he asked. "ʿAbdallāh b. Ubayy," he answered. "And what did he say?" he asked. He replied, "He said that if he returned to Medina, those who are stronger would drive out the weaker from it." Usayd said: "You, by God, O Messenger of God, will drive him out, if you wish. He is the weak one by God, and you are the strong." Then he said: "Messenger of God, be gentle with him. By God, God caused you to arrive at the very moment when his people were stringing precious stones to make him a crown; so he thinks that you deprived him of a kingdom."

The Messenger of God traveled all that day until evening with the people, all that night until dawn, and the first part of the day until the sun hurt them; then he halted with them, and they fell asleep as soon as they felt the touch of the ground. He did this only to distract them from the talk that had taken place the day before—what ʿAbdallāh b. Ubayy had said. In the afternoon he set out with the people, marched through the Ḥijāz, and halted at a watering place in the Ḥijāz called Naqʿāʾ, a little above al-Naqīʿ.[221] When the Messenger of God set out in the afternoon, a strong wind blew on the people, hurting them, and they became fearful about it. The Messenger of God said, "Do not be afraid: it blew only because of the death of one of the great men among the

221. The place is mentioned by Yāqūt, *Muʿjam a-buldān*, VIII, 309, as belonging to the tribe of Muzaynah.

[1514] unbelievers." When they reached Medina, they found that Rifā'ah b. Zayd b. al-Tābūt, one of the Banū Qaynuqā', a great man among the Jews and a cave of refuge to the hypocrites, had died on that day. The sura in which God mentions the hypocrites ("When the hypocrites come to you. . . . ") was revealed concerning 'Abdallāh b. Ubayy b. Salūl and those of like mind.[222] When this sura was revealed, the Messenger of God took hold of Zayd b. Arqam's ear and said, "This is he whose ear God has confirmed."[223]

According to Abū Kurayb[224]—Yaḥyā b. Ādam[225]—Isrā'īl[226]—Abū Isḥāq[227]—Zayd b. Arqam, who said: I went out with my paternal uncle on an expedition, and I heard 'Abdallāh b. Ubayy b. Salūl saying to his companions: "Do not spend on those who are with the Messenger of God. By God, if we return to Medina, the stronger will drive out the weaker from it."[228] I mentioned this to my uncle, and my uncle mentioned it to the Messenger of God. The latter sent for me; I spoke to him, and he sent to 'Abdallāh and his companions, who swore that they had not said it. The Messenger of God took me to be lying and believed him. I felt grief such as I never had felt, and I sat in the tent. My uncle asked, "What did you intend, acting so that the Messenger of God deemed you to be lying and hated your action?" Then God revealed [the sura that begins], "When the hypocrites come to you." The Messenger of God sent to me and recited it; then he said, "God has confirmed your truthfulness, Zayd."

Resumption of the account of Ibn Isḥāq: 'Abdallāh, the son of

---

222. Qur'ān, Sura 63, entitled *al-Munāfiqūn*, "The Hypocrites."

223. I.e., God has confirmed the truth of what he said he heard. Cf. ed. Leiden, *Glossarium*, p. DLXIII.

224. Abū Kurayb Muḥammad b. al-'Alā' b. Kurayb al-Hamdānī al-Kūfī died in 248/862. See Ibn Ḥajar, *Tahdhīb*, IX, 385–86.

225. Abū Zakariyā Yaḥyā b. Ādam b. Sulaymān al-Umawī al-Aḥwal was born ca. 140/757 in al-Kūfah and died in 203/818. He was a respected scholar of *fiqh*, *ḥadīth*, and Qur'ān. See Ibn Ḥajar, *Tahdhīb*, XI, 175–76; *GAS*, I, 520.

226. Isrā'īl b. Yūnus b. Abī Isḥāq al-Sabī'ī al-Kūfī was born in 100/718 and died in 162/778. See al-Khaṭīb, *Ta'rīkh Baghdād*, VII, 20–25; Ibn Ḥajar, *Tahdhīb*, I, 261–63.

227. Abū Isḥāq 'Amr b. 'Abdallāh al-Hamdānī, the grandfather of Isrā'īl b. Yūnus, died between 126 and 129/743–47 at the age of ninety-six. See Ibn Ḥajar, *Tahdhīb*, I, 261–63.

228. See note 220, above.

'Abdallāh b. Ubayy, got word of what had happened involving his father.

According to Ibn Ḥumayd—Salamah—Muḥammad b. Isḥāq—'Āṣim b. 'Umar b. Qatādah: 'Abdallāh b. 'Abdallāh b. Ubayy b. Salūl came to the Messenger of God and said: "Messenger of God, I have been told that you want to kill 'Abdallāh b. Ubayy because of what has been reported to you concerning him. If you are going to do it, command me to do it and I will bring you his head. By God, al-Khazraj know that there has never been among them a man more dutiful to his father than I. I am afraid that you may order someone else to do it and that he may kill him; and then my soul will not allow me to look on the slayer of 'Abdallāh b. Ubayy walking among the people: I would kill him, killing a believer to avenge an unbeliever, and thereby enter the Fire [of Hell]." The Messenger of God said, "No, we will be gentle with him and associate with him on friendly terms as long as he stays with us." Thus, after that day whenever he did anything objectionable, it was his own tribesmen who reproved him, corrected him, censured him, and threatened him. When word of how they were behaving reached the Messenger of God, he said to 'Umar b. al-Khaṭṭāb: "What do you think, 'Umar? By God, had I killed him the day you ordered me to kill him, prominent men would have been upset, who, if I ordered them today to kill him, would do so." 'Umar said, "Now by God I know that what the Messenger of God ordered had more of a blessing in it that what I would have ordered." [1515]

Miqyas b. Ṣubābah came from Mecca, pretending to have become a Muslim, and said: "Messenger of God, I have come to you as a Muslim. I have come to seek blood money[229] for my brother, who was killed by mistake." The Messenger of God ordered him to be paid blood money for his brother Hishām b. Ṣubābah. He stayed briefly with the Messenger of God; then he attacked his

229. Arabic *diyah*: a specified amount of money or goods due in cases of homicide or other injuries to physical health unjustly committed upon the person of another. The payment for homicide was normally 100 camels, payable to the aggrieved family. The payment terminated all further vengeance. See *EI*[2], s.v. Diya.

brother's slayer, killed him, and left for Mecca as an apostate. He said while he was traveling:[230]

[1516] It has sated my soul that he has spent the night laid to rest in the valley,
with blood from his neck veins staining his two garments.
Before I killed him, soul's griefs
assailed me and forbade me the smoothness of beds.
With him I discharged my vengeance; I took my retaliation,
and was the first to return to the idols.
By [killing] him I took vengeance by force,[231] and I made to pay blood money for him
the princes of the Banū al-Najjār and the lords of Fāri'.[232]

Miqyas b. Ṣubābah also said:

I rained down on him a blow that settled accounts: because of it there was a dripping
of the belly's fresh blood that overspread him and flowed away.
And I said, as death came over his features,
"You cannot be safe from the Banū Bakr when they are wronged!"

Many of the Banū al-Muṣṭaliq were wounded on that day. 'Alī b. Abī Ṭālib killed two of them: Mālik and his son. The Messenger of God took many captives, and they were divided among all the Muslims. Juwayriyah bt. al-Ḥārith b. Abī Ḍirār, [who became] the wife of the Prophet, was one of the captives.

[1517] According to Ibn Ḥumayd—Salamah—Muḥammad b. Isḥāq—Muḥammad b. Ja'far b. al-Zubayr—'Urwah—the Prophet's wife 'Ā'ishah, who said: When the Messenger of God divided the captives of the Banū al-Muṣṭaliq, Juwayriyah bt. al-Ḥārith fell to the share of Thābit b. Qays b. al-Shammās (or to a cousin of his), and

230. Ed. Cairo: "He said in a poem," reading *fī shi'r*, for ed. Leiden's *fī safarihī*. Parallel text of this and the following poem with variants: W, I, 408; IH, III, 293–94 (tr. Guillaume, 492).

231. Thus ed. Leiden (*tha'artu bihī qahran*); al-Wāqidī, Ibn Hishām, and ed. Cairo read *fihran* ("I avenged Fihr with him"). Since Fihr was one of the early members of Quraysh; the line would then refer to exacting vengeance for his brother, a member of Quraysh, from the Banū al-Najjār of Medina.

232. Fāri' was one of the fortresses of Medina; see p. 22, above.

she contracted with him for her freedom.[233] She was a sweet, beautiful woman who captivated anyone who looked at her. She came to the Messenger of God seeking his help in the matter of her contract. By God, as soon as I saw her at the door of my chamber, I took a dislike to her, and I knew that he would see in her what I saw. She went before him and said, "Messenger of God, I am Juwayriyah, the daughter of al-Ḥārith b. Abī Ḍirār, the chief of his tribesmen. You can see what misfortune has befallen me. I have fallen to the share of Thābit b. Qays b. al-Shammās (or his cousin) and have contracted with him for my freedom. I have come to you to ask your aid with my contract." He said to her, "Would you like something better than that?" She said, "What is it, Messenger of God?" He said, "I will pay your contract and marry you." She said, "Yes, Messenger of God," and he said, "I do so." When the news got out to the people that the Messenger of God had married Juwayriyah bt. al-Ḥārith, they said, "Relatives by marriage of the Messenger of God!" and they set free those in their possession. When he married her, a hundred families of the Banū al-Muṣṭaliq were freed. I know of no woman who was a greater blessing to her people than she.

An Account of the Lie[234]

According to Ibn Ḥumayd—Salamah—Muḥammad b. Isḥāq, who said: The Messenger of God then set out on his way back from that journey (according to what my father Isḥāq [b. Yasār] transmitted to me from al-Zuhrī—'Urwah—'Ā'ishah). When he was near Medina ('Ā'ishah was along on that journey of his), the authors of the [1518]
lie said about her what they said.

233. Arabic *kātabathu 'alā nafsihā*: she made a contract with him (written or otherwise) that she would pay a certain sum as the price of herself and be free on payment of it (cf. Lane, *Lexicon*, VII, 2590). The practice (called *mukātabah*, "manumission by contract") is recommended by the Qur'ān (24:33) for any slave who wishes it. Cf. Schacht, *Introduction to Islamic Law*, 42f., 129f.; and *EI*², I, 30, s.v. 'Abd.

234. Parallels: W, II, 426–40; IH, III, 297–307 (tr. Guillaume, 493–99); al-Bukhārī, *Ṣaḥīḥ* (ed. Boulaq), V, 52; al-Ṭabarī, *Jāmi' al-bayān*, XVIII, 68–77. Cf. Stowasser, *Women in the Qur'an, Traditions, and Interpretation*, 94–95; and Spellberg, *Politics, Gender, and the Islamic Past*, 61–99.

According to Ibn Ḥumayd—Salamah—Muḥammad b. Isḥāq—al-Zuhrī—'Alqamah b. Waqqāṣ al-Laythī, Sa'īd b. al-Musayyab,[235] 'Urwah b. al-Zubayr, and 'Ubaydallāh b. 'Abdallāh b. 'Utbah[236] (al-Zuhrī said, "Each transmitted to me part of this account, some remembering more of it than others, and I have assembled for you everything they transmitted to me").

According to Ibn Ḥumayd—Salamah—Muḥammad b. Isḥāq—Yaḥyā b. 'Abbād b. 'Abdallāh b. al-Zubayr—his father—'Ā'ishah; also, [Muḥammad b. Isḥāq]—'Abdallāh b. Abī Bakr b. Muḥammad b. 'Amr b. Ḥazm al-Anṣārī—'Amrah bt. 'Abd al-Raḥmān[237]—'Ā'ishah ([Muḥammad b. Isḥāq] said: "The report of each has been assembled in the account of 'Ā'ishah's story about herself, when the authors of the lie said about her what they said. Each contributed to her account as transmitted from all these people. Some
[1519] of them relate what others do not. Each was a reliable informant concerning her, and each related about her what he had heard.")

'Ā'ishah said: Whenever the Messenger of God planned a journey, he had his wives draw lots among themselves; whichever one's lot came out, he took her with him. When the raid on the Banū al-Muṣṭaliq took place, he had his wives draw lots as he used to do; my lot came out over theirs, and the Messenger of God took me along. Women in those days used to eat only enough to stay alive; they were not bloated with meat so as to become heavy. While my camel was being saddled, I would sit in my litter; then the men who were to bind my litter onto my camel would come and carry me: they would take hold of the bottom of the litter, lift it, and place me on the back of the camel. Then they would tie it with its ropes, take hold of the camel's head, and set out with it.

---

235. Abū Muḥammad Sa'īd b. al-Musayyab b. Ḥazn al-Makhzūmī was born in 13/634 and died in 94/713 in Medina. He was a scholar of genealogy, history, traditions, and law and was closely connected with the caliph 'Umar. Al-Zuhrī was one of his students. See Ibn Ḥajar, *Tahdhīb*, IV, 84–88; *GAS*, I, 276.

236. 'Ubaydallāh b. 'Abdallāh b. 'Utbah died in the 90's/708–18. See Ibn Ḥajar, *Tahdhīb*, VII, 23–24, which quotes al-Ṭabarī's favorable opinion of him.

237. 'Amrah bt. 'Abd al-Raḥmān b. Sa'd b. Zurārah al-Anṣāriyyah was highly regarded as a transmitter of material from 'Ā'ishah. The caliph 'Umar b. 'Abd al-'Azīz is said to have asked for a written collection of her reports from 'Ā'ishah. She died in 98/716–17 (or later) at the age of seventy-seven. See Ibn Ḥajar, *Tahdhīb*, XII, 438–39.

When the Messenger of God had finished with his journey on that occasion, he turned back to return. When he was near Medina, he made camp and, having spent part of the night there, announced the departure. When the people had mounted, I went out to attend to a need of mine.[238] On my neck was a necklace of mine with onyx beads from Ẓafār.[239] When I was finished, it came undone from my neck without my noticing. When I returned to the encampment, I felt for it on my neck and did not find it. The people had already begun to leave. I retraced my steps to the place to which I had gone and looked for the necklace until I found it. While I was away, the men who used to saddle the camel for me came and finished saddling it. Assuming that I was in the litter as [1520] usual, they took hold of the litter, lifted it up, and tied it onto the camel, not doubting that I was in it. Then they took hold of the camel's head and set out. When I came back to camp, not a soul was there[240]—the people had departed. So I wrapped myself in my outer garment (*jilbāb*) and lay down in the place to which I had gone. I knew that if they missed me, they would return for me. By God, while I was lying down, Ṣafwān b. al-Muʿaṭṭal al-Sulamī passed by me—he had lagged behind away from the camp to attend to a need of his and had not spent the night with the people in camp. When he saw my form, he approached and stood near me and recognized me, for he used to see me before the curtain (*ḥijāb*) was imposed on us.[241] When he saw me, he said, "'Surely we belong to God, and to Him we return!'[242]—is it she who travels in the litter of the Messenger of God?" I was wrapped up in my garments. "What has caused you to stay behind?—may God have mercy on you!" he asked, but I did not talk to him. Then he brought the camel near and said, "Mount—may God have mercy on you!"—and he kept back from me. I mounted, and he came and took hold of the camel's head and set out with me, hastening in pursuit of the party. By God, we did not overtake them, neither

238. I.e., to relieve herself.

239. The city of Ẓafār, near San'ā' in Yemen (not to be confused with Ẓafār on the coast of Oman), was famous for its onyx. See Yāqūt, *Muʿjam al-buldān*, VI, 85–86.

240. Literally, "not a caller and not a responder."

241. See note 96, above.

242. See note 213, above.

was I was missed until morning. The people halted and, when they had settled down, the man came into view leading me. Then the authors of the lie said about me what they said, and the camp was disturbed; yet, by God, I knew nothing about it.

Then we came to Medina, and I immediately came down with a severe complaint. Nothing about the matter reached me, but the story reached the Messenger of God and my parents. My parents said not a word to me about it; however, I missed some of the
[1521] kindness toward me of the Messenger of God. Whenever I complained of an illness, he would be merciful to me and treat me with kindness, but he did not do so at the time of that complaint of mine, and I missed it. When he came to see me while my mother was nursing me, he would say "How is she?" and nothing more. Finally, troubled by his apparent coldness toward me, I said, "Messenger of God, I wish you would allow me to move to my mother's, so that she could nurse me." "Do what you like," he said. So I moved to my mother's, knowing nothing of what had happened, and after some twenty days I recovered from my pain.

We were Arab folk. We did not have in our houses these privies that the foreigners have; we loathed and disliked such things. Instead, we would go out into the fields of Medina. The women would go out every night to attend to their needs. One night I went out to attend to my needs along with Umm Misṭaḥ, the daughter of Abū Ruhm b. al-Muṭṭalib b. ʿAbd Manāf (her mother, the maternal aunt of Abū Bakr, was the daughter of Ṣakhr b. ʿĀmir b. Kaʿb b. Saʿd b. Taym). By God, as she was walking with me, she tripped over her garment and said, "May Misṭaḥ stumble and fall!" I said, "By the life of God, what a bad thing to say about an Emigrant who was present at Badr!"[243] She replied, "Daughter of Abū Bakr, hasn't the news reached you?" "What news?" I asked. She told me what the authors of the lie had been saying. I asked, "Has this really happened?" "Yes," she said, "by God, it really has happened." By God, I was unable to do what I had to do. I went back and kept crying until I thought that the crying would split my liver. I said to my mother: "May God forgive you. People spoke the things they spoke and you heard what you heard, yet you mention
[1522] nothing of it to me!" She said: "Dear daughter, take it lightly. By

243. See note 91, above.

God, whenever a beautiful woman married to a man who loves her has rival wives, they always gossip about her, and people do the same."

The Messenger of God stood up among the people to preach without my knowing about it. He said: "People, why are some men hurting me regarding my family and saying falsehood about them?[244] By God, I know only good about them. People are saying this about a man about whom, by God, I know only good and who has never entered any of my apartments except in my company."

The main offense lay with 'Abdallāh b. Ubayy b. Salūl and some men of al-Khazraj, along with what Misṭaḥ and Ḥamnah bt. Jaḥsh had said. Ḥamnah's sister, Zaynab bt. Jaḥsh, was the wife of the Messenger of God.[245] Ḥamnah therefore spread her rumors trying to hurt me for the sake of her sister Zaynab bt. Jaḥsh, and I became distressed by it.

When the Messenger of God had finished his speech, Usayd b. Ḥuḍayr, a member of the Banū 'Abd al-Ashhal,[246] said: "Messenger of God, if they belong to al-Aws, we will take care of them for you; if they belong to our brothers, al-Khazraj, give us your command. By God, they deserve to have their heads cut off!"

Sa'd b. 'Ubādah stood up—previously he was thought to be a righteous man—and said: "You lie! By God's life, their heads shall not be cut off. By God, you have said these words only because you already know that they belong to al-Khazraj; had they been your tribesmen, you would not have said it." Usayd said: "You lie, by [1523]
God's life! But you are a hypocrite arguing for hypocrites." The men jumped up at each other, so that violence almost took place between the tribes of al-Aws and al-Khazraj.

The Messenger of God descended [from the pulpit] and came in to see me. He called 'Alī b. Abī Ṭālib and Usāmah b. Zayd and asked their advice. Usāmah spoke in praise, saying, "Messenger of God, they are your family, and we know nothing but good about them,[247] and this is lying and falsehood." As for 'Alī, he said:

---

244. The pronoun "them" is in the feminine plural, indicating that "my family" is a polite way of saying "my wives."

245. IH adds: "None of his wives but she could rival me in status. As for Zaynab herself, God protected her; but Ḥamnah bt. Jaḥsh spread her rumors. . . . "

246. The Banū 'Abd al-Ashhal were a division of al-Aws.

247. As before, "them" (feminine plural) refers to Muḥammad's wives.

"Messenger of God, women are many, and you can get a replacement. Ask the slave girl; she will tell you the truth." So the Messenger of God called Barīrah to question her. 'Alī went up to her and struck her hard, saying, "Speak the truth to the Messenger of God." "By God," she said, "I know nothing but good. The only fault I ever found in 'Ā'ishah is that, when I was kneading my dough and ordered her to watch it, she fell asleep over it, and the pet sheep[248] came and ate it."

Then the Messenger of God came into my room. My parents were with me, along with a woman from the Anṣār. I was crying, and she was crying with me. Having seated himself, he praised and lauded God and then said: "'Ā'ishah, as you know, people have been saying things. Fear God, and if you have committed an evil deed such as people say, repent to God, for God accepts repentance from his servants." By God, as soon as he said that, my tears diminished, so that I felt nothing of them. I waited for my parents to reply to the Messenger of God, but they did not speak. I swear to
[1524] God, I considered myself too lowly and unimportant for God, who is mighty and exalted, to reveal a Qur'ān[249] about me to be recited in mosques and used in worship; but I hoped that the Messenger of God would see something in a dream whereby God, knowing my innocence, would refute [the accusations] about me or that he would be given a message. As for a Qur'ān to be revealed about me, by God, I considered myself too lowly for that.

When I saw that my parents did not speak, I said, "Will you not reply to the Messenger of God?" They said to me, "By God, we do not know what to reply to him." (I swear to God, I know of no family that suffered what the family of Abū Bakr suffered during those days.) When they were unable to speak on my behalf, my eyes filled with tears and I wept. "By God," I said, "I will never repent to God of that which you have spoken of. By God, if I confess to what people are saying, so that you believe me—and God knows that I am innocent of it—I shall be saying what did not

248. Arabic: *dājin*, an animal (usually a sheep or goat) that one keeps in one's house.

249. I.e., a Qur'ānic revelation, a single passage of Qur'ān to be recited in liturgical worship; see Bell and Watt, *Introduction to the Qur'ān*, 135–36.

happen; and if I deny what you are saying, you will not believe me." Then I tried to recall the name of Jacob, but I could not remember it; instead, I said: "As the father of Joseph said, 'Comely patience! And God it is whose help is to be sought in that which you describe.' "[250]

By God, before the Messenger of God left the place where he was sitting, there came over him from God what used to come over him. They covered him with his garment and set a leather cushion under his head. As for me, when I saw that happen, by God I did not become very frightened or troubled, for I knew that I was innocent and that God would not wrong me. As for my parents, by the One who holds 'Ā'ishah's soul in His hand, as soon as the Messenger of God came to, I thought their souls would depart for fear that confirmation of what people had said would come from God.

The Messenger of God came to and sat up. [Drops of sweat] were [1525]
falling from him like silver beads on a day of hail. He began wiping the perspiration from his brow and said: "Rejoice, 'Ā'ishah! God has revealed your innocence." I said, "To God's praise and your[251] blame!" Then he went out to the people and preached to them. He recited to them the Qur'ān that God had revealed concerning me. He gave orders concerning Misṭaḥ b. Uthāthah, Ḥassān b. Thābit, and Ḥamnah bt. Jaḥsh (they were among those who had spoken evil openly) and they received their prescribed flogging.[252]

According to Ibn Ḥumayd—Salamah—Muḥammad b. Isḥāq—his father [Isḥāq b. Yasār]—some men of the Banū al-Najjār: Umm Ayyūb, the wife of Abū Ayyūb Khālid b. Zayd, said to her husband,

---

250. Qur'ān 12:18.

251. The pronoun is plural.

252. Literally: "they were beaten with their *ḥadd.*" *Ḥadd,* meaning "hindrance, impediment, limit, boundary," is used in the plural in the Qur'ān to designate the restrictive ordinances of God (*ḥudūd Allāh*). In Islamic jurisprudence, *ḥadd* is a technical term for the punishment of certain acts that have been forbidden or sanctioned by punishments in the Qur'ān and have thereby become crimes against religion. These are unlawful intercourse (*zinā*), false accusation of unlawful intercourse (*qadhf*), wine drinking (*khamr*), theft (*sariqah*), and highway robbery (*qaṭ' al-ṭarīq*). The punishment for false accusation of unlawful intercourse was set at eighty lashes by Qur'ān 24:4, which some say was revealed on this occasion (see al-Ṭabarī, *Jāmi' al-bayān,* XVIII, 59–60, ad loc.). See *EI*², s. vv. Ḥadd, Ḳadhf; Schacht, *Introduction to Islamic Law,* 179.

"Abū Ayyūb, don't you hear what people are saying about 'Ā'ishah?" "Yes," he replied, "and it is falsehood. Would you, Umm Ayyūb, do such a thing?" She said, "No, by God, I wouldn't do it." "And 'Ā'ishah," he said, "is better than you, by God!"

When the Qur'ān was revealed, God mentioned the authors of the slander who spoke their evil, saying: "Those who came with the slander are a band of you"—and the rest of the verse.[253] This refers to Ḥassān b. Thābit and his companions who said what they said. Then God said, "Why, when you heard it, did the believers, men and women, not of their own account think good thoughts?"—and the rest of the verse.[254] That is, [why did they not speak] as Abū Ayyūb and his wife spoke? Then He said: "When you received it on your tongues"—and the rest of the verse.[255]

When this was revealed concerning 'Ā'ishah and those who had said what they said about her, Abū Bakr, who had been supporting Misṭaḥ because of his close kinship with him and his poverty,
[1526] said, "By God, I will never support Misṭaḥ with anything or help him in any way after what he said about 'Ā'ishah, making us suffer as we did." Then God revealed concerning this: "Let not those of you who possess bounty and plenty swear off giving kinsmen"—and the rest of the verse.[256] Abū Bakr therefore said, "By God, I want God to forgive me"—and he restored Misṭaḥ's support that he had been paying him, saying, "By God, I will never withdraw it from him."

Ṣafwān b. al-Mu'aṭṭal advanced on Ḥassān b. Thābit with a sword when he learned what Ḥassān was saying about him. In addition, Ḥassān had composed poetry with insinuations against

---

253. Qur'ān 24:11: "Those who came with the slander are a band of you; do not reckon it evil for you; rather it is good for you. Every man of them shall have the sin that he has earned charged to him; and whosoever of them took upon himself the greater part of it, him there awaits a mighty chastisement."

254. Qur'ān 24:12, which continues: "and say, 'This is a manifest calumny'?"

255. Qur'ān 24:15: "When you received it on your tongues, and were speaking with your mouths that whereof you had no knowledge, and reckoned it a light thing, and with God it was a mighty thing."

256. Qur'ān 24:22: "Let not those of you who possess bounty and plenty swear off giving kinsmen and the poor and those who emigrate in the way of God; but let them pardon and forgive. Do you not wish that God should forgive you? God is All-forgiving, All-compassionate."

Ibn al-Mu'aṭṭal and the Arabs of Muḍar[257] who had become Muslims. He had said:[258]

The [wearers of the] *jilbāb*[259] have become strong and
numerous,
and Ibn al-Furay'ah[260] has become [as alone as] an
[ostrich's] egg in the land.[261]
Bereft of her son is the mother of the one whose companion I
become,[262]
or [of anyone who] becomes caught in the claws of a lion.
For my victim, the one whom I take early in the morning,
no blood money shall be paid and no revenge [shall be
taken].
Not even the sea, when the wind blows from the north,
so that it becomes heaped up and spatters the shore with
foam,
Is more overwhelming ever than I, when you see me [1527]
amaze with [my] rage[263] like a cloud that brings amazing
[amounts of] hail.

Ṣafwān b. al-Mu'aṭṭal therefore advanced on him with a sword, struck him, and said (according to Ibn Ḥumayd—Salamah—Muḥammad b. Isḥāq):

---

257. I.e., the Emigrants of Quraysh. Muḍar was a large grouping of North Arabian tribes including Qays 'Aylān, Hudhayl, Khuzaymah, Asad, Kinānah, Quraysh, Ḍabbah, and Tamīm. See *EI*[1] Suppl., s.v. Rabī'a and Muḍar. Ḥassān b. Thābit belonged to al-Khazraj of Medina.

258. Parallels: *Aghānī*, IV, 11–13 (with narrative of the circumstances of the poem's composition, variant readings, and six additional lines); *Dīwān*, I, 284–86 and II, 212–13 (twelve verses and extensive comment); W, II, 436; IH, III, 304–5. See also W. Arafat, "A Controversial Incident."

259. See note 219. An alternate reading, preferred by Arafat in his edition of the *Dīwān* is *khalābīs*, "a mixed multitude, scum."

260. I.e., Ḥassān b. Thābit, whose mother was named al-Furay'ah. Cf. *Aghānī*, IV, 2.

261. Arabic *bayḍat al-balad* is a common metaphor for isolation or insignificance, although it can also mean something precious. See Arafat, "A Controversial Incident," 197.

262. Ed. Cairo (change of vocalization): "you become."

263. The interpretation follows the suggestion in the notes to the *Dīwān* of Ḥassān b. Thābit concerning the meaning of *farā, yafrī*. See *Dīwān*, II, 212–13; Lane, *Lexicon*, VI, 2391.

Receive the sword's edge from me: I am
a young man who, when I am satirized, am no poet.

According to Ibn Ḥumayd—Salamah—Muḥammad b. Isḥāq—Muḥammad b. Ibrāhīm b. al-Ḥārith al-Taymī:[264] Thābit b. Qays b. al-Shammās (a member of the Banū al-Ḥārith[265] b. al-Khazraj) assaulted Ṣafwān b. al-Mu'aṭṭal because of his having struck Ḥassān, and, having tied Ṣafwān's hands to his neck, set out with him for the territory of the Banū al-Ḥārith b. al-Khazraj. 'Abdallāh b. Rawāḥah met him. "What is this?" he asked. Thābit replied: "Hasn't the striking of Ḥassān b. Thābit with the sword made you indignant? By God, I think it nearly killed him!" 'Abdallāh b. Rawāḥah said to him, "Does the Messenger of God know anything about what you have done?" He replied, "No, by God." 'Abdallāh said: "You have acted too boldly. Release the man!" So Thābit b. Qays released him. They came to the Messenger of God and told him what had happened. He called on Ḥassān and Ṣafwān b. al-Mu'aṭṭal [to speak]. Ibn al-Mu'aṭṭal said, "Messenger of God, he insulted me and satirized me, so that rage overcame me and I struck him." The Messenger of God said to Ḥassān, "Ḥassān, have you treated my own tribesmen harshly because God has guided
[1528] them to Islam?" Then he said, "Ḥassān, treat well[266] the one who struck you." "I will, Messenger of God," he answered.

According to Ibn Ḥumayd—Salamah—Muḥammad b. Isḥāq—Muḥammad b. Ibrāhīm b. al-Ḥārith: In compensation for [the blow], the Messenger of God gave [Ḥassān] Bayraḥā,[267] which today is the palace of the Banū Ḥudaylah in Medina. It had been the property of Abū Ṭalḥah b. Sahl, who donated it to the Messenger of God, who in turn gave it to Ḥassān for his blow. He also gave him Sīrīn, a Coptic slave girl, and she bore him 'Abd al-Raḥmān b. Ḥassān.

'Ā'ishah used to say: They inquired about Ṣafwān b. al-Mu'aṭṭal

---

264. Muḥammad b. Ibrāhīm b. al-Ḥārith al-Taymī, died ca. 120/738, was the grandson of an Emigrant. See Ibn Ḥajar, *Tahdhīb*, IX, 5–7.

265. The tribal name is abbreviated here to Balḥārith. I have normalized it to Banū al-Ḥārith throughout, which is the form used later in the sentence.

266. Arabic: *aḥsin yā Ḥassān*. Muḥammad is punning on Ḥassān's name, which comes from the same root as the verb *aḥsana*, "do good, treat well."

267. Variant (al-Wāqidī, *Aghānī*): Bayraḥā'.

and found him to be an impotent man who had no intercourse with women. He was killed afterward as a martyr [in battle].

According to Ibn Ḥumayd—Salamah—Ibn Isḥāq—'Abd al-Wāḥid b. Ḥamzah:[268] 'Ā'ishah's account was given on the Pilgrimage of Fulfillment.[269]

According to Abū Ja'far [al-Ṭabarī]: The Messenger of God stayed the months of Ramaḍān and Shawwāl in Medina. He set out to perform the lesser pilgrimage (*'umrah*) in Dhū al-Qa'dah of the year 6.[270]

The Prophet's Lesser Pilgrimage from Which the Polytheists Turned Him Back: The Story of al-Ḥudaybiyah[271]

According to Ibn Ḥumayd—al-Ḥakam b. Bashīr[272]—'Umar b. Dharr al-Hamdānī[273]—Mujāhid:[274] The Prophet made three lesser pilgrimages, all of them in [the month of] Dhū al-Qa'dah, returning from each of them to Medina.

According to Ibn Ḥumayd—Salamah—Ibn Isḥāq, who said: The Prophet set out to make the lesser pilgrimage in Dhū al-Qa'dah, [1529]
not intending to make war. He had called on the Arabs and Bedouin desert dwellers who were around him to help by setting out

268. On the Medinan transmitter 'Abd al-Wāḥid b. Ḥamzah b. 'Abdallāh b. al-Zubayr al-Asadī Abū Ḥamzah see Ibn Ḥajar, *Tahdhīb*, VI, 434.

269. Arabic: *'umrat al-qaḍā'*, the lesser pilgrimage that Muḥammad performed in 7/629 (called the Pilgrimage of Fulfillment because it took the place of the pilgrimage he had been prevented from making). See pp. 133–38, below.

270. Ramaḍān of A.H. 6 began on 14 January 628, Shawwāl on 13 February, and Dhū al-Qa'dah on 13 March.

271. Parallels: W, II, 571–633; IH, III, 308–27 (tr. Guillaume, 499–510). Al-Ḥudaybiyah was a small town with a well one stage from Mecca and nine stages from Medina. It was on the edge of the Meccan *ḥaram* or sacred territory. See *EI²*, s.v. al-Ḥudaybiya.

272. Perhaps the same as the Kūfan scholar al-Ḥakam b. Bishr b. Sulaymān al-Nahdī whom Ibn Ḥajar lists as one of the sources consulted by Muḥammad b. Ḥumayd. See Ibn Ḥajar, *Tahdhīb*, II, 424.

273. 'Umar b. Dharr b. 'Abdallāh b. Zurārah al-Hamdānī was a Kūfan who died ca. 153/770. See Ibn Ḥajar, *Tahdhīb*, VII, 444–45.

274. Abū al-Ḥajjāj Mujāhid b. Jabr al-Makkī was born ca. 21/642 in Mecca and died in 104/722. He was a student of Ibn al-'Abbās and author of a commentary on the Qur'ān. See Ibn Ḥajar, *Tahdhīb*, X, 42–44; *GAS*, I, 29.

with him, for he feared that Quraysh would oppose him with fighting or turn him away from the [Holy] House[275]—which they did. Many of the Bedouins were slow in coming to him. The Messenger of God, the Emigrants and Anṣār who were with him, and the Arabs who joined him set out. He took sacrificial animals with him and put on pilgrim garb[276] so that people would have no apprehension about his fighting and would know that he had come only to visit and venerate the House.

According to Ibn Ḥumayd—Salamah—Muḥammad b. Isḥāq—Muḥammad b. Muslim al-Zuhrī—'Urwah b. al-Zubayr—al-Miswar b. Makhramah[277] and Marwān b. al-Ḥakam,[278] who said: The Messenger of God set out in the Year of al-Ḥudaybiyah, intending to visit the House, not intending to fight. He drove with him seventy fattened camels. The party numbered seven hundred men; each fattened camel was for ten men.

However, according to Ibn 'Abd al-A'lā[279] (who transmitted his report to us from Muḥammad b. Thawr[280]—Ma'mar[281]—al-Zuhrī—'Urwah b. al-Zubayr—al-Miswar b. Makhramah); and according to Ya'qūb[282] (who transmitted his report from Yaḥyā b.

275. Arabic: *al-bayt*, the Ka'bah.

276. Arabic *aḥrama*: "he entered the state of *iḥrām*," a state of ritual consecration marked by the wearing of a simple two-piece garment and abstention from cutting the hair, shedding blood, sexual relations, and a number of other activities. See *EI*², s.v. Iḥrām.

277. Al-Miswar b. Makhramah b. Nawfal al-Zuhrī was the nephew of 'Abd al-Raḥmān b. 'Awf through his mother. Born in 2/623–24 in Mecca, he was taken to Medina in 8/629–30 and died in 64/683–84 in Mecca. He was a close friend of 'Umar. See Ibn Ḥajar, *Tahdhīb*, X, 151–52.

278. Marwān b. al-Ḥakam b. Abī al-'Āṣ b. Umayyah, was governor of Medina under Mu'āwiyah and became caliph in 64/684, reigning nine months. He died in Ramaḍān 65/685. See Ibn Ḥajar, *Tahdhīb*, X, 91–92; *EI*², s.v.

279. Muḥammad b. 'Abd al-A'lā al-Ṣan'ānī (cf. p. 74, below, where the same isnād occurs in fuller form) died in 245/859 in al-Baṣrah, where al-Ṭabarī met him. See Ibn Ḥajar, *Tahdhīb*, IX, 289; Rosenthal, *General Introduction*, 20.

280. Muḥammad b. Thawr al-Ṣan'ānī died ca. 190/805. See Ibn Ḥajar, *Tahdhīb*, IX, 87.

281. Abū 'Urwah Ma'mar b. Rāshid, born in 96/714 and died in 154/770, a pupil of al-Zuhrī, was a historian and traditionist. See Ibn Ḥajar, *Tahdhīb*, X, 243–46; *GAS*, I, 290–91.

282. I.e., Ya'qūb b. Ibrāhīm al-Dawraqī (cf. the fuller version of the same *isnād* at p. 74, below) was born in 166/782 and died in 252/866. See al-Khaṭīb al-Baghdādī, *Ta'rīkh Baghdād*, XIV, 277–80; Ibn Ḥajar, *Tahdhīb*, XI, 381–82.

Sa'īd[283]—'Abdallāh b. Mubārak[284]—Ma'mar—al-Zuhrī—'Urwah b. al-Zubayr—al-Miswar b. Makhramah and Marwān b. al-Ḥakam, both of whom said): The Messenger of God set out from al-Ḥudaybiyah with between thirteen and nineteen hundred[285] of his companions. (The [same] report then follows.)

According to al-Ḥasan b. Yaḥyā—Abū 'Āmir [al-'Aqadī]—'Ikrimah b. 'Ammār al-Yamāmī—Iyās b. Salamah—his father [1530] [Salamah b. al-Akwa'], who said: We came to al-Ḥudaybiyah with the Messenger of God. We were fourteen hundred.[286]

According to Yūsuf b. Mūsā al-Qaṭṭān[287]—Hishām b. 'Abd al-Malik and Sa'īd b. Shuraḥbīl al-Miṣrī—al-Layth b. Sa'd al-Miṣrī[288]—Abū al-Zubayr[289]—Jābir,[290] who said: On the day of al-Ḥudaybiyah we were one thousand and four hundred.

According to Muḥammad b. Sa'd[291]—his father—his paternal

---

283. Yaḥyā b. Sa'īd b. Farrūkh al-Qaṭṭān, who was born in 120/737 and died in 198/813, was a pupil of Sufyān al-Thawrī. See al-Khaṭīb al-Baghdādī, *Ta'rīkh Baghdād*, XIV, 135–44; Ibn Ḥajar, *Tahdhīb*, XI, 216–20; *GAS*, I, 75.

284. Abū 'Abd al-Raḥmān 'Abdallāh b. al-Mubārak b. Wāḍiḥ al-Ḥanẓalī al-Tamīmī, who was born in 118/736 and died in 181/797, was a traditionist, historian, and Sufi. See Ibn Ḥajar, *Tahdhīb*, V, 382–87; *EI*², s.v. Ibn al-Mubārak; *GAS*, I, 95.

285. Following the text of ed. Leiden (*fī biḍ'a 'ashrata mi'atan*). The reading of ed. Cairo (*fī biḍ'ata 'ashara wa-mi'atin*, "with between thirteen and nineteen and one hundred," i.e., with between 113 and 119) seems to be a misprint.

286. For ed. Leiden's *arba'a 'ashrata mi'atan* (14 hundred), ed. Cairo reads *arba'ata 'ashara wa-mi'atun* (14 and a hundred, i.e., 114).

287. Yūsuf b. Mūsā b. Rāshid b. Bilāl al-Qaṭṭān Abū Ya'qūb was born in al-Kūfah, lived in Rayy, then went to Baghdād, where he died in Ṣafar of 253/867. See Ibn Ḥajar, *Tahdhīb*, XI, 425.

288. Al-Layth b. Sa'd b. 'Abd al-Raḥmān al-Fahmī Abū al-Ḥārith (born in Qalqashandah, Egypt, in 94/713, and died in 175/791) was one of the most famous traditionists and jurists of his time. See Ibn Ḥajar, *Tahdhīb*, VIII, 459–65; *EI*², s.v. al-Layth b. Sa'd; *GAS*, I, 520.

289. Abū al-Zubayr Muḥammad b. Muslim b. Tadrus al-Asadī, a traditionist, died in 126/743 or 128. See Ibn Ḥajar, *Tahdhīb*, IX, 440–43; *GAS*, I, 86–87.

290. I.e., the companion of the Prophet, Jābir b. 'Abdallāh b. 'Amr al-Khazrajī, one of the Medinans who swore allegiance to Muḥammad at the first Pledge of 'Aqabah. See *GAS*, I, 85.

291. Abū 'Abdallāh Muḥammad b. Sa'd b. Manī' al-Baṣrī al-Zuhrī (known as "Kātib al-Wāqidī" after his teacher) was born in al-Baṣrah in 168/784 and died in 230/845 in Baghdād. He was the author of *Kitāb al-ṭabaqāt al-kabīr*, containing biographies of the Prophet and of his companions. See Ibn Ḥajar, *Tahdhīb*, IX, 182–83; *GAS*, I, 300–301.

uncle—his father—his father—Ibn 'Abbās,[292] who said: The people who swore allegiance under the tree were one thousand five hundred and twenty-five.

According to Ibn al-Muthannā[293]—Abū Dāwūd[294]—Shu'bah[295]—'Amr b. Murrah,[296] who said: I heard 'Abdallāh b. Abī Awfā say: "On the Day of the Tree we were one thousand three hundred. Aslam[297] was an eighth of the Emigrants."

According to Ibn Ḥumayd—Salamah—Muḥammad b. Isḥāq—al-A'mash[298]—Abū Sufyān[299]—Jābir b. 'Abdallāh al-Anṣārī, who said: We, the people of al-Ḥudaybiyah, were fourteen hundred.[300]

According to al-Zuhrī: The Messenger of God set out. When he
[1531] was at 'Usfān, Bishr b. Sufyān al-Ka'bī met him and said: "Messenger of God, Quraysh have heard about your journey and have gone out with their 'foals and dams.'[301] They have put on leopard skins and encamped at Dhū Ṭuwā,[302] swearing by God that you shall never enter the city in defiance of them. Khālid b. al-

292. 'Abdallāh b. 'Abbās (or al-'Abbās), a cousin of the Prophet, was born three years before the Hijrah. He spent much of his life at al-Ṭā'if as a scholar and authority on Qur'ān interpretation. He died in 68/687 (or in 69 or 70). See *GAS*, I, 25–28; *EI*², s.v. 'Abd Allāh b. al-'Abbās.

293. Muḥammad b. al-Muthannā Abū Mūsā al-Baṣrī died ca. 252/866. See Ibn Ḥajar, *Tahdhīb*, IX, 425–27.

294. Abū Dāwūd Sulaymān b. Dāwūd b. al-Jārūd al-Ṭayālisī was born in 133/750 and died in 203/818 or 204. See Ibn Ḥajar, *Tahdhīb*, IV, 182–86; *GAS*, I, 97–98.

295. Shu'bah b. al-Ḥajjāj al-Baṣrī died in 160/776. See Ibn Ḥajar, *Tahdhīb*, IV, 233–34.

296. 'Amr b. Murrah b. 'Abdallāh al-Murādī al-Kūfī died ca. 118/736. See Ibn Ḥajar, *Tahdhīb*, VIII, 102–3.

297. Aslam was a division of Khuzā'ah with territory to the west of Medina and Mecca. On the Emigrant status of members of other non-Medinan tribes than Quraysh who adhered to Muḥammad, see Watt, *Muhammad at Medina*, 86.

298. Sulaymān b. Mihrān al-Asadī al-A'mash died in 148/765. See al-Dhahabī, *Tadhkirah*, 154; Ibn Ḥajar, *Tahdhīb*, XI, 123.

299. For Abū Sufyān b. Sa'īd b. al-Mughīrah al-Thaqafī, see Ibn Ḥajar, *Tahdhīb*, XII, 112; *GAS*, I, 63–64, 85.

300. For ed. Leiden's *arba'a 'ashrata mi'atan* (14 hundred), ed. Cairo reads *arba'ata 'ashara wa-mi'atan* (14 and a hundred, i.e., 114).

301. Arabic: *al-'ūdh al-maṭāfīl*, literally, "[camels] that have recently foaled and [camels] that have foals with them." The commentators take the phrase as figurative for "women and children"; see Lane, *Lexicon*, V, 2193, s.v. *'ā'idh*.

302. At place near Mecca, sometimes vocalized Dhū Ṭawā; not the same as the valley where Moses is said to have met God (Qur'ān 20:12, 79:16); see Yāqūt, *Mu'jam al-buldān*, VI, 64.

Walīd[303] is with their horsemen, whom they have sent forward to Kurā' al-Ghamīm."[304]

According to Abū Ja'far [al-Ṭabarī]: Some have said that Khālid b. al-Walīd on that day was with the Messenger of God as a Muslim.

A Report That Khālid b. al-Walīd Was Already a Muslim

According to Ibn Ḥumayd—Ya'qūb al-Qummī[305]—Ja'far (i.e., Ibn Abī al-Mughīrah)[306]—Ibn Abzā,[307] who said: When the Messenger of God set out with camels for sacrifice and reached Dhū al-Ḥulayfah,[308] 'Umar said to him, "Messenger of God, will you without arms or horses enter the territory of people who are at war with you?" So the Prophet sent to Medina and left no horses or weapons there untaken. When he approached Mecca, they prohibited him from entering; so he marched to Minā[309] and halted there. His spy brought him word, saying, "'Ikrimah b. Abī Jahl has come out against you with five hundred men." The Messenger of God said to Khālid b. al-Walīd, "Khālid, here is your paternal uncle's son come against you with horsemen." Khālid said, "I am the sword of God and the sword of His Messenger!"—he received the name *Sword of God* on that day—"Messenger of God, direct me wherever you wish!" He sent him in command of horsemen, and he met 'Ikrimah in the canyon and routed him, so that he drove 'Ikrimah back into the walled gardens of Mecca. 'Ikrimah returned again, and Khālid routed him, driving him back into the

---

303. On the later military career of Khālid b. al-Walīd see *EI²*, s.v.

304. See note 187, above.

305. Ya'qūb b. 'Abdallāh al-Qummī died in 174/790. See Ibn Ḥajar, *Tahdhīb*, XI, 390–91.

306. Ja'far b. Abī al-Mughīrah al-Khuzā'ī al-Qummī is listed without dates in Ibn Ḥajar, *Tahdhīb*, II, 108.

307. 'Abd al-Raḥmān b. Abzā is listed without exact dates in Ibn Ḥajar, *Tahdhīb*, VI, 132–33.

308. Dhū al-Ḥulayfah is six or seven miles from Medina on the way to Mecca; see Yāqūt, *Mu'jam al-buldān*, III, 329.

309. Minā is located in a narrow valley about five miles east of Mecca and lies on the traditional pilgrimage route between Mecca and 'Arafāt. See *EI²*, s.v. Minā.

walled gardens of Mecca. 'Ikrimah returned a third time, and
[1532] Khālid routed him, so that he drove him back into the walled gardens of Mecca. God revealed concerning him: "It is He who restrained their hands from you, and your hands from them, in the hollow of Mecca, after He made you victors over them"—until the words "painful punishment."[310] Having made the Prophet victor over them, God restrained him from them on account of remnants of the Muslims who remained in Mecca after He had made Muḥammad victor over the Meccans; for God did not want the horsemen to trample them unwittingly.

Resumption of the account of Ibn Isḥāq: The Messenger of God said: "Woe to Quraysh! War has eaten them up! What would they lose if they left me to deal with the rest of the Arabs? If the Arabs defeat me, that will be what they want. If God makes me prevail over [the Arabs], [Quraysh] can enter Islam en masse; or, if they do not, they can fight, having regained their strength. What do Quraysh think? By God, I shall not cease to strive against them for the sake of that with which God has sent me until God makes it prevail or this side of my neck becomes separated."[311] Then he said, "Who is a man who will lead us forth on a way other than the one on which they are?"

According to Ibn Ḥumayd—Salamah—Ibn Isḥāq—'Abdallāh b. Abī Bakr: A man from Aslam said, "I will, Messenger of God." He took them on a rough and rugged path among canyons. When they emerged from it—it was exhausting for the Muslims—and reached level ground at the end of the valley, the Messenger of God said to the people, "Say, 'We ask God to forgive us, and we repent to him.'" They did this. The Messenger of God said, "By God, this is the [petition for] 'putting down' [a heavy burden of

---

310. Qur'ān 48:24–25. The passage continues: "God sees the things you do. They are the ones who disbelieved, and barred you from the Holy Mosque and the offering, detained so as not to reach its place of sacrifice. If it had not been for certain men believers and certain women believers whom you knew not, lest you should trample them, and there befall you guilt unwittingly on their account (that God may admit into His mercy whom He will), had they been separated clearly, then We would have chastised the unbelievers among them with a painful chastisement."

311. I.e., until death; see Lane, *Lexicon*, IV, 1409.

sin][312] that was offered to the Children of Israel and which they did not say." [1533]

According to Ibn Shihāb [al-Zuhrī]: Then the Messenger of God gave orders to the people, saying, "Turn right, amid the salt-bush,[313] on a path that will bring [the army] out over al-Murār Pass[314] to the descent of al-Ḥudaybiyah below Mecca." So the army traveled that path. When the horsemen of Quraysh saw the dust of the army and that the Messenger of God had turned away from their path, they galloped back to Quraysh. The Messenger of God set out, but when he entered al-Murār Pass, his camel kneeled down. The people said, "She has balked." "She has not balked," he said, "and that is not her nature; but the One who restrained the elephant from Mecca has restrained her.[315] I will grant to Quraysh any matter to which they invite me today asking me to show kindness to kindred." Then he told the people to halt. He was told, "Messenger of God, there is no water in the valley for us to halt by." So he took an arrow out of his quiver and gave it to one of his companions; the man went down into an old well, inserted the arrow into the middle of it, and the water flowed abundantly, so that the people quenched their thirst and halted there.

---

312. Arabic: *al-ḥiṭṭatu allatī 'uriḍat 'alā Banī Isrā'īl.* The consonants *ḥ.ṭ.h* (read as *ḥiṭṭatun*) occur in Qur'ān 2:58 and 7:161, where God commands the Children of Israel to say the word *ḥ.ṭ.h* (*ḥiṭṭatun*) as a sign of humility or repentance. The word caused difficulty; a few commentators even suggested that it was a foreign word, though curiously none seems to have referred to Hebrew *ḥeṭ'* "sin," or to *ḥaṭā'āh* and *ḥaṭṭāt*, "sin, sin offering" (see Ṭabarī, *Jāmi' al-bayān*, I, 237–39). Most explained it as a noun derived from the verb *ḥaṭṭ*, "set down (e.g., a load)," and as meaning "a petition for the putting down of a heavy burden from one; or, of the heavy burden of sin" (see Lane, *Lexicon*, II, 592). James Bellamy suggests reading *khiṭ'atan* (this involves no change in the underlying unpointed text of the Qur'ān, where the dots distinguishing *ḥ* and *kh* were not written and *hamzah* was not indicated). Grammatically, the word would be a *maṣdar* to an understood finite verb: *khaṭi'na khiṭ'atan*, "we have truly sinned" (cf. Bellamy, "Some Proposed Emendations," 566–67).

313. Arabic: *ḥamḍ*, any of a variety of shrubs with salty leaves on which camels can feed; see Lane, *Lexicon*, II, 644.

314. Thaniyyat al-Murār (Bitter-Bush Pass) is mentioned by Yāqūt (*Mu'jam al-buldān*, VIII, 3) but not located precisely.

315. Ca. A.D. 570 (the year of Muḥammad's birth), God is said to have thwarted an attack on Mecca that included an elephant: the elephant is said to have balked at advancing toward Mecca (see al-Ṭabarī, I, 941). The event is commemorated in Sura 105 of the Qur'ān. See *EI²*, s.v. al-Fīl.

According to Ibn Ḥumayd—Salamah—Muḥammad b. Isḥāq—a person of learning—a man from Aslam: The person who went down into the old well with the arrow of the Messenger of God was Nājiyah[316] b. 'Umayr b. Ya'mar b. Dārim. He was the driver of the sacrificial camels of the Messenger of God.

[1534] A certain person of learning alleged to me that al-Barā' b. 'Āzib[317] used to say, "I was the one who went down with the arrow of the Messenger of God."

Aslam recited some verses of poetry that Nājiyah composed, [saying,] "We thought he [viz. Nājiyah] was the one who went down with the arrow of the Messenger of God." Aslam alleged that a slave girl from the Anṣār came with her bucket while Nājiyah was in the well drawing water for the people. She said:

O drawer of water, my bucket is near you:
I saw the people praising you,
Speaking well of you, and glorifying you.

Nājiyah replied while he was in the well drawing water for the people:

A Yemeni slave girl knows
that I am the water drawer and that my name is Nājiyah:
Many a broad, blood-sprinkling wound
have I struck under the breast of the enemy.

According to Muḥammad b. 'Abd al-A'lā al-Ṣan'ānī—Muḥammad b. Thawr—Ma'mar—al-Zuhrī—'Urwah [b. al-Zubayr]—al-Miswar b. Makhramah; and according to Ya'qūb b. Ibrāhīm—Yaḥyā b. Sa'īd al-Qaṭṭān—'Abdallāh b. al-Mubārak—Ma'mar—al-Zuhrī—'Urwah—al-Miswar b. Makhramah and Marwān b. al-Ḥakam, who said: The Messenger of God halted at the edge of al-Ḥudaybiyah at a seasonal pool with a little water. The people were able to draw only small amounts of water before exhausting it, and so they complained of thirst to the Messenger of God. He drew an arrow from his quiver and commanded them to

316. IH, III, 310, inserts "b. Jundab."
317. For the later life of al-Barā' b. 'Āzib b. al-Ḥārith al-Awsī, who became a partisan of 'Alī and died in al-Kūfah ca. 72/691, see *EI²*, s.v. al-Barā' b. 'Āzib.

set it in the pool. By God, the pool continued to flow abundantly [1535]
for them until they departed from it.

While they were there, Budayl b. Warqā' al-Khuzā'ī came to them with a band of his tribesmen from Khuzā'ah. (They were the faithful friends of the Messenger of God among the people of Tihāmah.) Budayl said: "I left Ka'b b. Lu'ayy and 'Āmir b. Lu'ayy encamped at the all-season wells of al-Ḥudaybiyah with their 'foals and dams.'[318] They intend to fight you and turn you away from the House." The Prophet said: "We have not come to fight anyone; we have come to make the lesser pilgrimage. War has exhausted and harmed Quraysh. If they wish, we will grant them a delay, and they can leave me to deal with the people.[319] If I am victorious, if they wish to enter that which the people enter[320] they can do so; if not, they will have rested and recovered their strength. If they refuse [the delay], by Him who holds my soul in His hand, I shall fight them for the sake of this affair of mine until the side of my neck becomes separated[321] or God effects his command." Budayl said, "We will inform them of what you say."

Budayl then set out and went to Quraysh and said: "We come to you from this man. We have heard him make a statement—if you want us to present it to you, we will." The foolish among them said, "We have no need for you to say anything to us from him." But someone intelligent among them said, "Present what you have heard him say." So he said, "I heard him say the following"—and he told them what the Prophet had said. 'Urwah b. Mas'ūd al-Thaqafī stood up and said, "My people, are you not the father?" "Yes," they said. "And am I not the son?" he asked. "Yes," they said.[322] "And do you doubt me?" he asked. "No," they said. "Do you not know," he said, "that [once] I called on the people of 'Ukāẓ[323] for assistance; and, when they gave me no help,

318. See note 301, above.
319. I.e., the Arabs.
320. I.e., Islam.
321. See note 311, above.
322. As the next report indicates, 'Urwah's mother, Subay'ah bt. 'Abd Shams, was from Quraysh, while his father, Mas'ūd, was from the tribe of Thaqīf from al-Ṭā'if.
323. 'Ukāẓ was the site of a yearly market a day's journey from the city of al-Ṭā'if and three days from Mecca (Yāqūt, *Mu'jam al-buldān*, VI, 203).

[1536] I came to you with my family and children and those who obeyed me?" "Yes," they said. (According to Ibn Ḥumayd—Salamah—Muḥammad b. Isḥāq—al-Zuhrī, who said in his report of this incident: 'Urwah b. Mas'ūd was the son of Subay'ah bt. 'Abd Shams.)

Resumption of the account of Ibn 'Abd al-A'lā and Ya'qūb: 'Urwah said: "This man has offered you a sensible proposal. Accept it, and let me go to him." They said, "Go to him." So 'Urwah went to the Prophet and began speaking to him. The Prophet spoke as he had spoken to Budayl. Then 'Urwah said: "Muḥammad, tell me: if you extirpate your tribesmen, have you ever heard of any of the Arabs who destroyed his own race before you? And if the contrary comes to pass,[324] by God I see both prominent people and rabble who are likely to flee and leave you." Abū Bakr said, "Go suck the clitoris of al-Lāt!"—al-Lāt[325] was the idol of Thaqīf, which they used to worship—"Would we flee and leave him?" "Who is this?" asked 'Urwah. They said, "Abū Bakr." 'Urwah said, "By the One who holds my soul in His hand, were it not for a favor you did me for which I have not repaid you, I would answer you."[326]

'Urwah [again] began speaking to the Prophet. As often as he spoke to him, he took hold of his beard. Al-Mughīrah b. Shu'bah was standing next to the Prophet with his sword, wearing a mail neck-protector, and whenever 'Urwah extended his hand toward
[1537] the Prophet's beard, al-Mughīrah struck his hand with the lower end of the scabbard and said, "Take your hand away from his beard!" 'Urwah raised his head and asked, "Who is this?" They said, "Al-Mughīrah b. Shu'bah." 'Urwah said, "Treacherous man, am I not trying to rectify your act of treachery?" (During the Time of Ignorance[327] al-Mughīrah b. Shu'bah had accompanied some men and killed them and taken their money. Later he had come

324. I.e., if Quraysh prove too powerful for you.

325. Al-Lāt (called *al-Ṭāghiyah*, the dominator) was a female fertility and warrior goddess worshiped especially at al-Ṭā'if. See *EI²*, s.v. al-Lāt; and T. Fahd, *Le panthéon de l'Arabie centrale à la veille de l'Hégire,* 111–20.

326. The favor was that Abū Bakr had helped 'Urwah b. Mas'ūd pay the blood money with which 'Urwah had ended the feud caused by his nephew, al-Mughīrah b. Shu'bah. See W, II, 595.

327. See note 109, above.

and accepted Islam. The Prophet had said, "As for your Islam, we accept it; but the money is money of treachery for which we have no need."[328])

'Urwah began looking at the companions of the Prophet. "By God," he said, "if the Prophet coughs up a bit of phlegm and it falls onto the hand of one of them, he rubs his face and skin with it. If he gives them an order, they vie with each other to be the first to carry it out. If he performs ablutions, they almost fight over the water he used for them. If they speak in his presence, they lower their voices and do not look sharply at him out of respect for him."

'Urwah went back to his comrades and said: "My people, by God I have gone as an envoy to kings. I have gone as an envoy to Kisrā, Caesar, and the Negus,[329] but, by God, never have I seen a king whose companions respect him as Muḥammad's companions respect Muḥammad. By God, if he coughs up a bit of phlegm and it falls onto the hand of one of them, he rubs his face and skin with it. If he gives them an order, they vie with each other to be the first to carry it out. If he performs ablutions, they almost fight over the water he used for them. If they speak in his presence, they lower their voices and do not look sharply at him out of respect for him. [1538]
He has offered you a sensible proposal; accept it!"

Then a man from Kinānah[330] said, "Let me go to him." "Go to him" they said. When he came in sight of the Prophet and his companions, the Prophet said: "This is so and so. He is from a people who venerate sacrificial camels; so send them out to him." They were sent out to him. People went out to meet him shouting [the pilgrim's cry] *labbayka*.[331] When [the man from Kinānah] saw that, he said: "Praise God! These people should not be turned away from the House."

According to Ibn Ḥumayd—Salamah—Ibn Isḥāq—al-Zuhrī, who said in his report: Then they sent to him al-Ḥulays b. 'Alqa-

328. The parallels in IH, III, 313 (from al-Zuhrī), and in W, II, 595–98 (very elaborate), tell how al-Mughīrah b. Shu'bah, the nephew (or perhaps grandnephew) of 'Urwah b. Mas'ūd, once killed thirteen men and took their money, causing a feud that his uncle 'Urwah ended by paying blood money for the slain men.

329. The rulers of Persia, Byzantium, and Ethiopia respectively.

330. Kinānah (b. Khuzaymah) was a tribe near Mecca. See *EI*², s.v. Kināna.

331. Literally, "at your service [O Lord]," an ancient ritual chant used by pilgrims to Mecca in pre-Islamic times and preserved in the Islamic pilgrimage.

mah (or b. Zabbān), who was the chief of the Aḥābīsh[332] at that time. He was one of the Banū al-Ḥārith b. 'Abd Manāt b. Kinānah. When the Messenger of God saw him, he said: "Surely this man is from a people who devote themselves to piety. Send the sacrificial victims toward him for him to see." When he saw the sacrificial victims streaming toward him from the side of the valley with their necklaces and having eaten away their hair from being penned up so long, he returned to Quraysh without having reached the Messenger of God, so greatly was he impressed by what he had seen. "People of Quraysh," he said, "I have seen what it is not lawful to turn away: sacrificial victims with their necklaces, having eaten away their hair from being long penned up away from their place [of sacrifice]." They said to him, "Sit down; you are only a Bedouin who knows nothing!"

According to Ibn Ḥumayd—Salamah—Muḥammad b. Isḥāq—
[1539] 'Abdallāh b. Abī Bakr: Al-Ḥulays became angry at this and said: "People of Quraysh, by God, not on these terms did we became your confederates! Not on these terms did we league together with you—that you should turn away from the House of God those who have come to venerate it! By Him who holds the soul of al-Ḥulays in His hand, you shall leave Muḥammad free to accomplish what he came for, or I will leave, taking every last man of the Aḥābīsh!" They said to him: "Wait! Leave us alone, Ḥulays, until we obtain terms for ourselves with which we can be satisfied."

Resumption of the account of Ibn 'Abd al-A'lā and Ya'qūb: One of them named Mikraz b. Ḥafṣ stood up and said to them, "Let me go to him." "Go to him!" they said. When he came into view, the Prophet said: "This is Mikraz b. Ḥafṣ. He is a dissolute man." Mikraz came and began speaking to the Prophet, but while he was speaking to him, Suhayl b. 'Amr came. (According to Ayyūb[333]—'Ikrimah:[334] When Suhayl came, the Prophet said, "Your business has now become easy for you."[335])

---

332. See note 74, above.

333. Ayyūb b. Abī Tamīmah Kaysān al-Sakhtiyānī was born in 66/685 (or 68) and died in 131/748. See Ibn Ḥajar, *Tahdhīb*, I, 397–99; *GAS*, I, 87–88.

334. 'Ikrimah, a *mawlā* of Ibn 'Abbās and one of the most distinguished transmitters, is said to have died around 104–7/722-25 at the age of eighty. See Ibn Ḥajar, *Tahdhīb*, VII, 263–73; and *EI²*, s.v. 'Ikrima.

335. Arabic *sahula* "it has become easy" is a pun on the name Suhayl.

According to Muḥammad b. 'Umārah al-Asadī[336] and Muḥammad b. Manṣūr[337] (the wording of the account belongs to Ibn 'Umārah)—'Ubaydallāh b. Mūsā[338]—Mūsā b. 'Ubaydah[339]—Iyās b. Salamah b. al-Akwa'—his father [Salamah b. al-Akwa'], who said: Quraysh sent Suhayl b. 'Amr, Ḥuwayṭib b. 'Abd al-'Uzzā, and Ḥafṣ b. Fulān to the Prophet to make peace with him. When the Messenger of God saw that Suhayl b. 'Amr was among them, he said: "God has made your business easy for you. The men intend to gain access to you by their kinship[340] with you and intend to ask you for peace. Send forth the sacrificial animals and proclaim the [pilgrim's cry of] *labbayka*; perhaps that will soften their hearts." So they cried out *labbayka* from throughout the camp until their voices resounded with the call.

Then [the three emissaries of Quraysh] came and asked him for [1540] peace. When the people had made peace and while there were among the Muslims some of the polytheists and among the polytheists some of the Muslims, Abū Sufyān plotted treachery against him. Suddenly the valley was flowing with men and weapons.

According to Iyās [b. Salamah]—Salamah [b. al-Akwa']: I came bringing six of the polytheists, they being armed, I leading them, and they having no power to do any good or any mischief. I brought them to the Prophet, and he neither plundered nor killed, but forgave.

As for the report of al-Ḥasan b. Yaḥyā—Abū 'Āmir [al-'Aqadī]—

---

336. For Muḥammad b. 'Umārah b. 'Amr b. Ḥazm al-Anṣārī, see Ibn Ḥajar, *Tahdhīb*, IX, 359–60.

337. Muḥammad b. Manṣūr b. Dāwūd b. Ibrāhīm al-Ṭūsī Abū Ja'far al-'Ābid lived at Baghdād and died in 254/868 or 256/870 at age eighty. See Ibn Ḥajar, *Tahdhīb*, IX, 472.

338. 'Ubaydallāh b. Mūsā b. Bādhām/Bādhān was born in 128/745 and died in 213 or 214/828–29. See Ibn Ḥajar, *Tahdhīb*, VII, 50–53.

339. Mūsā b. 'Ubaydah b. Nashīṭ b. 'Amr b. al-Ḥārith al-Rabadhī Abū 'Abd al-'Azīz was born in Medina and died in 152/769 or 153. See Ibn Ḥajar, *Tahdhīb*, X, 356–60.

340. This may allude to the fact that Muḥammad's second wife, Sawdah bt. Zam'ah, whom he married shortly after the death of Khadījah, had been the sister-in-law of Suhayl b. 'Amr. Although Suhayl (the head of the Banū 'Āmir clan of Quraysh) remained a pagan, his brother, al-Sakrān b. 'Amr, had become a Muslim and took part in the second Muslim emigration to Ethiopia. After al-Sakrān's death, Muḥammad married his widow. See *EI*[1], s.v. Sawda bint Zam'a.

'Ikrimah b. 'Ammār al-Yamāmī—Iyās b. Salamah—his father [Salamah b. al-Akwa']), it is that [Salamah] said: After we and the people of Mecca had made peace with each other, I went to the tree, cleared away its thorns, and lay down in its shade. Four polytheists, people of Mecca, came to me and began speaking evil of the Messenger of God. Finding them hateful, I moved to another tree. They hung up their weapons and lay down. While they were lying there, suddenly someone called out from the lower part of the valley: "Help, Emigrants! Ibn Zunaym has been killed." I drew my sword, ran at the four—they were lying down—and took their weapons, which I made a bundle in my hands. Then I said, "By Him who honored Muḥammad, if any of you raises his head, I will strike off his skull."[341] I led them away to the Messenger of God.
[1541] My uncle 'Āmir brought in a man clothed in mail named Mikraz from the al-'Abalāt.[342] We made them stand before the Messenger of God along with seventy of the polytheists. The Messenger of God looked at them and said, "Let the first violating [of the peace] be theirs"—and he pardoned them. Thus God revealed: "It is He who restrained their hands from you, and your hands from them, in the hollow of Mecca."[343]

Resumption of the account of Muḥammad b. 'Umārah and Muḥammad b. Manṣūr, from 'Ubaydallāh [b. Mūsā]: Salamah [b. al-Akwa'] said: We rushed toward those of our side who were in the hands of the polytheists, and we rescued every one of our men who was in their hands. We overpowered those of their side who were in our hands. Then Quraysh sent Suhayl b. 'Amr and Ḥuwayṭib and put them in charge of their [side of the] peace; the Prophet sent 'Alī for his [side of the] peace.

According to Bishr b. Mu'ādh[344]—Yazīd b. Zuray'[345]—Sa'īd[346]—Qatādah,[347] who said: We were told that one of the

---

341. Literally, "I will strike off that wherein are his two eyes."

342. Al-'Abalāt was a division of the clan of Banū Umayyah al-Ṣughrā of Quraysh (*Lisan*, IV, 2790).

343. Qur'ān 48:24.

344. Bishr b. Mu'ādh al-'Aqadī, with whom al-Ṭabarī studied in al-Baṣrah, died in or before 245/859. See Ibn Ḥajar, *Tahdhīb*, I, 458.

345. Abū Mu'āwiyah Yazīd b. Zuray' al-Baṣrī was born in 101/720 and died in 182/798. See Ibn Ḥajar, *Tahdhīb*, XI, 325–28.

346. Sa'īd b. Abī 'Arūbah died in the 150s (ca. 772). See Ibn Ḥajar, *Tahdhīb*, IV, 63–66.

347. Abū al-Khaṭṭāb Qatādah b. Di'āmah b. Qatādah al-Sadūsī (born 60/679, died 118/736) was a Qur'ān commentator and scholar of poetry, genealogy, and

companions of the Prophet, a man named Zunaym, had gone up into the pass from al-Ḥudaybiyah and that the polytheists shot and killed him. The Messenger of God sent out horsemen, and they brought him twelve horsemen of the unbelievers. God's Prophet asked them: "Do I owe you any treaty obligations? Do I owe you any protection?" "No," they replied. Then the Messenger of God released them. God revealed concerning this the [following words of] Qur'ān: "It is He who restrained their hands from you, [1542] and your hands from them, in the hollow of Mecca"—until the words, "He sees the things you do."[348]

As for Ibn Isḥāq, he has mentioned that Quraysh sent Suhayl b. 'Amr only after a message that the Messenger of God had sent to them with 'Uthmān b. 'Affān.

According to Ibn Ḥumayd—Salamah—Muḥammad b. Isḥāq—a certain man of learning: The Messenger of God summoned Khirāsh b. Umayyah al-Khuzā'ī and sent him to Quraysh in Mecca, mounting him on a camel of his called al-Tha'lab,[349] to inform their dignitaries from him of why he had come. Quraysh, however, hamstrung the camel of the Messenger of God that Khirāsh was riding. They intended to kill Khirāsh, but the Aḥābīsh protected him; so they released him, and he returned to the Messenger of God.

According to Ibn Ḥumayd—Salamah—Muḥammad b. Isḥāq—someone I do not doubt—'Ikrimah, the *mawlā* of Ibn 'Abbās: Quraysh sent forty or fifty of their men and commanded them to surround[350] the camp of the Messenger of God in order to injure[351] for themselves some[352] of his companions; however, these men were taken prisoner and brought to the Messenger of God. He pardoned them and released them. They had thrown stones and shot arrows into the camp of the Messenger of God.

Then the Prophet summoned 'Umar b. al-Khaṭṭāb, to send him to Mecca to inform the dignitaries of Quraysh from him of why he

---

history. The *isnād* is to a Qur'ān commentary by him. See Ibn Ḥajar, *Tahdhīb*, VIII, 351–56; *GAS*, I, 31–32.

348. Qur'ān 48:24.

349. The name means "fox."

350. Arabic *yuṭīfū* can also mean "go around, circumambulate."

351. Arabic *yuṣībū* has a range of meanings from "obtain" through "injure," and even "kill."

352. IH, III, 314, reads "one."

had come. 'Umar said: "Messenger of God, I fear for my life from Quraysh. There is no one of the Banū 'Adī b. Ka'b[353] in Mecca who will protect me now that Quraysh know of my hostility and roughness to them. But I can recommend to you a man they will like better than me—'Uthmān b. 'Affān."[354] So the Messenger of God summoned 'Uthmān and sent him to Abū Sufyān and the dignitaries of Quraysh, to inform them that he had come not for
[1543] war but only to visit the House and venerate its sanctity. 'Uthmān set out for Mecca. When he entered Mecca (or before he entered it), Abān b. Sa'īd b. al-'Āṣ met him and, dismounting from his animal, mounted 'Uthmān in front of him and rode [on the same animal] behind him. He protected 'Uthmān until the latter had delivered the message of the Messenger of God. 'Uthmān hastened to Abū Sufyān and the powerful men of Quraysh and informed them of the message with which he had been sent from the Messenger of God. When 'Uthmān had finished the message of the Messenger of God to them, they said to him, "If you wish to circumambulate the House, do so." He replied, "I will not do it until the Messenger of God circumambulates it." Quraysh then imprisoned him, and a report reached the Messenger of God and the Muslims that 'Uthmān had been killed.

According to Ibn Ḥumayd—Salamah—Muḥammad b. Isḥāq—'Abdallāh b. Abī Bakr: When the Messenger of God received a report that 'Uthmān had been killed, he said, "We will not leave until we fight it out with the enemy"—and he summoned the people to swear allegiance. Thus the Pledge of al-Riḍwān[355] took place under the tree.

According to Ibn 'Umārah al-Asadī—'Ubaydallāh b. Mūsā—Mūsā b. 'Ubaydah—Iyās b. Salamah—Salamah b. al-Akwa', who

353. The Banū 'Adī b. Ka'b were 'Umar's clan. They belonged to the group of less influential clans known as Quraysh al-Ẓawāhir ("of the outskirts"), whose quarters were far from the central area of Mecca.

354. 'Uthmān was a member of the influential clan of Banū Umayyah b. 'Abd Shams (the clan of Abū Sufyān) and would thus be a more respected emissary. As the sequel shows, 'Uthmān was immediately taken under the protection of his cousin, Abān b. Sa'īd b. al-'Āṣ b. Umayyah.

355. I.e., the Pledge of [God's] Being Well Pleased [with the Muslims], alluding to the verse of Qur'ān revealed concerning the occasion (Qur'ān 48:18), as explained in the next paragraph. Watt in his *EI*² article on al-Ḥudaybiya calls it the Pledge of Good Pleasure.

said: While we were returning from al-Ḥudaybiyah, the Prophet's crier announced: "People, an oath of allegiance! An oath of allegiance! The Holy Spirit[356] has descended!" So we hastened to the Messenger of God, who was under an acacia tree, and swore allegiance to him. This was what God referred to when He said: "God was well pleased with the believers when they were swearing allegiance to you under the tree."[357] [1544]

According to 'Abd al-Ḥamīd b. Bayān[358]—Muḥammad b. Yazīd[359]—Ismā'īl b. Abī Khālid[360]—'Āmir,[361] who said: The first to swear the Pledge of al-Riḍwān was a man from the Banū Asad named Abū Sinān b. Wahb.

According to Yūnus b. 'Abd al-A'lā—Ibn Wahb—al-Qāsim b. 'Abdallāh b. 'Umar[362]—Muḥammad b. al-Munkadir[363]—Jābir b. 'Abdallāh: They were fourteen hundred on the day of al-Ḥudaybiyah.[364] [Jābir] said: We swore allegiance to the Messenger of God while 'Umar was holding his hand under the tree, which was an acacia. We swore allegiance to him—except al-Jadd b. Qays al-Anṣārī, who hid under the belly of his camel.

Jābir said: We swore allegiance to the Messenger of God that we would not flee; we did not swear allegiance to him to the death.

Another account of this is as follows. According to al-Ḥasan b. Yaḥyā—Abū 'Āmir—'Ikrimah b. 'Ammār al-Yamāmī—Iyās b. Salamah b. al-Akwa'—his father [Salamah b. al-Akwa']: The Prophet summoned the people to swear allegiance at the foot of the tree. I swore allegiance to him among the first of the people;

---

356. Arabic: *rūḥ al-qudus*, normally referring to the Angel Gabriel as the intermediary who delivered the Qur'ānic revelations to Muḥammad.

357. Qur'ān 48:18.

358. 'Abd al-Ḥamīd b. Bayān died in 244/858. See Ibn Ḥajar, *Tahdhīb*, VI, 111.

359. Muḥammad b. Yazīd al-Kulā'ī Abū Sa'īd al-Wāsiṭī was a *mawlā* of Syrian origin who died in 188/803–4. See Ibn Ḥajar, *Tahdhīb*, X, 527–28.

360. Ismā'īl b. Abī Khālid al-Aḥmasī, a *mawlā* known for his superior knowledge of reports from al-Sha'bī, died in 146/763. See Ibn Ḥajar, *Tahdhīb*, I, 291–92.

361. Abū 'Amr 'Āmir b. Sharāḥīl b. 'Amr al-Sha'bī, a member of the South Arabian tribe of Hamdān, was born in al-Kūfah in 19/640, and died in 103/721. In addition to political activity, he was a transmitter of *ḥadīth* and a major source for later historians. See Ibn Ḥajar, *Tahdhīb*, V, 65–69; *EI*[1], s.v. al-Sha'bī; *GAS*, I, 277.

362. Al-Qāsim b. 'Abdallāh b. 'Umar b. Ḥafṣ b. 'Āṣim b. 'Umar b. al-Khaṭṭāb died between 150/767 and 160/776–77. See Ibn Ḥajar, *Tahdhīb*, VIII, 320–21.

363. Muḥammad b. al-Munkadir b. 'Abdallāh al-Taymī died ca. 130/747–48 at the age of seventy-six. See Ibn Ḥajar, *Tahdhīb*, IX, 473–75.

364. Ed. Cairo: "they were fourteen and a hundred"—i.e., 114.

then he received more and more pledges of allegiance, until, when he was in the middle of the people, he said, "Swear allegiance, Salamah!" I said, "I did swear allegiance to you, Messenger of God, among the first of the people." He said, "Again!" Seeing me unarmed, the Prophet gave me a [shield of the kind called] *ḥajafah* or *daraqah*.[365] The Messenger of God received the people's pledges of allegiance until, having arrived at the last of them, he said, "Aren't you going to swear allegiance, Salamah?" I said, "Messenger of God, I did swear allegiance to you among the first of the people and in the middle group." "Again!" he said. So I swore allegiance to him for the third time. The Messenger of God said, "Where are the *daraqah* and[366] *ḥajafah* that I gave you?" I said,
[1545] "My uncle 'Āmir came up to me without a weapon, and I gave it[367] to him." The Messenger of God laughed and said, "You are like the one who said of old, 'O God, help me find a friend who shall be dearer to me than myself.'"

Resumption of the account of Ibn Isḥāq: The people swore allegiance to the Messenger of God. None of the Muslims who were present on the occasion hung back except al-Jadd b. Qays, a member of the Banū Salimah. Jābir b. 'Abdallāh used to say: "It is as if I could see him now, clinging to the armpit of his camel. He had taken refuge there to hide from the people by means of her." Word then came to the Messenger of God that the report about 'Uthmān was false.

According to Ibn Isḥāq—al-Zuhrī: Quraysh then sent Suhayl b. 'Amr, a member of the Banū 'Āmir b. Lu'ayy, to the Messenger of God. They instructed Suhayl: "Go to Muḥammad and make peace with him. Let the only provision of the peace with him be that he shall go away from us this year; for, by God, the Arabs must never say that he entered our territory by force."

---

365. Both terms, which can be synonymous, refer to a shield made of heavy animal skins without wood. Insofar as the dictionaries distinguish between them, the *ḥajafah* was taken to be the native Arab shield made of layered camel hides, while the *daraqah* was said to be made of hippopotamus or crocodile skins imported from Ethiopia. See Lane, *Lexicon*, II, 520; III, 872.

366. The parallel in Muslim, *Ṣaḥīḥ*, reads "your *ḥajafah* or *daraqah*"—ed. Leiden, note.

367. The pronoun *-hā* (feminine singular or collective plural, but not dual) implies that only one shield was given.

Suhayl b. 'Amr approached. When the Messenger of God saw him coming, he said, "The people [of Quraysh] intended peace when they sent this man." When Suhayl reached the Messenger of God, he spoke for a long time. The two men negotiated with each other, and peace was made between them. When the matter had been arranged and only the writing of the document remained, 'Umar b. al-Khaṭṭāb jumped up and went to Abū Bakr and said, "Abū Bakr, isn't he the Messenger of God?" "Yes," he replied. "And are we not Muslims?" he asked. "Yes," he replied. "And are they not polytheists?" he asked. "Yes," he replied. "Then why," asked 'Umar, "should we grant what is detrimental to our religion?" Abū Bakr said, "'Umar, stick to what he says,[368] for I bear witness that he is the Messenger of God." 'Umar said, "I, too, bear witness that he is the Messenger of God."

'Umar then went to the Messenger of God and said, "Messenger of God, are you not the Messenger of God?" "Yes," he replied. [1546] "And are we not Muslims?" asked 'Umar. "Yes," he replied. "And are they not polytheists?" he asked. "Yes," he replied. "Then why," asked 'Umar, "should we grant what is detrimental to our religion?" He replied: "I am God's servant and messenger. I will never disobey His command, and He will not allow me to perish." ('Umar used to say, "I continued to fast, give alms, pray, and free slaves because of what I did on that day, for fear of the words I had spoken, until I hoped it would be set right.")

According to Ibn Ḥumayd—Salamah—Muḥammad b. Isḥāq—Buraydah b. Sufyān b. Farwah al-Aslamī[369]—Muḥammad b. Ka'b al-Quraẓī—'Alqamah b. Qays al-Nakha'ī—'Alī b. Abī Ṭālib, who said: Then the Messenger of God summoned me and said, "Write, 'In the name of God, the Merciful and Compassionate.'" Suhayl said: "I do not know this one.[370] Write rather, 'In Thy name, O God.'" So the Messenger of God said, "Write, 'In Thy name, O

---

368. Literally, "hold closely to his stirrup." See Lane, *Lexicon*, VI, 2246, s.v. *gharz* for the idiom.

369. Buraydah b. Sufyān b. Farwah al-Aslamī is mentioned as a *tābi'ī* (but without dates) in Ibn Ḥajar, *Tahdhīb*, I, 433–34.

370. Suhayl's objection is to the peculiarly Muslim formula, "the Merciful and Compassionate," (cf. the parallel in W, II, 610, "I do not know 'the Merciful [al-Raḥmān]'") not to the invocation of God under the name Allāh. Suhayl's formula itself uses the name Allāh.

God' "—and I wrote it. Then he said, "Write, 'This is that whereon Muḥammad the Messenger of God has made peace with Suhayl b. 'Amr.' " Suhayl b. 'Amr said: "If I testified that you are the Messenger of God, I would not fight you. Write rather your name and the name of your father." So the Messenger of God said, "Write: This is that whereon Muḥammad b. 'Abdallāh has made peace with Suhayl b. 'Amr. The two have agreed on these terms: that warfare shall be laid aside by the people for ten years, during which the people shall be safe and refrain from [attacking] each other; that whoever shall come to the Messenger of God from Quraysh without the permission of his guardian, [Muḥammad] shall return him to them; that whoever shall come to Quraysh from those who are with the Messenger of God, they shall not return him to [Muḥammad]; that there shall be between us a breast bound [to fulfill the terms of this writing];[371] that there shall be neither clandestine theft nor betrayal;[372] and that anyone who wishes to enter into treaty and pact with the Messenger of
[1547] God may do so, and anyone who wishes to enter into treaty and pact with Quraysh may do so." (The Khuzā'ah jumped up and said, "We have a treaty and pact with the Messenger of God." The Banū Bakr jumped up and said, "We have a treaty and compact with Quraysh.")[373] "You shall go back, leaving us this year and not entering Mecca against us. When the next year comes, we will go out, away from you, and you shall enter Mecca with your companions and stay there for three nights: you shall have with you the weapons of a rider, with the swords in scabbards; you shall not enter with other weapons."

While the Messenger of God was writing the document—he and

371. Arabic: *anna baynanā 'aybatan makfūfatan*, literally "a receptacle closed (or tied up)." The phrase is enigmatic. Lane, *Lexicon*, V, 2206, lists three quite different explanations. The first is that it means there shall be between us as it were a receptacle closed and fastened by its loops over its contents—i.e., a breast bound to fulfill the terms of the treaty. Another interpretation is that as a receptacle is tied up so shall evil be tied up between the two sides. Yet another interpretation is that there shall be sincere friendship between the two sides (a friend being often compared to a receptacle in which one can deposit one's secrets).

372. Arabic: *lā islāla wa-lā ighlāla*, thus interpreted by Abū Dharr's commentary on the *Sīrah*. Alternatively, the two terms may be taken as referring to secret and open violations.

373. This notice anticipates the violence between the Banū Bakr b. 'Abd Manāt b. Kinānah (allies of Quraysh) and the Banū Khuzā'ah (allies of Muḥammad) in A.H. 8, which precipitated the Muslim conquest of Mecca. See p. 160, below.

Suhayl b. 'Amr—suddenly Abū Jandal, the son of Suhayl b. 'Amr, came walking with short steps in shackles. He had escaped to the Messenger of God. The companions of the Messenger of God had set out not doubting that they would conquer, because of a vision the Messenger of God had seen. Therefore, when they saw what they saw—the peace, the retreat, and the obligations the Messenger of God had taken on himself—the people felt so grieved about it that they were close to despair. When Suhayl saw Abū Jandal, he went up to him, struck him on the face, and grabbed him by the front of his garment. "Muḥammad," he said, "the pact was ratified between me and you before this fellow came to you." "You are right," he replied. Suhayl began pulling and dragging [his son Abū Jandal] by the front of his garment to return him to Quraysh. Abū Jandal began screaming at the top of his voice, "People of the Muslims, shall I be returned to the polytheists for them [1548]
to torment me for my religion?" This made the people feel even worse. The Messenger of God said: "Abū Jandal, count on a reward, for God will give you and those who are oppressed with you relief and a way out. We have made a treaty and peace between ourselves and these people; we have given them and they have given us a promise, and we will not act treacherously toward them."

'Umar b. al-Khaṭṭāb jumped up with Abū Jandal, walking beside him, and saying, "Be patient, Abū Jandal! They are only polytheists, and the blood of any of them is no more than the blood of a dog!" He held the hilt of his sword close to him. ('Umar used to say, "I hoped he would take the sword and strike his father with it, but the man was too attached to his father.")

When the writing was finished, he had some of the Muslims and some of the polytheists witness the peace: Abū Bakr b. Abī Quḥāfah, 'Umar b. al-Khaṭṭāb, 'Abd al-Raḥmān b. 'Awf, 'Abdallāh b. Suhayl b. 'Amr, Sa'd b. Abī Waqqāṣ, Maḥmūd b. Maslamah (a member of the Banū 'Abd al-Ashhal), Mikraz b. Ḥafṣ b. al-Akhyaf (a polytheist, a member the Banū 'Āmir b. Lu'ayy), and 'Alī b. Abī Ṭālib, who wrote—he was the writer of the document.

According to Hārūn b. Isḥāq[374]—Muṣ'ab b. al-Miqdām;[375] and

---

374. Hārūn b. Isḥāq b. Muḥammad al-Hamdānī al-Kūfī died in 285/898. See Ibn Ḥajar, *Tahdhīb*, X, 2–3.

375. Muṣ'ab b. al-Miqdām al-Khath'amī al-Kūfī died in 203/818. See Ibn Ḥajar, *Tahdhīb*, X, 165–66.

according to Sufyān b. Wakī'—his father [Wakī' b. al-Jarrāḥ];[376] each of the two said: according to Isrā'īl—Abū Isḥāq—al-Barā', who said:[377] The Messenger of God set out to perform the lesser pilgrimage during Dhū al-Qa'dah. The people of Mecca refused to allow him to enter Mecca until he made a pact with them that he would stay there [only] three days. When he wrote the document,
[1549] he wrote, "This is what Muḥammad the Messenger of God has agreed to." They said, "If we knew that you are the Messenger of God, we would not prevent you; but you are Muḥammad b. 'Abdallāh." He replied, "I am the Messenger of God, and I am Muḥammad b. 'Abdallāh." He said to 'Alī, "Erase 'Messenger of God.'" "No," he replied, "by God, I will never erase *you*!" So the Messenger of God took the document—he did not write well—and wrote "Muḥammad" in place of "the Messenger of God."[378] Then he wrote: "This is what Muḥammad has agreed to: he shall not enter Mecca with weapons, except swords in scabbards; he shall not depart from its people taking anyone who wants to follow him; and he shall not hinder any of his companions who wants to stay in Mecca." When Muḥammad entered Mecca and the time elapsed, they came to 'Alī and said to him, "Tell your master to leave us, for the time has elapsed." So the Messenger of God left.

According to Muḥammad b. 'Abd al-A'lā—Muḥammad b. Thawr—Ma'mar—al-Zuhrī—'Urwah b. al-Zubayr—al-Miswar b. Makhramah; and according to Ya'qūb b. Ibrāhīm—Yaḥyā b. Sa'īd—'Abdallāh b. al-Mubārak—Ma'mar—al-Zuhrī—'Urwah—al-Miswar b. Makhramah and Marwān b. al-Ḥakam in the story of al-Ḥudaybiyah:[379] When the Messenger of God had finished his pact, he said to his companions, "Arise, sacrifice, and shave." By

376. Wakī' b. al-Jarrāḥ b. Mulayḥ (or Malīḥ) al-Ru'āsī Abū Sufyān was born ca. 129/746 in al-Kūfah. Regarded as one of the leading *ḥadīth* scholars of his time, he died ca. 197/812. See Ibn Ḥajar, *Tahdhīb*, XI, 123–31; *GAS*, I, 96–97.

377. Parallel in al-Bukhārī, *Ṣaḥīḥ* (ed. Būlāq), III, 154.

378. The text as it stands is illogical. The parallel in al-Bukhārī omits "Muḥammad" (yielding, "he wrote [something] in place of 'the Messenger of God'"). As the Leiden editor notes, one could restore the logic of the passage by assuming that the treaty as originally drafted began, "This is what the Messenger of God has agreed to" (omitting "Muḥammad"). The sense of the report thus would be that Muḥammad replaced "the Messenger of God" with "Muḥammad."

379. Parallel: al-Bukhārī, *Ṣaḥīḥ* (ed. Būlāq), III, 167.

God, not a man stood up until he had said it three times. When no one stood up, he arose and went into [the tent of] Umm Salamah and told her what he had encountered from the people. Umm Salamah said to him: "Prophet of God, do you approve of this? Go out, and speak not a word to any of them until you have slaughtered your fattened camel and summoned your shaver to shave you." He arose, went out, and spoke not a word to anyone until he [1550] had done this. He slaughtered his fattened camel and called his shaver, who shaved him. When they saw this, they rose up and slaughtered, and they began to shave each other, until they almost killed each other for grief.

According to Ibn Ḥumayd—Salamah—Ibn Isḥāq: The person who shaved him that day—according to my information—was Khirāsh b. Umayyah b. al-Faḍl al-Khuzāʿī.

According to Ibn Ḥumayd—Salamah—Ibn Isḥāq—ʿAbdallāh b. Abī Najīḥ[380]—Mujāhid—Ibn ʿAbbās, who said:[381] On the day of al-Ḥudaybiyah, some men shaved [their heads] and others shortened [their hair by cutting it]. The Messenger of God said, "God will have mercy on those who shave." They asked, "And those who shorten, Messenger of God?" He replied, "God will have mercy on those who shave." They asked, "And those who shorten, Messenger of God?" He replied, "God will have mercy on those who shave." They asked, "Messenger of God, and those who shorten?" He replied, "And those who shorten." They asked, "Messenger of God, why did you explicitly mention mercy for those who shave and not those who shorten?" He replied, "Because they did not doubt."

According to Ibn Ḥumayd—Salamah—Ibn Isḥāq—ʿAbdallāh b. Abī Najīḥ—Mujāhid—Ibn ʿAbbās, who said: Among the victims that he sacrificed the year of al-Ḥudaybiyah, the Messenger of God sacrificed a camel stallion belonging to Abū Jahl[382] which had a silver nose ring, and this he did to anger the polytheists.

---

380. ʿAbdallāh b. Abī Najīḥ died in 131 or 132/748–50. See Ibn Saʿd, *Ṭabaqāt*, V, 355; Ibn Ḥajar, *Tahdhīb*, VI, 54–55. Sezgin (*GAS*, I, 20) argues that Ibn Abī Najīḥ was the author of a commentary on the Qurʾān commentary of Mujāhid.

381. Parallel: IH, III, 319 (tr. Guillaume, 505).

382. Abū Jahl (or Abū al-Ḥakam) ʿAmr b. Hishām b. al-Mughīrah, the leader of the Banū Makhzūm clan of Quraysh, was a prominent opponent of Muḥammad.

Resumption of the account of al-Zuhrī that we have mentioned previously: Then the Prophet returned to Medina.

In his account, Ibn Ḥumayd (on the authority of Salamah—Ibn Isḥāq—al-Zuhrī) adds that al-Zuhrī used to say: No victory greater than this one had been won previously in Islam. There had been only fighting when the people met together; however, when the
[1551] truce took place, and war laid down its burdens, and all the people felt safe with each other, they met with each other in conversation and debate, and no one possessing understanding was told about Islam but embraced it. Thus, in those two years as many or more entered Islam as had been in it before.

All [transmitters of the account] from al-Zuhrī—'Urwah—al-Miswar and Marwān say: When the Messenger of God arrived in Medina, Abū Baṣīr, a man from Quraysh, came to him.

According to Ibn Isḥāq in his report:[383] Abū Baṣīr 'Utbah b. Asīd[384] b. Jāriyah, a Muslim, was one of those confined in Mecca. When he came to the Messenger of God, Azhar b. 'Abd 'Awf and al-Akhnas b. Sharīq b. 'Amr b. Wahb al-Thaqafī wrote concerning him to the Messenger of God and sent a man from the Banū 'Āmir b. Lu'ayy along with a *mawlā* of that clan. The two brought the letter of al-Azhar and al-Akhnas to the Messenger of God. The Messenger of God said: "Abū Baṣīr, you know what we have given these people. Breaking a promise is not right in our religion. God will give you and those who are oppressed with you relief and a way out."

Abū Baṣīr departed with the two men. When he was at Dhū al-
[1552] Ḥulayfah, he sat against a wall, and his two companions sat with him. Abū Baṣīr said, "Is this sword of yours sharp, O tribesman of the Banū 'Āmir?" "Yes," he replied. "May I look at it?" he said. "If you wish," he replied. Abū Baṣīr unsheathed it, attacked the man with it, and killed him. The *mawlā* hurried away and came to the Messenger of God while the latter was sitting in the mosque. When the Messenger of God caught sight of him, he said, "This man has seen something fearful." When he reached the Messenger

---

Presumably, the camel had been captured at the Battle of Badr, where Abū Jahl had been killed. See al-Ṭabarī, I, 1187; *EI*², s.v. Abū Dj̲ahl.

383. IH, III, 323–24 (tr. Guillaume, 507–8); parallel in W, II, 624–29.

384. Ed. Cairo: Usayd. Al-Dhahabī, *al-Mushtabih*, 12, gives Asīd as the name of Abū Baṣīr's father.

of God, the latter asked, "Alas, what has happened to you?" The man replied, "Your companion killed my companion." By God, while the man was still there, Abū Baṣīr appeared girded with the sword and halted before the Messenger of God, saying: "Messenger of God, your obligation has been fulfilled and has been discharged from you.[385] You surrendered me and returned me to them, but God rescued me from them." The Prophet said: "Woe to his mother! A kindler of war's fire"—Ibn Isḥāq, in his account, said "a stirrer up of war"—"if he had men with him!" When Abū Baṣīr heard this, he knew that he would return him to them. So Abū Baṣīr went out and encamped at al-ʿĪṣ,[386] in the vicinity of Dhū al-Marwah, on the coast of the sea, on the route that Quraysh used to take to Syria. The words that the Messenger of God had spoken to Abū Baṣīr—"Woe to his mother! A stirrer up of war if he had men with him!"—were reported to the Muslims who were confined in Mecca, and they went out to Abū Baṣīr at al-ʿĪṣ. Abū Jandal b. Suhayl b. ʿAmr escaped and joined Abū Baṣīr. Nearly seventy such men gathered around him, and they harassed Quraysh. By God, whenever they heard of a caravan of Quraysh that had set out for Syria, they intercepted it, killed the men, and took their goods. Quraysh therefore sent to the Prophet, imploring him for the sake of God and the bond of kinship to send word to them that whoever came to him would be safe.[387] So the Messenger of God gave them refuge, and they came to him in Medina.

Ibn Isḥāq added in his account: When word of how Abū Baṣīr [1553]
had killed their companion from the Banū ʿĀmir reached Suhayl b. ʿAmr, he leaned his back against the Kaʿbah and said, "I will not remove my back from the Kaʿbah until they pay blood money for this man."[388] Abū Sufyān b. Ḥarb said: "By God, this is foolishness. By God, no blood money will be paid for him." He said it three times.

---

385. Ibn Hishām: "and God has discharged it for you."

386. Al-ʿĪṣ is said to be four nights' journey from Medina and two nights' journey from Dhū al-Marwah (a village in Wādī al-Qurā, the long valley extending north from Medina toward Syria)—see Ibn Saʿd, *Ṭabaqāt*, II, 23.

387. I.e., he would not be returned to Mecca.

388. As the leader of the Banū ʿĀmir, Suhayl b. ʿAmr had responsibility for demanding compensation for the murder of a fellow clansman.

According to Ibn 'Abd al-A'lā and Ya'qūb in their account:[389] Believing women then came to him (that is, the Messenger of God). God therefore revealed to him: "O believers, when believing women come to you as emigrants"—until the words, "to the ties of unbelieving women."[390] On that day 'Umar b. al-Khaṭṭāb divorced two women who had been his wives in polytheism. Thus, He forbade them to send the women back, but commanded them to return the bride price at that time. (A man asked al-Zuhrī, "Was that because of conjugal relations?" "Yes," he replied.[391]) Mu'āwiyah b. Abī Sufyān married one of the women; Ṣafwān b. Umayyah married the other.

Ibn Isḥāq added in his account: Umm Kulthūm bt. 'Uqbah b. Abī Mu'ayṭ emigrated to the Messenger of God during that period. Her brothers, 'Umārah and al-Walīd b. 'Uqbah, went to the Messenger of God to ask him to return her to them according to the treaty made between him and Quraysh at al-Ḥudaybiyah, but he did not do so: God had rejected it.

Ibn Isḥāq also said in his report: Among those who divorced [their unbelieving wives] was 'Umar b. al-Khaṭṭāb, who divorced
[1554] his wives Quraybah bt. Abī Umayyah b. al-Mughīrah (Mu'āwiyah b. Abī Sufyān married her afterward in Mecca while both of them were still polytheists) and Umm Kulthūm bt. 'Amr b. Jarwal al-Khuzā'iyyah,[392] the mother of 'Ubaydallāh b. 'Umar (Abū Jahm b. Ḥudhāfah b. Ghānim, one of her tribesmen, married her in Mecca while both of them were still polytheists).

According to al-Wāqidī:[393] In this year, in the month of Rabī'

389. Parallel: al-Bukhārī, *Ṣaḥīḥ* (ed. Būlāq), III, 127.

390. Qur'ān 60:10. The passage reads: "O believers, when believing women come to you as emigrants, test them. God knows very well their belief. Then, if you know them to be believers, return them not to the unbelievers. They are not permitted to the unbelievers, nor are the unbelievers permitted to them. Give the unbelievers what they have expended (on them); and there is no fault in you to marry them when you have given them their due. Do not hold fast to the ties of unbelieving women."

391. I.e., the bride price (*ṣadāq*), being the husband's payment to the woman for sexual rights, should be returned to indemnify the unbelieving husband for the loss of his now Muslim wife.

392. IH, II, 327, reads: Umm Kulthūm bt. Jarwal (omitting 'Amr). The Leiden editor prefers Ibn Hishām's reading.

393. Parallel with fuller text: W, II, 550.

II,[394] the Messenger of God sent out 'Ukkāshah b. Miḥṣan with forty men to al-Ghamr.[395] Among them were Thābit b. Aqram and Shujā' b. Wahb. He traveled quickly, but the enemy became aware and fled. He encamped by their water and sent out scouts. They captured a spy who guided them to some of their cattle. They found two hundred camels and brought them down to Medina.

In this year the Messenger of God sent out Muḥammad b. Maslamah with ten men in Rabī' I.[396] The enemy lay in wait for them until he and his companions went to sleep. Before they suspected anything, there was the enemy. The companions of Muḥammad b. Maslamah were killed; Muḥammad escaped wounded.

According to al-Wāqidī:[397] In this year the Messenger of God dispatched the raiding party of Abū 'Ubaydah b. al-Jarrāḥ to Dhū al-Qaṣṣah in the month of Rabī' II with forty men. They traveled through the night on foot and reached Dhū al-Qaṣṣah just before dawn. They raided the inhabitants, who escaped them by fleeing [1555] to the mountains, and took cattle, old clothes, and a single man. He became a Muslim, and the Messenger of God released him.

In this year a raiding party led by Zayd b. Ḥārithah went to al-Jamūm.[398] He captured a woman of the Muzaynah named Ḥalīmah, who guided them to an encampment of the Banū Sulaym, where they captured cattle, sheep, and prisoners. Among the prisoners was Ḥalīmah's husband. When Zayd brought back what he had taken, the Messenger of God granted to the woman of Muzaynah her husband and her freedom.

In this year a raiding party led by Zayd b. Ḥārithah went to al-'Īṣ in Jumādā I.[399] During it, the property that was with Abū al-'Āṣ b.

394. Rabī' II of A.H. 6 began on 20 August 627.

395. Al-Ghamr was a watering place belonging to the Banū Asad b. Khuzaymah to the east of Medina in the Yamāmah (central Arabia); see Yāqūt, *Mu'jam al-buldān*, VI, 304.

396. Rabī' I of A.H. 6 began on 21 July 627. Parallel with fuller text: W, II, 551–52, where the destination of this raid, like the following one, is given as Dhū al-Qaṣṣah of the Banū Tha'labah and 'Uwāl (subtribes of Ghaṭafān), a night's march east of Medina.

397. Parallel with fuller text: W, II, 552. Another account (perhaps the same raid) of a raid by Abū 'Ubaydah to the coast is in IH, IV, 632–33 (tr. Guillaume, 673).

398. The nature and date of this raid are uncertain.

399. Jumādā I of A.H. 6 began on 18 September 627. Parallel (with fuller text): W, II, 553–55.

al-Rabī' was taken. He asked the Prophet's daughter Zaynab to grant him refuge, and she did so.[400]

In this year a fifteen-man raiding party led by Zayd b. Ḥārithah went to al-Ṭaraf in Jumādā II against the Banū Tha'labah.[401] The Bedouins fled, fearing that the Messenger of God had set out against them. Zayd took twenty camels from their herds. He was away four nights.

In this year a raiding party led by Zayd b. Ḥārithah went to Ḥismā in Jumādā II.[402] According to [al-Wāqidī]—Mūsā b. Muḥammad—his father [Muḥammad b. Ibrāhīm], who said: The beginning of this incident was when Diḥyah al-Kalbī came back from the court of Caesar,[403] who had presented Diḥyah with gifts of merchandise and clothing. When Diḥyah reached Ḥismā, men from Judhām[404] intercepted him and robbed him, leaving him
[1556] with nothing. He came to the Messenger of God even before entering his own house [in Medina] and informed him. The Messenger of God then sent Zayd b. Ḥārithah to Ḥismā.

In this year 'Umar b. al-Khaṭṭāb married Jamīlah bt. Thābit b. Abī al-Aqlaḥ. She was the sister of 'Āṣim b. Thābit. Jamīlah bore him 'Āṣim b. 'Umar; then 'Umar divorced her. Yazīd b. Jāriyah

---

400. Zaynab was Muḥammad's daughter by Khadījah, his first wife, and her marriage to Abū al-'Āṣ b. al-Rabī' b. 'Abd al-'Uzzā b. 'Abd Shams, an influential merchant, had taken place before Muḥammad began to receive revelations. Although Abū al-'Āṣ remained a pagan, Zaynab continued to live with him in Mecca even after Muḥammad's emigration to Medina. After Abū al-'Āṣ was captured at the Battle of Badr, it was arranged that he would be released in return for Zaynab's leaving him and coming to Medina. See al-Ṭabarī, I, 1347–51; IH, II, 651–60 (tr. Guillaume, 313–18); Ibn Sa'd, *Ṭabaqāt*, VIII, 20–24; *EI*[1], s.v. Zainab bint Muḥammad.

401. Jumādā II of A.H. 6 began on 18 October 627. Parallel: W, II, 555. According to Ibn Sa'd (*Ṭabaqāt*, II, 63) al-Ṭaraf was a watering place near al-Marāḍ, before al-Nakhīl, thirty-six miles from Medina; according to IH, IV, 616, it was near Nakhl on the road to Iraq.

402. Parallel with fuller text: W, II, 555–60. Ḥismā was on the route to Syria, west of Tabūk. Another account, probably of the same raid, can be found in IH, IV, 612–16 (tr. Guillaume, pp. 662–64). See Watt, *Muhammad at Medina*, 43f.

403. On Diḥyah's mission to the court of the Byzantine emperor Heraclius, who was in Palestine at the time, see pp. 100, 104–6, below.

404. Judhām was a nomadic tribe on the borders of the Byzantine empire. They ranged from places like Madyan, 'Ammān, Ma'ān, and Adhruḥ as far south as Tabūk and Wādī al-Qurā. They were among the Arab allies of the Byzantines. See *EI*[2], s.v. Djudhām.

married her after him, and she bore him ʿAbd al-Raḥmān b. Yazīd, who was ʿĀṣim's half-brother through his mother.

In this year a raiding party led by Zayd b. Ḥārithah went to Wādī al-Qurā[405] in Rajab.[406]

In this year a raiding party led by ʿAbd al-Raḥmān b. ʿAwf went to Dūmat al-Jandal in Shaʿbān.[407] The Messenger of God said to him, "If they obey you, marry the daughter of their king." The people became Muslims, and therefore ʿAbd al-Raḥmān married Tumāḍir bt. al-Aṣbagh. She became the mother of Abū Salamah [b. ʿAbd al-Raḥmān b. ʿAwf]. Her father was their chief and king.[408]

In this year the people suffered a severe drought. The Messenger of God therefore led the people in prayers for rain in the month of Ramaḍān.[409]

In this year a raiding party led by ʿAlī b. Abī Ṭālib went to Fadak in Shaʿbān.[410] According to [al-Wāqidī]—ʿAbdallāh b. Jaʿfar[411]—Yaʿqūb b. ʿUtbah,[412] who said: ʿAlī b. Abī Ṭālib set out for Fadak with a hundred men against a clan of the Banū Saʿd b. Bakr. This was because the Messenger of God had received information that a force of theirs intended to aid the Jews of Khaybar. ʿAlī traveled toward them by night and lay in wait during the day. He captured a spy, who confessed to them that he had been sent to Khaybar to offer the people their aid on condition that they would give them the date harvest of Khaybar.

In this year a raiding party led by Zayd b. Ḥārithah set out [1557]

405. Wādī al-Qurā ("the Valley of the Villages") was a fertile valley stretching north from Medina on the road to Syria; see *EI*[1] s.v. Wādī 'l-Ḳurā.

406. Rajab of A.H. 6 began on 16 November 627.

407. For Dūmat al-Jandal, see note 16, above. Shaʿbān of A.H. 6 began on 16 December 627. Parallel with fuller text: W, II, 560–62; IH, IV, 631–32 (tr. Guillaume, 672).

408. His full name was al-Aṣbagh b. ʿAmr al-Kalbī. See *EI*[2], II, s.v. Dūmat al-Djandal.

409. Ramaḍān of A.H. 6 began on 14 January 628.

410. Parallel with fuller text: W, II, 562–63. Fadak was a village near Khaybar, north of Medina. See *EI*[2], s.v. Fadak.

411. Ed. Cairo, index, identifies him as ʿAbdallāh b. Jaʿfar al-Zuhrī, based on the *isnād* in al-Ṭabarī, I, 1081.

412. Yaʿqūb b. ʿUtbah b. al-Mughīrah al-Thaqafī, a contemporary of al-Zuhrī, was an expert on the biography of the Prophet. He died in 128/745. See Ibn Ḥajar, *Tahdhīb*, XI, 392; *GAS*, I, 283. (Ed. Cairo's reading "b. ʿUqbah" is a misprint.)

against Umm Qirfah in the month of Ramaḍān.[413] During it, Umm Qirfah (Fāṭimah bt. Rabī'ah b. Badr) suffered a cruel death. He tied her legs with rope and then tied her between two camels until they split her in two. She was a very old woman.

Her story is as follows. According to Ibn Ḥumayd—Salamah—Ibn Isḥāq—'Abdallāh b. Abī Bakr, who said: The Messenger of God sent Zayd b. Ḥārithah to Wādī al-Qurā, where he encountered the Banū Fazārah. Some of his companions were killed there, and Zayd was carried away wounded from among the slain. One of those killed was Ward b. 'Amr, one of the Banū Sa'd b. Hudhaym:[414] he was killed by one of the Banū Badr [b. Fazārah]. When Zayd returned, he vowed that no washing [to cleanse him] from impurity should touch his head until he had raided the Fazārah.[415] After he recovered from his wounds, the Messenger of God sent him with an army against the Banū Fazārah. He met them in Wādī al-Qurā and inflicted casualties on them. Qays b. al-Musaḥḥar al-Ya'murī killed Mas'adah b. Ḥakamah b. Mālik b. Badr and took Umm Qirfah prisoner. (Her name was Fāṭimah bt. Rabī'ah b. Badr. She was married to Mālik b. Ḥudhayfah b. Badr. She was very old woman.) He also took one of Umm Qirfah's daughters and 'Abdallāh b. Mas'adah prisoner. Zayd b. Ḥārithah ordered Qays to kill Umm Qirfah, and he killed her cruelly. He
[1558] tied each of her legs with a rope and tied the ropes to two camels, and they split her in two. Then they brought Umm Qirfah's daughter and 'Abdallāh b. Mas'adah to the Messenger of God. Umm Qirfah's daughter belonged to Salamah b. 'Amr b. al-Akwa', who had taken her—she was a member of a distinguished family among her people: the Arabs used to say, "Had you been more powerful than Umm Qirfah, you could have done no more."[416] The Messenger of God asked Salamah for her, and Salamah gave

413. Parallels with fuller text: W, II, 564–65; IH, IV, 617–18 (tr. Guillaume, 664–65).

414. Ibn Hudhaym is Ibn Hishām's correction (accepted by the Leiden editor) of Ibn Isḥāq's original reading "Ibn Hudhayl."

415. This implies that he vowed to abstain from sexual relations, since the word for "major ritual impurity" (*janābah*) refers specifically to the impurity contracted by sexual relations, which requires full washing of the body.

416. The proverb is discussed in Freytag, *Arabum Proverbia*, II, 151 and 710.

her to him. He then gave her to his maternal uncle, Ḥazn b. Abī Wahb, and she bore him 'Abd al-Raḥmān b. Ḥazn.

The other version of the story of this expedition—from Salamah b. al-Akwa'—is that its commander was Abū Bakr b. Abī Quḥāfah.[417] According to al-Ḥasan b. Yaḥyā—Abū 'Āmir—'Ikrimah b. 'Ammār—Iyās b. Salamah—his father [Salamah b. al-Akwa'], who said: The Messenger of God appointed Abū Bakr as our commander, and we raided some of the Banū Fazārah. When we came near the watering place, Abū Bakr ordered us to halt for a rest. After we prayed the dawn prayer, Abū Bakr ordered us to launch the raid against them. We went down to the watering place, and there we killed some people. I saw a group of people, women and children among them, who had almost outstripped us to the mountain; so I sent an arrow between them and the mountain. When they saw the arrow, they stopped, and I led them back to Abū Bakr. Among them was a woman of the Banū Fazārah [1559] wearing a worn-out piece of leather.[418] With her was her daughter, among the fairest of the Arabs. Abū Bakr gave me her daughter as booty. When I returned to Medina, the Messenger of God met me in the market and said, "Salamah—how excellent the father who begot you!—give me the woman." I said, "Messenger of God, I like her, by God, and I have not uncovered her garment." He said nothing to me until the next day, when he met me in the market and said, "Salamah—how excellent a father begot you!—give me the woman." I said: "Messenger of God, I have not uncovered her garment. She is yours, Messenger of God." The Messenger of God sent her to Mecca, and with her he ransomed some Muslim captives who were in the hands of the polytheists. (This version of the story comes from Salamah.)

According to Muḥammad b. 'Umar [al-Wāqidī]: In this year a raiding party led by Kurz b. Jābir al-Fihrī set out against the members of the Banū 'Uraynah who had killed the herdsman of the

417. Parallel in Muslim, *Ṣaḥīḥ*, IV, 197.

418. Her garment is called a *qash'*. *Lisān*, V, 3637, cites this tradition without the words "of leather" and argues that the word means "old, worn-out fur." Another meaning is "a piece of old, worn-out leather," which fits in this version. See ed. Leiden, *Glossarium*, p. CDXXIV.

Messenger of God and driven off camels in Shawwāl of the year 6.[419] The Messenger of God sent Kurz with twenty horsemen.

The Missions to Foreign Rulers

In this year the Messenger of God sent out messengers.[420] He sent out six persons in the month of Dhū al-Ḥijjah,[421] three of them setting out together: Ḥāṭib b. Abī Balta'ah of Lakhm, a confederate of the Banū Asad b. 'Abd al-'Uzzā, to al-Muqawqis;[422] Shujā' b. Wahb of the Banū Asad b. Khuzaymah, a confederate of Ḥarb b. Umayyah and veteran of Badr, to al-Ḥārith b. Abī Shimr al-
[1560] Ghassānī;[423] and Diḥyah b. Khalīfah al-Kalbī to Caesar.[424] He sent out Salīṭ b. 'Amr al-'Āmirī (of 'Āmir b. Lu'ayy) to Hawdhah b. 'Alī al-Ḥanafī,[425] and he sent out 'Abdallāh b. Ḥudhāfah al-Sahmī to Kisrā,[426] and 'Amr b. Umayyah al-Ḍamrī to the Negus.[427]

As for what Ibn Isḥāq has alleged (according to Ibn Ḥumayd—Salamah—Ibn Isḥāq), it is: Between [the truce of] al-Ḥudaybiyah and his death, the Messenger of God dispersed some of his companions to the kings of the Arabs and the foreigners to call them to God.

---

419. Shawwāl of A.H. 6 began on 13 February 628. Parallel with fuller text: W, II, 568–71; cf. IH, IV, 640–41 (tr. Guillaume, 677–78)—apparently the same events.

420. Parallel: IH, IV, 606–8 (tr. Guillaume, 652–59); Ibn Sa'd, *Ṭabaqāt*, I/2, 15–86. For a discussion of the historicity of these reports, see Watt, *Muhammad at Medina*, 345–47.

421. Dhū al-Ḥijjah of A.H. 6 began on 12 April 628.

422. Al-Muqawqis was the Arabic term for the Melkite (i.e., Byzantine) patriarch of Alexandria. Its derivation from the name of Patriarch Cyrus ("of the Caucasus"), who arrived in Egypt in 631, is discussed by K. Öhrnberg in *EI*², s.v. al-Muḳawḳis. If this derivation of the name is correct, this account, which places the mission in 627–28, involves an anachronism.

423. Ed. Cairo vocalizes the name as Shamir. The mission was to the ruler of the Banū Ghassān, an Arab tribal kingdom with its capital at Buṣrā (Bostra) in Syria. The Ghassānids were Monophysite Christians and ruled a client state of the Byzantine Empire. See *EI*² s.v. Ghassān.

424. I.e., the Byzantine emperor.

425. I.e., the chief of the Banū Ḥanīfah b. Lujaym (part of Bakr b. Wā'il), a tribe in al-Yamāmah (central Arabia) centered on the town of al-Hajr. Hawdhah was apparently a Christian and was aligned with the Persians, for whom he conducted caravans. See *EI*², s.v. Ḥanīfa b. Ludjaym.

426. Kisrā (Persian "Khusrau," Greek "Chosroes") was the Arabic designation for the ruler of the Sassanian (Persian) Empire. See *EI*², s.v. Kisrā.

427. Negus (Arabic *al-Najāshī* from Ge'ez *nägāsī*) was the Arabic term for the ruler of Ethiopia. See *EI*², s.v. al-Nadjāshī.

According to Ibn Ḥumayd—Salamah—Ibn Isḥāq—Yazīd b. Abī Ḥabīb al-Miṣrī:[428] [Yazīd b. Ḥabīb al-Miṣrī] found a letter containing a list of those whom the Messenger of God sent to the kings [of the unbelievers][429] and what he said to his companions when he sent them out. [Yazīd] sent the letter to Ibn Shihāb al-Zuhrī via a trustworthy countryman of his, and al-Zuhrī recognized the letter [as genuine]. The letter stated that the Messenger of God went out to his companions one morning and said to them: "I have been sent as a mercy and for all. Therefore, convey [the message] from me, and God shall have mercy on you. Do not become disobedient to me as the disciples became disobedient to Jesus the son of Mary." They asked, "Messenger of God, how were they disobedient?" He replied: "He called [them] to the like of what I have called you to. Those whom he sent close by were pleased and accepted; those whom he sent far off were displeased and refused. Jesus complained of their behavior to God, and when they awoke the next morning, each of them could speak the language of the people to whom he had been sent. Then Jesus said, 'This is an affair that God has determined for you; so go forth!'"

According to Ibn Isḥāq: The Messenger of God gave his companions different destinations. He sent Salīṭ b. 'Amr b. 'Abd Shams b. 'Abd Wudd (a member of the Banū 'Āmir b. Lu'ayy) to Hawdhah [1561] b. 'Alī, the ruler of al-Yamāmah. He sent al-'Alā' b. al-Ḥaḍramī to al-Mundhir b. Sāwā[430] (a member of the Banū 'Abd al-Qays), the ruler of al-Baḥrayn; and 'Amr b. al-'Āṣ[431] to Jayfar b. Julandā al-

---

428. Abū Rajā' Yazīd b. Abī Ḥabīb (Suwayd) al-Azdī al-Miṣrī was born in 53/672 and died in 128/745. He composed a history of the conquest of Egypt and was a teacher of Muḥammad b. Isḥāq. See Ibn Ḥajar, *Tahdhīb*, XI, 318–19; *GAS*, I, 341–42.

429. The reading of the Leiden editor (*al-khā'ibīn*, "those disappointed, who suffer loss," occasionally a synonym for *kāfirīn* "unbelievers") is conjectural. Of the two manuscripts, one gives the word's unpointed ductus, which could also be read as *al-jānibayn*, "of both sides," or, in the larger sense, "of all sides or directions"—cf. Lane, *Lexicon*, II, 466a. The other manuscript reads *al-nās* ("of the people"). Ibn Hishām reads "kings of the Arabs and foreigners."

430. Al-Mundhir b. Sāwā, chief of the tribal division Dārim of Tamīm, was in close relation with the Persian empire and controlled the market of Ḥajar (now al-Ḥasā) and Baḥrayn. See *EI*², s.v. al-Baḥrayn.

431. Cf. the notices below, pp. 142 and 143 [I, 1600 and 1601], dating this event and the coming of 'Amr b. al-'Āṣ to Medina as a Muslim in A.H. 8. Cf. *EI*², s.v. 'Amr b. al-'Āṣ.

Azdī and ʿAbbād b. Julandā al-Azdī, the rulers of ʿUmān. He sent Ḥāṭib b. Abī Baltaʿah to al-Muqawqis, the ruler of Alexandria. Ḥāṭib delivered to him the letter of the Messenger of God, and al-Muqawqis gave the Messenger of God four slave girls, including Māriyah, the mother of Ibrāhīm, the son of the Messenger of God. The Messenger of God sent Diḥyah b. Khalīfah al-Kalbī (and al-Khazrajī)[432] to Caesar, who was Heraclius, the king of the Romans.[433] When Diḥyah brought him the letter of the Messenger of God, he looked into it and then placed it between his thighs and his flanks.

According to Ibn Ḥumayd—Salamah—Muḥammad b. Isḥāq—Ibn Shihāb al-Zuhrī—ʿUbaydallāh b. ʿAbdallāh b. ʿUtbah b. Masʿūd—ʿAbdallāh b. ʿAbbās—Abū Sufyān b. Ḥarb, who said:[434] We were merchant folk. The warfare between us and the Messenger of God had prevented us from journeying, so that our wealth became depleted. After the truce between us and the Messenger of God, we feared that we might not encounter security.[435] I set out for Syria with a group of merchants of Quraysh. Our specific destination was Gaza, and we arrived there at the time of Heraclius' victory over the Persians who were in his land—he expelled them and regained from them his Great Cross, which they had carried off.[436] Having accomplished this against them

432. Arabic: *al-Kalbī thumma al-Khazrajī*: "of the tribe of Kalb and of the subdivision Khazraj" (cf. Wright, *Arabic Grammar*, I, 293). Cf. the genealogy given in Ibn Ḥajar, *Iṣābah*, II, 161–62: Diḥyah b. Khalīfah b. Farwah b. Faḍālah b. Zayd b. Imru' al-Qays b. al-Khazraj b. ʿĀmir b. Bakr b. ʿĀmir al-Akbar b. ʿAwf al-Kalbī. Ed. Cairo emends *al-Khazrajī* to *al-Khazjī* (the *Qāmūs* lists al-Khazj b. ʿĀmir as an ancestor of Diḥyah).

433. The Byzantine emperor Heraclius (Arabic Hiraql) ruled 610–41. See *EI*², s.v. Ḳayṣar, for a list of all the versions of the account of this embassy.

434. Parallel: *Aghānī*, VI, 94–96.

435. Arabic: *lam na'man an lā najida amnan*. Ed. Leiden, *Glossarium*, p. cxx, renders this as *persuasum nobis fuit nos securitatem inventuros*, which would mean, "we were convinced that we should find/encounter security." The compilers of the *Glossarium* apparently took the second negative as pleonastic. I do not think it is. The sense of this passage and of the similarly worded one at p. 103, below, is that Abū Sufyān feared a possible violation of the truce.

436. "In 627 Heraclius invaded the Persian empire, and in December of that year won an important victory near ancient Nineveh, but had to retreat shortly afterwards. In February 628, however, the Persian emperor was assassinated, and the son who succeeded him desired peace. By about March 628 Heraclius could regard himself as victorious, but the negotiations for the evacuation of the Byzantine

and having received word that his cross had been rescued from them (he was staying at Ḥimṣ[437]), he set out from there on foot in thanksgiving to God for restoring it to him, to pray in Jerusalem.[438] Carpets were spread out for him, and fragrant herbs were strewn on them.[439] When he reached Jerusalem and performed his worship—with him were his military commanders and the nobles of the Romans—he arose troubled one morning, turning his gaze to the sky. His military commanders said to him, "By God, you have arisen troubled this morning, O King." "Yes," he replied, "I was shown in a dream last night that the kingdom of the circumcision will be victorious." They said to him: "O King, we know of no nation that practices circumcision but the Jews, and they are under your control and authority. Send to all over whom you have authority in your lands and command them to behead all the Jews under their control, and be rid of this care." By God, even as they were debating this proposal, a messenger from the ruler of Buṣrā[440] arrived leading an Arab—the kings used to send each other reports—and said: "O King, this man of the Arabs, the people of sheep and camels, will report about something marvelous that happened in his country. Ask him about it." When the messenger of the ruler of Buṣrā had brought the man to Heraclius, the latter said to his interpreter, "Ask him what was this event that happened in his country." So he asked him, and the man said: "A man has appeared among us claiming to be a prophet. Some people have followed him and believed him; others have opposed him, and between them there have been bloody battles in many places. That was their state when I left them." After he had given Her- [1562]

empire by the Persians were not completed until June 629. In September 629 Heraclius entered Constantinople as victor, and in March 630 restored the Holy Rood to Jerusalem." (Watt, *Muhammad at Medina*, 113–14). See also Ostrogorsky, *History of the Byzantine State*, 103–4.

437. Ḥimṣ (Emesa) is in Syria, approximately halfway between Damascus and Aleppo. See *EI*², s.v. Ḥimṣ.

438. I have used the conventional name for the city. The Arabic reads Bayt al-Maqdis ("House of the Holy Place") in this sentence and Īliyā' (from Aelia, the name the Romans gave the city after its recapture in A.D. 70) in the next sentence. Perhaps Bayt al-Maqdis here refers specifically to the Temple area or to the Church of the Holy Sepulchre. See *EI*², s.v. Ḳuds.

439. I.e., he vowed to walk to Jerusalem, but tempered the rigor of the vow by having herb-strewn carpets spread along the way.

440. See note 423, above.

aclius his report, the latter said, "Strip him!" They stripped him, and behold he was circumcised. Heraclius said: "This, by God, is what I was shown [in the dream]; not what you say! Give him his garment, and be gone!"

[1563] Then Heraclius summoned his chief of police and said to him, "Turn Syria upside down for me, until you bring me someone from the people of this man"—he meant the Prophet. By God, while we were still at Gaza, his chief of police assaulted us and said, "Are you are from the people of this man in the Ḥijāz?" "Yes," we said. "Off to the king with us!" he said. So we set out with him. When we reached the king, he said, "Are you from the kindred of this man?" "Yes," we said. "Which of you," he asked, "is closest to him in kinship?" "I am," I said. I swear to God, I never saw a man I should consider more astute than that uncircumcised one—Heraclius, that is. "Bring him near," he said. He seated me before him and seated my companions behind me; then he said: "I will question him. If he lies, refute him." By God, had I lied, they would not have refuted me; however, I was a lordly person, too noble to lie. Also I knew that, if I lied, the least of the matter was that they would hold it against me and speak of it concerning me; so I did not lie to him.

Heraclius said, "Tell me about this man who has emerged among you claiming what he claims." I began minimizing his importance to him and disparaging him. "O King," I said, "do not worry about him. His importance is too small to affect you." Paying no attention to this, he said, "Tell me whatever I ask you about him." I said, "Ask whatever you wish." He said, "What is his lineage among you?" I said, "Pure—the best of us in lineage." He asked, "Tell me: has anyone from his family ever said the like of what he says, so that he would be imitating him?" "No," I said. He said, "Did he have authority among you, of which you then stripped him, so that he brought this discourse in order that you might restore to him his authority?" "No," I said. He said, "Tell me about his followers among you, who they are." I said, "The weak, poor, young boys, and women. As for those of his people
[1564] who have years and honor, none of them has followed him." He said, "Tell me about those who follow him: Do they love him and adhere to him, or do they fall out with him and abandon him?" I said, "No man has followed him and then abandoned him." He

said, "Tell me how the war between you and him is going." I said, "Variously—sometimes it is his luck to prevail against us, and sometimes our luck to prevail against him." He said, "Tell me, does he act treacherously?" (I found nothing in what he asked me about him in which I could impugn [Muḥammad's] character except that.) I said, "No; we are in a state of truce with him, and [yet] we fear he may act treacherously."

By God, Heraclius paid no attention to what I had said but repeated the conversation to me. He said: "I asked what his lineage was among you, and you stated that he was pure, one of your best in lineage; but that is how God chooses a prophet when He chooses one—He chooses him only from the best of his people in lineage. I asked you whether anyone from his family had ever said what he says, so that he would be imitating him; and you said no. I asked you whether he had had authority among you, of which you stripped him, so that he brought this discourse, seeking thereby to regain his authority; and you said no. I asked you about his followers, and you stated that they were the weak, poor, juveniles, and women; but such have been the followers of the prophets in every age. I asked you about those who follow him, whether they love him and adhere to him or fall out with him and abandon him, and you stated that no man follows him and then abandons him; but such is the sweetness of faith. It does not enter a heart and then depart from it. I asked you whether he acts treacherously, and you said no. And so, if you have told me the truth about him, he shall surely wrest from me this very ground under my feet.
Would that I were with him that I might wash his feet! Depart to [1565]
your business!" So I left his presence, clapping my hands together and saying, "O worshipers of God, the affair of the son of Abū Kabshah[441] has become serious. Now the kings of the Greeks[442] fear him in their domain in Syria!"

---

441. I.e., Muḥammad. The dictionaries give various explanations of why the Meccan pagans nicknamed Muḥammad "the son of Abū Kabshah." Abū Kabshah is supposed to have been a man from the tribe of Khuzā'ah who abandoned the idolatry of Quraysh and worshiped instead the star Sirius. The pagans called Muḥammad "son of Abū Kabshah" because he, like Abū Kabshah, had departed from their manner of worship. Others say that Abū Kabshah was the nickname of Muḥammad's maternal grandfather, Wahb b. 'Abd Manāf, or that Abū Kabshah was the husband of Muḥammad's wet nurse. See *Lisān*, V, 3812.

442. Arabic: *banū al-aṣfar* "sons of yellow"; various explanations are given in

Heraclius received the following letter from the Messenger of God via Diḥyah b. Khalīfah al-Kalbī:

> In the name of God, the Merciful and Compassionate. From Muḥammad, the Messenger of God, to Heraclius, the ruler of the Romans. Peace to whoever follows right guidance!
>
> To proceed: Submit yourself, and you shall be safe.[443] Submit yourself, and God shall give you your reward twice over.[444] But, if you turn away, the sin of the Husbandmen shall be upon you.[445]

According to Sufyān b. Wakī'—Yaḥyā b. Ādam—'Abdallāh b. Idrīs[446]—Muḥammad b. Isḥāq—al-Zuhrī—'Ubaydallāh b. 'Abdallāh b. 'Utbah—Ibn 'Abbās—Abū Sufyān b. Ḥarb, who said: When the truce between us and the Messenger of God took place in the year of al-Ḥudaybiyah, I set out for Syria as a merchant. (Abū Sufyān then mentioned a report similar to the one transmitted on the authority of Ibn Ḥumayd—Salamah, except that he added at the end of it: He took the letter and put it between his thighs and flanks.)

According to Ibn Ḥumayd—Salamah—Ibn Isḥāq—Ibn Shihāb al-Zuhrī, who said: A Christian bishop whom I met in the time of 'Abd al-Malik b. Marwān[447] told me that he was acquainted with that affair involving the Messenger of God and Heraclius and his

---

addition to the reference to the comparatively light complexion of the Greeks. See Lane, *Lexicon*, IV, 1699.

443. Arabic: *aslim taslam*. The meaning of this lapidary and punning utterance is usually given as "Become a Muslim (or accept Islam), and you shall be safe." However, because the broader meaning of the verb *aslama* is "resign, or submit oneself [to God]," and the remainder of the letter contrasts submission and turning away, I have translated "submit yourself" to preserve the logic of the letter.

444. I.e., in this world and in the next.

445. The Arabic text adds a gloss: "i.e., the bearing of it." The sin of the Husbandmen (*akkārūn*) may allude to the parable of the Wicked Husbandmen in Matthew 22:33–41 (Guillaume's suggestion). The word *akkārūn* is a Syriac or Aramaic loanword; cf. Payne Smith, *Syriac Dictionary*, 17, s.v. *akkārā*, "ploughman, husbandman," which is "often metaphorical of the apostles, of ministers of evil, etc." The precise allusion is unclear to me.

446. 'Abdallāh b. Idrīs, a judge of al-Kūfah, lived from ca. 115/733 to 192/807. See al-Khaṭīb, *Ta'rīkh Baghdād*, III, 266–69; Ibn Ḥajar, *Tahdhīb*, V, 144–46.

447. The Umayyad caliph 'Abd al-Malik b. Marwān ruled from 65/685 to 86/705.

intelligence.[448] According to the bishop: When Heraclius received the letter of the Messenger of God via Diḥyah b. Khalīfah, he took it and put it between his thighs and flanks. Then he wrote to a man in Rome who used to read from the Hebrew what they used to read,[449] mentioning the affair of the man, describing him, and [1566] informing him of what he had received from him. The ruler of Rome wrote back to him: "He is indeed the prophet we have been awaiting. There is no doubt about it. Follow him, and believe him."

Heraclius then gave orders to gather the commanders of the Romans for him in a palatial building,[450] and he ordered its doors to be closed on them. He looked down on them from an upper chamber of his—he was mortally afraid of them—and said: "People of the Romans, I have assembled you for something good. I have received this man's letter calling me to his religion. By God, he is indeed the prophet whom we have been awaiting and whom we find in our books. Come, let us follow him and believe him, that our life in this world and the next may be secure." Without exception they snorted angrily and hastened to the doors of the building to leave it, but they found that they had been locked. Heraclius said, "Bring them back to me"—he was mortally afraid of them—and he said: "People of the Romans, I spoke to you the speech I spoke to see how steadfast you are in your religion because of this affair that has occurred. Now I have seen what gladdens me on your part." They fell down in obeisance to him; he ordered the doors of the building to be opened, and they departed.

According to Ibn Ḥumayd—Salamah—Muḥammad b. Isḥāq—a learned person: Heraclius said to Diḥyah b. Khalīfah when the latter brought him the letter of the Messenger of God: "Alas, by God, I know that your master is a prophet who has been sent and that he is the one whom we have been awaiting and whom we find in our book, but I am mortally afraid of the Romans; but for that, I

448. Translating *wa-'aqlihī*, the voweling of ed. Leiden; ed. Cairo vowels *wa-'aqalahū*, "and he understood it."

449. The exact sense of the Arabic, *kāna yaqra'u min al-'ibrāniyyati mā yaqra-'ūnahū*, is unclear. Perhaps it means not only knowledge of the Hebrew language, but knowledge of specific prophecies of an Arabian prophet contained in the Bible.

450. Arabic: *daskarah*.

would follow him. Go to Ḍaghāṭir[451] the bishop, and tell him of the affair of your master; for he, by God, is greater among the Romans than I, and his word has more authority with them. See
[1567] what he says to you."

So Diḥyah went to Ḍaghāṭir and told him what he had brought to Heraclius from the Messenger of God and to what he was summoning him. Ḍaghāṭir said: "Your master, by God, is a prophet who has been sent. We know him by his description, and we find him by name in our books." Ḍaghāṭir then went inside, laid off the black robes he was wearing, put on white ones, took his staff, and came out before the Romans while they were in the church. "People of the Romans," he said, "a letter has come to us from Aḥmad,[452] summoning us to God. I bear witness that there is no god but God and that Aḥmad is his servant and messenger." As one man they leaped up, attacked him, and beat him to death. When Diḥyah returned to Heraclius and told him the news, Heraclius said to him, "I told you that we are in mortal fear of them—and Ḍaghāṭir, by God, was greater in their estimation, and his word more authoritative than mine!"

According to Ibn Ḥumayd—Salamah—Muḥammad b. Isḥāq—Khālid b. Yasār—a very old Syrian, who said: When Heraclius was about to leave the land of Syria for Constantinople because of the report he had received about the Messenger of God, he assembled the Romans and said: "People of the Romans, I shall present certain matters to you. Consider what I have decided." "What are they?" they asked. He said: "You know, by God, that this man is a prophet who has been sent. We find him in our book. We know him by the description whereby he has been described to us. Let us

---

451. Ed. Cairo: Ṣaghāṭir.

452. Aḥmad must be taken as a proper name synonymous with Muḥammad. Etymologically, both words are adjectival forms from the root *ḥ-m-d* ("praise") and both mean "highly, or most praised." Ḍaghāṭir's behavior implies that he expects his audience to recognize the name Aḥmad. Cf. Qur'ān 61:6, where Jesus says to the Jews that he brings "good tidings of a messenger who comes after me, whose name is Aḥmad"—or one might translate, "whose name is more praiseworthy." Al-Ṭabarī, I, 1141, records a tradition (placed on the lips of one of the pre-Islamic monotheists of Mecca) predicting the coming of a prophet Aḥmad from the descendants of Ishmael. (Cf. Watt, "His Name is Aḥmad," *Muslim World*, xliii (1953): 110–17.) Another speculation about allusions to Muḥammad's name in the Christian scriptures is recorded in IH, I, 232–33 (tr. Guillaume, 103–4). See also *EI²*, s.v. Aḥmad.

follow him, that our life in this world and the next may be secure." They said, "Shall we be under the hands of the Arabs, when we are mankind's greatest kingdom, most numerous nation, and best land?" He said, "Then let me give him tribute[453] each year, so that I can avert his vehemence from me and find rest from his warfare by means of money that I give to him." They said: "Shall [1568] we concede to the Arabs [our own] humiliation and abasement by a tax[454] that they take from us, when we are mankind's most numerous nation, greatest kingdom, and most impregnable land? By God, we will never do it!" He said, "Then let me make peace with him on condition that I give him the land of Syria and that he leave me with the land of al-Sha'm." (The land of Syria was the land of Palestine, Jordan, Damascus, Ḥimṣ, and whatever of the land of Syria was on this side of al-Darb,[455] while they considered whatever was beyond al-Darb to be al-Sha'm.[456]) They said to him: "Shall we give him the land of Syria, when you know that it is the navel of al-Sha'm? By God, we will never do it!" They having refused him, he said, "By God, you shall see that, if you hold back from him, you will be defeated in your own city." Then he mounted a mule of his and departed. When he came in sight of al-Darb, he turned toward the land of al-Sha'm and said, "Peace be with you, land of Syria!"—a farewell salutation—and galloped back to Constantinople.

According to Ibn Isḥāq: The Messenger of God sent Shujā' b. Wahb, a member of the Banū Asad b. Khuzaymah, to al-Mundhir b. al-Ḥārith b. Abī Shimr al-Ghassānī, the ruler of Damascus.

According to Muḥammad b. 'Umar al-Wāqidī: He wrote to him via Shujā':

---

453. Arabic *jizyah*, later the technical term for the poll tax paid by members of protected minorities, here is used in the general sense of tribute. See *EI*², s.v. Djizya.

454. Arabic: *kharj*.

455. Ancient Derbe, a town near the Cilician Gates, the principal pass between Anatolia and Syria. See Lane, *Lexicon*, III, 866.

456. Arabic al-Sha'm, which normally means Syria or Damascus, here seems to be used in the generic sense of "the north." The word used for Syria is Sūriyah. The passage seems to have puzzled the Arabic transmitters, who added the parenthetical note of explanation.

> Peace be with whoever follows right guidance and believes in it. I call you to believe in God alone, Who has no partner, and your kingdom shall remain yours.

Shujā' b. Wahb brought the letter to him, and he read it to them. Al-Mundhir said: "Who can wrest my kingdom from me? It is I who will go against him!" The Prophet said, "His kingdom has perished."[457]

According to Ibn Ḥumayd—Salamah—Ibn Isḥāq, who said: The
[1569] Messenger of God sent 'Amr b. Umayyah al-Ḍamrī to the Negus concerning Ja'far b. Abī Ṭālib[458] and his companions, writing the following letter for him to take:

> In the name of God, the Merciful and Compassionate. From Muḥammad, the Messenger of God, to the Negus al-Aṣḥam, king of the Ethiopians. May you be at peace! I praise to you God, the King, the Most Holy, the Peace, the Keeper of Faith, the Watcher,[459] and I bear witness that Jesus the son of Mary is the Spirit and Word of God, which He cast into the goodly and chaste Virgin Mary, so that she conceived Jesus; whom God created from His Spirit and breathed into him, even as He created Adam by His hand and breathed into him. I call you to God alone, Who has no partner, to continued obedience to Him, and that you follow me and believe in what has come to me; for I am the Messenger of God.
>
> I have sent you my cousin Ja'far and a group of Muslims with him. When he comes to you, show them hospitality, and do not oppress; for I call you and your armies to God. I have communicated sincere advice. Accept my advice! Peace be upon whoever follows right guidance!

The Negus wrote back to the Messenger of God:

> In the name of God, the Merciful and Compassionate. To Muḥammad, the Messenger of God, from the Negus al-

---

457. Another possible translation, "May his kingdom perish!"

458. A cousin of Muḥammad and brother of 'Alī, he had emigrated to Ethiopia with a group of Muslims to avoid persecution in Mecca. See al-Ṭabarī, I, 1180–84; IH, I, 321–41 (tr. Guillaume, 146–55); *EI*², s.v. Dja'far b. Abī Ṭālib.

459. Cf. Qur'ān 59:23.

Aṣḥam b. Abjar. Peace be upon you, O Prophet of God, and God's mercy and blessings—from God, other than Whom there is no god; Who has guided me to Islam.

To proceed: I have received your letter, O Messenger of God, containing what you said about Jesus. By the Lord of heaven and earth, Jesus does not exceed by a whit[460] what you said—he is as you have said. We have acknowledged [as true[461] the message] wherewith you have been sent to us, and we have treated your cousin and his companions hospitably. I bear witness that you are the Messenger of God, speaking truly and confirming truth. I have sworn allegiance to you and sworn allegiance to your cousin. I [1570]
have submitted myself at his behest to God, the Lord of the worlds. I have sent my son Arhā b. al-Aṣḥam b. Abjar to you. I have power only over myself. If you want me to come to you, I will, O Messenger of God; for I bear witness that what you say is true. Peace be upon you, O Messenger of God.

According to Ibn Isḥāq: I was told that the Negus sent his son with sixty Ethiopians in a ship. When they were in the middle of the sea, their ship sank, and they perished.

According to Muḥammad b. 'Umar [al-Wāqidī], who said: The Messenger of God sent a message to the Negus that he should marry to him Umm Ḥabībah, the daughter of Abū Sufyān, and should send her to him along with the Muslims who were with him. To inform Umm Ḥabībah of the marriage proposal, the Negus sent a slave girl of his named Abrahah to her. Umm Ḥabībah was so overjoyed by the news that she gave Abrahah some of her silver jewelry and a ring.[462] The Negus commanded Umm Ḥabībah to appoint someone as her agent to give her in marriage, and she appointed Khālid b. Sa'īd b. al-'Āṣ. He gave her in marriage: the Negus spoke on behalf of the Messenger of God, and Khālid spoke [for Umm Ḥabībah] and gave Umm Ḥabībah in mar-

---

460. Arabic: *thufrūq*, the round part of the covering at the base of a date, where it joins the stalk.

461. For this interpretation of *'arafnā mā bu'ithta bihi ilaynā*, see ed. Leiden, *Glossarium*, p. CCCLVIII, which tranlates *'arafa mā qāla* as *pro recto agnovit*.

462. Arabic: *awḍāḥ, fatakh*. The first term refers either to silver jewelry made from coins or to anklets; the second term refers to unjeweled rings for the fingers or toes.

riage. The Negus called for 400 dinars as her bride gift and handed them to Khālid b. Sa'īd. When the money came to Umm Ḥabībah—it was Abrahah who brought it—Umm Ḥabībah gave her fifty *mithqāls*,[463] saying, "I gave you that[464] when I possessed nothing, but now God, Who is mighty and exalted, has brought
[1571] this!" Abrahah said, "The king has commanded me not to take anything from you and to return to you what I took from you"—and she returned it.[465] "I am the mistress of the king's ointments and garments. I believe Muḥammad the Messenger of God and trust in him. All I ask you is to greet him for me." Umm Ḥabībah said that she would. [Abrahah said,] "The king has ordered his women to send you the aloes wood and ambergris they have." The Messenger of God used to perceive it on her and in her quarters, and he did not disapprove of it.

According to Umm Ḥabībah, who said: We departed in two ships, and he sent sailors with us. We landed at al-Jār[466] and rode animals to Medina. We found that the Messenger of God was at Khaybar, and some went out to him. I stayed in Medina until the Messenger of God returned and I entered his presence. He used to question me about the Negus. I greeted him from Abrahah, and he responded to her greeting.

When Abū Sufyān learned that the Prophet had been married to Umm Ḥabībah, he said, "That stallion's nose is not to be restrained!"[467]

In this year, the Messenger of God sent the following letter to Kisrā[468] via 'Abdallāh b. Ḥudhāfah al-Sahmī:

---

463. Usually *mithqāl* is a synonym for *dīnār*, although a smaller coin may be intended.

464. I.e., the silver jewelry and ring mentioned above.

465. Ed. Cairo: "and I have returned it" or "I hereby return it" (making these words part of the speech of Abrahah).

466. Al-Jār, on the bay of Buraykah south of modern Yanbu', was a Red Sea port a day's journey from Medina; see Yāqūt, *Mu'jam al-buldān*, III, 34–36; *EI*², s.v. al-Djār.

467. For the proverb, see Freytag, *Arabum Proverbia*, II, 869; *Lisān*, V, 3551 (s.v. q-d-') and 3595 (s.v. q-r-'). The meaning is that he is a match not to be rejected as unequal to the bride. The *Lisān* explains: "One would bring a thoroughbred camel mare to someone who had a stallion and ask him to have his stallion service the mare, but if he led out a stallion with no pedigree, one would strike it on the nose to signify that one did not want it."

468. See note 426, above.

> In the name of God, the Merciful and Compassionate. From Muḥammad, the Messenger of God, to Kisrā, the ruler of Persia. Peace be with whoever follows right guidance, believes in God and His Messenger, and testifies that there is no god but God and that I am the Messenger of God to all mankind, to warn whoever is alive.[469] Submit yourself, and you shall be safe. If you refuse, the sin of the Magians[470] shall be upon you.

Kisrā tore up the letter of the Messenger of God. The Messenger of God said, "His kingdom has been torn up."[471]

According to Ibn Ḥumayd—Salamah—Muḥammad b. Isḥāq—Yazīd b. Abī Ḥabīb, who said: He sent ʿAbdallāh b. Ḥudhāfah b. [1572] Qays b. ʿAdī b. Saʿd b. Sahm to Kisrā the son of Hurmuz, the king of Persia, with the following letter:

> In the name of God, the Merciful and Compassionate. From Muḥammad, the Messenger of God, to Kisrā, the ruler of Persia. Peace be upon whoever follows right guidance, believes in God and His Messenger, and testifies that there is no god but God alone, Who has no partner, and that Muḥammad is His servant and His messenger. I summon you with the summons of God; for I am the Messenger of God to all mankind, to warn whoever is alive, and that the word may be fulfilled against the unbelievers.[472] Submit yourself, and you shall be safe. If you refuse, the sin of the Magians shall be upon you.

When Kisrā read it, he tore it up and said, "He writes this to me when he is my servant!"

According to Ibn Ḥumayd—Salamah—Muḥammad b. Isḥāq—ʿAbdallāh b. Abī Bakr—al-Zuhrī—Abū Salamah b. ʿAbd al-Raḥmān b. ʿAwf:[473] ʿAbdallāh b. Ḥudhāfah delivered the letter of

---

469. Cf. Qur'ān 36:69.
470. Arabic: al-Majūs, the ordinary word for Zoroastrians. See *EI*², s.v. Madjūs.
471. Alternative translation: "May his kingdom be torn up!"
472. Cf. Qur'ān 36:69.
473. As mentioned earlier, p. 95, above, Abū Salamah b. ʿAbd al-Raḥmān b. ʿAwf was the son of the Emigrant ʿAbd al-Raḥmān b. ʿAwf by Tumāḍir bt. al-Aṣbagh al-Kalbiyyah. He died ca. 94/712–13. See Ibn Ḥajar, *Tahdhīb*, XII, 115–18.

the Messenger of God to Kisrā. When the latter had read it, he tore it in half. When the Messenger of God heard that he had torn his letter, he said, "His kingdom has been torn up."[474]

[Muḥammad b. Isḥāq] then resumed the report of Yazīd b. Abī Ḥabīb, who said: Kisrā then wrote to Bādhān, who was governor of Yemen, saying, "Send two strong men of yours after this man in the Ḥijāz, and have them bring him to me." So Bādhān sent his steward Bābawayh, who was a scribe and accountant, with the
[1573] writ of Persia, and with him he sent a Persian named Khurrakhusrah.[475] He wrote a letter to be taken by them to the Messenger of God, commanding him to go back with the two men to Kisrā. He said to Bābawayh, "Go to this man's land, speak to him, and bring me a report about him." So the two men set out. Having reached al-Ṭā'if,[476] they found some men of Quraysh at Nakhib[477] in the territory of al-Ṭā'if and asked them about him. They said that he was at Medina. The men of Quraysh were delighted and glad to have met the two men; they said to one another: "Rejoice! Kisrā, the king of kings, has become his enemy. You have become rid of the man."

The two men set out and reached the Messenger of God. Bābawayh addressed him, saying: "The shah of shahs and king of kings, Kisrā, has written to King Bādhān, commanding him to send someone to you to bring you to him. Bādhān has sent me to you so that you may go back with me. If you do, he will write concerning you to the king of kings on your behalf and will keep him from you. If you refuse, you know who he is! He will destroy you, destroy your people, and lay waste to your lands."

Now the two men had come before the Messenger of God having shaved their beards but left their mustaches, so that he disliked looking at them. He turned to them and said, "Alas, who ordered you to do this?" They said, "Our lord"—meaning Kisrā—"ordered us to do it." The Messenger of God said, "But my Lord

474. See note 471, above.

475. So vocalized by ed. Cairo.

476. The city of al-Ṭā'if lies in the mountains about forty miles southeast of Mecca. See *EI*[1] s.v.; Yāqūt, *Mu'jam al-buldān*, s.v.

477. Yāqūt, *Mu'jam al-buldān*, VIII, 272, lists a valley by this name in al-Ṭā'if.

has ordered me to leave my beard and clip my mustache."[478] Then he said to them, "Go away, and come to me tomorrow."

Then a message from heaven came to the Messenger of God that God had incited against Kisrā his son Shīrawayh. He had killed him in such and such a month, on such and such a night of the month, after such and such hours of the night had passed.[479] God [1574] incited his son Shīrawayh against him, and he killed him.

According to al-Wāqidī: Shīrawayh killed his father, Kisrā, the eve of Tuesday, the 10th day of Jumādā I of the year 7, at the sixth hour of the night.[480]

Resumption of the account of Muḥammad b. Isḥāq—Yazīd b. Abī Ḥabīb: He summoned the two men and told them the news. They said: "Do you know what you are saying? We have reproved you for what is less than this. Shall we write this on your authority and report it to the king?"[481] "Yes," he said, "report it to him from me, and tell him that my religion and my dominion shall reach as far as the kingdom of Kisrā has reached and extend to the utmost reach of camel's pad and horse's hoof. Say to him, 'If you submit yourself,[482] I will give you what you possess and make you

---

478. For a list of *ḥadīth*s on the subject see Wensinck, *Concordance*, III, 91, s.v. *shārib.*

479. The text has been corrupted by the copyist. I have translated the reconstruction proposed by the Leiden editor.

480. Al-Wāqidī's date (15 September 628) conflicts with a previously cited tradition (al-Ṭabarī, I, 1009), according to which Muḥammad learned of the death of Kisrā (i.e., Khusrau II Parvīz, ruled 591–628) "on the day of al-Ḥudaybiyah"—i.e., sometime in Dhū al-Qa'dah (began 13 March 628) of A.H. 6. This corresponds closely to the date of the deposition of Khusrau II in February 628 in a coup involving Khusrau's son, Kavādh II Shērōē (Qubādh II Shīrawayh), and generals exasperated by Khusrau's refusal to conclude peace with the Byzantine emperor Heraclius after his military defeats. Shīrawayh's letter, quoted in the next paragraph, alludes to the army's discontent. The exact date of Khusrau's death is unknown. The *History of Heraclius* by the Armenian bishop Sebeos says he was killed immediately. A tradition preserved in al-Ṭabarī, I, 1045–61, has Shīrawayh prepare a detailed indictment of Khusrau's misdeeds, to which Khusrau replied—implying a lapse of time between the deposition and the killing of Khusrau. Shērōē/Shīrawayh ruled only briefly (six or eight months) and was dead by the fall of 628. See Christensen, *L'Iran sous les Sassanides*, 493–97; *Cambridge History of Iran*, III/1, 170; and Ostrogorsky, *History of the Byzantine State*, 103.

481. I.e., to the governor of Yemen, who is given the title of *malik* (king) in the Arabic.

482. Or, "if you become a Muslim."

king over your people, the Abnā'.'"[483] Then he gave Khurrakhusrah a belt containing gold and silver that one of the kings had given him. The two men departed from him. They came to Bādhān and told him the news. He said: "By God, this is not the language of a king. I think the man is a prophet as he says. Let us await the event of what he has said. If it proves true, there is no disputing that he is indeed a prophet who has been sent. If it does not prove true, we shall consider what to do concerning him." Soon Bādhān received Shīrawayh's letter, which said:

> To proceed: I have killed Kisrā. I killed him only out of zeal for Persia, because he allowed himself to kill its nobles and detain them on the frontiers. When you receive this letter of mine, secure for me the obedience of those who are with you. See to the man about whom Kisrā wrote to you, and do not provoke him until you receive my order concerning him.

When Shīrawayh's letter reached Bādhān, he said, "This man is indeed a messenger," and he became a Muslim, and the Abnā'—
[1575] those from Persia who were in Yemen—became Muslims with him. (The people of Ḥimyar[484] used to call Khurrakhusrah Dhū al-Mi'jazah, because of the belt that the Messenger of God gave to him. 'Belt' in the language of Ḥimyar is *mi'jazah.* His sons today take their surname from it: [sons of] Khurrakhusrah Dhū al-Mi'jazah.) Bābawayh said to Bādhān, "Never have I spoken to a man more awesome to me than he was." Bādhān said, "Does he have picked troops?" "No," he replied.

According to al-Wāqidī: In this year he wrote to al-Muqawqis, the ruler of the Copts, summoning him to Islam, but he did not become a Muslim.

According to Abū Ja'far [al-Ṭabarī]: When the Messenger of God

483. The Abnā' ("Sons") were the Persian residents of Yemen, descendants of the Persians said to have come with Sayf b. Dhī Yazan. They were also called Abnā' al-Aḥrār ("Sons of the Free"). See ed. Leiden, *Glossarium,* p. CXLII; *EI*², s.v. al-Abnā'.

484. Ḥimyar was a south Arabian tribe whose kingdom flourished before Islam. Here it is used loosely for Yemen.

returned to Medina from the expedition to al-Ḥudaybiyah, he remained there for the month of Dhū al-Ḥijjah and part of al-Muḥarram (according to the account of Ibn Ḥumayd—Salamah—Ibn Isḥāq). The polytheists were in charge of the pilgrimage in that year.

The Events of the Year 7

(May 11, 628–April 30, 629)

The Expedition to Khaybar[485]

Then the year 7 began. The Messenger of God set out for Khaybar[486] in the remainder of al-Muḥarram, leaving Sibāʿ b. ʿUrfuṭah al-Ghifārī in charge of Medina. He traveled and halted with his army at a valley called al-Rajīʿ,[487] encamping between the people of Khaybar and [the tribe of] Ghaṭafān (according to the account from Ibn Ḥumayd—Salamah—Ibn Isḥāq) to prevent the latter from aiding the people of Khaybar, for they were going to back them against the Messenger of God.

It has been reported to me that, when Ghaṭafān heard that the [1576] Messenger of God had encamped near Khaybar, they assembled because of him and set out to aid the Jews against him. Having traveled a day's journey, they heard a sound behind them in their possessions and families. Thinking that the enemy had come at them from behind, they turned back and stayed with their families and possessions, leaving the way to Khaybar open to the

---

485. Parallels: W, II, 633–705; IH, III, 328–53 (tr. Guillaume, 510–23).

486. Khaybar is an oasis about 95 miles (150 km) north of Medina. Its inhabitants at this time were mostly Jews engaged in agriculture and commerce. L. Veccia Vaglieri's article in *EI*², s.v. Khaybar, discusses the attack and its motives.

487. This is not to be confused with the similarly named al-Rajīʿ near al-Ṭāʾif, where a small party of Muslims was betrayed in A.H. 4 (see al-Ṭabarī, I, 1473); see Yāqūt, *Muʿjam al-buldān*, IV, 228–29.

Messenger of God. The Messenger of God began taking herds and property bit by bit and conquering Khaybar fortress by fortress. The first of their fortresses that he conquered was the fortress of Nā'im. Maḥmūd b. Maslamah was killed at it—a millstone was hurled on him from it and killed him. Next was al-Qamūṣ, the fortress of Ibn Abī al-Ḥuqayq. The Messenger of God took some of its people captive, including Ṣafiyyah bt. Ḥuyayy b. Akhṭab (the wife of Kinānah b. al-Rabī' b. Abī al-Ḥuqayq) and two daughters of her paternal uncle. The Messenger of God chose Ṣafiyyah for himself. Diḥyah al-Kalbī had asked the Messenger of God for Ṣafiyyah; when the latter chose her for himself, he gave Diḥyah her two cousins. The captives of Khaybar were divided among the Muslims. Then the Messenger of God began taking the fortresses and property that were closest to him.

According to Ibn Ḥumayd—Salamah—Muḥammad b. Isḥāq—'Abdallāh b. Abī Bakr—a member of the Aslam: The Banū Sahm, who were a part of Aslam,[488] came to the Messenger of God and said, "Messenger of God, by God we have been struck by drought and possess nothing." But they found that the Messenger of God had nothing to give them. So the Prophet said: "O God, Thou knowest their condition—that they have no strength and that I have nothing to give them. Open to them [for conquest] the greatest of the fortresses of Khaybar, the one most abounding in food [1577]
and fat meat." The next morning God opened the fortress of al-Ṣa'b b. Mu'ādh for them [to conquer]. There was no fortress in Khaybar more abounding in food and fat meat than it.

After the Messenger of God had conquered some of their fortresses and taken some of the property, they reached their fortress[489] of al-Waṭīḥ and al-Sulālim, which was the last of the fortresses of Khaybar to be conquered. The Messenger of God besieged the inhabitants between thirteen and nineteen nights.

According to Ibn Ḥumayd—Salamah—Muḥammad b. Isḥāq—

---

488. See note 297, above.

489. IH, III, 332, reads "their two fortresses"; cf. p. 123, below. The confusion may be due to the division of the oasis into three regions (al-Naṭāh, al-Shiqq, and al-Katībah), each containing several fortresses and separated from the other regions by wadis, lava fields, or swamps. See *EI*², s.v. Khaybar.

'Abdallāh b. Sahl b. 'Abd al-Raḥmān b. Sahl (a member of the Banū Ḥārithah)—Jābir b. 'Abdallāh al-Anṣārī, who said: Marḥab the Jew sallied forth from their fortress[490] fully armed, reciting the following verses in *rajaz* meter:

Khaybar knows well that I am Marḥab,
    whose weapon is sharp, a warrior tested.
Sometimes I thrust with spear; sometimes I strike with sword.
    When lions advance in their rage,
My territory is territory unapproachable.

He said, "Is there anyone who will come out for single combat?" The Messenger of God said, "Who will take him on?" Muḥammad b. Maslamah stood up and said: "I will take him on, Messenger of God. By God, I have had a relative slain and seek revenge, for they killed my brother yesterday." The Messenger of God said: "Arise and go to him! O God, help him against him!" When each drew
[1578] near the other, an ancient *'ushar* bush[491] came between them. Each of them began using it as a refuge from the other; but, whenever one took refuge in it, the other would cut with his sword the part of it separating him from his adversary. Finally each was exposed to the other, and the bush between them came to be like a man standing, with no branches between the two. Then Marḥab attacked Muḥammad and struck him. Muḥammad warded him off with his shield,[492] and Marḥab's sword landed in the shield, which gripped it and held it fast. Muḥammad b. Maslamah struck him and killed him.

After the death of Marḥab, his brother Yāsir came forth reciting the following verses:

Khaybar knows well that I am Yāsir,
    whose weapon is sharp, a warrior-raider.
When lions advance swiftly
    and raiders shrink from my assault,
In my territory death is a dweller.

---

490. For a photograph of the ruins traditionally identified as Qaṣr Marḥab (Marḥab's Castle), see Hamidullah, *Battlefields*, 51.

491. Identified as *Asclepias gigantea* (giant swallowwort) and described in Lane, *Lexicon*, V, 2051.

492. Arabic: *daraqah*; see note 365, above.

According to Ibn Ḥumayd—Salamah—Muḥammad b. Isḥāq—Hishām b. 'Urwah:[493] Al-Zubayr b. al-'Awwām went out against Yāsir. Al-Zubayr's mother, Ṣafiyyah bt. 'Abd al-Muṭṭalib, asked, "Messenger of God, is he going to kill my son?" "No," he replied, "your son will kill him, God willing." Al-Zubayr went out reciting:

Khaybar knows well that I am Zabbār,[494]
chief of folk who do not turn back and flee;
A son of defenders of glory, a son of the best.
Yāsir, let the unbelievers' host not deceive you:
Their host is like a slow-moving mirage.

Then the two met, and al-Zubayr killed him. [1579]

According to Ibn Bashshār—Muḥammad b. Ja'far—'Awf[495]—Maymūn (Abū 'Abdallāh)[496]—'Abdallāh b. Buraydah[497]—Buraydah al-Aslamī,[498] who said: When the Messenger of God encamped at the fortress of the people of Khaybar, he gave the banner to 'Umar b. al-Khaṭṭāb. Some of the people set out with him, and they encountered the people of Khaybar. 'Umar and his companions were put to flight. When they returned to the Messenger of God, 'Umar's companions accused him of cowardice, and he accused them of the same. The Messenger of God said, "Tomorrow I shall give the banner to a man who loves God and His Messenger and whom God and His Messenger love." The next day, Abū Bakr and 'Umar vied for the banner, but the Messenger of God called 'Alī, who was suffering from inflamed eyes, and, having spat on his eyes, gave him the banner. Some of the people set

---

493. Hishām b. 'Urwah b. al-Zubayr, the son of 'Urwah b. al-Zubayr, was born ca. 61/680 in Medina and died in 146/763 in Baghdād. He was a transmitter of traditions and a jurist. See Ibn Ḥajar, *Tahdhīb*, XI, 48–51; *GAS*, I, 88–89.

494. *Zabbār* ("extremely strong") is an intensive adjective from the root of his name. The line ends in a pun, also conditioned by the need for a rhyme.

495. 'Awf b. Abī Jamīlah al-A'rābī lived from 59/678 to 146 or 147/763–65. See Ibn Ḥajar, *Tahdhīb*, VIII, 166–67.

496. Identified by the index to the Cairo ed. as Abū 'Abdallāh Maymūn, the *mawlā* of 'Abd al-Raḥmān b. Samurah.

497. 'Abdallāh b. Buraydah b. al-Ḥuṣayb al-Aslamī, supposedly born in 16/637, died as judge of Marv, perhaps as late as 115/733. See Ibn Ḥajar, *Tahdhīb*, V, 157–58.

498. Buraydah b. al-Ḥuṣayb al-Aslamī died between 60 and 64/679–84. See Ibn Ḥajar, *Tahdhīb*, I, 432–33.

out with him. When 'Alī met the people of Khaybar, there was Marḥab reciting his verses:

Khaybar knows well that I am Marḥab,
 whose weapon is sharp, a warrior tested.
Sometimes I thrust with spear; sometimes I strike with sword,
 when lions advance in burning rage.

He and 'Alī exchanged two blows. Then 'Alī struck him on his head, so that the sword bit firmly into it.[499] The people of the army heard his blow. Even before the last of the people had joined 'Alī, God gave him and them the victory.

According to Abū Kurayb—Yūnus b. Bukayr[500]—al-Musayyab b. Muslim al-Awdī—'Abdallāh b. Buraydah—his father [Buraydah b. al-Ḥuṣayb], who said: The Messenger of God often had migraines and would remain a day or two without coming out. When the Messenger of God encamped at Khaybar, he came down with
[1580] migraine and did not come out to the people. Abū Bakr took the banner of the Messenger of God, set out and fought vigorously, and then came back. Then 'Umar took it, fought with even more vigor than the first fighting, and then came back. When the Messenger of God was informed of this, he said, "By God, tomorrow I shall give it to a man who loves God and His Messenger, whom God and His Messenger love, and who will take it in humble obedience."[501] Because 'Alī was not there, the Quraysh[502] vied for it, each of them hoping to be its bearer. In the morning, 'Alī came on his camel and made it kneel down near the tent of the Messenger of God. He was suffering from inflamed eyes and had ban-

499. Literally, "bit into it with its teeth." Perhaps this alludes to the tradition that 'Alī's sword, D̲h̲ū al-Faqār, had notches or ridges or that it was two-pointed. Cf. *EI*², s.v. Dhu'l-Faḳār. Another possibility, suggested by the parallel below (p. 121), is that the sword "bit into the [rear] teeth of it [viz. his head]."

500. Yūnus b. Bukayr b. Wāṣil al-Shaybānī (died 199/815) transmitted a recension of Ibn Isḥāq's biography of the Prophet, later condensed by Ibn Hishām. See Ibn Ḥajar, *Tahdhīb*, XI, 434; *GAS*, I, 146, 289.

501. Arabic *'anwatan*, which can also mean "by force" or "by compulsion." It is possible that the second "it" refers, not to the banner, but to another feminine word left to be understood from the context, such as "the city" (*al-madīnah*)—cf. p. 121 below, where the word occurs. In that case, the fact that Khaybar fell to the Muslims "by compulsion" had legal implications for the disposition of the booty and the status of the inhabitants.

502. I.e., the Emigrants.

daged them with a strip of Qaṭarī cloth.[503] The Messenger of God asked, "What is wrong?" 'Alī replied, "My eyes are still inflamed." The Messenger of God said, "Come near me." 'Alī came near him, and he spat in his eyes. The pain departed immediately. He gave 'Alī the banner, and 'Alī set out with it. He was wearing a suit of reddish purple whose fringes[504] were of two colors, white and red.

When 'Alī came to the city of Khaybar, Marḥab, the master of the fortress, came out wearing a safflower-dyed Yemeni neck protector (*mighfar*) and a stone in which he had bored holes like a helmet on his head. He was reciting the following verse:

Khaybar knows well that I am Marḥab,
  whose weapon is sharp, a warrior tested.

'Alī recited:

I am he whose mother named him Lion:[505]
  I will mete you out sword blows by the bushel—
A lion in thickets, powerful, mighty.

They exchanged two blows. Then 'Alī struck him a swift blow [1581]
that split the stone, the neck protector, and his head and landed in his rear teeth; and he took the city.

According to Ibn Ḥumayd—Salamah—Muḥammad b. Isḥāq—'Abdallāh b. al-Ḥasan[506]—a member of his family—Abū Rāfi',[507] the *mawlā* of the Messenger of God, who said: We went out with 'Alī b. Abī Ṭālib, when the Messenger of God sent him forth with his banner. When he approached the fortress, its inhabitants came out against him, and he fought them. One of the Jews hit him and knocked his shield out of his hand; so 'Alī picked up a door that was by the fortress and shielded himself with it. It remained in his hand while he fought until God granted him victory; then he threw it aside when he was finished. I can see myself with seven

503. A kind of reddish cloth ornamented with large figures; see ed. Leiden, *Glossarium*, p. CDXXVII.

504. Arabic: *khaml*, perhaps "nap."

505. Arabic *ḥaydar.* The word used for lion in the last line of the poem is *layth*, another of the many synonyms in Arabic for the lion. See *EI*², s.v. Asad.

506. Identified in ed. Cairo, Index, as 'Abdallāh b. al-Ḥasan b. al-Ḥasan b. 'Alī b. Abī Ṭālib.

507. His name was Ruwayfi'. See the biography given in Poonawala, *Last Years*, 143 [I, 1778–79].

other men in a group straining to turn that door over and unable to do it.

According to Ibn Ḥumayd—Salamah—Ibn Isḥāq, who said: After the Messenger of God conquered al-Qamūṣ, the fortress of Ibn Abī al-Ḥuqayq, Ṣafiyyah bt. Ḥuyayy b. Akhṭab was brought to him, and another woman with her. Bilāl, who was the one who brought them, led them past some of the slain Jews. When the woman who was with Ṣafiyyah saw them, she cried out, struck her face, and poured dust on her head. When the Messenger of God saw her, he said, "Take this she-devil away from me!" He commanded that Ṣafiyyah should be kept behind him and that his cloak should be cast over her. Thus the Muslims knew that the Messenger of God had chosen her for himself. The Messenger of God said to Bilāl (according to what I have received) when he saw
[1582] the Jewish woman doing what he saw her do, "Are you devoid of mercy, Bilāl, that you take two women past their slain men?"

When Ṣafiyyah became the bride of Kinānah b. al-Rabīʿ b. Abī Ḥuqayq, she dreamt that a moon had fallen into her lap. She told her vision to her husband, and he said, "That is only because you are wishing for the king of the Ḥijāz, Muḥammad"—and he gave her face a slap that blackened her eye. She was brought to the Messenger of God with the traces of it still there; he asked her what it was, and she told him this story.

According to Ibn Isḥāq: Kinānah b. al-Rabīʿ b. Abī al-Ḥuqayq, who had the treasure of the Banū al-Naḍīr,[508] was brought to the Messenger of God, who questioned him; but he denied knowing where it was. Then the Messenger of God was brought a Jew who said to him, "I have seen Kinānah walk around this ruin every morning." The Messenger of God said to Kinānah: "What do you say? If we find it in your possession, I will kill you."[509] "All right," he answered. The Messenger of God commanded that the ruin should be dug up, and some of the treasure was extracted from it. Then he asked him for the rest of it. Kinānah refused to surrender it; so the Messenger of God gave orders concerning him to al-Zubayr b. al-ʿAwwām, saying, "Torture him until you root out

508. See note 26, above.
509. Ed. Cairo: "shall I kill you?"

what he has." Al-Zubayr kept twirling his firestick in his breast[510] until Kinānah almost expired; then the Messenger of God gave him to Muḥammad b. Maslamah, who beheaded him to avenge his brother Maḥmūd b. Maslamah.

The Messenger of God besieged the people of Khaybar in their two fortresses of al-Waṭīḥ and al-Sulālim. Finally, when they were certain that they would perish, they asked him to banish them and spare their lives, which he did. The Messenger of God had already taken all the property—al-Shiqq, Naṭāh, al-Katībah, and all their [1583] fortresses—except what belonged to those two fortresses. When the people of Fadak[511] heard of what they had done, they sent word to the Messenger of God, asking him to banish them and spare their lives, and they would leave him their property; and he did so. Among the men who mediated between them and the Messenger of God in the matter was Muḥayyiṣah b. Mas'ūd, a member of the Banū Ḥārithah. When the people of Khaybar surrendered on these terms, they asked the Messenger of God to employ them on the properties for a half share. They said, "We know more about them than you and are better cultivators of them." So the Messenger of God made peace with them for a half share, provided that "if we want to make you leave, we may." The people of Fadak made peace with him on similar terms. Khaybar became the booty (*fay'*) of the Muslims; Fadak belonged exclusively to the Messenger of God, because the Muslims had not attacked its people with horses or camels.[512]

When the Messenger of God rested from his labor, Zaynab bt. al-Ḥārith, the wife of Sallām b. Mishkam, served him a roast sheep. She had asked what part of the sheep the Messenger of God liked best and was told that it was the foreleg. So she loaded that part with poison, and she poisoned the rest of the sheep, too. Then she brought it. When she set it before the Messenger of God, he took the foreleg and chewed a bit of it, but he did not swallow it. With him was Bishr b. al-Barā' b. Ma'rūr, who, like the Messenger of

---

510. Possibly (as Guillaume translates the parallel from Ibn Hishām), "he kindled a fire" with his firestick on his chest (not, however, with flint and steel, as Guillaume would have it). The firestick (*zand*) was a stick of wood that could be twirled rapidly in an indentation in a second piece of wood to produce fire.

511. See note 410, above.

512. This echoes the language of Qur'ān 17:64.

God, took some of it; Bishr, however, swallowed it, while the Messenger of God spat it out, saying, "This bone informs me that it has been poisoned." Then he summoned the woman, and she confessed. He asked, "What led you to do this?" She said: "How
[1584] you have afflicted my people is not hidden from you. So I said, 'If he is a prophet, he will be informed; but if he is a king, I shall be rid of him.'" The Prophet forgave her. Bishr b. al-Barā' died of the food he had eaten.

According to Ibn Ḥumayd—Salamah—Muḥammad b. Isḥāq—Marwān b. 'Uthmān b. Abī Sa'īd b. al-Mu'allā,[513] who said: The Messenger of God said during the illness from which he died—the mother of Bishr b. al-Barā' had come in to visit him—"Umm Bishr, at this very moment I feel my aorta being severed[514] because of the food I ate with your son at Khaybar." The Muslims believed that in addition to the honor of prophethood that God had granted him the Messenger of God died a martyr.

According to Ibn Isḥāq: After the Messenger of God had finished with Khaybar, he returned to Wādī al-Qurā and besieged its people for some nights; then he returned to Medina.

The Expedition of the Messenger of God to Wādī al-Qurā

According to Ibn Ḥumayd—Salamah—Ibn Isḥāq—Thawr b. Zayd[515]—Sālim, the *mawlā* of 'Abdallāh b. Muṭī'[516]—Abū Hurayrah, who said: After we returned with the Messenger of God from Khaybar to Wādī al-Qurā, we halted late in the afternoon toward sunset. With the Messenger of God was a slave lad of his whom Rifā'ah b. Zayd al-Judhāmī (and al-Ḍubaybī)[517] had given

513. Marwān b. 'Uthmān b. Sa'īd b. al-Mu'allā al-Anṣārī al-Zurqī Abū 'Uthmān is listed in Ibn Ḥajar, *Tahdhīb*, X, 95, as being from Medina, but without dates.

514. The expression *qaṭa'a abharahū* "it severed his aorta" need not be taken literally; it is used metaphorically for extreme pain. See Lane, *Lexicon*, I, 266.

515. Thawr b. Zayd al-Dīlī was a *mawlā* born in Medina who died in 135/752–53. See Ibn Ḥajar, *Tahdhīb*, II, 31–32.

516. Sālim Abū al-Ghayth, *mawlā* of Ibn Muṭī', is listed without dates in Ibn Ḥajar, *Tahdhīb*, III, 445.

517. I.e., of the al-Ḍubayb subdivision of the tribe of Judhām. One manuscript reads al-Ḍabīnī, which is also possible.

him. Suddenly, as we were setting down the saddle of the Messenger of God, a stray arrow came and hit the slave, killing him. We said, "May he enjoy Paradise!" But the Messenger of God said, "No; by Him who holds Muḥammad's soul in His hand, his cloak is now being burnt on him in the Fire!" He had pilfered it from the booty of the Muslims at the battle of Khaybar. Having heard these words, one of the companions of the Messenger of God came to him and said, "Messenger of God, I took two thongs for my sandals." He replied, "Two similar ones of fire will be cut for you!" [1585]

During this journey, the Messenger of God and his companions overslept the dawn prayer until the sun had already risen.

According to Ibn Ḥumayd—Salamah—Ibn Isḥāq—al-Zuhrī—Sa'īd b. al-Musayyab, who said: After the Messenger of God had left Khaybar and was on the road, he said late at night, "Who will watch for dawn for us, so that we can sleep?" Bilāl said, "I will watch for you, Messenger of God." So the Messenger of God halted, and the people halted, and they went to sleep. Bilāl stood praying. Having prayed for a time, he leaned against his camel and turned himself in the direction of the dawn to watch for it, but his eye overcame him and he fell asleep. It was only the touch of the sun that woke them. The Messenger of God was the first among his companions to wake from sleep, and he asked, "What have you done to us, Bilāl?" "Messenger of God," he replied, "what overcame your soul overcame mine also." "You are right," he said. Then the Messenger of God led [his camel] a short distance and made it kneel down. He performed ablutions, and the people also performed them. Then he commanded Bilāl to give the call to prayer, and he led the people in worship. After he had recited the peace,[518] he turned to the people and said, "If you forget the prayer, pray it when you remember it; for God says, 'Perform the prayer on remembering Me.'"[519]

---

518. I.e., after he had finished praying: the ritual of *ṣalāh* ends with a twofold salutation, "Peace be upon you and God's mercy," usually explained as being recited by the worshiper to the attending angels at his right and left.

519. Qur'ān 20:14. The usual translation is "perform the prayer for/of (Arabic *li*-) My remembrance." However, the context implies reference to the time of prayer, not its purpose. Beside indicating purpose, *li*- can mark the time from which or at which something took place. Cf. Wright, *Grammar*, II, 151.

[1586] According to Ibn Isḥāq: The conquest of Khaybar took place in Ṣafar.[520] Some Muslim women were present with the Messenger of God. The Messenger of God gave them small gifts from the booty, but he did not assign them a share.

The Affair of al-Ḥajjāj b. ʿIlāṭ al-Sulamī

After Khaybar had been conquered, al-Ḥajjāj b. ʿIlāṭ al-Sulamī (and al-Bahzī)[521] said to the Messenger of God: "Messenger of God, I have property in Mecca with my wife Umm Shaybah bt. Abī Ṭalḥah"—she was his wife, and he had a son, Muʿarriḍ b. al-Ḥajjāj, by her—"and property dispersed among the merchants of Mecca. Give me leave to go, Messenger of God." The Messenger of God gave him leave. Then al-Ḥajjāj said, "It will be necessary for me for me to say [something]."[522] "Say [whatever you want],"[523] he said.

According to al-Ḥajjāj, who said: I departed and arrived in Mecca. On the mountain trail at al-Bayḍā'[524] I met some men from Quraysh who were eager to hear news and were asking about what had happened to the Messenger of God. They had heard that he had gone to Khaybar and knew that it was the leading town of the Ḥijāz in fertility, defenses, and men; so they were seeking news. When they saw me, they said: "Al-Ḥajjāj b. ʿIlāṭ!"—they had not learned that I had become a Muslim—"He, by God, must have news! Tell us what has happened to Muḥammad; for we have heard that that cutter [of kinship ties][525] has marched against Khaybar, a town of Jews and the most fertile land in the Ḥijāz."

I said, "I have heard about that, and I have news that will make you happy." They clung to the sides of my camel, saying, "Out with it, Ḥajjāj!" So I said: "They have been handed a defeat like no
[1587] defeat you have ever heard of. His companions have suffered

520. Ṣafar, A.H. 7, began on 10 June 628.

521. I.e., of the Bahz subdivision of the Banū Sulaym.

522. I.e., to lie. Al-Ḥajjāj may be intentionally avoiding the bluntness of the ordinary word for lying.

523. The bracketed words are from the parallel in W, II, 702.

524. According to Yāqūt (*Muʿjam al-buldān*, II, 335), al-Bayḍā' is another name for Tanʿīm, just outside the sacred territory (*ḥaram*) encircling Mecca.

525. Arabic: *al-qāṭiʿ*, "the cutter," which can be a shortened way of saying *qāṭiʿ al-raḥim*, "cutter, i.e., breaker of ties of kinship," or *qāṭiʿ al-ṭarīq*, "cutter of the road, i.e., highwayman." Either meaning would fit the context.

slaughter like no slaughter you have ever heard of. Muḥammad himself has been taken prisoner, but they have said, 'We will not kill him, but will send him to Mecca, so that they can kill him in their midst for those of their men whom he killed.'"

So the men went and proclaimed it in Mecca, saying: "Here is news for you! Muḥammad is on the way. All you have to do is wait for him to be brought to you to be put to death in your midst."

I said, "Help me collect my property in Mecca from my debtors; for I want to go to Khaybar and get something from Muḥammad's defeated army and companions before the merchants beat me to what there is." So they went and collected my property as quickly as I have ever heard of its being done. I went to my wife and said: "My property!"—for I had property of mine left with her. "Perhaps I can reach Khaybar and take advantage of the opportunities to buy before the merchants beat me to it."

When al-'Abbās b. 'Abd al-Muṭṭalib[526] heard the news—it was reported to him on my authority—he came and stood beside me while I was in one of the merchants' tents and said, "Ḥajjāj, what is this news you have brought?" I said, "Can you keep to yourself what I entrust to you?" "Yes," he replied. I said, "Leave me, and I will meet you in private; for I am in the midst of collecting my property, as you see." So he went away from me. When I had collected everything belonging to me in Mecca and was ready to leave, I met al-'Abbās and said, "Keep what I say to yourself for three nights, Abū al-Faḍl,[527] for I fear pursuit; then say whatever you want." "I will," he said. I said: "By God, I left your nephew [1588]
married to their king's daughter, Ṣafiyyah bt. Ḥuyayy b. Akhṭab. He has conquered Khaybar and plundered what it contains. It has become his and his companions'." "What are you saying, Ḥajjāj?" he said. I said: "It is so, by God! Keep my secret. I have become a Muslim and have come only to get my property for fear that it may be taken from me by force. After three days have passed, make what you know public; for the matter, by God, is as you would like it to be."

526. Al-'Abbās was Muḥammad's uncle. According to al-Ṭabarī, I, 1344, he became a Muslim sometime before the Battle of Badr but had been forced to fight on the Meccan side at that battle, professing his Islam openly only after he was captured. See *EI²*, s.v. al-'Abbās b. 'Abd al-Muṭṭalib.

527. Abū al-Faḍl is the *kunyah* of al-'Abbās.

On the third day, al-'Abbās put on a suit of clothes, perfumed himself, took his stick, left his house, went to the Ka'bah, and circumambulated it. When people saw him, they said, "Abū al-Faḍl, this, by God, is composure in the face of a searing misfortune!" "No," he replied, "by Him by whom you swore, Muḥammad has conquered Khaybar and has been made the husband of the daughter of their king. He has taken its wealth and what was in it; they have become his and his companions'." "Who brought you this news?" they asked. He said: "The one who brought you what he brought you. He came among you as a Muslim, took his property, and left to join the Messenger of God and his companions and be with him." They said: "Help, servants of God! The enemy of God has escaped! By God, had we known, we should have had a bone to pick with him." Soon the news of it reached them.

The Division of the Spoils of Khaybar

According to Ibn Ḥumayd—Salamah—Muḥammad b. Isḥāq—'Abdallāh b. Abī Bakr, who said: The property of Khaybar—[the fortresses of] al-Shiqq, Naṭāh, and al-Katībah—was divided as follows. Al-Shiqq and Naṭāh were among the shares of the Muslims. Al-Katībah was the fifth of God, the fifth of the Prophet, the share of kinsmen, orphans, the needy, and the wayfarer, food for the
[1589] wives of the Prophet, and food for the men who had mediated the peace between the Messenger of God and the people of Fadak[528] (they included Muḥayyiṣah b. Mas'ūd, whom the Messenger of God gave from it thirty camel loads of barley and thirty camel loads of dates). Khaybar was divided among the people who had been at al-Ḥudaybiyah, both those who were present at Khaybar

528. It is unlikely that the *ands* in the original connect equal units, implying (as Guillaume translates the parallel in Ibn Hishām) that the spoils of al-Katībah were divided into five equal parts—one-fifth for God, one-fifth for the Prophet, one-fifth for relatives, orphans, the needy, and wayfarers, one-fifth for the Prophet's wives, and one-fifth for the mediators between him and Fadak. Qur'ānic usage normally treats the one-fifth (*khums*) of God and the one-fifth of the Prophet as synonymous (e.g., Qur'ān 8:41: "a fifth is for God and for the Messenger and for the kinsman and orphans and the needy and the wayfarer"; similarly Qur'ān 59:7). The most likely meaning is that al-Katībah as a whole was treated as constituting the fifth of the booty reserved for Muḥammad to divide for special uses ("the fifth of God"). This interpretation is followed by Vaglieri, in *EI*², s.v. Khaybar, summarizes the varying traditions about the division of the spoils of Khaybar.

and those who were absent. Only Jābir b. ʿAbdallāh b. Ḥarām al-Anṣārī was absent, and the Messenger of God allotted him a share like that of those who were present.

After the Messenger of God had finished with Khaybar, God cast fear into the hearts of the people of Fadak when they received news of what God had brought upon the people of Khaybar; so they sent to the Messenger of God to make peace with him for a half share of Fadak. Their messengers came to him in Khaybar (or on the way,[529] or perhaps after he had arrived in Medina), and he accepted their terms. Fadak became the property of the Messenger of God exclusively, because no horses or camels had been spurred against it.[530]

According to Ibn Ḥumayd—Salamah—Muḥammad b. Isḥāq—ʿAbdallāh b. Abī Bakr, who said: The Messenger of God used to send ʿAbdallāh b. Rawāḥah to the people of Khaybar to estimate the quantity of the date harvest [to be divided] between the Muslims and the Jews. He would make his estimate for them; and if they said, "You have wronged us," he would say, "If you wish, it[531] is yours; and if you wish, it is ours." So the Jews used to say, "By this man heaven and earth stand firm!"[532] ʿAbdallāh b. Rawāḥah acted as their assessor for only [one year];[533] then he was killed at Mu'tah. Jabbār b. Ṣakhr b. Khansā' of the Banū Salimah became their assessor after ʿAbdallāh b. Rawāḥah. The Jews continued on these terms, and the Muslims found no fault with their sharecropping until, in the lifetime of the Messenger of God, they [1590] attacked ʿAbdallāh b. Sahl of the Banū Ḥārithah and killed him. The Messenger of God and the Muslims became suspicious of them because of him.

According to Ibn Ḥumayd—Salamah—Ibn Isḥāq, who said: I asked Ibn Shihāb al-Zuhrī how the Messenger of God's grant to

---

529. For "on the way" (*bi-al-ṭarīq*), IH reads "in al-Ṭā'if" (*bi-al-Ṭā'if*).

530. The language is similar to Qur'ān 59:7.

531. Apparently, "this heap." I.e., he divided the harvest into two heaps and gave the Jews the choice of which they wanted.

532. The pronoun *hādhā* ("this") refers, as is usual, to a person (ʿAbdallāh b. Rawāḥah). Guillaume's finding of a direct echo of *Pirqē Ābhōth* 1:19 (he translates as if *hādhā* meant "this foundation") is unlikely, although some echo of the Jewish topos of "things on which heaven and earth rest" is possible.

533. The bracketed words, which are syntactically necessary, are from the parallel in IH, III, 354.

the Jews of Khaybar of their date palms, when he granted them the palm trees with the proviso of a tax on them, had taken place: did he concede them these terms as established [only] until his death, or for some necessity did he grant them to them without such a proviso? Ibn Shihāb informed me that the Messenger of God conquered Khaybar by force after fighting. Khaybar was something that God gave as booty to His Messenger. The Messenger of God took one-fifth of it and divided [the remainder] among the Muslims. Those of the inhabitants who surrendered did so on condition that they should be expelled after having fought. The Messenger of God summoned them and said, "If you wish, we will deliver these properties to you on condition that you shall work them and that their produce shall be divided between us and you; I will allow you to remain as long as God allows you to remain." They accepted, and they worked the properties on those terms. The Messenger of God used to send 'Abdallāh b. Rawāḥah; he would divide the produce and assess it fairly for the inhabitants. After the death of the Prophet, Abū Bakr after the Prophet confirmed the properties in their hands on the same terms of sharecropping on which the Messenger of God had dealt with them. When Abū Bakr died, 'Umar confirmed the sharecropping arrangement in the beginning of his term as commander; then, however, 'Umar was informed that the Messenger of God had said during his final illness, "Two religions cannot coexist in the Arabian peninsula."[534] 'Umar investigated the matter until trustworthy evidence reached him;[535] then he sent to the Jews, saying: "God has given permission for you to be expelled; for I have received
[1591] word that the Messenger of God said that two religions cannot coexist in the Arabian peninsula. Let anyone who has a treaty from the Messenger of God bring it to me, and I will carry it out for him. Let any Jew who has no treaty from the Messenger of God make ready to leave." Thus 'Umar expelled any of them who had no treaty from the Messenger of God.

According to Abū Ja'far [al-Ṭabarī]: Then the Messenger of God returned to Medina.

---

534. Cf. the proverb (al-Maydani, II, 268): *lā yajtami'u faḥlāni fī shawl*, "Two stallions cannot live side by side in a herd."

535. Or, "until a trustworthy transmitter informed him."

Various Notices

According to al-Wāqidī: In this year the Messenger of God returned his daughter Zaynab to Abū al-ʿĀṣ b. al-Rabīʿ. This took place in Muḥarram.[536]

In this year Ḥāṭib b. Abī Baltaʿah came back from al-Muqawqis bringing Māriyah and her sister Sīrīn, his female mule Duldul, his donkey Yaʿfūr, and sets of garments. With the two women al-Muqawqis had sent a eunuch, and the latter stayed with them. Ḥāṭib had invited them to become Muslims before he arrived with them, and Māriyah and her sister did so. The Messenger of God lodged them with Umm Sulaym bt. Milḥān. Māriyah was beautiful. The Prophet sent her sister Sīrīn to Ḥassān b. Thābit, and she bore him ʿAbd al-Raḥmān b. Ḥassān.

In this year the Prophet had the pulpit[537] made on which he used to preach to the people: he had it made with two steps and his seat. Others say that it was made in the year 8, which we[538] think is the reliable report.

In this year the Messenger of God sent ʿUmar b. al-Khaṭṭāb with thirty men against the "rear" of Hawāzin[539] at Turabah.[540] He set out with a guide from the Banū Hilāl. They traveled by night and [1592] hid by day. However, word reached Hawāzin and they fled. ʿUmar returned without having encountered any fighting.

In this year a raiding party led by Abū Bakr b. Quḥāfah went to Najd in Shaʿbān.[541]

According to Salamah b. al-Akwaʿ: We raided with Abū Bakr in that year. According to Abū Jaʿfar [al-Ṭabarī]: An account of this has been given earlier.[542]

---

536. Muḥarram of A.H. 7 began on 11 May 628. Cf. pp. 93–94 and note 400, above. Apparently, Abū al-ʿĀṣ became a Muslim after his release, so that Zaynab could become his wife again.

537. See *EI*², s.v. Minbar, for a discussion by J. Pedersen of the derivation of the term and the various traditions about how the pulpit was introduced.

538. I.e., al-Wāqidī and his authorities.

539. The rear (*ʿajuz* or *ʿujz*) of the north Arabian tribe of Hawāzin consisted of the tribe's smaller divisions: Jusham, Naṣr, and Saʿd b. Bakr; see Watt, *Muhammad at Medina*, 99; *Lisān*, IV, 2819; and *EI*², s.v. Hawāzin. Parallel: W, II, 722.

540. Turabah was south of Mecca; see Yāqūt, *Muʿjam al-buldān*, II, 374.

541. Shaʿbān of A.H. 7 began on 4 December 628.

542. See p. 97, above.

According to al-Wāqidī: In this year a thirty-man raiding party led by Bashīr b. Sa'd[543] went to the Banū Murrah at Fadak in Sha'bān.[544] His companions were killed,[545] and he was carried away wounded with the dead. Then he returned to Medina.

According to Abū Ja'far [al-Ṭabarī]: In this year a raiding party led by Ghālib b. 'Abdallāh went to al-Mayfa'ah in the month of Ramaḍān.[546]

According to Ibn Ḥumayd—Salamah—Muḥammad b. Isḥāq—'Abdallāh b. Abī Bakr, who said:[547] The Messenger of God sent Ghālib b. 'Abdallāh al-Kalbī to the land of the Banū Murrah. During the raid, Usāmah b. Zayd and one of the Anṣār killed Mirdās b. Nahīk, an ally [of the Banū Murrah] from the al-Ḥuraqah [clan of the tribe] of Juhaynah.

According to Usāmah: When we overcame him, he said "I testify that there is no god but God," but we killed him before we left. When we came to the Messenger of God, we told him the story, and he said, "Usāmah, who will [say] to you 'There is no god but God'?"[548]

According to al-Wāqidī:[549] In this year the raiding party led by
[1593] Ghālib b. 'Abdallāh went to the Banū 'Abd b. Tha'labah. Accord-

543. On this Medinese companion of the Prophet (a member of al-Khazraj), see *EI*², s.v. Bashīr b. Sa'd.

544. Parallel: W, II, 723–26.

545. Or "wounded": Arabic *uṣība*, "were hit," is ambiguous. The parallel in al-Wāqidī implies many, but not all, were killed.

546. Ramaḍān of A.H. 7 began on 2 January 629. Al-Mayfa'ah is in Najd. Ibn Sa'd (*Ṭabaqāt*, II, 86) locates it beyond Baṭn Nakhl (which Yāqūt, *Mu'jam al-buldān*, II, 221, places "close" to Medina), toward al-Naqirah (which Yāqūt, VIII, 308, locates where the road from Iraq divides into two branches, one to Medina and one to Mecca; the modern toponym Nuqra in central Saudi Arabia may be the same place), eight post stages from Medina.

547. Parallel: IH, IV, 622–23 (without *isnād*).

548. I think this is the simplest interpretation of *man laka bi-lā ilāha illā Allāh*. Cf. Wright, *Arabic Grammar*, II, 163C; Reckendorf, *Arabische Syntax*, 240. Guillaume (p. 667) translates "who will absolve you from ignoring the confession of faith?"—which I think is too complicated. The idiom normally means "who will bring/get/procure something for someone?" Muḥammad's rebuke to Usāmah would therefore mean that if he kills prisoners who recite the Muslim creed, no one will ever bring him (i.e., say to him) these words and thus accept Islam in his presence.

549. Parallel: W, II, 626–27.

ing to al-Wāqidī—ʿAbdallāh b. Jaʿfar—Ibn Abī ʿAwn[550]—Yaʿqūb b. ʿUtbah, who said: Yasār, the *mawlā* of the Messenger of God, said, "Messenger of God, I know where the Banū ʿAbd b. Thaʿlabah can be taken by surprise." He sent with him Ghālib b. ʿAbdallāh with 130 men. They raided the Banū ʿAbd, drove off camels and sheep, and brought them back to Medina.

In this year a raiding party led by Bashīr b. Saʿd went to Yumn and Jināb in Shawwāl of the year 7.[551] According to [al-Wāqidī]—Yaḥyā b. ʿAbd al-ʿAzīz b. Saʿīd[552]—Saʿd b. ʿUbādah—Bashīr b. Muḥammad b. ʿAbdallāh b. Zayd, who said:[553] What prompted this raiding party was that Ḥusayl b. Nuwayrah al-Ashjaʿī, who had been the guide of the Messenger of God to Khaybar, came before the Prophet. The Prophet asked him, "What news do you bring?" He said, "I left a large gathering of Ghaṭafān at al-Jināb: ʿUyaynah b. Ḥiṣn has summoned them to march against you." So the Prophet summoned Bashīr b. Saʿd, and the guide, Ḥusayl b. Nuwayrah, went with him. They captured camels and sheep. A slave belonging to ʿUyaynah b. Ḥiṣn met them, and they killed him. Then they encountered ʿUyaynah's army, which was put to flight. Al-Ḥārith b. ʿAwf[554] met ʿUyaynah as he was fleeing and said, "The time has come, ʿUyaynah, for you to give up what you[555] plan."

The Lesser Pilgrimage of Fulfillment

According to Ibn Ḥumayd—Salamah—Ibn Isḥāq, who said:[556] When the Messenger of God returned to Medina from Khaybar, he

---

550. ʿAbd al-Wāḥid b. Abī ʿAwn al-Dawsī was born in Medina and died in 144/761–62. See Ibn Ḥajar, *Tahdhīb*, VI, 438.

551. Yumn (Yāqūt, *Muʿjam al-buldān*, VIII, 524) was a watering place of Ghaṭafān between Baṭn Qaww and Ruʾāf, on the road between Taymāʾ and Fayd; al-Jināb was near Khaybar (ibid., III, 130–31).

552. A Yaḥyā b. ʿAbd al-ʿAzīz Abū ʿAbd al-ʿAzīz al-Urdunnī (or al-Yamāmī) of Syrian origin—possibly they are two different men—is listed without dates in Ibn Ḥajar, *Tahdhīb*, XI, 251.

553. Parallel: W, II, 727–31.

554. Al-Ḥārith b. ʿAwf al-Murrī, the leader of the Banū Murrah, seems to have been an ally of ʿUyaynah; cf. the parallel in W, II, 729; also Watt, *Muhammad at Medina*, 94.

555. Variant, "we."

556. Parallel: IH, IV, 370 (tr. Guillaume, 530).

[1594] stayed there the months of Rabīʿ I, Rabīʿ II, Jumādā I, Jumādā II, Rajab, Shaʿbān, Ramaḍān, and Shawwāl,[557] sending out expeditions and raiding parties during the period. Then in Dhū al-Qaʿdah,[558] the month in which the polytheists had turned him back [in the previous year], he set out to perform the "Lesser Pilgrimage of Fulfillment" in place of the lesser pilgrimage from which they had turned him back.[559] The Muslims who had been with him on that lesser pilgrimage of his set out with him. It was the year 7. When the people of Mecca heard of it, they made way for him. The Quraysh spoke among themselves of how Muḥammad and his companions were in difficulty, distress, and want.

According to Ibn Ḥumayd—Salamah—Ibn Isḥāq—al-Ḥasan b. ʿUmārah[560]—al-Ḥakam b. ʿUtaybah[561]—Miqsam[562]—Ibn ʿAbbās, who said: They stood in rows at the House of Assembly (*Dār al-Nadwah*)[563] to look at the Messenger of God and his companions with him. When the Messenger of God entered the mosque, he put his cloak under his right arm and threw the bottom of it over his left shoulder,[564] leaving his right arm uncovered. Then he said, "May God have mercy on a man who today has shown them his

557. I.e., from 9 July 728 (the beginning of Rabīʿ I) to 1 March 729 (the end of Shawwāl).

558. Dhū al-Qaʿdah of A.H. 7 began on 2 March 629.

559. See pp. 67 ff., above. The phrase *ʿumrat al-qaḍāʾ* implies that it was seen as making up for the interrupted pilgrimage of the previous year. See *EI*², s.v. Ḳaḍāʾ. It was sometimes called *ʿumrat al-qaḍiyyah* (the Lesser Pilgrimage of the Pact—so on p. 138, below) to imply that there was no obligatory making up, merely the fulfilling of a bargain struck at al-Ḥudaybiyah the previous year. See Burton, *An Introduction to the Ḥadīth*, 14.

560. Al-Ḥasan b. ʿUmārah died in 153/752. See Ibn Ḥajar, *Tahdhīb*, II, 304–8.

561. Abū Muḥammad al-Ḥakam b. ʿUtaybah al-Kindī lived from around 47–50/667–70 to about 113–15/731–33. See Ibn Ḥajar, *Tahdhīb*, II, 432–34; *GAS*, I, 65–66, 403.

562. Abū al-Qāsim Miqsam b. Bujrah (*mawlā* of ʿAbdallāh b. al-Ḥārith b. Nawfal) died in 101/719. See Ibn Ḥajar, *Tahdhīb*, X, 288–89; *GAS*, I, 65.

563. The House of Assembly (Dār al-Nadwah), to the north of the Kaʿbah, was where the Meccan leaders gathered to deliberate and transact common business. See *EI*², s.v. Dār al-Nadwa.

564. The procedure is expressed by the Arabic phrase *iḍṭabaʿa bi-ridāʾihī*. As Lane (*Lexicon*, V, 1766) notes, it frees the right arm and shoulder for work. One might see it as a symbolic gesture proclaiming the worshiper's readiness to serve the deity.

own strength." He touched the stone at the corner[565] and set out at a quick walk,[566] his companions going at the same pace with him. Then, when the House[567] had hidden him from the people and he had touched the southern corner, he walked until he touched the Black [Stone]; then he went at a quick walk in similar fashion for three circuits. He walked the remainder of the circuits.[568] Ibn 'Abbās used to say: "People used to think that it[569] was not incumbent upon them—that the Messenger of God had done it only because of those people of Quraysh, on account of what had been reported to him about them.[570] However, when he performed his Farewell Pilgrimage,[571] he trotted [those circuits],[572] and it became *sunnah*[573] to do so."

According to Ibn Ḥumayd—Salamah—Ibn Isḥāq—'Abdallāh b. [1595]
Abī Bakr: When the Messenger of God entered Mecca on that lesser pilgrimage, he entered it while 'Abdallāh b. Rawāḥah was holding his camel's nose-ring and reciting:[574]

Make way, ye sons of unbelievers, for him:
I am a witness that he is His Messenger.
Make way: for all good is in His Messenger.
O Lord, I believe in what he says.
I know that God's truth is in accepting it.

---

565. The Black Stone at the corner of the Ka'bah. "He touched (*istalama*) it," may also mean "he kissed it, or wiped it with his hand." The verb implies a ritual gesture, and the dictionaries are uncertain of its derivation; cf. Lane, *Lexicon*, IV, 1413.

566. Arabic: *yuharwil*, going at the pace called *harwalah*, between a walk and a run.

567. I.e., the Ka'bah.

568. I.e., the four circuits remaining of the total of seven. See *EI*[1], s.v. 'Umra.

569. I.e., the quick walk.

570. I.e., to impress Quraysh that he was not exhausted, as they had rumored.

571. In A.H. 10 (February–March 632); cf. al-Ṭabarī, I, 1751 ff.

572. Arabic: *ramala*, usually taken to be synonymous with *harwala* and to refer to the same gait between a walk and a run; see Lane, *Lexicon*, III, 1159.

573. *Sunnah* (from *sanna*, to institute) originally meant "a way of acting or conduct . . . instituted by former people, and . . . pursued by those after them"—Lane, *Lexicon*, IV, 1438. The Islamic community applied the word to the normative actions and sayings of Muḥammad handed down within the community. See also, Bravmann, *The Spiritual Background of Early Islam*, 123–98.

574. Further discussion of the poem, its variants, and attributions of it to other poets may be found in the *Dīwān* of 'Abdallāh b. Rawāḥah, 101–2.

We have killed you in accordance with[575] its interpretation,
As we have killed you in accordance with its revelation,
with striking that removes the head from its resting place
and makes friend forget his friend.

According to Ibn Ḥumayd—Salamah—Muḥammad b. Isḥāq—Abān b. Ṣāliḥ[576] and 'Abdallāh b. Abī Najīḥ—'Aṭā' b. Abī Rabāḥ[577] and Mujāhid—Ibn 'Abbās: The Messenger of God married Maymūnah bt. al-Ḥārith on this journey while he was in a state of ritual purity; al-'Abbās b. 'Abd al-Muṭṭalib married her to him.[578]

According to Ibn Isḥāq: The Messenger of God stayed in Mecca three nights. On the third day, Ḥuwayṭib b. 'Abd al-'Uzzā b. Abī Qays b. 'Abd Wudd b. Naṣr b. Mālik b. Ḥisl came to him with a
[1596] group of Quraysh: Quraysh had deputed Ḥuwayṭib to make the Messenger of God leave Mecca. They said to him, "Your allotted time is up; so depart from us!" The Messenger of God said to them: "How would it harm you if you left me and I celebrated the wedding feast among you? We would prepare food for you, and you would attend it." They said, "We do not need your food; so depart from us!" The Messenger of God departed, leaving behind Abū

575. Arabic: *'ala ta'wīlihī*, can also be rendered "over its interpretation," and the next hemistich "over its revelation." My translation preserves the possibility that the verses could have been addressed to the pagan Meccans on this occasion. IH, IV, 371–72, however, accepts the translation "over." After quoting the verse (omitting the hemistich "I am a witness . . ."), Ibn Hishām pronounces only the first two verses genuine: the last two verses, he argues, must have been pronounced on another occasion because "the polytheists had not accepted the revelation, and one fights over interpretation only with those who have already accepted the revelation."

576. Abān b. Ṣāliḥ b. 'Umayr b. 'Ubayd al-Qurashī, a *mawlā*, was born in 60/679–80 and lived until ca. 110/728–29. See Ibn Ḥajar, *Tahdhīb*, I, 94–95.

577. Abū Muḥammad 'Aṭā' b. Abī Rabāḥ Aslam al-Qurashī was born in 27/647 and died in 114/732. He was a Qur'ān commentator and expert on law. See Ibn Ḥajar, *Tahdhīb*, VII, 199–203; *GAS*, I, 31.

578. Maymūnah, at this time a widow, was the sister of Umm al-Faḍl, the wife of al-'Abbās, Muḥammad's uncle. The authenticity of this tradition, which implies that it is permissible to contract (but not consummate) a marriage while one is in the state of ritual purity (*iḥrām*) necessary for performance of the pilgrimage (*'umrah* or *ḥajj*), was a subject of controversy among early Islamic schools of law. The various opinions are summarized by Schacht, *The Origins of Muhammadan Jurisprudence*, 153. See also *EI²*, s.v. Maymūna bint al-Ḥārith; Burton, *An Introduction to the Ḥadīth*, 78–81.

Rāfi' his *mawlā* to take charge of Maymūnah. Abū Rāfi' brought her to him at Sarif,[579] and the Messenger of God consummated his marriage with her there. The Messenger of God commanded that they should find a substitute for the sacrificial camels—he himself also found a substitute with them. Camels being scarce for them, he permitted them [to sacrifice] cattle. The Messenger of God returned to Medina in Dhū al-Ḥijjah and stayed there the remainder of Dhū al-Ḥijjah (the polytheists were in charge of the pilgrimage that year), Muḥarram, Ṣafar, and both months of Rabī'.[580] In Jumādā I he sent out his expedition to Syria, which came to grief at Mu'tah.

According to al-Wāqidī—Ibn Abī Dhi'b[581]—al-Zuhrī, who said: The Messenger of God commanded them that they should perform the lesser pilgrimage in the following year in fulfillment of [or, to make up for] the lesser pilgrimage of al-Ḥudaybiyah and that they should bring sacrificial animals.

According to [al-Wāqidī]—'Abdallāh b. Nāfi'[582]—his father [Nāfi'][583]—Ibn 'Umar,[584] who said: This lesser pilgrimage was not a fulfillment [or a making up]; rather, it had been stipulated that the Muslims should perform the lesser pilgrimage in the following year in the month in which the polytheists turned them back.

According to al-Wāqidī: The statement of Ibn Abī Dhi'b is preferable to us because they had been prevented [the previous year] and had not reached the Ka'bah.

According to al-Wāqidī—'Ubaydallāh b. 'Abd al-Raḥmān b.

579. Sarif is close to Mecca. Yāqūt (*Mu'jam al-buldān*, V, 70f.) gives the distance as six, seven, nine, or twelve miles.

580. I.e., he remained in Medina roughly from 1 April 629 to 5 September (the end of Rabī' II).

581. Ibn Abī Dhi'b is Muḥammad b. 'Abd al-Raḥmān b. al-Mughīrah, a judge of al-Kūfah, who died in 159/776. See Ibn Ḥajar, *Tahdhīb*, IX, 303–7; *GAS*, I, 204.

582. 'Abdallāh b. Nāfi' al-'Adawī was a *mawlā* born in Medina. He transmitted *ḥadīth* from his father, Nāfi', the *mawlā* of Ibn 'Umar, and died in 154/771. See Ibn Ḥajar, *Tahdhīb*, VI, 53–54.

583. Nāfi', the *mawlā* of 'Abdallāh b. 'Umar, died in 119 or 120/737–38. See Ibn Ḥajar, *Tahdhīb*, X, 412–15.

584. 'Abdallāh b. 'Umar b. al-Khaṭṭāb (a son of the caliph 'Umar) died in 73/692. See Ibn Ḥajar, *Tahdhīb*, V, 228–29; *EI*², s.v. 'Abdallāh b. 'Umar.

Mawhab[585]—Muḥammad b. Ibrāhīm, who said: The Messenger of God drove sixty fatted camels on the Lesser Pilgrimage of the Pact (*'umrat al-qaḍiyyah*).

[1597] According to [al-Wāqidī]—Mu'ādh b. Muḥammad al-Anṣārī[586]—'Āṣim b. 'Umar b. Qatādah, who said: He carried arms, helmets, and spears and led a hundred horses. He appointed Bashīr b. Sa'd to be in charge of the weapons, and Muḥammad b. Maslamah to be in charge of the horses. When Quraysh received word of this, it frightened them. They sent Mikraz b. Ḥafṣ b. al-Akhyaf, who met him at Marr al-Ẓahrān.[587] [The Messenger of God] said to him: "Young or old, I have never been known but for keeping a promise. I do not want to bring in weapons against them, but the weapons will be close to me." Mikraz returned to Quraysh and informed them.

According to al-Wāqidī: In this year the raid of Ibn Abī al-'Awjā' al-Sulamī on the Banū Sulaym took place in Dhū al-Qa'dah.[588] The Messenger of God sent him against them with fifty men after he returned from Mecca, and he set out against them.

According to Abū Ja'far [al-Ṭabarī]: According to what I have received from Ibn Ḥumayd—Salamah—Ibn Isḥāq—'Abdallāh b. Abī Bakr:[589] The Banū Sulaym met him during it, and he and his companions all were killed.

According to Abū Ja'far [al-Ṭabarī]: However, al-Wāqidī alleges that he escaped and returned to Medina, but his companions were killed.[590]

---

585. 'Ubaydallāh b. 'Abd al-Raḥmān b. Mawhab is listed without dates in Ibn Ḥajar, *Tahdhīb*, VII, 29.

586. For Mu'ādh b. Muḥammad al-Anṣārī, see Ibn Ḥajar, *Tahdhīb*, X, 193–94.

587. Marr al-Ẓahrān, according to Yāqūt, *Mu'jam al-buldān*, VIII, 21, is either one stage or five miles from Mecca.

588. Thus the manuscripts, but it is an error for "Dhū al-Ḥijjah," which is given in al-Wāqidī, Ibn Sa'd, Nuwayrī, and others, and which the sequence demands; cf. al-Ṭabarī, I, 1596. [Ed. Leiden note].

589. The tradition does not appear in the surviving recensions of the *Sīrah*.

590. Parallel: W, II, 741.

The Events of the Year 8

(May 1, 629–April 19, 630)

In this year (as alleged by al-Wāqidī—Yaḥyā b. ʿAbdallāh b. Abī Qatādah[591]—ʿAbdallāh b. Abī Bakr) Zaynab, the daughter of the Messenger of God, died.

The Expedition against the Banū al-Mulawwiḥ

In Ṣafar of this year the Messenger of God sent Ghālib b. ʿAbdallāh al-Laythī on a raid to al-Kadīd against the Banū al-Mulawwiḥ.[592] [1598]

According to Abū Jaʿfar [al-Ṭabarī]: The report of this raiding party and of Ghālib b. ʿAbdallāh was transmitted to me by Ibrāhīm

---

591. Yaḥyā b. ʿAbdallāh b. Abī Qatādah, the grandson of the companion Abū Qatādah, seems to be mentioned in Ibn Ḥajar, *Tahdhīb*, V, 360 as having transmitted *ḥadīth* from his father ʿAbdallāh. The name of ʿAbdallāh's second son, Yaḥyā, appears to have dropped out of the text of Ibn Ḥajar by haplography.

592. Ṣafar of A.H. 8 began on 31 May 629. The Banū al-Mulawwiḥ (also vocalized as al-Mulawwaḥ) were a part of the Banū Layth (in turn a part of Bakr b. ʿAbd Manāt) with territory west of Medina. Al-Kadīd is in the Ḥijāz, twenty-four miles from Mecca (Yāqūt, *Muʿjam al-buldān*, VII, 224). Parallels: W, 750–52; IH, IV, 609–12 (tr. Guillaume, 660–62).

b. Sa'īd al-Jawharī[593] and Sa'īd b. Yaḥyā b. Sa'īd.[594] (Ibrāhīm said he had received his report from Yaḥyā b. Sa'īd;[595] Sa'īd b. Yaḥyā said he had received his report from his father [Yaḥyā b. Sa'īd].) We also received this report from Ibn Ḥumayd—Salamah. All [these reports] are from Ibn Isḥāq—Ya'qūb b. 'Utbah b. al-Mughīrah—Muslim b. 'Abdallāh b. Khubayb al-Juhanī[596]—Jundab b. Makīth al-Juhanī,[597] who said: The Messenger of God sent out Ghālib b. 'Abdallāh al-Kalbī (of the Kalb [subdivision] of Layth) against the Banū al-Mulawwiḥ in al-Kadīd and commanded him to raid them. Ghālib set out; I was in his raiding party. We traveled on until, when we were at Qudayd,[598] we encountered al-Ḥārith b. Mālik, known as Ibn al-Barṣā' al-Laythī. We took him, but he said, "I came only to become a Muslim." Ghālib b. 'Abdallāh said, "If you have indeed come as a Muslim, it will not harm you to be bound for a day and night; if you have come for another purpose, we shall [thereby] be safe from you." So he secured him with a rope and left a little black man who was with us in charge of him, saying: "Stay with him until we pass by you. If he gives you trouble, cut off his head."

We continued on until we came to the bottomland of al-Kadīd and halted toward evening, after the midafternoon prayer. My companions sent me out as a scout. I went to a hill that gave me a view of the settlement and lay face down on the ground. It was just before sunset. One of their men came out, looked, and saw me
[1599] lying on the hill. He said to his wife: "By God, I see a shape on this hill that I did not see at the beginning of the day. See whether the dogs may not have dragged away one of your utensils." She looked and said, "By God, I am not missing anything." He said, "Hand me

593. Ibrāhīm b. Sa'īd al-Jawharī was originally from Ṭabaristān and died ca. 250/864. See al-Khaṭīb, *Ta'rīkh Baghdād*, VI, 93–96; Ibn Ḥajar, *Tahdhīb*, I, 123–25.

594. Sa'īd b. Yaḥyā b. Sa'īd al-Umawī died in 249/863. See Ibn Ḥajar, *Tahdhīb*, IV, 97–98.

595. Abū Ayyūb Yaḥyā b. Sa'īd b. Abān b. Sa'īd b. al-'Āṣ al-Umawī al-Kūfī was born ca. 114/732. He later moved to Baghdād, where he died in 194/809. See Ibn Ḥajar, *Tahdhīb*, XI, 213–14; *GAS*, I, 293.

596. Muslim b. 'Abdallāh b. Khubayb al-Juhanī is mentioned without dates in Ibn Ḥajar, *Tahdhīb*, X, 133.

597. Jundab b. Makīth b. Jarād b. Yarbū' al-Juhanī was a companion of the Prophet. See Ibn Ḥajar, *Tahdhīb*, II, 118.

598. Yāqūt (*Mu'jam al-buldān*, VII, 38) locates Qudayd near Mecca. Al-Samhūdī, *Khulāṣat al-wafā'*, 595, calls it "a large village with abundant water on the road to Mecca."

my bow and two of my arrows." She handed them to him, and he shot me with an arrow and hit my side. I pulled it out, put it down, and did not move. Then he shot me with the other and hit the top of my shoulder. I pulled it out, put it down, and did not move. He said: "By God, both my arrows penetrated it. If it were a living thing,[599] it would have moved. Go after my arrows in the morning and get them, so that the dogs do not chew them up for me."

We gave them time until their herds had come back from pasture in the evening. After they had milked the camels, set them to rest by the watering trough, and had stopped moving around, after the first part of the night had passed, we launched the raid on them. We killed some of them, drove away the camels, and set out to return. Meanwhile, the party carrying the people's appeal for aid set out to the tribe to get help.

We traveled quickly. When we passed by al-Ḥārith b. Mālik (Ibn al-Barṣā') and his companion, we took him with us. The party summoned to aid the people came at us. They were too powerful for us. However, when only the bottom of Qudayd Canyon was between us and them, God sent clouds from out of the blue, although we had seen neither rain nor clouds before that, and the result was [a torrent] that no one could risk [crossing]. We saw them looking at us, none of them able to risk it or advance, while we quickly drove off the camels. We took them up to al-Mushallal[600] and then brought them down from it, and we eluded the tribesmen with what we had taken. I shall never forget the [1600]
rajaz verses that one of the Muslims recited as he was driving the camels from behind:

Abū al-Qāsim[601] refuses to let you remain out all night
  in [pasture] whose plants are moist and luxuriant,
  their tops golden like the color of something gilded.

---

599. Reading *zā'ilah*, as suggested by ed. Leiden "Addenda et emendanda," ad loc. The original Leiden reading (echoed by ed. Cairo) was *rabī'ah*, "a scout."

600. Al-Mushallal is a mountain overlooking Qudayd; see Yāqūt, *Mu'jam al-buldān*, VIII, 67. Al-Samhūdī, *Khulāṣat al-wafā'*, 607, calls it a mountain pass (or trail) overlooking Qudayd and refers to the shrine to the goddess Manāt located there. See p. 188, below, for the report of its destruction. Cf. *EI*², VI, 373–74, s.v. Manāt, and T. Fahd, *Le panthéon de l'Arabie centrale*, 123. Fahd locates al-Mushallal seven Arab miles (ca. fifteen kilometers) from Medina, but Yāqūt and al-Samhūdī give no distance.

601. Abū al-Qāsim ("Father of al-Qāsim") was the *kunyah* of Muḥammad, taken from the name of his first male child; see al-Ṭabarī, I, 1128.

According to Ibn Ḥumayd—Salamah—Muḥammad b. Isḥāq—a man from Aslam—a shaykh of Aslam: The battle cry of the companions of the Messenger of God that night was "Kill! Kill!"

According to al-Wāqidī: The raiding party led by Ghālib b. 'Abdallāh consisted of between thirteen and nineteen men.

Other Notices

In this year the Messenger of God sent al-'Alā' b. al-Ḥaḍramī to al-Mundhir b. Sāwā al-'Abdī[602] and wrote to him a letter containing the following:

> In the name of God, the Merciful and Compassionate. From Muḥammad the Prophet, Messenger of God, to al-Mundhir b. Sāwā: Peace be upon you! I praise to you God, save Whom there is no god.
>
> To proceed: I have received your letter and your messengers. Whoever prays our prayer, eats of our sacrifice, and turns to our *qiblah* is a Muslim: permitted to him is what is permitted to Muslims, and incumbent on him is what is incumbent on Muslims. Incumbent on whoever refuses is [the payment of] tax.[603]

The Messenger of God made peace with them on condition that the Zoroastrians should be required [to pay] tax, that their sacrifices should not be eaten, and that one should not marry their women.

In this year the Messenger of God sent 'Amr b. al-'Āṣ to Jayfar
[1601] and 'Abbād, the sons of Julandā, in 'Umān. The two believed in the Prophet and affirmed what he had brought. He exacted the poor rate[604] on their wealth and collected tax (*jizyah*) from the Zoroastrians.

---

602. See note 430, above.

603. Arabic: *jizyah*, "the tax that is taken from the free non-Muslim subjects of a Muslim government, whereby they ratify the compact that ensures them protection" (Lane, *Lexicon*, II, 422). Cf. *EI²*, s.v. Djizya.

604. Arabic: *ṣaddaqa*, he collected *ṣadaqah*, "a gift to the poor for the sake of God." Later usage distinguished *ṣadaqah* from *zakāh*, the obligatory payment by Muslims of a fixed portion or their wealth for the poor, but here *ṣaddaqa* clearly refers to the collection of an obigatory payment; such instances are not uncommon in early usage. See Lane, *Lexicon*, IV, 1668; Watt, *Muhammad at Medina*, 369–72.

In this year a twenty-four-man raiding party led by Shujā' b. Wahb went to the Banū 'Āmir in the month of Rabī' I.[605] He launched a raid on them and took camels and sheep. The shares [of booty] came to fifteen camels for each man.

In this year a raiding party led by 'Amr b. Ka'b[606] al-Ghifārī went to Dhāt Aṭlāḥ. He set out with fifteen men, and when he reached Dhāt Aṭlāḥ he encountered a large force of men whom they summoned to Islam. They refused to respond and killed all of 'Amr's companions. He[607] managed to get away and returned to Medina.

According to al-Wāqidī: Dhāt Aṭlāḥ is in the direction of Syria. Its people belonged to [the tribe of] Quḍā'ah.[608] Their head was a man named Sadūs.

'Amr b. al-'Āṣ and Khālid b. al-Walīd Go to Medina as Muslims

In this year 'Amr b. al-'Āṣ came to the Messenger of God as a Muslim, having accepted Islam at the court of the Negus. With him came 'Uthmān b. Ṭalḥah al-'Abdarī and Khālid b. al-Walīd b. al-Mughīrah. They came to Medina at the beginning of Ṣafar.[609]

According to Abū Ja'far [al-Ṭabarī]: The circumstances of 'Amr b. al-'Āṣ's becoming a Muslim were as follows (according to Ibn Ḥumayd—Salamah—Ibn Isḥāq—Yazīd b. Abī Ḥabīb—Rāshid,

605. Rabī' I of A.H. 8 began on 29 June 629.

606. The name is given thus in the manuscripts of al-Ṭabarī and in the later historian Ibn al-Athīr. The correct reading, Ka'b b. 'Umayr, is preserved in Ibn Sa'd, and in W, II, 752, and IH, IV, 621 (tr. Guillaume, 667). See ed. Leiden, note *ad loc.*

607. Al-Ṭabarī implies that 'Amr was the man who escaped. Al-Wāqidī has: "The companions of the Prophet . . . fought very hard, until they were killed; one of them, who was wounded among the dead, escaped and managed to get away after nightfall"—similarly in Ibn Sa'd.

608. Quḍā'ah was a group of Arab tribes of obscure origin. Of its main divisions, Juhaynah controlled the coastal caravan route between Syria and Mecca, while Balī was located farther to the north, from Wādī Iḍam and Taymā'. Other divisions included 'Udhrah and Kalb. See *EI*[2], s.v. Ḳuḍā'a; Watt, *Muhammad at Medina,* 110–11.

609. Ṣafar of A.H. 8 began on 31 May 629.

the *mawlā* of Ibn Abī Aws[610]—Ḥabīb b. Abī Aws,[611] who said
[1602] that 'Amr b. al-'Āṣ himself had spoken in his hearing, saying]:[612] When we returned with the allies from the [Battle of the] Trench, I gathered some men of Quraysh who thought as I did and would heed my words. I said to them: "You know, by God, that I think Muḥammad's enterprise will prevail in an extraordinary manner. I have formed an idea: What do you think of it?" "What is your idea?" they asked. I said: "I think we should join the Negus and stay at his court. If Muḥammad defeats our people, we shall stay with the Negus; for it will be preferable for us to be under the power of the Negus than under the power of Muḥammad. If our people are victorious, we are people whom they know, and only good will come to us from them." They said, "This is good counsel indeed." So I said, "Gather up things that we can present to him as gifts." The gift he liked most from our land was tanned hides; so we gathered up many tanned hides for him. Then we set out, and we came to him. While we were at his court, by God, 'Amr b. Umayyah al-Ḍamrī came to him, sent to him by the Messenger of God in the matter of Ja'far b. Abī Ṭālib and his companions. 'Amr went before him and then came out of his presence. I said to my companions: "This is 'Amr b. Umayyah al-Ḍamrī. Perhaps I should go before the Negus and ask him for him. Perhaps he will give him to me and I can cut off his head. If I do it, Quraysh will think I have rendered them a service by killing Muḥammad's messenger."

So I went before the Negus and prostrated myself to him as I used to do. "Welcome to my friend!" he said. "Have you brought me something from your country as a gift?" "Yes, King," I said, "I have brought you many tanned skins." I presented them to him; they pleased him, and he desired them. Then I said to him: "O
[1603] King, I have seen a man who left your presence. He is the messenger of a man who is our enemy. Give him to me, so that I may kill him, for he has killed some of our dignitaries and best men." The Negus became angry and, reaching out with his hand, struck

---

610. Rāshid, the *mawlā* of Ḥabīb b. Aws (or b. Abī Aws), was Egyptian. He is listed without dates in Ibn Ḥajar, *Tahdhīb*, III, 225.

611. Ḥabīb b. Abī Aws (or b. Aws) al-Thaqafī participated in the conquest of Egypt. See Ibn Ḥajar, *Tahdhīb*, II, 177.

612. Parallels: W, II, 741–50; IH, III, 276–79 (tr. Guillaume, 484–85).

his nose such a blow with it that I thought he had broken it. Had the earth split open for me, I would have entered into it for fear of him! I said, "By God, O King, had I thought the matter would displease you, I would not have asked it of you." He said, "Will you ask me to hand over to you the messenger of a man to whom comes the Great *Nāmūs*,[613] who used to come to Moses, for you to kill him?" I said, "O King, is he indeed such?" He said: "Alas for you, ʿAmr! Obey me, and follow him! By God, he is right and will be victorious over whoever opposes him, even as Moses was victorious over Pharaoh and his hosts." I said, "Will you accept my oath of allegiance to him for Islam?" "Yes," he said. He extended his hand, and I swore allegiance to him for Islam. Then I went out to my companions, my outlook having changed, but I concealed my acceptance of Islam from my companions.

Then I set out, intending to go to the Messenger of God to accept Islam. I met Khālid b. al-Walīd—it was before the conquest [of Mecca]. He was coming from Mecca. I asked him, "Where to, Abū Sulaymān?" "By God," he replied, "the trail has become straight! The man is indeed a prophet. By God, I am going to become a Muslim. How much longer [can one delay]?" I said, "By God, I [too] have come only to become a Muslim!" So we came to the Messenger of God. Khālid b. al-Walīd went first, became a Muslim, and swore allegiance. Then I approached and said, "Messenger of God, I will pledge allegiance to you on condition that you forgive me my earlier sin; I will not mention what came later."[614] The Messenger of God said, "ʿAmr, swear allegiance; for acceptance of Islam entirely cuts off what went before it, and emigra- [1604]
tion,[615] too, entirely cuts off what went before it." So I swore allegiance to him and departed.

---

613. Arabic *nāmūs*, is derived (through Syriac *nāmūs*) from Greek *nómos*, "law" (i.e., the Pentateuch or Law of Moses); but Arabic uses it in this phrase as a title of the Angel Gabriel, and it is so glossed in al-Ṭabarī, I, 1151. See *EI*², s.v. Nāmūs.

614. This interpretation is grammatically more likely than Guillaume's, "on condition that my past faults are forgiven and no mention is made of what has gone before." In the parallel in W, III, 745, ʿAmr describes himself as having been so awed by the occasion that he forgot to mention all his sins: "As soon as I sat before him I was unable to raise my eyes to him from embarrassment. I swore allegiance to him on condition that my earlier sin should be forgiven me; the later one(s) did not enter my mind."

615. Arabic: *hijrah*.

According to Ibn Ḥumayd—Salamah—Muḥammad b. Isḥāq—someone I do not doubt: 'Uthmān b. Ṭalḥah b. Abī Ṭalḥah was with the two of them and accepted Islam when they did.

Other Events of the Year 8 of the Hijrah

Among the events of this year, the Messenger of God sent 'Amr b. al-'Āṣ in Jumādā II to al-Salāsil in the territory of [the tribe of] Quḍā'ah with 300 men.[616] The circumstances were as follows. According to reports, the mother of al-'Āṣ b. Wā'il[617] was a woman from Quḍā'ah. It has been reported that the Messenger of God wanted to win them over by that, and he therefore sent 'Amr b. al-'Āṣ, along with men of eminence among the Emigrants and Anṣār. 'Amr asked the Messenger of God for reinforcements, and the latter reinforced him with Abū 'Ubaydah b. al-Jarrāḥ in charge of the Emigrants and Anṣār, including Abū Bakr and 'Umar, with 200 men. The total number of men was 500.

The Expedition of Dhāt al-Salāsil

According to Ibn Ḥumayd—Salamah—Muḥammad b. Isḥāq—'Abdallāh b. Abī Bakr, who said: The Messenger of God sent 'Amr b. al-'Āṣ to the territory of Balī and 'Udhrah to seek their assistance [for an expedition] to Syria. The circumstances were as follows. The mother of al-'Āṣ b. Wā'il was a woman from [the tribe of] Balī. The Messenger of God therefore sent 'Amr b. al-'Āṣ to
[1605] them to try to gain their good will. When 'Amr was in the territory of [the tribe of] Judhām at a watering place called al-Salāsil (the expedition therefore came to be called Dhāt al-Salāsil[618])—when he was at the place, he became afraid and sent to the Messenger of God, asking him for reinforcements. The Messenger of God sent to him Abū 'Ubaydah b. al-Jarrāḥ with the first Emigrants, including Abū Bakr and 'Umar. When he sent out Abū 'Ubaydah, he said to him, "Let the two of you not disagree!" Abū 'Ubaydah set out.

---

616. Jumādā II of A.H. 8 began on 26 September 629. Parallels: W, III, 769–74; IH, IV, 623–26 (tr. Guillaume, 668–69).

617. Al-'Āṣ b. Wā'il was the father of 'Amr b. al-'Āṣ.

618. I.e., [the Expedition] Pertaining to al-Salāsil. According to Ibn Sa'd (*Ṭabaqāt*, II, 94) the site was ten-days' journey north of Medina.

When he reached 'Amr b. al-'Āṣ, the latter said to him, "You have come only to reinforce me." Abū 'Ubaydah said to him: "'Amr, the Messenger of God said to me, 'Let the two of you not disagree.' Even if you disobey me, I will obey you." 'Amr said, "Then I am your commander, and you are merely a reinforcement to me." Abū 'Ubaydah replied, "Have your way." So 'Amr b. al-'Āṣ led the men in worship.[619]

The Expedition Known as al-Khabaṭ

According to al-Wāqidī: In this year the expedition known as al-Khabaṭ took place.[620] Its commander was Abū 'Ubaydah b. al-Jarrāḥ. The Messenger of God dispatched him in Rajab[621] of this year with 300 Emigrants and Anṣār toward [the tribe of] Juhaynah. During the expedition they suffered such severe dearth and distress that they divided up the dates by number.

According to Aḥmad b. 'Abd al-Raḥmān[622]—his uncle, 'Abdallāh b. Wahb[623]—'Amr b. al-Ḥārith[624]—'Amr b. Dīnār[625]—Jābir b. 'Abdallāh, who said: We set out with an expedition. We were 300 men, with Abū 'Ubaydah b. al-Jarrāḥ as our commander. Hunger beset us, so that for three months we ate leaves that we beat down from the trees. Then a sea creature came forth, called an am- [1606]
bergris whale, and we continued eating it for half a month. One of the Anṣār slaughtered some camels; then he slaughtered again the next day. Abū 'Ubaydah forbade him, and he stopped. ('Amr b.

---

619. Leading worship was a sign of authority.

620. Parallel: W, II, 774–77; IH, IV, 632–33 (tr. Guillaume, 673). The raid took its name not from a place, but from the shortage of provisions. *Khabaṭ* means "leaves that have been made to fall from a tree by its being beaten with a staff or stick, used as food for camels" (Lane, *Lexicon*, II, 698).

621. Rajab of A.H. 8 began on 25 October 629.

622. Ahmad b. 'Abd al-Raḥmān b. Wahb died in 264/877. See Ibn Ḥajar, *Tahdhīb*, I, 54–55.

623. 'Abdallāh b. Wahb b. Muslim al-Fihrī was born in Egypt in 125/743 and died there in 197/812. He was a pupil of the jurist Mālik b. Anas. See Ibn Ḥajar, *Tahdhīb*, VI, 71–74; *GAS*, I, 466.

624. 'Amr b. al-Ḥārith b. Ya'qūb b. 'Abdallāh al-Anṣārī, a *mawlā* of Qays Abū Umayyah al-Miṣrī, was of Medinese origin. He was born ca. 90/708–9 and died ca. 148/765–66. See Ibn Ḥajar, *Tahdhīb*, VIII, 14–15.

625. 'Amr b. Dīnār al-Makkī Abū Muḥammad al-Athram al-Jumaḥī was born in 46/666–67 and died in 126/743–44. See Ibn Ḥajar, *Tahdhīb*, VIII, 28–30; *GAS*, I, 594 and Index.

Dīnār said that he heard Dhakwān Abū Ṣāliḥ say that the man was Qays b. Sa'd.)

'Amr [b. al-Ḥārith] said that he received a similar report from Bakr b. Sawādah al-Judhāmī[626]—Abū Jamrah[627]—Jābir b. 'Abdallāh, except that [in it] he said: They became exhausted. Qays b. Sa'd was their commander, and he slaughtered nine riding camels for them.

He also said: They had been sent on an expedition to the seacoast, and the sea cast up a creature to them. They stayed near it for three days, eating of it, making jerky, and scooping out its fat. When they returned to the Messenger of God, they told him what Qays b. Sa'd had done, and the Messenger of God said that generosity was the nature of that family. Concerning the whale he said, "If we knew that we could reach it before it began to smell, we should like to have some of it." [The narrator of this version] did not mention the leaves beaten down from the trees or anything except that.

According to Ibn al-Muthannā—al-Ḍaḥḥāk b. Makhlad[628]—Ibn Jurayj[629]—Abū al-Zubayr—Jābir b. 'Abdallāh, who said: The Prophet provisioned us with bags of dates. Abū 'Ubaydah doled them out to us handful by handful, then date by date. We would suck on them and drink water with them until night. Finally, when the contents of the bags were exhausted, we collected leaves beaten down from the trees. We became very hungry. Then the sea cast up a dead whale for us. Abū 'Ubaydah said, "Hungry ones, eat!"—and we ate. Abū 'Ubaydah would set up one of its ribs, and
[1607] a rider on his camel could pass under it. Five men could sit in its eye socket. We ate and oiled ourselves until our bodies became healthy, and we came away fat. When we returned to Medina (so said Jābir), we mentioned this to the Prophet, and he said: "Eat a sustenance that God brought out for you. Do you have any of it

---

626. Bakr b. Sawādah b. Thumāmah al-Judhāmī died in North Africa during the caliphate of Hishām (reigned 105/724 to 125/743). See Ibn Ḥajar, *Tahdhīb*, I, 483–84.

627. Abū Jamrah al-Ḍuba'ī died ca. 128/745. See Ibn Ḥajar, *Tahdhīb*, X, 431–32.

628. Al-Ḍaḥḥāk b. Makhlad, called Abū 'Āṣim al-Nabīl, lived from 122/740 to between 212 and 214/827–29. See Ibn Ḥajar, *Tahdhīb*, IV, 450–53; *EI*², Suppl., I, s.v. Abū 'Āṣim al-Nabīl.

629. Ibn Jurayj, 'Abd al-Malik b. 'Abd al-'Azīz, was born in 80/699 and died in 150 or 151/767–68. See Ibn Ḥajar, *Tahdhīb*, VI, 402–6; *GAS*, I, 91.

with you?" We had some of it with us. He sent one of the people to get it, and he ate some of it.

According to al-Wāqidī: It was called the expedition of *al-Khabaṭ* because they ate leaves beaten down from the trees (*khabaṭ*) until the linings of their mouths were like those of camels that have pastured on thorn trees.

Expeditions Involving Ibn Abī Ḥadrad and Abū Qatādah

In Sha'bān of this year[630] the Messenger of God sent out a party of men under the command of Abū Qatādah.

According to Ibn Ḥumayd—Salamah—Ibn Isḥāq—Yaḥyā b. Sa'īd al-Anṣārī[631]—Muḥammad b. Ibrāhīm—'Abdallāh b. Abī Ḥadrad al-Aslamī, who said:[632] I married a woman from my tribe, promising her a nuptial gift (*ṣadāq*) of 200 dirhams. Then I came to the Messenger of God to seek his assistance with my marriage. He said, "How much did you set as the nuptial gift?" I said, "Two hundred dirhams, Messenger of God." "Praise God!" said he, "if you could take dirhams from a creek bed, you could not have gone higher! By God, I have nothing with which to help you."

I waited a few days. Then a man named Rifā'ah b. Qays or Qays b. Rifā'ah from the Banū Jusham b. Mu'āwiyah arrived with a large group from Jusham.[633] He encamped at al-Ghābah[634] with his tribesmen and companions, intending to gather [the tribe of] Qays to make war on the Messenger of God. He was a man of name and standing in [the tribe of] Jusham. The Messenger of God summoned me and two other Muslims and said, "Go out to this man and either bring him to us or bring us a report and information [1608] about him." He presented us with an emaciated old camel and mounted one of us on it. By God, it was so weak that it could not stand up with him until the men propped it up from behind with

630. Sha'bān of A.H. 8 began on 24 November 629.

631. Yaḥyā b. Sa'īd b. Qays al-Anṣārī Abū Sa'īd, who died in 143/760, was a Medinan judge who later served under al-Manṣūr in al-Hāshimiyyah in Iraq. See Ibn Ḥajar, *Tahdhīb*, XI, 221–24; *GAS*, I, 407.

632. Parallels: W, II, 777–80; IH, IV, 629–31 (tr. Guillaume, 671–72).

633. The Banū Jusham were a division of the large tribe of Hawāzin. See Watt, *Muhammad at Medina*, 99.

634. See note 73, above.

their hands, and then it raised itself, though barely. Then he said, "Make do with her, and take turns riding."

We set out, armed with arrows and swords. We approached the encampment at evening as the sun was setting. I hid myself in one place and commanded my two companions to hide themselves somewhere else near the men's encampment. I told them, "If you hear me shout 'God is greatest!' and attack the encampment, shout 'God is greatest!' and attack with me."

By God, we kept watching for some heedlessness on their part or some way to strike them until night fell over us and the time of the darkness of the night prayer passed. One of their herdsman who had gone out in the area in the morning was late coming back, so that they became worried about him. Their leader, Rifāʿah b. Qays, stood up, took his sword, put [its belt] on his neck, and said: "By God, I am going to follow the tracks of this herdsman of ours. Some evil must have befallen him." Some of his companions said: "By God, do not go. We will take care of it for you." He said, "By God, no one but I shall go." They said, "And we with you!" "By God," he said, "none of you shall follow me!" He set out and passed by me. When he came within range, I shot him with an arrow and put it into his heart. By God, he spoke not a word. I leaped at him and cut off his head. Then I rushed toward the encampment and shouted "God is great!" My two companions rushed and shouted "God is great!" In no time at all, those who were in the encampment were shouting "Save yourself!" and "Quick, quick!" and taking all they could—wives, children, and any property light enough to carry. We drove away a great herd of
[1609] camels and many sheep and goats and brought them to the Messenger of God. I brought him Rifāʿah's head, which I carried with me. The Messenger of God gave me thirteen camels from that herd as aid, and I consummated my marriage.

As for al-Wāqidī, his account is as follows. According to al-Wāqidī—Muḥammad b. Yaḥyā b. Sahl b. Abī Ḥathmah—his father [Yaḥyā b. Sahl b. Abī Ḥathmah[635]]: The Prophet sent Ibn Abī Ḥadrad in this party with Abū Qatādah. The party consisted of

---

635. Yaḥyā would be the son of Sahl b. Abī Ḥathmah, a companion of the Prophet, who died during the early part of Muʿāwiyah's reign (from 41/661 to 60/680). See Ibn Ḥajar, *Tahdhīb*, IV, 248–49.

sixteen men, and they were away fifteen nights. Their shares [of booty] were twelve camels [for each man], each camel being accounted equal to ten sheep or goats. When the people fled in various directions, they took four women, including one young woman who was very beautiful. She fell to Abū Qatādah. Then Maḥmiyah b. al-Jaz' spoke of her to the Messenger of God, and the Messenger of God asked Abū Qatādah about her. Abū Qatādah said, "I purchased her from the spoils." The Messenger of God said, "Give her to me." So he gave her to him, and the Messenger of God gave her to Maḥmiyah b. Jaz' al-Zubaydī.

In this year the Messenger of God sent Abū Qatādah with a company of men to raid the lowland of Iḍam.[636]

According to Ibn Ḥumayd—Salamah—Ibn Isḥāq—Yazīd b. 'Abdallāh b. Qusayṭ—Abū al-Qa'qā' b. 'Abdallāh b. Abī Ḥadrad al-Aslamī (some authorities give the chain of transmission as Ibn al-Qa'qā'—his father—'Abdallāh b. Abī Ḥadrad),[637] who said: The Messenger of God sent us to Iḍam. I set out with a group of Muslims, including Abū Qatādah al-Ḥārith b. Rib'ī and Muḥallim b. Jaththāmah b. Qays al-Laythī. We set out and came to the lowland of Iḍam. This was before the conquest [of Mecca]. 'Āmir b. al- [1610]
Aḍbaṭ al-Ashja'ī passed us by on a young camel of his. He had a bit of food with him and a skin of sour milk. As he passed us, he greeted us with the greeting of Islam;[638] so we held back from him. But Muḥallim b. Jaththāmah attacked him because of some quarrel between them, killed him, and took his camel and food. When we returned to the Messenger of God and told him the story, the [following passage of] Qur'ān was revealed concerning us: "O believers, when you are journeying in the path of God, be discriminating"—and the rest of the verse.[639]

636. Parallels: W, II, 796–97; IH, IV, 397 and 626–29 (tr. Guillaume, 544, 669–71). Yāqūt, *Mu'jam al-buldān*, I, 281, lists a number of places with the name, both in the Ḥijāz and Central Arabia. Iḍam is probably to be located at the present Wādī al-Ḥamḍ, which enters the Red Sea 50 kilometers south of al-Wajh in northwestern Arabia. See *EI*², s.v. Ḥamḍ, Wādī al-.

637. In the present recension of Ibn Hishām's *Sīrah*, the isnād reads: Yazīd b. 'Abdallāh b. Qusayṭ—al-Qa'qā' b. 'Abdallāh b. Abī Ḥadrad—his father 'Abdallāh.

638. I.e., *al-salāmu 'alaykum*, "Peace be upon you!"

639. Qur'ān 4:94, which continues: "and do not say to him who offers you a greeting, 'You are not a believer,' seeking the chance goods of the present life."

According to al-Wāqidī: The Messenger of God sent out this party only when he set out for the conquest of Mecca in the month of Ramaḍān.[640] They numbered eight men.

The Expedition to Mu'tah[641]

According to Ibn Ḥumayd—Salamah—Ibn Isḥāq, who said: After the Messenger of God returned to Medina from Khaybar, he stayed in Medina for the two months of Rabī'; then, in Jumādā I,[642] he sent out his expedition to Syria whose members met with disaster at Mu'tah.

According to Ibn Ḥumayd—Salamah—Muḥammad b. Isḥāq—Muḥammad b. Ja'far b. al-Zubayr—'Urwah b. al-Zubayr, who said: The Messenger of God sent his expedition to Mu'tah in Jumādā I of the year 8. He put Zayd b. Ḥārithah in command of the men and said, "If Zayd b. Ḥārithah is killed, Ja'far b. Abī Ṭālib shall be in command of the men; if Ja'far is killed, 'Abdallāh b. Rawāḥah shall be in command." The men equipped themselves and made ready to set out. They numbered 3,000. When the time for their departure came, the people said goodbye to the commanders of the Messenger of God, wishing them safety and bidding them farewell. When 'Abdallāh b. Rawāḥah said goodbye with the other
[1611] commanders of the Messenger of God who were doing so, he wept. They said to him, "What is making you weep, Ibn Rawāḥah?" He said, "By God, I have no love of this world or excessive love for you, but I heard the Messenger of God recite a verse from the Book of God that mentioned the Fire [of Hell]—'Not one of you there is, but he shall go down to it; that for thy Lord is a thing decreed, determined'[643]—and I do not know how I can come out after going down." The Muslims said, "May God accompany you, defend

---

640. Ramaḍān of A.H. 8 began on 23 December 629.

641. Parallels: W, II, 755–69; IH, IV, 373–89 (tr. Guillaume, 531–40). Mu'tah is a village in the area known as al-Balqā' (Yāqūt, *Mu'jam al-buldān*, VIII, 190). The modern town of Mu'tah, Jordan, about 10 km south of Karak and 20 km east of the southern end of the Dead Sea, is on the site. See *EI*², s.v. Mu'ta, for a bibliography of the Arabic and Byzantine sources.

642. I.e., he remained in Medina from about 29 June to 26 August, dispatching the expedition to Mu'tah in the month that began on 27 August 629.

643. Qur'ān 19:71.

you, and bring you back to us in good health." Then 'Abdallāh b. Rawāḥah recited:[644]

But I ask the Merciful One for pardon,
    and for a sword blow that makes a wide wound that shoots out foaming [blood];
Or a deadly thrust by a thirsty one,
    by a lance that pierces right through the guts and the liver;
So that people shall say, when they pass my grave:
    "God guided you aright, O warrior who followed the right way."

Then the men made ready to depart. 'Abdallāh b. Rawāḥah went to the Messenger of God and said goodbye to him. The men set out, and the Messenger of God went out to see them off; having bidden them farewell, he returned from them. 'Abdallāh b. Rawāḥah recited:[645]

May [He who is] Peace supply the place [of the departing ones]
    to a man to whom I bade farewell
    among the palm trees—the best escort and friend!

They journeyed on and encamped at Mu'ān[646] in the land of Syria. The men learned that Heraclius had encamped with 100,000 Byzantines at Ma'āb[647] in the territory of al-Balqā'. Joined to him were Arab auxiliaries from [the tribes of] Lakhm, Judhām, Balqayn, Bahrā', and Balī, numbering 100,000 and commanded by a man from [the tribe of] Balī and of the subdivision Irāshah, named Mālik b. Rāfilah.[648] When the Muslims received word of

---

644. Other sources, variants, and commentary on the poem may be found in the *Dīwān* of 'Abdallāh b. Rawāḥah, 88.

645. For variants and commentary see *Dīwān* of 'Abdallāh b. Rawāḥah, 100. The line is a prayer that God (here paradoxically addressed by his name al-Salām, Peace) may supply the place of the departing men. The opening formula is a variant on a common formula of consolation for the loss of a relative—*khalafa Allāhu 'alayka* ("may God supply the place [of the one you have lost]"). See Lane, *Lexicon*, II, 792.

646. The name is also given as Ma'ān, which is the form used for the city in modern Jordan that perpetuates the name.

647. This is the ancient town of Rabbath Moab, now al-Rabbah, a dozen kilometers north of Karak in Jordan. See Le Strange, *Palestine under the Moslems*, 494–95, 509–10; Yāqūt, *Mu'jam al-buldān*, VII, 249–50; *EI*², VII, s.v. Mu'ta.

648. Ibn Hishām: Zāfilah.

[1612] this, they stayed at Mu'ān two nights, considering what to do. They said: "We will write to the Messenger of God and inform him of the number of our enemy. Either he will reinforce us with men or he will give us his command that we should return to him." 'Abdallāh b. Rawāḥah encouraged the men, saying: "Men, by God, what you loathe is the very thing you came out to seek—martyrdom. We do not fight the enemy by number, strength, or multitude; we fight them only by this religion with which God has honored us. Go forward, for it is one of two good things: victory or martyrdom." The men said, "By God, Ibn Rawāḥah has spoken the truth." So the men went forward. Concerning how they held back, 'Abdallāh b. Rawāḥah recited the following verses:[649]

We urged our horses on from the fortresses of Qurḥ,[650]
their packs crammed with grass.
Because of the flintstone we shod them with hide
as slippery as if its surface were leather.[651]
They stayed two nights at Mu'ān,
and energy replaced their fatigue.
Then we went forth with steeds given free rein,[652]
the simoom breathing in their nostrils.
No, by my father! Ma'āb—we will come to it
though Arabs and Romans be in it.
We set their reins in order, and they came
grim-faced, the dust being a second color for them,[653]

649. The poem, with significant variants, occurs in IH, IV, 375–76 (tr. Guillaume, 533) and in later texts. See *Dīwān* of 'Abdallāh b. Rawāḥah, 102–4.

650. Qurḥ was a market town in Wādī al-Qurā, the valley stretching north of Medina toward Syria. The verse is quoted in Yāqūt's article on Qurḥ (*Mu'jam al-buldān*, VII, 48–49). Ibn Hishām's text reads: "We urged on our horses from Aja' and Far'"—two mountains in the territory of the tribe of Ṭayyi'.

651. The line was obscure to the commentators. On journeys over stony ground the Arabs normally "shod" their camels and horses with protective "boots" of leather.

652. Arabic *musawwam* has a variety of meanings: pastured, sent forth, or marked (with brands or distinguishing colors).

653. The commentator suggests that the color of dust mixed with the color of their coats, forming a pattern that looked like *barīm*, a two-colored rope used by women as an ornament. Perhaps the meaning is less specific and refers to patches of dust covering the coats of the horses and making them appear dappled. See Lane, *Lexicon*, I, 195.

Bearing a clamorous [army]: as if the helmets in it, [1613]
when their tops became apparent, were the stars.
A life of ease and contentment
our spears have divorced, to marry or remain unmarried.

Then the people proceeded on their way.

According to Ibn Ḥumayd—Salamah—Ibn Isḥāq—ʿAbdallāh b. Abī Bakr—Zayd b. Arqam, who said: I was an orphan under the care and protection of ʿAbdallāh b. Rawāḥah. He set out on that journey of his, mounting me behind him on the back of his camel saddle. By God, as he traveled by night, I heard him recite these verses of his:[654]

When you have delivered me and carried my saddle
a four-day's journey after al-Ḥisā',[655]
May yours be an easy life, and may blame pass away from you—
and may I not return to my family behind me.
May the Muslims come and leave me
in the land of Syria, where I desire to remain.
May you be led back by men who, having close relationship
to the Merciful One, are cut off from kindred.
There I shall care neither for the spathes of rain-watered palms
nor for palm trees whose roots are irrigated.

When I heard him recite the verses, I wept. He tapped me with the whip and said: "What's wrong, little fellow? God is going to reward me with martyrdom, and you are going back between the two horns of the camel saddle!" Then ʿAbdallāh said in one of his poems in *rajaz* meter:[656]

O Zayd, Zayd of the swift, lean camels,[657] [1614]
the night has become protracted; so dismount—may you be guided!

---

654. For other sources of the poem, variants, and commentary, see *Dīwān* of ʿAbdallāh b. Rawāḥah, 79–80. The verses are addressed to his riding camel.

655. *Al-Ḥisā'*, meaning "a flow of water that disappears under the sand but can be reached by digging," is modern Wādī al-Ḥasā at the southern end of the Dead Sea; cf. Yāqūt, *Muʿjam al-buldān*, III, 274–75, quoting this verse.

656. Text and discussion in *Dīwān* of ʿAbdallāh b. Rawāḥah, 99–100.

657. The editor of the *Dīwān* explains this as a compliment—i.e., Zayd who knows how to take care of such camels.

The men journeyed on. When they were within the boundaries of al-Balqā',[658] they were met by Heraclius' armies of Romans and Arabs at a village of al-Balqā' called Mashārif. When the enemy drew near, the Muslims withdrew to a village called Mu'tah, and the two sides encountered each other there. The Muslims disposed their forces: in command of their right wing they set a man from the Banū 'Udhrah named Quṭbah b. Qatādah; in command of their left wing they set a man from the Anṣār named 'Abāyah[659] b. Mālik. The two sides met and fought. Zayd b. Ḥārithah fought with the banner of the Messenger of God until he perished among the enemy's javelins. Ja'far b. Abī Ṭālib took up the banner and fought with it. When the fighting forced him into difficulties from which he could not extricate himself, he leaped from his sorrel mare, hamstrung it, and fought the enemy until he was killed. Ja'far was the first Muslim to hamstring his horse in the time of Islam.[660]

According to Ibn Ḥumayd—Salamah and Abū Tumaylah[661]—Muḥammad b. Isḥāq—Yaḥyā b. 'Abbād—his father ['Abbād b. 'Abdallāh b. al-Zubayr]—his foster-father, who was from the Banū Murrah b. 'Awf and went on the expedition to Mu'tah and who said: By God, it is as if I could still see Ja'far when he leaped from his sorrel mare, hamstrung her, and fought the enemy until he was killed. When Ja'far was killed, 'Abdallāh b. Rawāḥah took up the banner and advanced with it on horseback. He kept urging his soul to obey. He hesitated a bit, and then he said:[662]

I swear, soul, that you shall become obedient
    willingly, or you shall be compelled.
[1615] If men raise a clamor and utter cries,
    why do I see you averse to Paradise?
Too long have you been at ease!

---

658. Al-Balqā' is the old Arabic name for most of modern Jordan, roughly the plateau between Wādī al-Zarqā' (or Jabbok) in the north to Wādī al-Mūjib (or Arnon) in the south. In Byzantine times, the Arnon formed the boundary between the province of Arabia and Palestina Tertia. See *EI*², s.v. al-Balḳā'.

659. Ibn Hishām notes that the name is also given as 'Ubādah.

660. See note 93, above.

661. For Abū Tumaylah Yaḥyā b. Wāḍiḥ see Ibn Ḥajar, *Tahdhīb*, XI, 293–94.

662. For other sources of the poem, variants, and commentary, see *Dīwān* of 'Abdallāh b. Rawāḥah, 108–9.

Are you anything but a drop of moisture in an old water skin?

He also said:[663]

My soul, unless you are killed, you will die:
this is the destiny of death by which you have been tried.
You have been granted what you wished:
If you act as those two did, you will have been guided aright.[664]

Then he dismounted. When he had dismounted, a cousin of his brought him a joint of meat, saying, "Strengthen yourself with it, for you have endured much in these days." Having taken it from the cousin's hand, he took a bite of it. Then he heard the rushing of the troops. "And you are [still] in this world!" he said—and he threw the meat away. Then he took up his sword, advanced, and fought until he was killed. Thābit b. Aqram, of the Banū al-'Ajlān,[665] then took up the banner. He said, "O Muslims, agree on a man from among yourselves!" They said, "You!" He said, "I cannot do it." So the people agreed on Khālid b. al-Walīd. When he [1616]
took the banner, he fended off the enemy and tried to deflect them.[666] Then he withdrew and there was a withdrawal [by the enemy] from him, so that he got away with his forces.

According to al-Qāsim b. Bishr b. Ma'rūf[667]—Sulaymān b. Ḥarb[668]—al-Aswad b. Shaybān[669]—Khālid b. Sumayr,[670] who

663. Ibid., 87 (with additional verses).

664. The reference is to Zayd b. Ḥārithah and Ja'far b. Abī Ṭālib, who died carrying the Prophet's banner.

665. The name is also given as Thābit b. Arqam. The Banū al-'Ajlān (here abbreviated as Bal'ajlān) were a subdivision of Balī.

666. The textual witnesses are evenly divided between *ḥāshā*, "he tried to divert," and *khāshā*, "he was cautious or wary" of them (and therefore turned away and withdrew); see ed. Leiden note *ad loc.*

667. For al-Qāsim b. Bishr [b. Aḥmad] b. Ma'rūf see Ibn Ḥajar, *Tahdhīb*, VIII, 308.

668. Sulaymān b. Ḥarb b. Bujayl al-Azdī al-Wāshiḥī Abū Ayyūb was born in 140/757–58. Of Baṣran origin, he served as judge in Mecca, then returned to al-Baṣrah, where he died in 224/839. See Ibn Ḥajar, *Tahdhīb*, IV, 178–80.

669. Al-Aswad b. Shaybān al-Sadūsī al-Baṣrī Abū Shaybān died in 165/781–82. See Ibn Ḥajar, *Tahdhīb*, I, 339–40.

670. Khālid b. Sumayr (or Shumayr) al-Sadūsī al-Baṣrī is listed without dates in Ibn Ḥajar, *Tahdhīb*, III, 97.

said: ʿAbdallāh b. Rabāḥ al-Anṣārī,[671] whom the Anṣār had instructed [in religious matters], once arrived in our midst. The people came to him, and he said that he had received a report from Abū Qatādah, the horseman of the Messenger of God, who said: The Messenger of God sent out the Army of Commanders[672] and said, "Your commander is Zayd b. Ḥārithah; if he is killed, it is Jaʿfar b. Abī Ṭālib; and if Jaʿfar is killed, it is ʿAbdallāh b. Rawāḥah." Jaʿfar jumped up and said, "Messenger of God, I will not go if you appoint Zayd commander over me." "Go," he replied, "for you do not know what is best."

So they set out. After they had been away for some time, the Messenger of God ascended the pulpit. He ordered that the call to congregational prayer should be given, and the people gathered to hear the Messenger of God. He said: "A gate to good fortune! A gate to good fortune! A gate to good fortune! I bring you news of your campaigning army. They have set out and have met the enemy. Zayd has died a martyr's death"—he prayed for forgiveness for him. "Then Jaʿfar took up the banner and attacked the enemy until he died a martyr's death"—he testified that he had attained martyrdom and prayed for forgiveness for him. "Then ʿAbdallāh b. Rawāḥah took up the banner and planted his legs firmly until he died a martyr's death"—he prayed for forgiveness for him. "Then Khālid b. al-Walīd took up the banner: he was not one of the commanders, but he showed himself to be a real commander." Then the Messenger of God said, "O God, he is one of Thy swords,
[1617] and Thou wilt aid him." From that day on, Khālid was named "the Sword of God." Then the Messenger of God said: "Hasten to reinforce your brothers! Let none of you hang back." So they went forth to fight both on foot and mounted. It was in a time of extreme heat.

According to Ibn Ḥumayd—Salamah—Ibn Isḥāq—ʿAbdallāh b. Abī Bakr, who said: When the Messenger of God received word of the death of Jaʿfar, he said, "Last night Jaʿfar, with two wings whose forefeathers were stained with blood, passed by among a

671. ʿAbdallāh b. Rabāḥ al-Anṣārī Abū Khālid, of Medinese origin, moved to al-Baṣrah. He died ca. 90/708–9. See Ibn Ḥajar, *Tahdhīb*, V, 206–7.

672. *Jaysh al-umarāʾ*: apparently a title given to the Muʾtah expedition because of the presence of close relatives of Muḥammad appointed as commanders.

band of angels, all of them headed for Bīshah." [Bīshah is] a place in Yemen.[673]

Quṭbah b. Qatādah al-'Udhrī, the commander of the Muslims' right wing, attacked Mālik b. Rāfilah, the commander of the Arab auxiliaries, and killed him.

A woman soothsayer[674] from Ḥadas, having heard of the approach of the army of the Messenger of God, said to her people, who were a clan of Ḥadas known as the Banū Ghanm:[675] "I warn you of a folk with narrow eyes, who look askance, who lead horses whose tails have been cut off, and who spill blood copiously." They heeded her words and separated from the rest of Lakhm. Afterward, they remained the wealthiest [clan] of the Ḥadas. Those who felt the heat of battle that day were the Banū Tha'labah clan of Ḥadas, and afterward they remained few in number.

After Khālid b. al-Walīd withdrew with the men, he returned, bringing them back.

According to Ibn Ḥumayd—Salamah—Muḥammad b. Isḥāq—Muḥammad b. Ja'far b. al-Zubayr—'Urwah b. al-Zubayr, who said: When they were about to enter Medina, the Messenger of God and [1618] the Muslims met them. The young boys ran to meet them, and the Messenger of God came with the men on a mount. "Take up the boys," he said, "and have them ride. Give me Ja'far's son." 'Abdallāh b. Ja'far was brought, and the Messenger of God took him and mounted him in front of him.

The people began to throw dust at the army, saying, "Fleers in the way of God!" But the Messenger of God said: "They are not fleers. God willing, they are ones who will turn to fight again."

According to Ibn Ḥumayd—Salamah—Muḥammad b. Isḥāq—'Abdallāh b. Abī Bakr—'Āmir b. 'Abdallāh b. al-Zubayr[676]—some

---

673. Bīshah is located at the junction of the routes from al-Ṭā'if and al-Riyāḍ to Abhā, Najrān, and southwest Arabia. See *EI*², s.v. Bīsha.

674. Arabic: *kāhinah*. See *EI*², s.v. Kāhin.

675. Ḥadas was a section of the tribe of Lakhm settled in Byzantine Syria. The woman's words that follow are in rhymed prose (*saj'*), which is typically used for such mantic utterances.

676. 'Āmir b. 'Abdallāh b. al-Zubayr b. al-'Awwām al-Asadī Abū al-Ḥārith transmitted *ḥadīth* from his father and from his maternal uncle Abū Bakr b. 'Abd al-Raḥmān b. Hishām (his mother was Ḥantamah bt. 'Abd al-Raḥmān). He died about the same time as the caliph Hishām in 125/742–43. See Ibn Ḥajar, *Tahdhīb*, V, 74.

members of the family of al-Ḥārith b. Hishām[677] (namely, his maternal uncles)—Umm Salamah, the wife of the Prophet: Umm Salamah said to the wife of Salamah b. Hishām b. al-Mughīrah,[678] "Why don't I see Salamah attending worship with the Messenger of God and with the Muslims?" "By God," she replied, "he cannot leave the house! Every time he goes out, people shout, 'Did you flee in the way of God?' So he has stayed in his house and does not go out."

In this year the Messenger of God went on expedition against the people of Mecca.

The Conquest of Mecca[679]

According to Ibn Ḥumayd—Salamah—Ibn Isḥāq, who said: After sending his expedition to Mu'tah, the Messenger of God stayed in Medina during Jumādā II and Rajab.[680] Then the Banū Bakr b. 'Abd Manāt b. Kinānah assaulted [the tribe of] Khuzā'ah while the latter were at a watering place called al-Watīr belonging to Khuzā'ah
[1619] in Lower Mecca. The cause of the strife between the Banū Bakr and the Banū Khuzā'ah was a man from the Banū al-Ḥaḍramī named Mālik b. 'Abbād. This man of the Banū al-Ḥaḍramī had a covenant of protection at that time with al-Aswad b. Razn.[681] Mālik set out on a journey as a merchant. When he was in the middle of Khuzā'ah territory, the Khuzā'ah assaulted him, killed him, and took his property. The Banū Bakr therefore attacked and killed a man from Khuzā'ah. Just before Islam, the Khuzā'ah in turn assaulted Salmā, Kulthūm, and Dhu'ayb, the sons of al-Aswad b. Razn al-Dīlī—they were the leading men and dignitaries

677. Al-Ḥārith b. Hishām b. al-Mughīrah al-Makhzūmī, a member of an important Meccan family, fought on the pagan side at the battles of Badr and Uḥud. He was the nephew of the Prophet's wife Umm Salamah bt. al-Mughīrah and became a Muslim at the time of the conquest of Mecca.

678. I.e., to her nephew's wife. Umm Salamah was the daughter of al-Mughīrah.

679. Parallels: W, II, 780–871; III, 873–75; IH, IV, 389–428 (tr. Guillaume, 540–61).

680. I.e., from 26 September (the beginning of Jumādā II) to 23 November 629 (the end of Rajab).

681. I.e., with one of the chiefs of Kinānah, al-Aswad b. Razn al-Dīlī, the Banū al-Dīl being a part of the Banū Bakr b. 'Abd Manāt b. Kinānah.

of the Banū Bakr—and killed them at ʿArafah, by the border markers of the sacred territory.[682]

According to Ibn Ḥumayd—Salamah—Muḥammad b. Isḥāq—a man from the Banū al-Dīl, who said: In pagan times two payments of blood money would be paid for each of the sons of al-Aswad, while a single payment of blood money would be paid for us; and that because of their excellence [compared with us].[683]

Matters stood thus between the Banū Bakr and Khuzāʿah when Islam intervened to separate them and occupy people's minds. When the peace of al-Ḥudaybiyah was concluded between the Messenger of God and Quraysh (this information is according to Ibn Ḥumayd—Salamah—Muḥammad b. Isḥāq—Muḥammad b. Muslim b. ʿAbdallāh b. Shihāb al-Zuhrī—ʿUrwah b. al-Zubayr—al-Miswar b. Makhramah, Marwān b. al-Ḥakam, and other learned men of ours), among the terms they imposed on the Messenger of God and that he granted to them was that whoever wanted to enter into a treaty and pact with the Messenger of God [1620] might do so, and whoever wanted to enter into a treaty and pact with Quraysh might do so. The Banū Bakr entered into a pact with Quraysh, and Khuzāʿah entered into a pact with the Messenger of God.

The truce having been concluded, the Banū al-Dīl of the Banū Bakr took advantage of it against Khuzāʿah. To retaliate for the sons of al-Aswad b. Razn they wanted to kill the persons from Khuzāʿah who had killed their men. Nawfal b. Muʿāwiyah al-Dīlī set out with the Banū al-Dīl (at that time he was leader of the Banū al-Dīl, though not all the Banū Bakr followed him). He made a night raid on Khuzāʿah while the latter were at their watering place of al-Watīr, and they killed a man [of the Khuzāʿah]. They tried to drive each other away and fought. Quraysh aided the Banū Bakr with weapons, and some members of Quraysh fought on their side under cover of darkness until they drove Khuzāʿah into the sacred territory.

According to al-Wāqidī: Among the members of Quraysh who helped the Banū Bakr against Khuzāʿah that night, concealing

---

682. Mecca is surrounded by a sacred territory (*ḥaram*) in which killing is prohibited. The murderers killed their victims just outside this territory.

683. The addition is from Ibn Hishām.

their identity, were Ṣafwān b. Umayyah, 'Ikrimah b. Abī Jahl, Suhayl b. 'Amr, and others, along with their slaves.

Resumption of the account of Ibn Isḥāq, who said: When they reached the sacred territory, the Banū Bakr said: "Nawfal, we have entered the sacred territory. Be mindful of your God! Be mindful of your God!" To which he replied blasphemously: "Today he has no God![684] Banū Bakr, take your revenge! By my life, you steal in the sacred territory; will you not take your revenge in it?"

The night that the Banū Bakr attacked the Khuzā'ah at al-Watīr, they killed a man of Khuzā'ah named Munabbih. Munabbih was a man with a weak heart. He had gone out with a tribesman of his
[1621] named Tamīm b. Asad. Munabbih said to him: "Tamīm, save yourself! As for me, by God, I am a dead man whether they kill me or spare me, for my heart has ceased beating." Tamīm ran away and escaped; Munabbih they caught and killed. When the Khuzā'ah entered Mecca, they took refuge in the house of Budayl b. Warqā' al-Khuzā'ī and the house of one of their *mawlās* named Rāfi'.

When Quraysh leagued together [with the Banū Bakr][685] against Khuzā'ah and killed some of their men, breaking the treaty and covenant that existed between them and the Messenger of God by violating the Khuzā'ah, who had a pact and treaty with him, 'Amr b. Sālim al-Khuzā'ī, one of the Banū Ka'b,[686] went to the Messenger of God in Medina. This was one of the things that prompted the conquest of Mecca. 'Amr stood before the Messenger of God while he was in the mosque sitting among the people, and he recited:

O God, I will remind Muḥammad
  of the venerable alliance of our father and his father.
Parent were we, and you were child;[687]

---

684. I.e., "Today *I* have no God," referring to himself in the third person, as is frequent in oaths; see ed. Leiden, *Glossarium*, p. CXXI.

685. Addition from IH, IV, 394.

686. The Banū Ka'b b. 'Amr were a subdivision of Khuzā'ah.

687. Cf. the variant in IH, IV, 394: "You were progeny, and we were parent." According to the note in IH, ad loc., this refers to the fact that the mother of the Banū 'Abd Manāf (which included the Prophet's clan of the Banū Hāshim and the clans of 'Abd Shams, al-Muṭṭalib, and Nawfal) was a woman from Khuzā'ah. Quṣayy, the father of 'Abd Manāf, likewise had a mother from the Khuzā'ah. For

then we became Muslims and did not withdraw our hand.
Help, Messenger of God, with ready help!
Summon God's worshipers to come with assistance!
Among them the Messenger of God has come forth [1622]
bright as the full moon—waxing, ascending.
If he is wronged, his face takes on a dusky hue,
among an army huge like the sea that runs foaming.
Quraysh have violated the promise to you;
they have broken the solemn covenant with you.
They have set a watch for me at Kadā'[688]
and have said that I can call on no one.
Most contemptible are they and fewest in number.
They attacked us at al-Watīr while we were praying at night,
Killing many of us while we were bowing and prostrating ourselves.

(By this he was saying that they had killed them after they had become Muslims.) When the Messenger of God heard this, he said, "You have received help, 'Amr b. Sālim!" Then a cloud appeared to the Messenger of God in the sky, and he said, "This cloud signals the beginning of help for the Banū Ka'b."

Then Budayl b. Warqā' set out with a group of men from Khuzā'ah. They came to the Messenger of God in Medina and told him what had befallen them and how Quraysh had backed the Banū Bakr against them; then they departed to return to Mecca. The Messenger of God had told them, "I think you will see Abū Sufyān come to strengthen the pact and extend the term." As Budayl b. Warqā' and his companions traveled, they met Abū Sufyān at 'Usfān: Quraysh had sent him to the Messenger of God to strengthen the pact and extend the term, for they had become fearful of what they had done. When Abū Sufyān met Budayl, he said, "Where have you come from, Budayl?"—for he guessed that [1623]
he had gone to the Messenger of God. Budayl said, "I traveled with the Khuzā'ah along this shore and along the bottom of this val-

---

wālid as referring either to a male or female parent (the latter without the feminine termination), see Lane, *Lexicon*, VIII, 2967, s.v.

688. Kadā' is a mountain overlooking Mecca from the north; see Yāqūt, *Mu'jam al-buldān*, VII, 220.

ley." Abū Sufyān asked, "Didn't you go to Muḥammad?" "No," he replied.

When Budayl set out for Mecca, Abū Sufyān said, "If in fact he went to Medina, he will have fed his camel date pits there." So he went to the place where his camel had rested, picked up some of its droppings, crumbled them, and saw date pits in them. "I swear by God," he said, "Budayl went to Muḥammad!"

Abū Sufyān then set out and went to the Messenger of God in Medina. Abū Sufyān [first] visited his own daughter, Umm Ḥabībah bt. Abī Sufyān.[689] When he was about to sit on the bed of the Messenger of God, she folded it up to stop him. He said, "My daughter, by God, I don't know whether you think I am too good for this bed or you think it is too good for me." She said: "It is the bed of the Messenger of God, and you are an unclean polytheist. I did not want you to sit on the bed of the Messenger of God." He said, "My daughter, by God, evil came over you after you left me."

Then he went out and came to the Messenger of God. He spoke to him, but the Messenger of God gave him no reply. Then he went to Abū Bakr and asked him to speak to the Messenger of God for him, but Abū Bakr said, "I will not do it." Then he went to 'Umar b. al-Khaṭṭāb and spoke to him. 'Umar said: "I intercede for you with the Messenger of God! By God, if I found only ant grubs [to eat], I would fight you!" Abū Sufyān then left and went to see 'Alī b. Abī Ṭālib. Fāṭimah, the daughter of the Messenger of God, was with him, and with her was al-Ḥasan b. 'Alī, a young child crawling before her. Abū Sufyān said: "'Alī, you are the nearest of the men to me in kinship and the closest of them in relationship. I
[1624] have come with a request, and I will not go back empty-handed as I came. Intercede for us with the Messenger of God!" He said: "Woe to you, Abū Sufyān. By God, the Messenger of God has determined on a matter about which we cannot speak to him." Abū Sufyān then turned to Fāṭimah and said, "Daughter of Muḥammad, don't you want to command your little son here to make peace among the people,[690] so that he will be lord of the

689. Cf. the account of her marriage to Muḥammad at pp. 109–10, above.

690. The sense of the passage depends on the fact that Arabic *yujīru bayna al-nās*, means literally, "extend protection among the people (so that neither side commits aggression against the other)" but also has the extended sense of "procure

Arabs forever?" "By God," she said, "my little son is not old enough to make peace among the people, and no one can do so against the will of the Messenger of God." Abū Sufyān said [addressing ʿAlī]: "Abū al-Ḥasan, I see that matters have become difficult for me. Give me advice!" ʿAlī said to him: "By God, I know of nothing that will be of any use to you. However, since you are the lord of the Banū Kinānah, go and make peace among the people, and then return to your country." Abū Sufyān asked, "Do you think that will be of any use to me?" "No, by God," replied ʿAlī, "I do not think so, but I can find nothing else for you to do." So Abū Sufyān stood up in the mosque and said, "People, I hereby make peace among the people." Then he mounted his camel and departed.

When Abū Sufyān came to Quraysh, they asked, "What is your news?" He said: "I went to Muḥammad and spoke to him; and, by God, he gave me no reply. Then I went to Ibn Abī Quḥāfah and got nothing good from him. Then I went to Ibn al-Khaṭṭāb, whom I found to be the most hostile of them. Then I went to ʿAlī b. Abī Ṭālib, whom I found to be the mildest of them. He advised me to do something that I have done, but, by God, I do not know whether it will be of any use to me or not." They asked, "What did he command you?" He replied, "He commanded me to make peace among the people, and I did it." They asked, "Has Muḥammad approved it?" "No," he said. "Woe to you!" they said. "By God, he did no more than play with you. What you have said is of no use to us." Abū Sufyān replied, "No, by God, I found nothing else to do."

The Messenger of God commanded the people to prepare for [1625]
travel, and he commanded his family to make his travel preparations. Abū Bakr visited his daughter ʿĀʾishah while she was moving some of the travel gear of the Messenger of God. "Daughter," asked Abū Bakr, "has the Messenger of God commanded you to make preparations for him to travel?" "Yes," she said, "so make yourself ready to travel!" "Where," he asked, "do you think he intends to go?" She said, "By God, I do not know."

---

or mediate peace"—see ed. Leiden, *Glossarium*, p. CLXXV; Lane, *Lexicon*, II, 483; *EI*[2], s.v. Djiwār.

Then the Messenger of God informed the people that he would travel to Mecca. He commanded them to prepare themselves quickly, and he said, "O God, keep spies and news from Quraysh until we take them by surprise in their territory." So the people made preparations for travel. Ḥassān b. Thābit al-Anṣārī composed the following verses to rouse the people, mentioning the killing of the men of Khuzā'ah.[691]

I received word, though I was not present, that in the plain of Mecca
  are men of the Banū Ka'b whose necks were cut
At the hands of men who did not unsheathe their swords,
  and [there were] many slain men whose graveclothes were not hidden [in earth].[692]
Would that I knew whether my help [to Khuzā'ah] will harm
  Suhayl b. 'Amr—with its heat and its punishment—
And Ṣafwān, an old camel the edge of whose anus has been cut.
  For this is the time for war—its milking girth has been firmly tied.[693]
You will not be safe from us, son of Umm Mujālid,
  when it is milked, yielding pure milk, and its teeth become strong.
[1626] So do not become impatient with it! Our swords
  have a fall the gate of which opens to reveal death.

Ḥassān's words, "at the hands of men who did not unsheathe their swords," refer to Quraysh; "son of Umm Mujālid" refers to 'Ikrimah b. Abī Jahl.

According to Ibn Ḥumayd—Salamah—Muḥammad b. Isḥāq—Muḥammad b. Ja'far b. al-Zubayr—'Urwah b. al-Zubayr and others of our scholars, who said: When the Messenger of God had decided to go to Mecca, Ḥāṭib b. Abī Balta'ah wrote a letter to

691. For variant readings, one additional verse, and comment, see *Dīwān of Ḥaṣṣān b. Thābit*, I, 296–97, and II, 218.

692. I.e., they were killed indirectly by Quraysh, who, although they did not draw their own swords, aided the Banū Bakr. The second part of the verse refers to the dead who remained unburied.

693. The metaphor is complex: the *'iṣāb* is a cord used to tie the leg of the camel during milking. War is not only compared to a camel (a common metaphor) but to a camel ready to be milked, so that war (the death-bringer) is compared paradoxically to milk (the sustainer of life).

Quraysh informing them of the decision of the Messenger of God to go to them, and he gave the letter to a woman. (Muḥammad b. Ja'far alleged she was from [the tribe of] Muzaynah; others asserted that she was Sārah, a *mawlāh* of one of the sons of 'Abd al-Muṭṭalib.) He paid her to deliver it to Quraysh. She put it on her head, twisted the hair on the sides of her head over it, and set out carrying it. But word of what Ḥāṭib had done came to the Messenger of God from heaven, and he sent out 'Alī b. Abī Ṭālib and al-Zubayr b. al-'Awwām, saying, "Overtake a woman with whom Ḥāṭib has sent a letter to Quraysh warning them of what we have decided about them." The two went out and overtook her at al-Ḥulayfah, al-Ḥulayfah of Ibn Abī Aḥmad.[694] They made her dismount and searched her saddle, but found nothing. 'Alī b. Abī [1627]
Ṭālib said to her: "I swear that the Messenger of God did not lie, nor have we lied. You shall produce this letter to me, or we will strip you." When she saw that he was serious, she said, "Turn away from me." He turned away from her, and she untied the side-locks of her head, took out the letter, and handed it to him. He brought it to the Messenger of God.

The Messenger of God summoned Ḥāṭib and said, "Ḥāṭib, what made you do this?" He said: "Messenger of God, by God, I am a believer in God and His Messenger. I have not changed or altered. But I was a man with no roots or clan among the people, while I had family and children among them.[695] And so I did them this favor for their sake." 'Umar b. al-Khaṭṭāb said, "Messenger of God, let me cut off his head, for the man has played the hypocrite." The Messenger of God said: "How do you know, 'Umar? Perhaps God looked down on those who were at Badr[696] on the day of the battle and said, 'Do what you will, for I have forgiven you.'" Concerning Ḥāṭib, God revealed: "O believers, take not My enemy and your

---

694. If the reading al-Ḥulayfah is correct (and is the same place as the well-known Dhū al-Ḥulayfah), she was overtaken about six miles from Medina. Ibn Hishām reads al-Khalīqah, which is 12 miles from Medina (cf. al-Samhūdī, *Khulāṣat al-wafā'*, 542, 546). The identification of the place as belonging to "Ibn Abī Aḥmad" renders both identifications doubtful.

695. I.e., the Meccans.

696. For the presence of Ḥāṭib at the Battle of Badr, see W, I, 140, 154; Ibn Ḥajar, *Iṣābah*, I, 314.

enemy for friends"—to the words, "to Thee we turn," and the end of the story.[697]

According to Ibn Ḥumayd—Salamah—Muḥammad b. Isḥāq—Muḥammad b. Muslim al-Zuhrī—'Ubaydallāh b. 'Abdallāh b. 'Utbah b. Mas'ūd—Ibn 'Abbās, who said: Then the Messenger of God went on his journey and left Abū Ruhm Kulthūm b. Ḥuṣayn b. Khalaf al-Ghifārī in charge of Medina. He departed on the tenth day of the month of Ramaḍān.[698] The Messenger of God fasted,
[1628] and the people fasted with him. When he was at al-Kadīd, between 'Usfān and Amaj, the Messenger of God broke his fast. He proceeded on and encamped at Marr al-Ẓahrān with 10,000 Muslims. [Members of the tribe of] Sulaym numbered 700, [members of the tribe] of Muzaynah 1,000, and in all the tribes there were a number of men and Muslims. The Emigrants and Anṣār went forth all together with the Messenger of God; not one of them hung back from him. When the Messenger of God encamped at Marr al-Ẓahrān, reports had been kept hidden from Quraysh; no news was reaching them about the Messenger of God, and they did not know what he would do. That night, Abū Sufyān b. Ḥarb, Ḥakīm b. Ḥizām, and Budayl b. Warqā' went out to seek news, hoping to find a report or hear of one.

According to Ibn Ḥumayd—Salamah—Muḥammad b. Isḥāq—al-'Abbās b. 'Abdallāh b. Ma'bad b. al-'Abbās b. 'Abd al-Muṭṭalib[699]—Ibn 'Abbās: Al-'Abbās b. 'Abd al-Muṭṭalib met the Messenger of God along the way. Abū Sufyān b. al-Ḥārith[700] and 'Abdallāh b. Abī Umayyah b. al-Mughīrah[701] had met the Mes-

697. Qur'ān 60:1–4. The passage uses the story of Abraham and his followers as an example of the enmity between believers and nonbelievers: "You have a good example in Abraham, and those with him, when they said to their people, 'We are quit of you and that you serve, apart from God. We disbelieve in you, and between us and you enmity has shown itself, and hatred for ever, until you believe in God alone. . . . Our Lord, in Thee we trust; to Thee we turn.'"

698. 10 Ramaḍān of A.H. 8 fell on 1 January 630.

699. Al-'Abbās b. 'Abdallāh b. Ma'bad b. 'Abbās b. 'Abd al-Muṭṭalib al-Hāshimī of Medina is mentioned without dates in Ibn Ḥajar, *Tahdhīb*, V, 120. According to *Tahdhīb*, VI, 39, his grandfather, Ma'bad, was the brother of 'Abdallāh b. 'Abbās.

700. Abū Sufyān [al-Mughīrah] b. al-Ḥārith b. 'Abd al-Muṭṭalib, Muḥammad's cousin (son of his paternal uncle), was a poet and had written satires against Muḥammad. See W, II, 806–12; Ibn Ḥajar, *Iṣābah*, VII, 86–87; *GAS*, II, 275.

701. 'Abdallāh b. Abī Umayyah b. al-Mughīrah was the half-brother of Muḥammad's wife Umm Salamah by Muḥammad's paternal aunt 'Ātikah bt. 'Abd al-

senger of God at Nīq al-'Uqāb, between Mecca and Medina.[702] They sought to have an interview with the Messenger of God, and Umm Salamah spoke to him about them, saying, "Messenger of God, the son of your paternal uncle and the son of your paternal aunt and relative by marriage!" He said: "I have no need for the two. As for the son of my paternal uncle, he injured my honor; as for the son of my paternal aunt and my relative by marriage, he is the one who said what he said to me in Mecca." When word of this came out to them—Abū Sufyān [b. al-Ḥārith] had a young son of [1629]
his with him—he said, "By God, he shall let me in, or I will take the hand of this son of mine and we will go into the open country until we die of thirst and hunger." When this was reported to the Messenger of God, he softened toward the two of them. He gave permission, and they came before him and became Muslims. Abū Sufyān [b. al-Ḥārith] recited to him the following verses, which he composed about his becoming a Muslim and to excuse himself for what he had done in the past:[703]

By my life, the day I carried a banner
  that the horsemen of al-Lāt[704] might overcome the horsemen of Muḥammad,
I was like a perplexed traveler in a dark night;
  but now the time has come when I am guided and find the way.
A Guide other than myself guided me; there overcame me,

Muṭṭalib. His sceptical arguments against Islam during Muḥammad's days in Mecca—they are said to have grieved Muḥammad greatly—are recorded in IH, I, 298 (tr. Guillaume, 134–35). After his conversion, he was killed fighting as a Muslim at the siege of al-Ṭā'if in A.H. 8/630—see IH, IV, 486 (tr. Guillaume, 591).

702. A place between Mecca and Medina, near al-Juḥfah; cf. Yāqūt, *Mu'jam al-buldān*, VIII, 360.

703. The poem should be read in connection with the first of the two accounts in al-Wāqidī of the conversion of Abū Sufyān b. al-Ḥārith, which is quite different from the second account (the one that al-Ṭabarī includes). In al-Wāqidī's first account, Abū Sufyān repeatedly attempted to find favor with Muḥammad on the eve of the conquest of Mecca but was not successful until his wife interceded for him during the women's pledge of allegiance after the conquest. He subsequently accompanied Muḥammad to the Battle of Ḥunayn against the tribes of Hawāzin and Thaqīf (the latter from the town of al-Ṭā'if). Thus the poem apparently refers to events that took place after the conquest of Mecca and cannot belong to the conversion story given by al-Ṭabarī.

704. See note 325, above.

with God, one whom I had expelled utterly.
I used to shun and diligently keep my distance from
Muḥammad;
yet I was called related to Muḥammad, though I did not
declare my kinship.[705]
They—what sort are they? Whoever does not profess their false
opinion,
though he be of sound judgment, is blamed and ridiculed.
I wanted to please them, but I could not adhere [to him]
with the people, so long as I was not guided in every place
of abode.
Say then to Thaqīf that I do not want to fight them,
and say this to Thaqīf: "Threaten others than me."
I was not in the army that overcame 'Āmir;
it did not happen because of my tongue or my hand:
[It was] tribes that came from far away lands—
strangers who came from Suhām and Surdad.[706]

[1630] Some have alleged that when he recited to the Messenger of God the words, "there overcame me, with God, one whom I had expelled utterly," the Prophet struck his chest and said, "You expelled me utterly?"[707]

According to al-Wāqidī:[708] When the Messenger of God set out for Mecca, some said his destination was Quraysh, some said it was Hawāzin, and some said it was Thaqīf. He sent to the tribes, but they hung back from him, and he appointed no one to military commands and displayed no banners. Then, when he reached Qudayd, the Banū Sulaym met him with horses and full arma-

---

705. According to material in W, II, 811, this refers to an occasion when Abū Sufyān b. al-Ḥārith fled to the court of the Byzantine emperor. Asked to identify himself, he gave his name as Abū Sufyān, son of al-Ḥārith, son of 'Abd al-Muṭṭalib. The emperor immediately said, "If you are telling the truth, you must be the cousin of Muḥammad, the son of 'Abdallāh, the son of 'Abd al-Muṭṭalib." Impressed by the fact that although he had fled from Muḥammad's reach and was so far away, he was known to the emperor only by his relation to Muḥammad, Abū Sufyān began to doubt the truth of paganism and lean toward Islam.

706. Suhām (also vocalized as Sahām) and Surdad were two places in Yemen. See Yāqūt, *Mu'jam al-buldān*, V, 67, 184.

707. As the parallel in W, II, 811, makes clear, the sentence is a rhetorical question. In al-Wāqidī, Muḥammad adds, "Rather, God has utterly expelled *you*!"

708. Cf. W, II, 812 ff.

ment. 'Uyaynah [b. Ḥiṣn][709] joined the Messenger of God at al-'Arj with a group of his companions. Al-Aqra' b. Ḥābis[710] joined him at al-Suqyā. 'Uyaynah said: "Messenger of God, by God I see neither the implements of war nor preparation to enter a state of consecration. Where then are you heading, Messenger of God?" The Messenger of God said, "Where God wills." The Messenger of God ordered that the information be kept ambiguous, and he encamped at Marr al-Ẓahrān. Al-'Abbās met him at al-Suqyā, and Makhramah b. Nawfal met him at Nīq al-'Uqāb. When he encamped at Marr al-Ẓahrān, Abū Sufyān b. Ḥarb came out with Ḥakīm b. Ḥizām.

According to Abū Kurayb—Yūnus b. Bukayr—Muḥammad b. Isḥāq—Ḥusayn b. 'Abdallāh b. 'Ubaydallāh b. 'Abbās[711]—'Ikrimah—Ibn 'Abbās, who said:[712] When the Messenger of God encamped at Marr al-Ẓahrān, al-'Abbās b. 'Abd al-Muṭṭalib said, the Messenger of God having departed from Medina: "Woe to Quraysh! If the Messenger of God surprises them in their territory and enters Mecca by force, it means the destruction of Quraysh forever." So he seated himself on the white mule of the Messenger [1631]
of God and said, "I will go out to al-Arāk;[713] perhaps I shall see a firewood gleaner, or someone bringing milk, or someone coming in who will enter Mecca and inform them where the Messenger of God is, so that they will go to him and ask him for a promise of safety."

[Continuing, al-'Abbās related:] So I set out. By God, while I was going through al-Arāk seeking what I had come out to find, I heard the voices of Abū Sufyān b. Ḥarb, Ḥakīm b. Ḥizām, and Budayl b. Warqā', who had come out in search of information about the Messenger of God. I heard Abū Sufyān say, "By God, I have never seen fires like those I see today!" Budayl said, "These, by God, are the fires of Khuzā'ah gathered for war." Abū Sufyān said,

709. Cf. W, II, 803–4.

710. Al-Aqra' b. Ḥābis was said to be the first Muslim from the tribe of Tamīm. See Watt, *Muhammad at Medina*, 137–38.

711. Ḥusayn b. 'Abdallāh b. 'Ubaydallāh b. 'Abbās died ca. 140/757. See Ibn Ḥajar, *Tahdhīb*, II, 341–42.

712. Parallel: *Aghānī*, VI, 97–98.

713. Wādī al-Arāk (Arāk-Tree Valley) is a valley near Mecca; see Yāqūt, *Mu'jam al-buldān*, I, 169.

"Khuzā'ah are too lowly and abject for that." Recognizing his voice, I said, "Abū Ḥanẓalah!"[714] He said, "Abū al-Faḍl!"[715] "Yes!" I said. He said: "At your service, may my father and mother be your ransom! What news do you have?" I said: "Here is the Messenger of God behind me. He has come against you with a force you cannot resist—10,000 Muslims." "What," he asked, "do you command me?" I said, "Mount the rump of this mule, and I will ask the Messenger of God to grant you a promise of safety; for, by God, if he gets hold of you, he will cut off your head." He mounted behind me, and I set out with him, urging the mule of the Messenger of God toward the Messenger of God. Whenever I passed one of the fires of the Muslims, they looked at me and said, "The uncle of the Messenger of God on the mule of the Messenger of God!" Finally, I passed the fire of 'Umar b. al-Khaṭṭāb, who said: "Abū Sufyān! Praise be to God, who has delivered you up without treaty or covenant!" He ran toward the Prophet, and I urged the
[1632] mule, Abū Sufyān riding behind me, until I jumped off at the door of the tent, having outdistanced 'Umar by as much as a slow mount can outdistance a slow man. 'Umar went before the Messenger of God and said: "Messenger of God, here is Abū Sufyān, the enemy of God. God has delivered him up without treaty or covenant. Let me cut off his head!" I said, "Messenger of God, I have granted him protection." Then I sat by the Messenger of God and took hold of his head. I said, "By God, no one but I shall speak confidentially to him today." When 'Umar kept speaking to him at length, I said: "Take it easy, 'Umar! By God, you are doing this only because he is from the Banū 'Abd Manāf; if he had been from the Banū 'Adī b. Ka'b,[716] you would not have said this." He said: "Take it easy, 'Abbās! By God, your [conversion to] Islam, the day you became a Muslim, was more pleasing to me than the conversion of [my father] al-Khaṭṭāb would have been, had he become a Muslim; for I know that your [conversion to] Islam was more pleasing to the Messenger of God than that of al-Khaṭṭāb would have been, had he become a Muslim." The Messenger of God said:

714. Abū Ḥanẓalah is the *kunyah* of Abū Sufyān.
715. Abū al-Faḍl is the *kunyah* of al-'Abbās.
716. The Banū 'Adī b. Ka'b were 'Umar's clan.

"Go, for we have promised him safety. Bring him to me tomorrow morning."

So 'Umar took Abū Sufyān back to his dwelling. In the morning, he brought him to the Messenger of God, who, when he saw him, said, "Alas, Abū Sufyān, hasn't the time come for you to know that there is no god but God?" Abū Sufyān said: "May my father and mother be your ransom! How concerned you are for your kin, how forbearing, and how generous! By God, I think that if there were another god along with God, he would have availed me somewhat." "Alas, Abū Sufyān," he said, "hasn't the time come for you to know that I am the Messenger of God?" Abū Sufyān said: "May my father and mother be your ransom! How concerned you are for your kin, how forbearing, and how generous! As for this matter, there is something of it in my mind."

(Al-'Abbās continued his narrative, saying:) So I said to him: "Woe to you! Recite the testimony of truth before, by God, your head is cut off!" And he recited the *shahādah.*[717]

The Messenger of God said to al-'Abbās, when Abū Sufyān re- [1633]
cited the *shahādah*, "Go back, 'Abbās, and detain him by the spur of the mountain in the narrow part of the valley until the troops of God pass by him.[718]

[Al-'Abbās continued his narrative, saying:] So I said to him, "Messenger of God, Abū Sufyān is a man who loves glory. Grant him something that shall be [a cause of glory for him] among his clansmen." He said, "Yes; whoever enters the house of Abū Sufyān shall be safe; anyone who enters the sanctuary[719] shall be safe; and anyone who locks his door behind him shall be safe."

I went out and detained Abū Sufyān by the spur of the mountain in the narrow part of the valley, and the tribes passed by him. He would ask, "Who are these, 'Abbās?" I would say, "Sulaym," and he would say, "What have I to do with Sulaym?" A tribe would pass by him, and he would ask, "Who are these?" I would say, "Aslam," and he would say, "What have I to do with Aslam?"

---

717. I.e., the formula of testimony or profession of faith whereby one becomes a Muslim: "There is no god but God; Muḥammad is the Messenger of God."

718. The parallel in IH, IV, 403, adds: "and he sees them," implying that the purpose is to impress Abū Sufyān.

719. Arabic: *masjid*, here meaning the area around the Ka'bah in Mecca; in later usage, a mosque. On the development of the term see *EI²*, s.v. Masdjid.

Juhaynah would pass by him, and he would say, "What have I to do with Juhaynah?" Finally, the Messenger of God passed by with *al-Khaḍrā'*,[720] the squadron of the Messenger of God, composed of Emigrants and Anṣār in iron [armor], with only their eyes visible. He asked, "Who are these, Abū al-Faḍl?" I said, "This is the Messenger of God amid the Emigrants and Anṣār." He said, "Abū al-Faḍl, your nephew's kingdom has become great!" I said: "Woe to you! It is prophethood."[721] He said, "All right then." I said, "Go join your people now, and warn them!"

Abū Sufyān departed in haste. When he reached Mecca, he shouted in the sanctuary, "People of Quraysh, behold Muḥammad has come upon you with forces you cannot resist." "What then?" they asked. He said, "Anyone who enters my house will be safe." They said, "Alas, what will your house avail us?" He said, "Anyone who enters the sanctuary will be safe, and anyone who locks his door behind him will be safe."

[1634] According to 'Abd al-Wārith b. 'Abd al-Ṣamad b. 'Abd al-Wārith[722]—his father ['Abd al-Ṣamad b. 'Abd al-Wārith][723]—Abān al-'Aṭṭār[724]—Hishām b. 'Urwah—'Urwah [b. al-Zubayr], who wrote [the following letter] to 'Abd al-Malik b. Marwān:[725] To proceed: You wrote to me asking about Khālid b. al-Walīd, whether he fought on the day of the conquest, and under whose command he fought. As regards Khālid on the day of the conquest, he was on the side of the Prophet. When the Prophet traveled the Marr basin heading for Mecca, Quraysh had already sent Abū Sufyān and Ḥakīm b. Ḥizām to meet the Messenger of God, not knowing, when they sent the two, where the Prophet was heading, whether to them or to al-Ṭā'if—that was at the time of the con-

---

720. The name means "green, greenish black, tawny" and is said to be derived from the appearance of their armor; see Ibn Hishām's comment, IH, IV, 404 (tr. Guillaume, 548, and note ad loc.).

721. I.e., not secular kingship such as had been claimed by powerful Arab chieftains in the past. On the disapproval of kings and kingship in early Islam, see *EI*², s.v. Malik.

722. 'Abd al-Wārith b. 'Abd al-Ṣamad b. 'Abd al-Wārith died in 252/866. See Ibn Ḥajar, *Tahdhīb*, VII, 390.

723. 'Abd al-Ṣamad b. 'Abd al-Wārith b. Sa'īd al-'Anbārī al-Baṣrī died in 206 or 207/821–22. See Ibn Ḥajar, *Tahdhīb*, VI, 327–28.

724. For Abān b. Yazīd al-'Aṭṭār al-Baṣrī, see Ibn Ḥajar, *Tahdhīb*, I, 101–2.

725. See note 447, above.

quest. Abū Sufyān and Ḥakīm b. Ḥizām asked Budayl b. Warqā' to follow—they wanted him to accompany them. They were only Abū Sufyān, Ḥakīm b. Ḥizām, and Budayl. When [Quraysh] sent them to the Messenger of God, they said to them, "Let us not be approached from behind you; for we do not know against whom Muḥammad intends to go, whether he intends to go against us, against Hawāzin, or against Thaqīf." Between the Prophet and Quraysh there was a peace made on the day of al-Ḥudaybiyah, with a pact and a fixed period of time. The Banū Bakr were in that peace on the side of Quraysh. Then a group of the Banū Ka'b and a group of the Banū Bakr fought with each other. Among the terms on which the Messenger of God and Quraysh had made peace was that there should be neither betrayal nor clandestine theft.[726] Quraysh aided the Banū Bakr with weapons, and the Banū Ka'b suspected Quraysh. That is why the Messenger of God attacked the people of Mecca. During this expedition of his, he met Abū Sufyān, Ḥakīm, and Budayl at Marr al-Ẓahrān. They had no idea that the Messenger of God had encamped at Marr until they sud- [1635]
denly came upon him. When they saw him at Marr, Abū Sufyān, Budayl, and Ḥakīm went before him in his dwelling at Marr al-Ẓahrān and swore allegiance to him. After they swore allegiance to him, he sent them ahead of him to Quraysh, to summon them to Islam. I have been told that he said, "Whoever enters the house of Abū Sufyān shall be safe"—his house was in the upper part of Mecca—"and whoever enters the house of Ḥakīm"—it was in the lower part of Mecca—"shall be safe, and whoever locks his door and withholds his hand shall be safe."

After Abū Sufyān and Ḥakīm left the presence of the Prophet heading for Mecca, he sent al-Zubayr after them, gave him his banner, and appointed him commander over the horsemen of the Emigrants and Anṣār. He commanded him to plant his banner in the upper part of Mecca at al-Ḥajūn.[727] He said to al-Zubayr, "Do not depart from where I have commanded you to plant my banner until I come to you." (The Messenger of God entered [Mecca] from there.) He commanded Khālid b. al-Walīd, along with those of [the tribe of] Quḍā'ah and the Banū Sulaym who had become Muslims

726. See p. 86 and note 372, above.
727. Al-Ḥajūn is a mountain overlooking Mecca.

and some people who had become Muslims only a short time before, to enter through the lower part of Mecca—that was where the Banū Bakr were, whom Quraysh had called on for aid, the Banū al-Ḥārith b. 'Abd Manāt, and the Aḥābīsh[728] whom Quraysh had commanded to be in the lower part of Mecca. So Khālid entered against them by the lower part of Mecca.

I have been told that the Prophet said to Khālid and al-Zubayr when he dispatched them, "Fight only those who fight you." When Khālid came upon the Banū Bakr and the Aḥābīsh in the lower part of Mecca, he fought them, and God put them to flight. That was the only fighting that took place in Mecca. However, Kurz b. Jābir, one of the Banū Muḥārib b. Fihr, and Ibn al-Ash'ar, a man from the Banū Ka'b—the two were among al-Zubayr's
[1636] horsemen—took the road to Kadā'.[729] They did not take the route that al-Zubayr took, which he had been commanded to take. They encountered a squadron of Quraysh on the slope of Kadā' and were killed. There was no fighting by al-Zubayr in the upper part of Mecca. The Prophet arrived from there. The people stood before him to swear allegiance to him, and so the people of Mecca became Muslims. The Prophet stayed among them half a month, no more—until Hawāzin and Thaqīf came and encamped at Ḥunayn.

According to Ibn Ḥumayd—Salamah—Muḥammad b. Isḥāq—'Abdallāh b. Abī Najīḥ: When the Prophet sent his army in divisions from Dhū Ṭuwā, he commanded al-Zubayr, who was in charge of the left wing, to make his entry with some of the forces by way of Kudā.[730] He commanded Sa'd b. 'Ubādah to make his entry with some of the forces by way of Kadā'. Some scholars assert that when Sa'd was sent out, he said as he made his entry, "Today is the day of battle; today the sacred territory is deemed profane."[731] Hearing this, one of the Emigrants said: "Messenger of God, hear what Sa'd b. 'Ubādah has said! We fear that he may assault Quraysh." The Messenger of God said to 'Alī b. Abī Ṭālib:

728. See note 74, above.

729. See note 688, above.

730. Kudā (distinct from Kadā', with which it is sometimes confused, as shown by the *apparatus criticus* of the Leiden edition) is a mountain in the lower (i.e., southern) part of Mecca. Kadā' is in the upper (i.e., northern) part. See Yāqūt, *Mu'jam al-buldān*, VII, 220–21; map in *EI*², VI, 163.

731. The slogan is in rhymed prose (*saj'*).

"Overtake him, and take the banner. You be the one who takes it in!"

According to Ibn Ḥumayd—Salamah—Ibn Isḥāq—'Abdallāh b. Abī Najīḥ: The Messenger of God commanded Khālid b. al-Walīd to enter the lower part of Mecca by way of al-Līṭ[732] with some of [1637]
the forces. Khālid was in charge of the right wing, which included Aslam, Ghifār, Muzaynah, Juhaynah, and other [tribes] of the Arabs. Abū 'Ubaydah b. al-Jarrāḥ advanced with the line of Muslims, moving toward Mecca in front of the Messenger of God. The Messenger of God entered by way of Adhākhir[733] and halted in the upper part of Mecca: there his round tent was pitched.

According to Ibn Ḥumayd—Salamah—Ibn Isḥāq—'Abdallāh b. Abī Najīḥ and 'Abdallāh b. Abī Bakr: Ṣafwān b. Umayyah, 'Ikrimah b. Abī Jahl, and Suhayl b. 'Amr had gathered men at al-Khandamah[734] to fight. Ḥimās b. Qays b. Khālid, a member of the Banū Bakr, was readying weapons before the Messenger of God entered Mecca and set it in order. His wife said to him, "Why are you readying what I see?" He said, "On account of Muḥammad and his forces." "By God," she replied, "I think nothing can stand up to Muḥammad and his forces." He said, "By God, I hope to make some of them serve you!" Then he said:

If you advance today, I have no excuse!
  Here is full panoply: a long-bladed spear,
  and a two-edged [sword] quick to be drawn.

He took up a position at al-Khandamah with Ṣafwān, Suhayl b. 'Amr, and 'Ikrimah. When the Muslims, forces of Khālid b. al-Walīd, met them, they skirmished. Kurz b. Jābir b. Ḥisl b. al-Ajabb b. Ḥabīb b. 'Amr b. Shaybān b. Muḥārib b. Fihr and Khunays[735] b. [1638]
Khālid (who is al-Ash'ar) b. Rabī'ah b. Aṣram b. Ḍabīs b. Ḥarām b. Ḥabashiyyah b. Ka'b b. 'Amr (an ally of the Banū Munqidh) were killed. The two were among the horsemen of Khālid b. al-Walīd, but they became separated from him and took a different route

---

732. I.e., by the main thoroughfare from the south. See Hamidullah, *Battlefields*, 39.

733. The vocalization Adhākhir is given by Yāqūt, *Mu'jam al-buldān*, I, 158–59.

734. Al-Khandamah is a mountain east of Mecca. See Yāqūt, *Mu'jam al-buldān*, III, 470–71; map in *EI*², VI, 163.

735. Ms. C and ed. Cairo: Ḥubaysh.

from his. Both of them were killed. Khunays was killed before Kurz b. Jābir. Kurz set him in front of him[736] and, reciting the following verses of *rajaz*, fought until he was killed:

A light-complexioned woman of the Banū Fihr,
spotless of face, spotless of breast, knows
that today I will strike to protect Abū Ṣakhr.

(Khunays was nicknamed Abū Ṣakhr.) Of [the tribe of] Juhaynah, Salamah b. al-Maylā', one of the horsemen of Khālid b. al-Walīd, was killed. About twelve or thirteen of the polytheists were killed, and then the polytheists were routed. Ḥimās left the scene in flight. He entered his house and said to his wife, "Lock my door behind me." "And where," she asked, "is what you used to say?" So he said:

[1639] Had you been present at the battle of al-Khandamah,
when Ṣafwān fled and 'Ikrimah fled;
While Abū Yazīd[737] was standing like a pillar,[738]
and the Muslims met them with swords
That cut off every arm and skull
with their blows, with only battle cries to be heard;
Behind us their roaring and snarling—
you would not have spoken the least word of blame.

According to Ibn Ḥumayd—Salamah—Ibn Isḥāq, who said: When the Messenger of God ordered his commanders to enter Mecca, he charged them to kill no one except those who fought them; however, he gave charge concerning a group of men whom he named: he ordered that they should be killed even if they were found under the curtains of the Ka'bah. Among them was 'Abdallāh b. Sa'd b. Abī Sarḥ b. Ḥubayb b. Jadhīmah b. Naṣr b. Mālik b. Ḥisl b. 'Āmir b. Lu'ayy. The Messenger of God ordered that he should be killed only because he had become a Muslim and then had reverted to being a polytheist. He fled to 'Uthmān, who was

736. I.e., mounted him in front of him. This seems to be the sense of *bayna rijlayhi*, "between his legs."
737. Abū Yazīd refers to Suhayl b. 'Amr.
738. Arabic: *ma'tamah*. The reading is explained in ed. Leiden, *Glossarium*, pp. CII–CIII.

his foster-brother,[739] and 'Uthmān hid him. 'Uthmān later brought him to the Messenger of God after the people of Mecca had become calm. He asked the Messenger of God to grant him a promise of safety. The Messenger of God is said to have remained [1640] silent for a long time and then to have said yes. After 'Uthmān had taken him away, the Messenger of God said to his companions who were around him, "By God, I kept silent so that one of you might go up to him and cut off his head!" One of the Anṣār said, "Why didn't you give me a signal, Messenger of God?" He replied, "A prophet does not kill by making signs."

Also among them was 'Abdallāh b. Khaṭal, a member of the Banū Taym b. Ghālib. The Messenger of God ordered that he should be killed only for the following reason: He was a Muslim, and the Messenger of God had sent him to collect alms,[740] sending with him one of the Anṣār. With him went a *mawlā* of his, also a Muslim, to serve him. He halted at a resting place and commanded the *mawlā* to slaughter him a goat and make him a meal; then he went to sleep. When he woke up, the *mawlā* had done nothing for him; so he attacked him and killed him. Then he reverted to being a polytheist. He had two singing girls, Fartanā and another with her. The two used to sing satire about the Messenger of God; so the latter commanded that the two of them should be killed along with him.

Also among them was al-Ḥuwayrith b. Nuqaydh b. Wahb b. 'Abd b. Quṣayy. He was one of the men who used to molest the Messenger of God in Mecca.

Also among them was Miqyas b. Ṣubābah. The Messenger of God commanded that he should be killed only because he had killed the member of the Anṣār who had killed his brother by mistake and had then returned to Quraysh as a renegade.

Also among them were 'Ikrimah b. Abī Jahl and Sārah, a *mawlāh* of one of the sons of 'Abd al-Muṭṭalib. She was one of those who used to molest the Messenger of God in Mecca. 'Ikrimah b. Abī Jahl fled to Yemen. His wife, Umm Ḥakīm bt. al-

---

739. I.e., the same woman had nursed them as infants.

740. Arabic *ṣadaqah* (here translated as "alms") is ambiguous. In later usage it usually refers to voluntary contributions. In early usage, however, it is often a synonym for the obligatory contributions known as *zakāh*. See the references in note 604, above.

Ḥārith b. Hishām, became a Muslim. She asked the Messenger of God to grant 'Ikrimah a promise of safety, and he did so. She set out to find him and then brought him to the Messenger of God. 'Ikrimah, as people relate, used to say that what brought him back to Islam after his departure for Yemen was—in his own words: I
[1641] was about to set sail for Ethiopia. When I came to board the ship, its captain said, "Servant of God, do not board my ship until you declare God to be one and repudiate any peers to Him; for I fear that if you do not do so, we shall perish in it." So I asked, "Does no one board until he declares God to be one and repudiates all others?" "Yes," he said, "no one boards until he clears himself." So I asked: Why then should I depart from Muḥammad? By God, this is the very message he brought to us: that our God on the sea is [the same as] our God on land! At that moment I came to know Islam, and it entered into my heart.

'Abdallāh b. Khaṭal was killed by Sa'īd b. Ḥurayth al-Makhzūmī and Abū Barzah al-Aslamī: the two shared in his blood. Miqyas b. Ṣubābah was killed by Numaylah b. 'Abdallāh, a man of his own clan. The sister of Miqyas said:

By my life, Numaylah shamed his clan
    and distressed winter guests by [killing] Miqyas.
How excellent it was for one to see a man like Miqyas
    in times when no food was prepared even for women in childbirth![741]

As for Ibn Khaṭal's two singing girls, one was killed and the other fled. The Messenger of God later was asked to grant her a promise of safety, and he did so. [As for Sārah, he was asked to grant her a promise of safety, and he did so.][742] She lived until someone in the

741. The line is proverbial for a time of such famine that no food is prepared even for those in greatest need of it, or when everyone looks out only for himself. Cf. Freytag, *Arabum Proverbia*, I, 217. The meaning is that Miqyas was generous even in times of extreme hardship.

742. The Leiden editor restored the sentence from the parallel in IH, IV, 411. The text in the manuscripts of al-Ṭabarī implies that it was one of the singing girls (Fartanā, according to Ibn al-Athīr) who later was trampled to death. The loss of the sentence (if it ever existed in the text of al-Ṭabarī) must have taken place early, since the later historian Ibn al-Athīr reflects the loss. The account in W, III, 860, accords with the text without the sentence. According to al-Wāqidī, Sārah was killed, as was one of the singing girls; the other singing girl (cf. the next paragraph

time of 'Umar b. al-Khaṭṭāb caused his horse to trample her at al-Abṭaḥ[743] and killed her. Al-Ḥuwayrith b. Nuqaydh was killed by 'Alī b. Abī Ṭālib.

According to al-Wāqidī: The Messenger of God commanded that six men and four women should be killed. Of the men, [al-Wāqidī] mentioned those whom Ibn Isḥāq named. The women he mentioned were Hind bt. 'Utbah b. Rabī'ah, who became a Muslim and swore allegiance; Sārah, the *mawlāh* of 'Amr b. Hāshim b. 'Abd al-Muṭṭalib b. 'Abd Manāf, who was killed on that day; Quraybah, who was killed on that day; and Fartanā, who lived until the caliphate of 'Uthmān. [1642]

According to Ibn Ḥumayd—Salamah—Ibn Isḥāq—'Umar b. Mūsā b. al-Wajīh—Qatādah al-Sadūsī: Having halted by the door of the Ka'bah, the Messenger of God stood up and said: "There is no god but God alone; He has no partner. He has fulfilled His promise and helped His servant. He alone has put to flight the parties who leagued together. Behold, every alleged claim of hereditary privilege, or blood, or wealth is abolished,[744] except the custodianship of the Ka'bah and the right of supplying water to pilgrims.[745] Behold, the one slain by an error that is like intention, [by] whip or staff—for both cases the blood money shall be made rigorous: [a hundred camels],[746] forty of them with their foals in their wombs. People of Quraysh, God has taken from you the haughtiness of the Time of Ignorance and its pride in ancestors. Mankind is from Adam, and Adam was created from dust." Then the Messenger of God recited:[747] "O mankind, We have created

---

of al-Ṭabarī) was granted a pardon; only to die of a broken rib in the time of 'Uthmān (not 'Umar).

743. Al-Abṭaḥ (*abṭaḥ* is a wash, a broad, dry stream bed with pebbles and gravel) is an area north of Mecca on the way to Minā. See Yāqūt, *Mu'jam al-buldān*, I, 85–86; map in *EI*², VI, 163.

744. Literally, "is [as dust] under these my feet." Cf. al-Zamakhsharī, *Asās al-balāghah*, 496: "'Put it under your feet' means 'turn from it.'"

745. On the custodianship (*sidānah*) of the Ka'bah and the right of supplying water (*siqāyah*) to pilgrims, see *EI*², s.v. Ka'ba. Muḥammad's uncle, al-'Abbās, was confirmed in his possession of the *siqāyah*. The custodianship of the Ka'bah was given to 'Uthmān b. Ṭalḥah.

746. The addition from the parallel in Ibn Hishām is not strictly necessary, since the Arabic *diyah mughallaẓah* "blood money that is made hard, rigorous, or severe" regularly implies a total of 100 camels. Cf. Lane, *Lexicon*, VI, 2283.

747. Qur'ān 49:13.

you male and female, and made you nations and tribes, that you may know one another. Surely the noblest among you in the sight of God is the most god-fearing of you"—to the end of the verse. "People of Quraysh and people of Mecca, what do you think I intend to do with you?" "Good," they said, "[for you are] a generous fellow tribesman and the son of a generous fellow tribesman!" Then he said, "Go, for you are 'those whose bonds have been loosed.'"[748] Thus the Messenger of God emancipated them,
[1643] although God had enabled him to take their persons by force and they were his booty. Therefore the people of Mecca are known as *al-Ṭulaqā'* (Those Whose Bonds Have Been Loosed).

The people assembled in Mecca to swear allegiance to the Messenger of God in Islam. As I have been informed, he sat for them on al-Ṣafā.[749] 'Umar b. al-Khaṭṭāb was below the Messenger of God, lower than the place where he sat, administering the oath to the people. He received from them the oath of allegiance to the Messenger of God, to heed and obey God and His Messenger to the extent of their ability. That was the oath he administered to those who swore allegiance to the Messenger of God in Islam.

When the Messenger of God was finished with the men's swearing of allegiance, the women swore allegiance. Some of the women of Quraysh assembled before him. Among them was Hind bt. 'Utbah, veiled and disguised because of her offense and what she had done to Ḥamzah; for she feared that the Messenger of God would punish her for her offense.[750] When the women approached to swear allegiance to him, the Messenger of God said, as I have been informed, "You are swearing allegiance to me on condition that you will associate nothing with God as a partner." Hind said:

---

748. Arabic *ṭulaqā'* (plural of *ṭalīq*), meaning "a captive having his bond loosed from him," or "a man freed from slavery, emancipated," became a technical term for those Quraysh who became Muslims at the time of the conquest of Mecca. See ed. Leiden, *Glossarium*, p. CCCXLII.

749. Al-Ṣafā was a low hill to the southeast of the Meccan sanctuary. Together with its neighboring hill to the north, Marwah, it still forms part of the sacred terrain of the pilgrimage as the site of the *sa'y* or ritual running between al-Ṣafā and Marwah to commemorate Hagar's frantic search for water for her son Ismā'īl (Ishmael). See Peters, *The Hajj*, 18–19.

750. For the part of Abū Sufyān's wife Hind in mutilating the bodies of the Muslims slain at the Battle of Uḥud, including the body of Muḥammad's uncle Ḥamzah, see al-Ṭabarī, I, 1415; IH, III, 91–92 (tr. Guillaume, 385–86); and *EI²*, s.v. Hind bt. 'Utba.

"By God, you are imposing something on us that you are not imposing on the men. We will grant it to you." He said, "Do not steal." She said, "By God, I used to take one trifle or another from Abū Sufyān's property, and I do not know whether it was permitted for me or not!" Abū Sufyān, who witnessed what she was saying, said, "As for what you took in the past, you are absolved regarding it." The Messenger of God said, "Surely you are Hind bt. 'Utbah!" She replied: "I am Hind bt. 'Utbah. Forgive what is past—may God forgive you." He said, "Do not commit adultery." She said, "Messenger of God, does a free woman commit adultery?" He said, "Do not kill your children." She said, "We raised them when they were young, and you killed them at the Battle of Badr when they were grown; so you and they know better about it!" 'Umar b. al-Khaṭṭāb laughed immoderately at her words. The [1644]
Messenger of God said, "Do not bring slander that you invent now and henceforth."[751] She said: "Bringing slander is truly ugly. Sometimes it is better to pass over a thing." He said, "Do not disobey me in a good action." She said, "We have not taken our seats in this place intending to disobey you in a good action." The Messenger of God said to 'Umar, "Receive their oath of allegiance." The Messenger of God prayed for their forgiveness, and 'Umar received their oath of allegiance; for the Messenger of God would not shake hands with women or touch a woman, nor would any woman touch him, except one whom God had made permissible to him [through marriage] or one too closely related for him to marry.[752]

---

751. The Arabic: *bayna aydīkunna wa-arjulikunna* "between your hands and your feet" (here translated as "now and henceforth," following the suggestion of the Leiden editor, *Glossarium*, p. DLXX) is obscure. The phrase occurs in Qur'ān 60:12, which contains a series of injunctions that echo the ones that Muḥammad imposes here. Commentators on the verse see the phrase as referring to a woman's foisting of a bastard child or foundling on her husband. The Leiden editor rejects this possibility because the phrase also occurs in masculine contexts. Another possibility is that it means "of your own doing"—hands and feet being a metonymy for the entire person.

752. Normally the oath of allegiance was sealed by a handclasp. Because of Muḥammad's scruples about contact with women, the actual administration of the oath was left to 'Umar. Women whose degree of relationship falls within the forbidden degrees of marriage (*dhāt maḥram*) are considered to be part of a man's extended family, and therefore he and they may mix more freely than may a man and an unrelated woman.

According to Ibn Ḥumayd—Salamah—Ibn Isḥāq—Abān b. Ṣāliḥ (as one scholar informed him): The women's oath of allegiance took place in two ways. A vessel containing water would be set before the Messenger of God. When he proposed the oath to them and they took it, he dipped his hand in the vessel and took it out; then the women dipped their hands in it. Later, he would propose the oath to them; and when they accepted his conditions, he would say, "Go, for I have accepted your oath of allegiance"—and that was all he did.

According to al-Wāqidī: In this year Khirāsh b. Umayyah al-Ka'bī killed Junaydib b. al-Adla' al-Hudhalī (his name, according to Ibn Isḥāq, was Ibn al-Athwa' al-Hudhalī).[753] Khirāsh killed Junaydib because of a blood feud that had occurred during the Time of Ignorance. The Prophet said: "Khirāsh is murderous! Khirāsh is murderous!"—thus reproaching him. The Prophet commanded [the tribe of] Khuzā'ah to pay blood money for the slain man.

According to Ibn Ḥumayd—Salamah—Muḥammad b. Isḥāq—Muḥammad b. Ja'far b. al-Zubayr (Muḥammad b. Isḥāq said, "I know nothing of the latter except that he transmitted traditions to
[1645] me from 'Urwah b. al-Zubayr"), who said:[754] Ṣafwān b. Umayyah left for Juddah to set sail from there to Yemen. 'Umayr b. Wahb said: "Prophet of God, Ṣafwān b. Umayyah, the lord of his people,[755] has left fleeing from you to hurl himself into the sea. Therefore—may God grant you peace—give him a promise of

753. IH, IV, 414–16, gives two variants of the name: first (in the main text of Ibn Isḥāq), Ibn al-Athwa', and then (in a note by Ibn Hishām) Ibn al-Akwa'. Parallel: W, II, 843–46.

754. The story, which is included to illustrate Muḥammad's forbearance and mildness, depends on one's knowing something of the past history of two prominent leaders of Quraysh. In A.H. 2, 'Umayr b. Wahb al-Jumaḥī, whose son Wahb had been captured by the Muslims at the Battle of Badr, went to Medina to assassinate Muḥammad with support from his cousin Ṣafwān b. Umayyah al-Jumaḥī (who agreed to support 'Umayr's family if the attempt came to grief; cf. al-Ṭabarī, I, 1352–54). 'Umayr was so impressed by Muḥammad's foreknowledge of his intentions that he converted to Islam on the spot and returned to Mecca to cause difficulties for the pagans. Ṣafwān, on the other hand, remained a pagan, commanded a Meccan contingent at the Battle of Uḥud in A.H. 3 (cf. Watt and McDonald, *The Foundation*, 105–7 [I, 1384–86]), and later went out of his way to purchase a captive Muslim and have him killed to avenge his father, Umayyah b. Khalaf, who had been killed at Badr (cf. ibid., pp. 144, 147 [I, 1433, 1437]).

755. I.e., the Banū Jumaḥ clan of Quraysh.

safety!" "He shall be safe," replied the Prophet. 'Umayr said, "Messenger of God, give me something whereby he may know your promise of safety." So he gave 'Umayr the turban he had been wearing when he entered Mecca. 'Umayr set out with it and, having overtaken Ṣafwān as he was about to set sail at Juddah, said to him: "Ṣafwān, may my father and mother be your ransom! I beg you for God's sake not to destroy yourself. Here is a promise of safety from the Messenger of God which I have brought to you!" Ṣafwān said: "Woe to you! Go away, and do not talk to me!" 'Umayr said: "Ṣafwān, may my father and mother be your ransom! The most excellent of men, the most righteous, the most forbearing, and best of them is the son of your paternal aunt.[756] His strength is your strength, his honor your honor, and his dominion your dominion." Ṣafwān said, "I am in mortal fear of him." 'Umayr said, "He is too forbearing and generous for that." So 'Umayr brought Ṣafwān back with him and came before the Messenger of God with him. Ṣafwān said, "This man asserted that you have given me a promise of safety." "He spoke truly," said the Messenger of God. Ṣafwān said, "Give me two months to decide what to do." He replied, "You have four months to decide about it."

According to Ibn Ḥumayd—Salamah—Ibn Isḥāq—al-Zuhrī: Umm Ḥakīm bt. al-Ḥārith b. Hishām (the wife of 'Ikrimah b. Abī Jahl) and Fākhitah bt. al-Walīd (the wife of Ṣafwān b. Umayyah) became Muslims. Umm Ḥakīm asked the Messenger of God to
grant a promise of safety to 'Ikrimah b. Abī Jahl, and he did so. She [1646]
then joined 'Ikrimah in Yemen and brought him back. When 'Ikrimah and Ṣafwān became Muslims, the Messenger of God confirmed the two women as wives of the two men as they had been originally.

According to Ibn Ḥumayd—Salamah—Muḥammad b. Isḥāq: When the Messenger of God entered Mecca, Hubayrah b. Abī Wahb al-Makhzūmī and 'Abdallāh b. al-Ziba'rā al-Sahmī fled to Najrān.[757]

---

756. IH, IV, 418: "your paternal uncle."

757. Najrān, near the northern border of Yemen, is about 180 miles south of Mecca.

According to Ibn Ḥumayd—Salamah—Muḥammad b. Isḥāq—Sa'īd b. 'Abd al-Raḥmān b. Ḥassān b. Thābit al-Anṣārī, who said: Ḥassān [b. Thābit] let fly a single verse, no more, against 'Abdallāh b. al-Ziba'rā in Najrān:[758]

May you never be deprived of a man whose hatred has made
you inhabit
Najrān in a life that is scanty and base!

When Ibn al-Ziba'rā learned of this, he returned to the Messenger of God. He said when he became a Muslim:

O Messenger of the King, my tongue
shall repair what I rent when I was perishing;
When I was trying to outstrip Satan in the way of the wind[759]—
and whoever turns aside with Satan shall perish.
My flesh and my bones have believed in my Lord,
and my soul is witness that you are the warner.
[1647] I will restrain from you—there is a clan
descended from Lu'ayy—all of them are in error.[760]

As for Hubayrah b. Abī Wahb, he stayed there as an unbeliever. When he learned that his wife, Umm Hāni' bt. Abī Ṭālib (her given name was Hind), had become a Muslim, he said:[761]

Does Hind miss you? or is she far from asking about you?
Such is absence—her ties and [then] her turning away.

According to Ibn Ḥumayd—Salamah—Ibn Isḥāq, who said: The total number of Muslims present at the conquest of Mecca was 10,000. There were 400 of the Banū Ghifār, 400 from Aslam, 1,003 from Muzaynah, 700 from the Banū Sulaym, and 1,400 from

758. The verse occurs in IH, IV, 418 (tr. Guillaume, 556). See *Dīwān of Ḥassān b. Thābit*, I, 140–41, and II, 214. Guillaume, noting that the version in the *Dīwān* consists of three verses, comments, "It looks almost as though Ḥassān's grandson knew that they [viz. the extra two verses] had been grafted on to Ḥassān's line and resented the impertinence."

759. Variant: "in the way of error."

760. The text of the verse appears to be corrupt. The parallel in IH, IV, 419, reads: "I will drive away from you there a clan descended from Lu'ayy, all of whom are in error." Lu'ayy was an ancestor of most of the clans of Quraysh.

761. The line is the beginning of a longer poem, seven lines of which are quoted by W, II, 849, and eleven lines by IH, IV, 420–21 (tr. Guillaume, 557).

Juhaynah; the remainder were from Quraysh, the Anṣār and their allies, and groups of Arabs from the Banū Tamīm, Qays, and Asad.

According to al-Wāqidī: In this year the Messenger of God married Mulaykah bt. Dāwūd al-Laythiyyah. One of the Prophet's wives came to Mulaykah and said to her, "Are you not ashamed to marry a man who killed your father?" She therefore "took refuge [in God]" from him.[762] She was beautiful and young. The Messenger of God separated from her. He had killed her father the day of the conquest of Mecca.

The Destruction of Idolatrous Shrines

In this year, five nights before the end of Ramaḍān, Khālid b. al- [1648]
Walīd destroyed al-'Uzzā in the lowland of Nakhlah.[763] Al-'Uzzā was an idol of the Banū Shaybān, a subdivision of Sulaym, allies of the Banū Hāshim. The Banū Asad b. 'Abd al-'Uzzā used to say it was their idol. Khālid set out for it, and then he said, "I have destroyed it." [The Messenger of God] said, "Did you see anything?" "No," said Khālid. "Then," he said, "go back and destroy it." So Khālid returned to the idol, destroyed its temple, and broke the idol. The keeper began saying, "Rage, O 'Uzzā, with one of thy fits of rage!"—whereupon a naked, wailing Ethiopian woman came out before him. Khālid killed her and took the jewels that were on her. Then he went to the Messenger of God and gave him a report of what had happened. "That was al-'Uzzā," he said, "and al-'Uzzā will never be worshiped [again]."

According to Ibn Ḥumayd—Salamah—Ibn Isḥāq, who said:[764] The Messenger of God sent Khālid b. al-Walīd to [deal with] al-'Uzzā, who was at Nakhlah. She was a temple venerated by the tribes of Quraysh, Kinānah, and all Muḍar.[765] Her keepers were of

---

762. Arabic: *ista'ādhat minhu.* This apparently alludes to pre-Islamic practice whereby a wife could repudiate her husband before the consummation of marriage by pronouncing the words *a'ūdhu billāhi minka,* "I seek refuge with God from you." For a discussion of three instances reported by Ibn Sa'd in which arranged tribal marriages were terminated by this formula, see Stowasser, *Women in the Qur'an, Traditions, and Interpretation,* 111–12.

763. Parallel: W, III, 873–74. 25 Ramaḍān of A.H. 8 fell on 16 January 630. Nakhlah is close to Mecca, on the way to al-Ṭā'if. On the cult of the goddess al-'Uzzā, see *EI*[1], s.v. al-'Uzzā; Fahd, *Panthéon,* 163–82.

764. Parallel: IH, IV, 436–37 (tr. Guillaume, 565).

765. See note 257, above.

the Banū Shaybān, a division of the Banū Sulaym, allies of the Banū Hāshim. When the master of the temple heard that Khālid was coming to deal with al-'Uzzā, he hung his sword on her and climbed the mountain near which al-'Uzzā was located. As he went up he said:

O 'Uzzā, attack with an attack that hits no unvital place,
against Khālid! Throw down thy veil, and gird up thy train!
O 'Uzzā, if today thou wilt not slay Khālid,
bear a swift punishment, or become a Christian!

Having reached al-'Uzzā, Khālid destroyed her and returned to the Messenger of God.

According to al-Wāqidī:[766] In this year [the idol] Suwā' was destroyed.[767] He was at Ruhāṭ[768] and belonged to [the tribe of]
[1649] Hudhayl. He was a stone. The person who destroyed it was 'Amr b. al-'Āṣ. When he reached the idol, the keeper asked him, "What do you want?" 'Amr replied, "To destroy Suwā'." The keeper said, "You cannot destroy him." 'Amr b. al-'Āṣ said to him, "You are still in falsehood." 'Amr destroyed him but found nothing in his treasury. Then 'Amr said to the keeper, "What do you think?" He replied, "I have become a Muslim, by God."

In this year [the idol] Manāt was destroyed by Sa'd b. Zayd al-Ashhalī at al-Mushallal.[769] It belonged to [the tribes of] al-Aws and al-Khazraj.

The Expedition against the Banū Jadhīmah

In this year the expedition of Khālid b. al-Walīd against the Banū Jadhīmah took place.[770] The following is an account of events concerning him and them according to Ibn Ḥumayd—Salamah—Muḥammad b. Isḥāq, who said:[771] The Messenger of God had sent

---

766. Parallel: W, II, 870.

767. On the cult of the Suwā', see Fahd, *Panthéon*, 155–56.

768. Ruhāṭ was a place three nights from Mecca in the direction of Medina; see Yāqūt, *Mu'jam al-buldān*, IV, 341.

769. On al-Mushallal see note 600, above. Manāt, one of the ancient deities of the Semitic pantheon, was a goddess of destiny and fate. See *EI²*, s.v. Manāt; Fahd, *Panthéon*, 123–28.

770. See *EI²*, s.v. Djadhīma b. 'Āmir.

771. Parallels: W, III, 875–84; IH, IV, 428–36 (tr. Guillaume, 561–65).

out detachments to the areas around Mecca to summon people to God; he did not command the detachments to fight. One of those whom he sent out was Khālid b. al-Walīd, whom he commanded to travel through the lowlands of Tihāmah to summon people; he did not send Khālid to fight. Khālid, however, mistreated the Banū Jadhīmah and killed some of them.

According to Ibn Ḥumayd—Salamah—Muḥammad b. Isḥāq—Ḥakīm b. Ḥakīm b. 'Abbād b. Ḥunayf[772]—Abū Ja'far Muḥammad b. 'Alī b. Ḥusayn,[773] who said: After he conquered Mecca, the Messenger of God sent out Khālid b. al-Walīd to summon people; he did not send him to fight. With him were Arabs of the tribes of Sulaym, Mudlij, and other tribes. They halted at al-Ghumayṣā', a watering place of the Banū Jadhīmah b. 'Āmir b. 'Abd Manāt b. Kinānah, by their main body. Now the Banū Jadhīmah in the Time [1650] of Ignorance had killed 'Awf b. 'Abd 'Awf (the father of 'Abd al-Raḥmān b. 'Awf) and al-Fākih b. al-Mughīrah.[774] The two had come from Yemen as merchants; when they had halted among the Banū Jadhīmah, the latter had killed them and taken their possessions. When Islam came and the Messenger of God sent out Khālid b. al-Walīd, Khālid traveled and halted at that watering place. When the Banū Jadhīmah saw him, they took up their weapons. Khālid said to them, "Put down your weapons, for the people have become Muslims."

According to Ibn Ḥumayd—Salamah—Muḥammad b. Isḥāq—a certain scholar—a man from the Banū Jadhīmah, who said: When Khālid commanded us to put down our weapons, one of our men, named Jaḥdam, said: "Alas for you, Banū Jadhīmah! It is Khālid. By God, after you lay down your weapons, it will be nothing but leather manacles, and after leather manacles it will be nothing but the smiting of necks. By God, I will never lay down my weapon!" Some of his fellow tribesmen took him and said: "Jaḥdam, do you

---

772. Ḥakīm b. Ḥakīm b. 'Abbād b. Ḥunayf al-Anṣārī al-Awsī is listed without dates in Ibn Ḥajar, *Tahdhīb*, 448–49.

773. Abū Ja'far Muḥammad b. 'Alī b. Ḥusayn b. 'Alī b. Abī Ṭālib, surnamed Muḥammad al-Bāqir, was the fifth imam of the Shī'ah. He was born in 57/676 and died between 114/732 and 126/743. See Ibn Ḥajar, *Tahdhīb*, IX, 350–52; Momen, *Introduction to Shi'i Islam*, 37–38.

774. 'Abd al-Raḥmān b. 'Awf was a Meccan who became a Muslim, emigrated to Medina, and fought at Badr. See al-Ṭabarī, I, 1325–27. Al-Fākih b. al-Mughīrah, as mentioned below, was the paternal uncle of Khālid b. al-Walīd.

want to cause our blood to be shed? The people have become Muslims. The war has ended, and the people are at peace." The people did not desist from him until they had taken away his weapon and had laid down their weapons because of what Khālid had said.

After the Banū Jadhīmah had laid down their weapons, Khālid ordered that their hands should be tied behind their backs; then he put them to the sword, killing some of them. When the news reached the Messenger of God, he raised his hands to heaven and said, "O God, I declare to Thee that I am innocent of what Khālid b. al-Walīd has done." Then he summoned 'Alī b. Abī Ṭālib and said, "'Alī, go out to these people, look into what has happened to them, and make an end to the ways of the Time of Ignorance." 'Alī set out and came to them; with him he had money that the Mes-
[1651] senger of God had sent with him. He paid the Banū Jadhīmah blood money and compensation for their property that had been taken, down to a dog's water bowl; there remained no life or property for which he did not pay compensation. Because he had some money left over, 'Alī said to them when he finished, "Do any of you still have lives or property for which you have not been compensated?" "No," they replied. He said, "Then I give you the remainder of this money as a precaution for the Messenger of God with regard to what he does not know and you do not know." Having done this, he returned to the Messenger of God and gave him a report. "You have done right and well," he said. Then the Messenger of God turned toward the *qiblah*, standing and raising his hands until the whiteness under his shoulders could be seen, saying three times, "O God, I declare to Thee that I am innocent of what Khālid b. al-Walīd has done."

According to Ibn Isḥāq: Someone who excuses Khālid said that Khālid said: "I did not fight until 'Abdallāh b. Ḥudhāfah al-Sahmī commanded me to do so. He said, 'The Messenger of God has commanded you to kill them[775] because of their resistance to Islam.'"

When they laid down their weapons, Jaḥdam, seeing what Khālid was doing to the Banū Jadhīmah, said to them: "Banū Jadhīmah, all is lost! I warned you of what you have fallen into."

---

775. The parallel in IH, IV, 430 (tr. Guillaume, 562), reads "to fight them."

According to Ibn Ḥumayd—Salamah—Ibn Isḥāq—'Abdallāh b. Abī Salamah,[776] who said: According to the report that I have received, an exchange took place over this between Khālid b. al-Walīd and 'Abd al-Raḥmān b. 'Awf. 'Abd al-Raḥmān said to Khālid, "You acted in the time of Islam according to the ways of the Time of Ignorance." Khālid replied, "I only took vengeance for your father." 'Abd al-Raḥmān b. 'Awf said: "You are lying. I have already killed my father's murderer. You only took vengeance for [1652] your paternal uncle, al-Fākih b. al-Mughīrah." This developed into a quarrel between them. When it was reported to the Messenger of God, he said: "Take it easy, Khālid. Leave my companions alone; for, by God, though you had a mountain of gold the size of Uḥud and spent it for the sake of God, you would in no wise become the equal of one of my companions."

According to Sa'īd b. Yaḥyā al-Umawi—his father [Yaḥyā b. Sa'īd]; and according to Ibn Ḥumayd—Salamah; both accounts coming from Ibn Isḥāq—Ya'qūb b. 'Utbah b. al-Mughīrah b. al-Akhnas b. Sharīq—Ibn Shihāb al-Zuhrī—Ibn 'Abdallāh b. Abī Ḥadrad al-Aslamī—his father, 'Abdallāh b. Abī Ḥadrad, who said: I was among Khālid's horsemen that day. One of their young men—he was among the prisoners, his hands were tied to his neck with a rope, and some women were gathered not far from him—said to me, "Young man!" "Yes," I said. He said: "Will you take hold of this rope and lead me by it to these women, so that I can entrust them with a needful matter of business? Then you can bring me back to do as you all please with me." I said, "By God, what you have asked is a small thing." I took hold of his rope and led him by it until I had brought him to stand near them. He said, "Farewell, Ḥubayshah, as life runs out!"[777]

Tell me: when I sought you and found you [1653]
at Ḥalyah,[778] or found you at al-Khawāniq,
Was it not right for a lover to be rewarded

---

776. 'Abdallāh b. Abī Salamah al-Mājishūn al-Taymī, a *mawlā* of the al-Munkadir family, died in 106/724–25. See Ibn Ḥajar, *Tahdhīb*, V, 243.

777. The poem, with variants, may also be found in W, III, 879; IH, IV, 433–34; and Ibn Sa'd, *Ṭabaqāt*, II, 107. In the first line, "you" (plural) refers to the tribe of the beloved.

778. Ḥalyah is a valley in Tihāmah. Its upper part belonged to Hudhayl, its lower part to Kinānah. Cf. Yāqūt, *Mu'jam al-buldān*, III, 331.

who tasked himself to travel in the nights and in the
noonday heat?
No guilt was mine when I said, our people being together,
"Requite with affection before some misfortune occurs!"
Requite with affection before remoteness becomes great;
before the commander takes the departing loved one far
away.
For I have divulged no secret lodged with me;
neither has anything pleased my eye after your face.
Now the misfortune that has befallen the people occupies my
mind,
and there is no memory except that of a tender lover.

She replied, "And you—may you be made to live ten and seven years uninterrupted and eight right after them!" Then I took him away. He was brought forward and beheaded.

According to Ibn Ḥumayd—Salamah—Ibn Isḥāq—Abū Firās b. Abī Sunbulah al-Aslamī—some of the old men [of the Banū Aslam]—some who were present there, who said: She went up to him when he was beheaded, and she threw herself down on him and kept kissing him until she died beside him.

According to Ibn Ḥumayd—Salamah—Ibn Isḥāq—al-Zuhrī—'Ubaydallāh b. 'Abdallāh b. 'Utbah b. Mas'ūd, who said: The Mes-
[1654] senger of God stayed in Mecca after its conquest for fifteen nights, shortening the prayers.[779]

According to Ibn Isḥāq: The conquest of Mecca took place ten nights before the end of the month of Ramaḍān in the year 8.[780]

---

779. Arabic: *yaqṣuru al-ṣalāh*, normally applied to the abbreviation of prayers allowed when one is on a journey (cf. Lane, *Lexicon*, VII, 2533). The implication is that Muḥammad did not consider his residence in Mecca permanent and intended to return to Medina.

780. I.e., 20 Ramaḍān (11 January 630).

Bibliography of Cited Works

I. Primary Sources: Texts and Translations

'Abdallah b. Rawāḥah. *Dīwān 'Abdallāh b. Rawāḥah al-Anṣārī al-Khazrajī.* Edited by Ḥasan Muḥammad Bājūrah. Cairo, 1972.

Aghānī. See al-Iṣbahānī.

al-Bukhārī, Muḥammad b. Ismā'īl. *Ṣaḥīḥ al-Bukhārī.* 9 vols. *Būlāq,* 1311–12/1893–94.

al-Dhahabī. *Al-Moschtabih* [i.e., *al-Mushtabih*]. Edited by P. de Jong. Leiden, 1881.

———. *Tadhkirat al-ḥuffāẓ.* 4 vols. Hyderabad, 1955–58.

Ḥassān b. Thābit. *Dīwān of Ḥassān ibn Thābit.* Edited by Walid N. 'Arafat. 2 vols. London, 1971.

Ibn al-Athīr, 'Izz al-Dīn. *Kitāb al-kāmil fī al-ta'rīkh.* Edited by C. J. Tornberg. 12 vols. Leiden, 1870–71.

Ibn Ḥajar al-'Asqalānī, Aḥmad b. 'Alī. *al-Iṣābah fī tamyīz al-Ṣaḥābah.* Edited by 'Alī Muḥammad al-Bijāwī. 8 vols. Cairo, [1970].

———. *Tahdhīb al-tahdhīb.* 12 vols. Hyderabad, 1325–27/1907–9.

Ibn Hishām, Abū Muḥammad b. 'Abd al-Malik. *Sīrat Rasūl Allāh.* Edited by Muṣṭafā al-Saqqā, Ibrāhīm al-Abyārī, and 'Abd al-Ḥafīẓ Shalabī. 4 vols. Cairo, 1936. Reprinted Beirut, n.d. Translated by A. Guillaume as *The Life of Muhammad: A Translation of . . .* Sīrat Rasūl Allāh. London, 1955. Reprinted Karachi, 1967.

Ibn Manẓūr, Jamāl al-Dīn Abū al-Faḍl Muḥammad b. Mukarram al-Anṣārī. *Lisān al-'arab.* 6 vols. Cairo, 1981.

Ibn Sa'd, Abū 'Abdallāh Muḥammad. *Kitāb al-ṭabaqāt al-kabīr.* Edited by Eduard Sachau. 9 vols. Leiden, 1904–40. Reprinted Beirut, 1978.

al-Iṣbahānī, Abū al-Faraj 'Alī b. al-Ḥusayn. *Kitāb al-aghānī.* Edited by Ibrāhīm al-Abyārī. 31 vols. Cairo, 1969.

al-Khaṭīb al-Baghdādī, Abu Bakr Aḥmad b. ʿAlī. *Taʾrīkh Baghdād.* 14 vols. Cairo, 1931.

Lisān. See Ibn Manẓūr.

al-Maydānī, Abū al-Faḍl Aḥmad b. Muḥammad. *Majmaʿ amthāl al-ʿArab.* Cairo, 1959. Translated by G. W. Freytag as *Arabum Proverbia.* 2 vols. Bonn, 1838–43.

Muslim b. al-Ḥajjāj. *Ṣaḥīḥ Muslim.* Edited by Muḥammad Fuʾād al-Bāqī. 5 vols. Cairo, 1374–75/1955–56.

Qurʾān. Verses are numbered according to the Egyptian national edition. The translation, with modifications, is based on A. J. Arberry, *The Koran Interpreted* (London, 1955).

al-Samhūdī, ʿAlī b. ʿAbdallāh. *Khulāṣat al-wafāʾ bi-akhbār dār al-muṣṭafā.* Damascus, 1392/1972.

al-Ṭabarī, Abū Jaʿfar Muḥammad b. Jarīr. *Jāmiʿ al-bayān fī tafsīr al-qurʾān.* 30 vols. Būlāq, 1323/1905. Reprinted Beirut, 1398/1978.

———. *Taʾrīkh al-rusul wa-al-mulūk.* Edited by M. J. de Goeje et al. under the title Annales quos scripsit Abu Djafar . . . at-Tabari. 13 vols. and 2 vols. *Indices* and *Introductio, glossarium, addenda et emendanda.* Leiden, 1879–1901. Also edited by Muḥammad Abū al-Faḍl Ibrāhīm. 10 vols. Cairo, 1960–69.

al-Wāqidī, Muḥammad b. ʿUmar. *Kitāb al-maghāzī.* Edited by Marsden Jones. 3 vols. London, 1966.

Yāqūt, Abū ʿAbdallāh Yāqūt b. ʿAbdallāh al-Ḥamawī al-Rūmī. *Muʿjam al-buldān.* Edited by Muḥammad Amīn al-Khānijī and Aḥmad b. al-Amīn al-Shanqīṭī. 8 vols. Cairo, 1323/1906.

al-Zamakhsharī, Jār Allāh Abū al-Qāsim Maḥmūd b. ʿUmar. *Asās al-balāghah.* Beirut, 1399/1979.

II. Secondary Sources and Reference Works

Abbott, Nabia. *Aishah the Beloved of Muhammad.* Chicago, 1942.

Arafat, W. "A Controversial Incident and the Related Poem in the Life of Ḥassān b. Thābit." BSOAS 17 (1955): 197–205.

Bell, Richard. *Bell's Introduction to the Qurʾān.* Revised and enlarged by W. Montgomery Watt. Edinburgh, 1970.

Bellamy, James A. "Some Proposed Emendations to the Text of the Koran." *Journal of the American Oriental Society* 113 (1993): 562–73.

Blachère, Régis, et al. *Dictionnaire arabe-français-anglais.* 4 vols. Paris, 1964–.

Bravmann, M. M. *The Spiritual Background of Early Islam: Studies in Ancient Arab Concepts.* Leiden, 1972.

Burton, John. *An Introduction to the Ḥadīth*. Edinburgh, 1994.

The Cambridge History of Iran. Vol. III/1. *The Seleucid, Parthian, and Sasanian Periods*. Edited by Ehsan Yarshater. Cambridge, 1983.

Christensen, Arthur. *L'Iran sous les Sassanides*. 2nd edition. Copenhagen, 1944.

Dozy, R. P. A. *Supplément aux dictionnaires arabes*. 2 vols. Leiden, 1881. Reprinted Beirut, 1968.

Duri, A. A. *The Rise of Historical Writing among the Arabs*. Edited and translated by Lawrence I. Conrad. Princeton, N.J., 1983.

Encyclopaedia of Islam. 1st edition. 4 vols. and Supplement. Leiden, 1913–42.

Encyclopaedia of Islam. 2nd edition. 8 vols. and Supplement. Leiden, 1960–.

Fahd, Toufic. *Le panthéon de l'Arabie centrale a la veille de l'hégire*. Paris, 1968.

Freytag, G. W. *Arabum Proverbia*. See al-Maydānī in Section I.

Goldziher, Ignaz. *Abhandlungen zur arabischen Philologie*. 2 vols. Leiden, 1896–99.

———. *Muslim Studies*. Translation of *Muhammedanische Studien* [1889–90]. Edited by S. M. Stern. Vol. I, Albany, N.Y., 1967. Vol II, Chicago, 1971.

von Grunebaum, Gustav E. *Muhammadan Festivals*. Chicago, 1951. Reprinted London, 1976.

Hamidullah, Muhammad. *The Battlefields of the Prophet Muhammad*. Revised edition. Hyderabad, 1392/1973.

Lane, Edward William. *An Arabic-English Lexicon*. London, 1863–93. Reprinted Beirut, 1968.

Le Strange, G. *Palestine under the Moslems*. London, 1890.

Lings, Martin. *Muhammad: His Life Based on the Earliest Sources*. New York, 1983.

Momen, Moojan. *An Introduction to Shi'i Islam: The History and Doctrines of Twelver Shi'ism*. New Haven, Conn., 1985.

Ostrogorsky, Georg. *History of the Byzantine State*. Translated by Joan Hussey. Revised edition. New Brunswick, N.J., 1969.

Payne Smith, R. *A Compendious Syriac Dictionary*. Oxford, 1903.

Peters, Francis E. *The Hajj: The Muslim Pilgrimage to Mecca and the Holy Places*. Princeton, N.J., 1994.

Poonawala, Ismail. *The Last Years of the Prophet: The Formation of the State*. Vol. 9 of *The History of al-Ṭabarī*. Albany, N.Y., 1990.

Reckendorf, H. *Arabische Syntax*. Heidelberg, 1921.

Rosenthal, Franz. *General Introduction and From the Creation to the Flood*. Vol. 1 of *The History of al-Ṭabarī*. Albany, N.Y., 1989.

Schacht, Joseph. *An Introduction to Islamic Law.* Oxford, 1964.
———. *The Origins of Muhammadan Jurisprudence.* Oxford, 1950.
Sezgin, Fuat. *Geschichte des arabischen Schrifttums.* Vol. 1. *Qur'ān-wissenschaften, Ḥadīṯ, Geschichte, Fiqh, Dogmatik, Mystik bis ca. 430 H.* Leiden, 1967. Vol. 2. *Poesie bis ca. 430 H.* Leiden, 1975.
Spellberg, D. A. *Politics, Gender, and the Islamic Past: The Legacy of 'A'isha bint Abi Bakr.* New York, 1994.
Stowasser, Barbara Freyer. *Women in the Qur'an, Traditions, and Interpretation.* New York and Oxford, 1994.
Watt, W. Montgomery. "His Name is Ahmad." *Muslim World* 43 (1953): 110–17.
———. *Muhammad at Mecca.* Oxford, 1953.
———. *Muhammad at Medina.* Oxford, 1956. Reprinted Karachi, 1981.
——— and M. V. McDonald. *The Foundation of the Community: Muhammad at al-Madina.* Vol. 7 of *The History of al-Ṭabarī.* Albany, N.Y., 1987.
Wensinck, A. J. *Concordance et indices de la tradition musulmane.* 8 vols. Leiden, 1936–88.
Wright, W. *A Grammar of the Arabic Language.* 3rd edition. Cambridge, 1896–98. Reprinted, 1967.
Wüstenfeld, F., and E. Mahler. *Vergleichungs-Tabellen der muhammedanischen und christlichen Zeitrechnung.* Leipzig, 1926. Arabic translation by A. M. Magued; Cairo, 1980.

Index

The index contains all names of persons, places, tribes, and other groups, as well as technical terms that occur in the introduction and the text (but only selected items from the footnotes). A separate index of Qur'ānic passages follows the general index.

*Names of places have been marked [P], names of tribes [T], and names of persons who appear only in chains of transmission (*isnāds*)*.*

The definite article al-, *the abbreviations* b. *(*ibn, *son of) and* bt. *(*bint, *daughter of), and everything in parentheses are disregarded for the purposes of alphabetization. Where a name occurs in both the text and the footnotes on the same page, only the page number is given.*

A

al-'Abalāt [T] 80
Abān [b. Yazīd] al-'Aṭṭār* 174
Abān b. Sa'īd b. al-'Āṣ 82
Abān b. Ṣāliḥ* 136, 184
'Abāyah b. Mālik 156
'Abbād b. 'Abdallāh b. al-Zubayr* 22, 58, 156
'Abbād b. Bishr b. Waqsh b. Zughbah b. Za'ūrā al-Ashhalī 49, 52
'Abbād b. Julandā al-Azdī 100, 142
al-'Abbās b. 'Abd al-Muṭṭalib xiii, 127–28, 136, 168, 171–74
al-'Abbās b. 'Abdallāh b. Ma'bad b. al-'Abbās b. 'Abd al-Muṭṭalib* 168
'Abd al-Ashhal (of al-Aws), Banū [T] 15, 34, 39, 49, 50, 61
'Abd al-Ḥamīd b. Bayān* 83
'Abd al-Malik b. Marwān (caliph) 104, 174
'Abd Manāf (of Quraysh), Banū [T] 172
'Abd al-Qays, Banū [T] 99
'Abd al-Raḥmān b. Abzā* 71
'Abd al-Raḥmān b. 'Amr b. Sa'd b. Mu'ādh* 34
'Abd al-Raḥmān b. 'Awf 87, 95, 189, 191
'Abd al-Raḥmān b. Ḥassān b. Thābit 66, 131
'Abd al-Raḥmān b. Ḥazn b. Abī Wahb 97
'Abd al-Raḥmān b. 'Uyaynah 44, 46
'Abd al-Raḥmān b. Yazīd b. Jāriyah 95
'Abd al-Raḥmān b. Zayd* 4
'Abd al-Ṣamad b. 'Abd al-Wārith* 174

'Abd b. Tha'labah, Banū [T], raid on 132, 133
'Abd al-Wāḥid b. Abī 'Awn*; see Ibn Abī 'Awn
'Abd al-Wāḥid b. Ḥamzah* 67
'Abd al-Wārith b. 'Abd al-Ṣamad b. 'Abd al-Wārith* 174
'Abdallāh b. 'Abbās b. 'Abd al-Muṭṭalib* 70, 89, 100, 104, 134, 135, 136, 168, 171
'Abdallāh b. 'Abdallāh b. Ubayy b. Salūl 54–55
'Abdallāh b. Abī Awfā* 70
'Abdallāh b. Abī Bakr b. Muḥammad b. 'Amr b. Ḥazm* 6, 43, 51, 58, 72, 78, 82, 96, 111, 117, 128, 129, 132, 135, 138, 139, 146, 155, 158, 159, 177
'Abdallāh b. Abī Ḥadrad al-Aslamī 149–51, 191
'Abdallāh b. Abī Najīḥ* 89, 136, 176, 177
'Abdallāh b. Abī Salamah* 191
'Abdallāh b. Abī Umayyah b. al-Mughīrah 168–69
'Abdallāh b. 'Āmir al-Aslamī* 1
'Abdallāh b. 'Amr b. 'Awf al-Muzanī* 10
'Abdallāh b. Buraydah al-Aslamī* 119, 120
'Abdallāh b. al-Ḥasan* 121
'Abdallāh b. Ḥudhāfah b. Qays b. 'Adī b. Sa'd al-Sahmī 98, 110–11, 190
'Abdallāh b. Idrīs* 104
'Abdallāh b. Ja'far b. Abī Ṭālib 159
'Abdallāh b. Ja'far al-Zuhrī* 95, 133
'Abdallāh b. Khaṭal (of Banū Taym b. Ghālib) 179, 180
'Abdallāh b. Mas'adah b. Ḥakamah b. Mālik b. Badr al-Fazārī 96
'Abdallāh b. (al-)Mubārak* 69, 74, 88
'Abdallāh b. Nāfi'* 137
'Abdallāh b. Rabāḥ al-Anṣārī* 158
'Abdallāh b. Rawāḥah (of Banū al-Ḥārith b. al-Khazraj) xviii, 15, 66, 129, 130, 135, 152–58
'Abdallāh b. Sa'd b. Abī Sarḥ b. Ḥubayb b. Jadhīmah b. Naṣr b. Mālik b. Ḥisl b. 'Āmir b. Lu'ayy 178, 179
'Abdallāh b. Sahl b. 'Abd al-Raḥmān b. Sahl (Abū Laylā) al-Ḥārithī al-Anṣārī* 19, 118
'Abdallāh b. Sahl al-Ḥārithī 129
'Abdallāh b. Suhayl b. 'Amr 87
'Abdallāh b. Ubayy b. Salūl xi, 33, 52–55, 61
'Abdallāh b. 'Umar b. al-Khaṭṭāb* 137
'Abdallāh b. Wahb* 4, 83, 147
'Abdallāh b. al-Ziba'rā al-Sahmī 185–86
Abnā' (Persian residents of Yemen) [T] 114
Abrahah (slave girl of Negus) 109–10
al-Abṭaḥ [P] 181
Abū 'Āmir al-'Aqadī* 44, 69, 79, 83, 97
Abū 'Ammār al-Wā'ilī 7
Abū al-'Āṣ b. al-Rabī' 93–94, 131
Abū 'Ayyāsh; see 'Ubayd b. Zayd
Abū Ayyūb Khālid b. Zayd 63–64
Abū Bakr b. Abī Quḥāfah 37, 40, 60, 62–64, 76, 85, 87, 97, 119, 120, 130, 131, 146, 164, 165
Abū Barzah al-Aslamī 180
Abū Baṣīr 'Utbah b. Asīd b. Jāriyah 90–91
Abū Dāwūd (Sulaymān b. Dāwūd b. al-Jārūd al-Ṭayālisī)* 70
Abū al-Faḍl (*kunyah* of al-'Abbās b. 'Abd al-Muṭṭalib, q.v.) 127, 172, 174
Abū Firās b. Abī Sunbulah al-Aslamī* 192
Abū Ḥanẓalah (*kunyah* of Abū Sufyān b. Ḥarb, q.v.) 172
Abū Hurayrah* 13, 124
Abū Isḥāq ('Amr b. 'Abdallāh al-Hamdānī)* 54, 88
Abū Ja'far*; see al-Ṭabarī
Abū Ja'far Muḥammad b. 'Alī b. Ḥusayn* 189
Abū Jahl ('Amr b. Hishām b. al-Mughīrah) 89
Abū Jahm b. Ḥudhāfah b. Ghānim al-Khuzā'ī 92
Abū Jamrah al-Ḍuba'ī* 148
Abū Jandal b. Suhayl b. 'Amr 87, 91
Abū Kabshah, son of (name for Muḥam-

mad) 103
Abū Kurayb (Muḥammad b. al-'Alā' b. Kurayb)* xx, 54, 120, 171
Abū Laylā*; see 'Abdallāh b. Sahl b. 'Abd al-Raḥmān
Abū Lubābah b. 'Abd al-Mundhir 29, 31–32
Abū al-Qa'qā' b. 'Abdallāh b. Abī Ḥadrad al-Aslamī* 151
Abū al-Qāsim (*kunyah* of Muḥammad the Prophet, q.v.) 141
Abū Qatādah al-Ḥārith b. Rib'ī al-Anṣārī 46, 47, 49, 50, 149–51, 158
Abū Rāfi' (*mawlā* of the Prophet) 121, 136–37
Abū Ruhm Kulthūm b. Ḥuṣayn b. Khalaf al-Ghifārī 168
Abū Ruhm b. al-Muṭṭalib b. 'Abd Manāf 60
Abū Sa'īd al-Khudrī* 34
Abū Salamah b. 'Abd al-Raḥmān b. 'Awf 95, 111
Abū Sinān b. Miḥṣan b. Ḥurthān (of Banū Asad b. Khuzaymah) 40
Abū Sinān b. Wahb al-Asadī 83
Abū Sufyān b. Ḥarb xix, 8, 24, 26, 79, 82, 91, 100, 102–4, 110, 163–65, 168, 171–75, 183
Abū Sufyān b. al-Ḥārith b. 'Abd al-Muṭṭalib 168–70
Abū Sufyān b. Sa'īd b. al-Mughīrah al-Thaqafī* 70
Abū Sulaymān (*kunyah* of Khālid b. al-Walīd, q.v.) 145
Abū Ṭalḥah b. Sahl 66
Abū Tumaylah (Yaḥyā b. Wāḍiḥ)* 156
Abū 'Ubaydah b. al-Jarrāḥ 93, 146–48, 177
Abū Usāmah al-Jushamī 22
Abū Yazīd (*kunyah* of Suhayl b. 'Amr, q.v.) 178
Abū al-Zubayr (Muḥammad b. Muslim b. Tadrus al-Asadī)* 69, 148
'Aḍal [T] 13 n. 74, 16
Adam (first man) 108, 181
al-'Aḍbā' (camel of Muḥammad) 47
Adhākhir [P] 177
'Adī b. Ka'b (of Quraysh), Banū [T] 82, 172
'Adī b. al-Najjār, Banū [T] 38
adoption xiii, 2 n. 5, 3
Aḥābīsh [T] 13, 78, 81, 176
ahl al-bayt (Prophet's household) 10
Aḥmad (name for the Prophet) 106
Aḥmad b. 'Abd al-Raḥmān* 147
aḥzāb (allied clans, parties who leagued together) xiv, 10, 12, 144, 181
'Ā'idh (or Mu'ādh) b. Mā'iṣ b. Qays b. Khaldah 49
'Ā'ishah bt. Abī Bakr (wife of the Prophet) 3, 19–21, 29, 30, 36, 39, 40, 56, 57, 165; lie/slander against xii–xiii, xv–xvi, 57–67
al-'Ajlān (of Balī), Banū [T] 157
al-Akhnas b. Sharīq b. 'Amr b. Wahb al-Thaqafī 90
al-Akhram al-Asadī 46
akkārūn (husbandmen), sin of 104
al-'Alā' b. al-Ḥaḍramī 99, 142
Alexandria [P] 98 n. 422, 100
'Alī b. Abī Ṭālib 18–19, 28, 41, 56, 61–62, 80, 85–88, 95, 119–21, 164–65, 167, 176–77, 181, 190
'Alī b. Mujāhid* 51
allegiance, oath of (*bay'ah*) 70, 82–84, 109, 145, 175, 176, 181–84; of women 38; see also women
'Alqamah b. Qays al-Nakha'ī* 21 n. 104, 85
'Alqamah b. Waqqāṣ al-Laythī* 21, 29, 34, 35, 39, 40, 58
Amaj [P] 43, 168
al-A'mash (Sulaymān b. Mihrān al-Asadī)* 70
'Āmir (uncle of Salamah b. al-Akwa') 46, 80, 84
'Āmir b. 'Abdallāh b. al-Zubayr* 159
'Āmir b. al-Aḍbaṭ al-Ashja'ī 151
'Āmir b. Lu'ayy (of Quraysh), Banū [T] 18, 20, 75, 79 n. 340, 84, 87, 90, 91, 98, 99
'Āmir b. Ṣa'ṣa'ah, Banū [T] 170; raid on 143
'Āmir b. Sharāḥīl b. 'Amr al-Sha'bī* 83

'Amr b. 'Abd Wudd b. Abī Qays (of Banū 'Āmir b. Lu'ayy) 18–19
'Amr b. 'Alqamah* 20, 29, 34, 39
'Amr b. al-'Āṣ 99, 142–47, 188
'Amr b. Awbār 50
'Amr b. 'Awf (clan of al-Aws), Banū [T] 15, 16, 31
'Amr b. 'Awf al-Muzanī* 10
'Amr b. Dīnār* 147–48
'Amr b. al-Ḥārith 147, 148
'Amr b. Ka'b al-Ghifārī 143
'Amr b. Murrah* 70
'Amr b. Qurayẓah, Banū [T] 37, 39
'Amr b. Sālim al-Khuzā'ī 162–63
'Amr b. Su'dā al-Quraẓī 32–33
'Amr b. Umayyah al-Ḍamrī 98, 108, 144
'Amrah bt. 'Abd al-Raḥmān* 58
angels 26 n. 121, 27, 29, 159; *see also* Gabriel
Anṣār [T] 10, 47, 49, 50, 51, 52, 53, 62, 68, 74, 132, 146, 147, 156, 158, 168, 174, 175, 179, 187
al-Aqra' b. Ḥābis al-Tamīmī 171
Arabian peninsula [P] xi, xviii, 130
Arabs xvii–xviii, 17–19, 60, 65, 67, 68, 72, 76, 84, 98, 101, 107, 165, 177, 187, 189; auxiliaries of Byzantines xviii, 153, 154, 156, 159
'Arafah [P] 161
al-Arāk [P] 171
Arhā b. al-Aṣḥam b. Abjar (son of Negus) 109
al-'Arj [P] 171
Army of Commanders (*jaysh al-umarā'*) 158
al-'Āṣ b. Wā'il (father of 'Amr b. al-Āṣ), mother of 146
Asad b. 'Abd al-'Uzzā (clan of Quraysh), Banū [T] 98, 187
Asad b. Khuzaymah, Banū [T] 40, 49, 83, 98, 107, 187
Asad b. 'Ubayd (of Banū Hadl) 32
al-Aṣbagh b. 'Amr al-Kalbī (king of Dūmat al-Jandal) 95
al-Aṣfar (Greeks), Banū [T] 103
al-Aṣḥam b. Abjar (Negus) 108–9
Ashja' [T] 8
Asīd b. Sa'yah; *see* Usayd b. Sa'yah
'Āṣim b. Thābit b. Abī al-Aqlaḥ 94
'Āṣim b. 'Umar b. al-Khaṭṭāb 94–95
'Āṣim b. 'Umar b. Qatādah* 6, 17, 20, 34, 43, 49, 51, 55, 138
Aslam [T] 70, 72, 74, 117, 142, 173, 177, 186, 192
al-Aswad b. Razn al-Dīlī 160–61
al-Aswad b. Shaybān* 157
'Aṭā' b. Abī Rabāḥ* 136
'Ātikah bt. 'Abd al-Muṭṭalib 168 n. 701, 169
Awbār 50
'Awf b. 'Abd 'Awf (father of 'Abd al-Raḥmān b. 'Awf) 189, 191
'Awf b. Abī Jamīlah al-A'rābī* 119
'Awf b. al-Khazraj, Banū [T] 52
al-Aws [T] xv, 15, 33, 61, 188
Aws b. Qayẓī (of Banū Ḥārithah b. al-Ḥārith) 16
Ayyūb b. 'Abd al-Raḥmān b. 'Abdallāh b. Abī Ṣa'ṣa'ah (of Banū 'Adī b. al-Najjār)* 38
Ayyūb b. Abī Tamīmah Kaysān al-Sakhtiyānī* 78
Azhar b. 'Abd 'Awf 90
'Azzāl b. Shamwīl al-Quraẓī 37

B

Bābawayh 112–14
Bādhān (governor of Yemen) 112, 114
Badr, battle of 18, 21, 60, 98, 167, 183
Badr b. Fazārah, Banū [T] 96
Bahrā' [T] 153
al-Baḥrayn [P] 99
Bakr b. 'Abd Manāt b. Kinānah, Banū [T] xviii–xix, 56, 86, 160–63, 175–77
Bakr b. Sawādah al-Judhāmī* 148
al-Balādhurī xxii
Bal'ajlān [T]; *see* al-'Ajlān
Balḥārith [T]; *see* al-Ḥārith b. al-Khazraj
Balī [T] 146, 153
Balmuṣṭaliq [T]; *see* al-Muṣṭaliq
al-Balqā' [P] 153, 156
Balqayn [T] 153
al-Barā' b. 'Āzib 74, 88

Barīrah (slave girl) 62
Bashīr b. Muḥammad b. ʻAbdallāh b. Zayd* 133
Bashīr b. Sa'd 132, 133, 138
al-Batrā' [P] 42
al-Bayḍā' [P] 126
Bayraḥā (palace in Medina) [P] 66
beard, shaving of 112–13
Bedouins 67, 68, 78, 94
Bilāl 47, 122, 125
Bi'r Annā (*or* Unā) [P] 28–29
Bīshah [P] 159
bishop, Christian 104–5
Bishr b. al-Barā' b. Ma'rūr 123–24; mother of (Umm Bishr) 124
Bishr b. Mu'ādh* 80
Bishr b. Sufyān al-Ka'bī 70
blood money (*diyah*) 55, 91, 161, 181, 184, 190
booty (*fay'*) 123, 130; division of 38–39; gifts to women from 126
bride gift/price (*ṣadāq*) 92, 110, 149
Bu'āth, battle of 36
Budayl b. Warqā' al-Khuzā'ī 75–76, 162, 163, 164, 168, 171, 175
Bunānah (wife of al-Ḥakam al-Quraẓī) 41
Buraydah b. al-Ḥuṣayb al-Aslamī* 119, 120
Buraydah b. Sufyān b. Farwah al-Aslamī* 85
Buṣrā [P] xviii, 101
Byzantines xi, xviii, 12, 153; *see also* Romans

C

Caesar (designation of Roman/Byzantine emperor) 16, 77, 94, 98, 100
calendar, Islamic xxii
circumcision 101–2
Constantinople [P] 106–7
Copts 114
Cross, Great (regained by Heraclius) 100–1

D

Ḍaghāṭir (bishop) 106
al-Ḍaḥḥāk b. Makhlad* 148
Damascus [P] 107
daraqah (kind of shield) 84, 118
al-Darb [P] 107
Dhakwān Abū Ṣāliḥ* 148
Dhanab Naqamā [P] 14, 15
Dhāt Aṭlāḥ [P], raid on 143
Dhāt al-Salāsil, expedition of 146–47
Dhū Athīr [P] 46
Dhū al-Faqār (sword of 'Alī) 120 n. 499
Dhū al-Ḥulayfah [P] 71, 90
Dhū al-Limmah (horse of Maḥmūd b. Maslamah) 50
Dhū al-Marwah [P] 91
Dhū Qarad [P], expedition to xv, 43–51
Dhū al-Qaṣṣah [P], raid on 93
Dhū Ṭuwā [P] 70, 176
Dhu'ayb b. al-Aswad b. Razn al-Dīlī 160–61
Dhūbāb [P] 11
Dhubyān [T] 5 n. 18
Diḥyah b. Khalīfah al-Kalbī 28, 29, 94, 98, 100, 104–6, 117
al-Dīl (of Banū Bakr b. 'Abd Manāt b. Kinānah), Banū [T] 160–61
Ḍirār b. al-Khaṭṭāb b. Mirdās (of Banū Muḥārib b. Fihr) 18
diyah; see blood money
dreams xvi, 62, 101, 102, 122
Duldul (mule) 131
Dūmat al-Jandal [P]; expedition to xi, 4–5; raid on 95

E

elephant (God's restraining from Mecca) 73
Emigrants (*muhājirūn*) 10, 50, 52, 60, 68, 70, 80, 120, 146, 147, 168, 174, 175, 176
Ethiopia/Ethiopians xi, 108, 109, 180; *see also* Negus

eunuch (sent by al-Muqawqis) 131

F

Fadak [P] 123, 128, 129, 132; raid on 95
Fākhitah bt. al-Walīd (wife of Ṣafwān b. Umayyah) 185
al-Fākih b. al-Mughīrah (paternal uncle of Khālid b. al-Walīd) 189, 191
Fāri' (fortress of Ḥassān b. Thābit) [P] 22–23, 56
Fartanā (singing girl of 'Abdallāh b. Khaṭal) 179–81
Fāṭimah bt. Muḥammad (daughter of the Prophet) 164–65
fay'; *see* booty
Fazārah, Banū [T] 5 n. 18, 8, 96–97
Fihr, Banū [T] 178
Fire (of Hell) 46, 55, 125, 152
flogging 63
al-Furay'ah (mother of Ḥassān b. Thābit) 65

G

Gabriel (angel) xv, 12, 27–29, 83, 145
Gaza [P] 102
Gehenna [P] 37
al-Ghābah [P] 13, 43, 44, 149
Ghālib b. 'Abdallāh al-Laythī al-Kalbī 132–33, 139, 140, 142
al-Ghamr [P], raid on 93
Ghanm (clan of al-Aws), Banū [T] 29
Ghanm (clan of Ḥadas), Banū [T] 159
ghashyah (fainting spell accompanying revelation) 3, 63
Ghassān, Banū [T] xviii, 98, 107–8
Ghaṭafān [T] xiv, xv, 5 n. 18, 8, 14–15, 17, 23–25, 27, 30, 43, 47, 51, 116, 133
Ghifār, Banū [T] 43, 51, 177, 186
al-Ghumayṣā' [P] 189
Ghurāb (mountain near Medina) [P] 42
Ghurān [P] 42–43
Greeks; *see* al-Aṣfar; Romans

H

Ḥabīb b. Abī Aws* 144
Ḥabīb b. 'Uyaynah b. Ḥiṣn 50
Ḥadas [T] 159
ḥadd (limit, prescribed punishment) 63 n. 252
Hadl, Banū [T] 32
al-Ḥaḍramī, Banū [T] 160
Ḥafṣ b. Fulān 79
Ḥafṣah bt. 'Umar (wife of the Prophet) xii
ḥajafah (kind of shield) 84
al-Ḥajjāj b. 'Ilāṭ al-Sulamī al-Bahzī 126–28
al-Ḥajūn [P] 175
al-Ḥakam b. Bashīr* 67
al-Ḥakam al-Quraẓī 41
al-Ḥakam b. 'Utaybah* 134
Ḥakīm b. Ḥakīm b. 'Abbād b. Ḥunayf* 189
Ḥakīm b. Ḥizām 168, 171, 174–75
Ḥalīmah (woman of Muzaynah) 93
Ḥalyah [P] 191
Ḥamnah bt. Jaḥsh 61, 63
Ḥamzah b. 'Abd al-Muṭṭalib 182
Ḥanīfah b. Lujaym, Banū [T] 98 n. 425
Ḥarb b. Umayyah (of Quraysh) [T] 98
al-Ḥārith, daughter of (of Banū al-Najjār) 35
al-Ḥārith b. 'Abd Manāt b. Kinānah, Banū [T] 13 n. 74, 78, 176
al-Ḥārith b. 'Abd al-Muṭṭalib 168 n. 700, 169
al-Ḥārith b. Abī Ḍirār 51
al-Ḥārith b. Abī Shimr al-Ghassānī 98
al-Ḥārith b. 'Awf b. Abī Ḥārithah al-Murrī 8, 17, 133
al-Ḥārith b. Aws 21
al-Ḥārith b. Hishām b. al-Mughīrah al-Makhzūmī, uncles of* 160
al-Ḥārith b. al-Khazraj, Banū [T] 15, 66
al-Ḥārith b. Mālik (Ibn al-Barṣā') al-Laythī 140–41
Ḥārithah b. al-Ḥārith (of al-Aws), Banū [T] 10, 16–17, 19, 49, 118, 123, 129
Hārūn b. Isḥāq* 87

harwalah (quick walk) 135
al-Ḥasan b. ʿAlī b. Abī Ṭālib 164–65
al-Ḥasan b. ʿUmārah* 134
al-Ḥasan b. Yaḥyā* 44, 69, 79, 83, 97
Hāshim (clan of Quraysh), Banū [T] 187, 188
Ḥassān b. Thābit al-Anṣārī 22–23, 63–66, 131, 166, 186
Ḥāṭib b. Abī Baltaʿah al-Lakhmī 98, 100, 131, 166–67
hātif (mysterious voice) 36
Hawāzin [T] 170, 175, 176; raid on "rear of" 131
Hawdhah b. ʿAlī al-Ḥanafī 98, 99
Hawdhah b. Qays al-Wāʾilī 7
Ḥazn b. Abī Wahb 97
heavens, seven (*raqīʿ*) 35
Hebrew (language) 105
Hell; *see* Fire; Gehenna
Heraclius (Byzantine emperor) 100–6, 153, 156
Ḥibbān b. Qays b. al-ʿAriqah (of Banū ʿĀmir b. Luʾayy) 20, 21
ḥijāb (curtain) 19, 32, 39, 59
Ḥijāz [P] 37, 53, 102, 112, 122, 126
Hilāl, Banū [T] 131
Ḥimās b. Qays b. Khālid al-Bakrī 177–78; wife of 177, 178
Ḥimṣ [P] 101, 107
Ḥimyar, language of 114
Hind bt. ʿUtbah b. Rabīʿah (wife of Abū Sufyān b. Ḥarb) 181–83
al-Ḥīrah [P] 12, 13
al-Ḥisāʾ [P] 155
Hishām b. ʿAbd al-Malik* 69
Hishām b. Ṣubābah 51, 55–56
Hishām b. ʿUrwah b. al-Zubayr* 119, 174
Ḥismā [P], raid on 94
Holy Spirit (*Rūḥ al-Qudus*, Gabriel) 83
House of Assembly (*Dār al-Nadwah*) [P] 134
Hubayrah b. Abī Wahb al-Makhzūmī 18, 185–86
Ḥubayshah (woman of Banū Jadhīmah) 191–92
al-Ḥudaybiyah [P] 67, 69–70, 73–75, 81, 83, 115, 128; treaty of xvi–xviii, 85–90, 92, 98, 100, 104, 161, 162, 163, 175; year of 44, 68
Ḥudaylah, palace of Banū [P] 66
Ḥudhayfah b. al-Yamān (Abū ʿAbdallāh) 10, 25–27
Hudhayl [T] 188
al-Ḥulayfah [P] 167
al-Ḥulays b. ʿAlqamah (or b. Zabbān) 77–78
Ḥunayn [P] xix, 176
Ḥuraqah (of Juhaynah) [T] 132
Hurmuz (Persian emperor) 111
Ḥusayl b. Nuwayrah al-Ashjaʿī 133
Ḥusayn b. ʿAbdallāh b. ʿUbaydallāh b. ʿAbbās* 171
al-Ḥuwayrith b. Nuqaydh b. Wahb b. ʿAbd b. Quṣayy 179, 181
Ḥuwayṭib b. ʿAbd al-ʿUzzā b. Abī Qays b. ʿAbd Wudd b. Naṣr b. Mālik b. Ḥisl 79, 80, 136
Ḥuyayy b. Akhṭab al-Naḍarī 7, 14–15, 30, 35–37
hypocrites (*munāfiqūn*) xi, xvii, 8, 9, 12, 13, 16, 33 n. 148, 54, 61, 167

I

Ibn ʿAbbās*; *see* ʿAbdallāh b. ʿAbbās
Ibn ʿAbd al-Aʿlā*; *see* Muḥammad b. ʿAbd al-Aʿlā
Ibn ʿAbdallāh b. Abī Ḥadrad al-Aslamī* 191
Ibn Abī Aḥmad 167
Ibn Abī al-ʿAwjāʾ al-Sulamī 138
Ibn Abī ʿAwn* 133
Ibn Abī Dhiʾb (Muḥammad b. ʿAbd al-Raḥmān b. al-Mughīrah)* 137
Ibn Abī Ḥadrad; *see* ʿAbdallāh b. Abī Ḥadrad
Ibn Abī al-Ḥuqayq 117, 122; fortress of; *see* al-Qamūṣ
Ibn Abī Quḥāfah; *see* Abū Bakr
Ibn Abzā*; *see* ʿAbd al-Raḥmān b. Abzā
Ibn al-Akwaʿ; *see* Salamah (b. ʿAmr) b. al-Akwaʿ

Ibn al-Ash'ar al-Ka'bī; *see* Khunays
Ibn Bashshār*; *see* Muḥammad b. Bashshār
Ibn Bishr*; *see* Muḥammad b. Bishr
Ibn Hishām xx, xxii
Ibn Ḥumayd xx, 5, 6, 13, 17, 19, 20, 22, 25, 27, 31, 34, 36, 38, 40, 41, 43, 49, 50, 51, 55, 56, 57, 58, 63, 65, 66, 67, 68, 70, 71, 72, 74, 76, 77, 78, 81, 82, 85, 89, 90, 96, 98, 99, 100, 104, 105, 106, 108, 111, 115, 116, 117, 119, 121, 122, 124, 125, 128, 129, 132, 133, 134, 135, 136, 138, 140, 142, 143, 146, 149, 151, 152, 155, 156, 158, 159, 160, 161, 166, 168, 176, 177, 178, 181, 184, 185, 186, 187, 188, 189, 191, 192
Ibn Isḥāq xx, 6, 8, 13, 17, 19, 20, 22, 23, 25, 27, 29, 30, 31, 32, 33, 34, 35, 36, 38, 40, 41, 43, 44, 48, 49, 50, 51, 54, 55, 56, 57, 58, 63, 65, 66, 67, 68, 70, 72, 74, 76, 77, 78, 81, 82, 84, 85, 89, 90, 91, 92, 96, 98, 99, 100, 104, 105, 106, 107, 108, 109, 111, 112, 113, 115, 116, 117, 119, 121, 122, 124, 125, 126, 128, 129, 132, 133, 134, 135, 136, 138, 140, 142, 143, 146, 149, 151, 152, 155, 156, 158, 159, 160, 161, 162, 166, 168, 171, 176, 177, 178, 181, 184, 185, 186, 187, 188, 189, 190, 191, 192
Ibn Jurayj ('Abd al-Malik b. 'Abd al-'Azīz)* 148
Ibn al-Khaṭṭāb; *see* 'Umar b. al-Khaṭṭāb
Ibn al-Muthannā* 70, 148
Ibn al-Qa'qā'* 151
Ibn Sa'd*; *see* Muḥammad b. Sa'd
Ibn 'Umar*; *see* 'Abdallāh b. 'Umar
Ibn 'Umārah*; *see* Muḥammad b. 'Umārah
Ibn Wahb*; *see* 'Abdallāh b. Wahb
Ibn Wakī'*; *see* Sufyān
Ibn Zayd*; *see* 'Abd al-Raḥmān b. Zayd
Ibn Zunaym 80; *see also* Zunaym
Ibrāhīm b. Ja'far* 5
Ibrāhīm b. Muḥammad (son of the Prophet) 100
Ibrāhīm b. Sa'īd al-Jawharī* 139–40
Iḍam [P], raid to 151–52
'iddah (period before remarriage of divorced woman) 3 n. 6
idols, destruction of 187–88
Ignorance, Time of; *see jāhiliyyah*
iḥrām (pilgrim garb, state of ritual consecration) xiii, xvii, 68, 136 n. 578, 171
'Ikrimah (*mawlā* of Ibn 'Abbās)* 78, 81, 171
'Ikrimah b. Abī Jahl al-Makhzūmī 18, 24, 71–72, 162, 166, 177–80, 185
'Ikrimah b. 'Ammār al-Yamāmī* 44, 69, 80, 83, 97
Irāshah (subdivision of Balī) [T] 153
al-'Īṣ [P] 91; raid on 93
Isḥāq b. Yasār* 29, 57, 63
Ismā'īl b. Abī Khālid* 83
Israel, Children of [T] 36, 73
Isrā'īl b. Yūnus* 54, 88
Iyās b. Salamah b. al-Akwa' 44, 69, 79, 80, 82, 83, 97

J

Jabal b. Jawwāl al-Tha'labī 36
Jabbār b. Ṣakhr b. Khansā' al-Salimī 129
Jābir b. 'Abdallāh b. 'Amr b. Ḥarām al-Khazrajī al-Anṣārī* 69, 70, 83, 84, 118, 129, 147, 148
Jacob 63
al-Jadd b. Qays al-Salimī al-Anṣārī 83, 84
Jadhīmah b. 'Āmir b. 'Abd Manāt b. Kinānah, Banū [T], expedition to 188–91
Ja'far b. Abī al-Mughīrah 71
Ja'far b. Abī Ṭālib xviii, 108–9, 144, 152, 156–59
Ja'far b. Maḥmūd (father of Ibrāhīm b. Ja'far)* 5
Jaḥdam (of Banū Jadhīmah) 189–90
jāhiliyyah (pagan times, time of ignorance) 22, 23, 36, 76, 161, 181, 184, 189–91

Jahjāh b. Sa'īd al-Ghifārī 51, 52
Jaḥsh b. Ri'āb 1 n. 1
Jamīlah bt. Thābit b. Abī al-Aqlaḥ 94–95
al-Jamūm [P], raid on 93
al-Janāḥ (horse of 'Ukkāshah b. Miḥṣan) 50
al-Jār [P] 110
jashīshah (gruel) 14
Jayfar b. Julandā al-Azdī 99, 142
Jerusalem [P] 101
Jesus 108–9; disciples of 99
Jews xi, xiv–xv, 7, 8, 22, 24, 30, 54, 95, 101, 116, 122, 126, 129, 130; *see also* Judaism; Sabbath; Torah
Jibrīl; *see* Gabriel
jilbāb (type of garment) 52, 59, 65
al-Jināb [P], raid to 133
jizyah (tax/tribute) 107, 142
Jordan [P] 107
Joseph 63
Ju'ayl, renamed 'Amr by Muḥammad 9
Judaism 39
Juddah [P] 184–85
Judhām [T] 94, 146, 153
Juhaynah [T] 132, 147, 174, 177, 178, 187
Jumaḥ (clan of Quraysh), Banū [T] 184
Junaydib b. al-Adla' (or al-Athwa') al-Hudhalī 184
Jundab b. Makīth al-Juhanī 140, 141
al-Juruf [P] 13
Jusham b. Mu'āwiyah, Banū [T] 149
Juwayriyah bt. al-Ḥārith b. Abī Ḍirār (wife of the Prophet) xii–xiii, 51, 56–57

K

Ka'b b. 'Abd al-Ashhal, Banū [T] 49
Ka'b b. 'Amr (of Khuzā'ah), Banū [T] 162–63, 166, 175–76
Ka'b b. Asad al-Quraẓī 14–15, 30, 35, 37
Ka'b b. Lu'ayy (of Quraysh) [T] 75
Ka'b b. Qurayẓah, Banū [T] 37
Ka'bah xix, 68, 75, 77, 78, 82, 91, 128, 137, 173, 174, 178; Black Stone of 135; custodianship of (*sidānah*) 181
Kadā' [P] 163, 176
al-Kadīd [P] 139–40, 168
Kalb b. 'Awf b. 'Āmir b. Layth b. Bakr, Banū [T] 51
Kathīr b. 'Abdallāh b. 'Amr b. 'Awf al-Muzanī* 10
al-Katībah (fortress at Khaybar) [P] 117 n. 489, 123, 128
Kavādh II Shērōē (Qubādh II Shīrawayh); *see* Shīrawayh
al-Khabaṭ, expedition of 147–49
Khadījah (wife of the Prophet) 2 n. 5, 94 n. 400
al-Khaḍrā' (squadron of the Prophet's troops) 174
Khālid b. Sa'īd b. al-'Āṣ 109–10
Khālid b. Sumayr* 157
Khālid b. al-Walīd b. al-Mughīrah 70–72, 143, 145–46, 157, 159, 174–78, 187–91; named "Sword of God" 158
Khālid b. Yasār* 106
Khallād b. Suwayd b. Tha'labah b. 'Amr b. Balḥārith b. al-Khazraj 40, 41
al-Khandamah [P] 177, 178
al-Khaṭṭāb (father of 'Umar b. al-Khaṭṭāb) 172
al-Khawāniq [P] 191
Khawwāt b. Jubayr 15
Khaybar [P] xv, 48, 95, 110; expedition to xi–xii, xvii, 116–26, 128–30, 133, 152
al-Khazraj [T] 15, 33, 55, 61, 188
Khirāsh b. Umayyah b. al-Faḍl al-Ka'bī al-Khuzā'ī 81, 89, 184
Khubayb b. 'Adī 16, 42
Khudrah, Banū 34 n. 152
khums (fifth of booty) 38–39, 128, 130
Khunays b. Khālid (al-Ash'ar) b. Rabī'ah b. Aṣram b. Ḍabīs b. Ḥabashiyyah b. Ka'b b. 'Amr 176, 177–78
Khurrakhusrah 112–14; called Dhū al-Mi'jazah 114
Khusrau II Parvīz; *see* Kisrā

Khuzā'ah, Banū [T] xviii–xix, 41, 51, 75, 86, 92, 160–63, 166, 171–72
Kinānah, Banū [T] 13, 18, 77, 165, 187
Kinānah b. al-Rabī' b. Abī al-Ḥuqayq al-Naḍarī 7, 117, 122–23
Kisrā (Persian emperor) 12, 13, 16, 77, 98, 110–14
Kudā [P] 176
al-Kūfah [P] 25
Kulthūm b. al-Aswad b. Razn al-Dīlī 160–61
Kurā' al-Ghamīm [P] 43, 71
Kurz b. Jābir b. Ḥisl b. al-Ajabb b. Ḥabīb b. 'Amr b. Shaybān b. Muḥārib al-Fihrī 97–98, 176–78

L

labbayka (pilgrim's cry) 77, 79
Lakhm [T] 98, 153, 159
al-Lāt (pagan goddess) 76, 169
al-Layth b. Sa'd al-Miṣrī* 69
Lesser Pilgrimage of the Pact (*'umrat al-qaḍiyyah*), for Lesser Pilgrimage of Fulfillment (*'umrat al-qaḍā'*) 134 n. 559, 138
Liḥyān, Banū [T] 16 n. 84; expedition against xv, 42, 43
al-Līt [P] 177
Lu'ayy (ancestor of clans of Quraysh) 186

M

Ma'āb [P] 153, 154
Ma'ān [P]; *see* Mu'ān
Ma'bad b. Ka'b b. Mālik al-Anṣārī* 29
al-Madā'in [P] 12, 13
al-Madhād [P] 10
Magians 111; *see also* Zoroastrians
Maḥmiyah b. al-Jaz' al-Zubaydī 151
Maḥmūd b. Maslamah al-Ashhalī 49, 50, 87, 117, 123
Makhīḍ [P] 42
Makhramah b. Nawfal 171
Makhzūm (clan of Quraysh), Banū [T] 18, 19, 22
Mālik (of Banū al-Muṣṭaliq) 56
Mālik b. 'Abbād al-Ḥaḍramī 160
Mālik b. Ḥudhayfah b. Badr 96
Mālik b. Rāfilah 153, 159
Ma'mar b. Rāshid* 68, 69, 74, 88
Manāt (pagan goddess) 188
al-Marāḍ [P] 5
Marḥab the Jew 118, 121
Māriyah the Copt (wife of the Prophet) xiii, 100, 131
Marr al-Ẓahrān [P] 138, 168, 171, 174, 175
martyrdom 46, 67, 154, 155, 158
Marwān b. al-Ḥakam* 68, 69, 74, 88, 90, 161
Marwān b. 'Uthmān b. Abī Sa'īd b. al-Mu'allā* 124
Mary (mother of Jesus) 108
Mas'adah b. Ḥakamah b. Mālik b. Badr 96
Mashārif [P] 156
Mas'ūd b. Rukhaylah b. Nuwayrah b. Ṭarīf b. Suḥmah b. 'Abdallāh b. Hilāl b. Khalāwah b. Ashja' b. Rayth b. Ghaṭafān 8
mawlā, pl. *mawālī* (client[s]) 6, 33, 34, 81, 90, 121, 124, 133, 137, 144, 162, 179; *mawlāh* (f.) 167, 179, 181
al-Mayfa'ah [P] 132
Maymūn (Abū 'Abdallāh)* 119
Maymūnah bt. al-Ḥārith (wife of the Prophet) xiii, 136, 137
Mecca xvi–xvii, xix, 7, 42–44, 55, 56, 71–73, 80–82, 86, 88, 90–92, 97, 126, 127, 134, 136, 138, 189; conquest of 40, 145, 151, 152, 160–87, 189, 192; sacred territory (*ḥaram*) surrounding xvii, 161–62, 176
Medina xi, xiv–xvi, xix, 5, 8, 17, 27, 41–45, 48, 51–54, 57, 59, 60, 66, 67, 71, 90, 91, 93, 94, 97, 110, 112, 115, 116, 124, 129, 130, 132, 133, 137, 138, 143, 148, 152, 159, 160,

163, 164, 168, 169, 171; date harvest of xiv, 17; fortresses/strongholds of 10, 14, 15, 19, 22, 23, 28, 30; lava flows surrounding 11–12; marketplace of 35; mosque of 29, 31–33, 40, 90, 162, 165
mighfar (neck armor) 21, 76, 121
Mikraz (of al-'Abalāt) 80
Mikraz b. Ḥafṣ b. al-Akhyaf al-'Āmirī 78, 87, 138
Minā [P] 71
al-Miqdād b. 'Amr (al-Aswad) al-Kindī 46, 49
Miqsam* 134
Miqyas b. Ṣubābah 55–56, 179, 180; sister of 180
Mirdās b. Nahīk 132
Misṭaḥ b. Uthāthah 60, 61, 63, 64
al-Miswar b. Makhramah* 68, 69, 74, 88, 90, 161
Moses 145
Mother of the Faithful (title of wives of the Prophet) 19, 40
Mu'ādh b. Mā'iṣ b. Qays b. Khaldah 49
Mu'ādh b. Muḥammad al-Anṣārī* 138
Mu'ān [P] 153, 154
Mu'arriḍ b. al-Ḥajjāj b. 'Ilāṭ al-Sulamī 126
Mu'attib b. Qushayr (of Banū 'Amr b. 'Awf) 16
Mu'āwiyah b. Abī Sufyān 92
Muḍar [T] 65, 187
Mudlij [T] 189
al-Mughīrah b. Shu'bah 76
Muḥallim b. Jaththāmah b. Qays al-Laythī 151
Muḥammad (the Prophet) 91–97, 101–3, 131–33, 139–41, 143–51, 188–91; at Battle of the Trench xiv, 5–27; called "king of Ḥijāz" xi, 122, 124; conquers Mecca xii, xix, 160–87, 192; expedition to Banū Liḥyān 42, 43; expedition to Banū al-Muṣṭaliq 51–57; expedition to Banū Qurayẓah xv, 27–41; expedition to Dhū Qarad 43–51; expedition to Dūmat al-Jandal 4, 5; expedition to Khaybar 116–24, 126–30; expedition to al-Muraysī' 41; expedition to Mu'tah 152–60; expedition to Wādī al-Qurā 124, 125; on Farewell Pilgrimage 135; foretold in Christian scriptures 105–6; on Lesser Pilgrimage of Fulfillment 133–38; and lie/slander against 'Ā'ishah xii, xv–xvi, 57–67; marries Juwayriyah bt. al-Ḥārith xii–xiii, 57; marries Maymūnah bt. al-Ḥārith 136–37; marries Mulaykah bt. Dāwūd al-Laythiyyah 187; marries Umm Ḥabībah bt. Abī Sufyān 109–10; marries Zaynab bt. Jaḥsh xii–xiii, 1–4, 19 n. 96; messages to foreign rulers xi–xii, xvii–xviii, 98–100, 104–14, 142; migraines 120; pilgrimage halted at al-Ḥudaybiyah/treaty of al-Ḥudaybiyah xvi–xvii, 67–90, 115, 134, 137
Muḥammad b. 'Abd al-A'lā al-Ṣan'ānī* 68, 74, 76, 78, 88, 92
Muḥammad b. 'Amr* 20, 21, 29, 34, 39
Muḥammad b. Bashshār* 10, 119
Muḥammad b. Bishr* 20, 29, 34, 39
Muḥammad b. Ḥumayd*; *see* Ibn Ḥumayd
Muḥammad b. Ibrāhīm b. al-Ḥārith al-Taymī* 66, 94, 138, 149
Muḥammad b. Isḥāq*; *see* Ibn Isḥāq
Muḥammad b. Ja'far (Ghundar)* 119
Muḥammad b. Ja'far b. al-Zubayr* 36, 56, 152, 159, 166, 167, 184
Muḥammad b. Ka'b al-Quraẓī* 6, 25, 85
Muḥammad b. Khālid Ibn 'Athmah* 10
Muḥammad b. Manṣūr* 79, 80
Muḥammad b. Maslamah al-Anṣārī 32, 93, 118, 123, 138
Muḥammad b. al-Munkadir* 83
Muḥammad b. Muslim al-Zuhrī*; *see* al-Zuhrī
Muḥammad b. Sa'd* xxii, 69
Muḥammad b. Thawr* 68, 74, 88
Muḥammad b. 'Umar*; *see* al-Wāqidī

Muḥammad b. 'Umārah al-Asadī* 79, 80, 82
Muḥammad b. Yaḥyā b. Ḥabbān* 1, 51
Muḥammad b. Yaḥyā b. Sahl b. Abī Ḥathmah* 150
Muḥammad b. Yazīd* 83
Muḥārib b. Fihr (of Quraysh), Banū [T] 18, 176
Muḥayyiṣah b. Mas'ūd al-Ḥārithī 123, 128
Muḥriz b. Naḍlah (called al-Akhram, Qumayr) 49–50
Mujāhid* 67, 89, 136
mukātabah (manumission by contract) 57
al-Mulawwiḥ, Banū [T], expedition against 139–40
Mulaykah bt. Dāwūd al-Laythiyyah (wife of the Prophet) 187
Munabbih al-Khuzā'ī 162
Munabbih b. 'Uthmān b. 'Ubayd b. al-Sabbāq b. 'Abd al-Dār 19
munāfiqūn; *see* hypocrites
al-Mundhir (son of Salmā bt. Qays) 38
al-Mundhir b. al-Ḥārith b. Abī Shimr al-Ghassānī 107–8
al-Mundhir b. Sāwā al-'Abdī 99, 142
Munqidh, Banū [T] 177
al-Muqawqis 98, 100, 114, 131
al-Murār Pass [P] 73
al-Muraysī' [P] xv, 41, 51, 52
Murrah b. 'Awf, Banū [T] 8, 156; raid against 132
Mūsā b. Muḥammad* 94
Mūsā b. 'Ubaydah* 79, 82
Muṣ'ab b. al-Miqdām* 87
al-Musayyab b. Muslim al-Awdī* 120
al-Mushallal* 141, 188
mushrikūn; *see* polytheism/polytheists Muslim b. 'Abdallāh b. Khubayb al-Juhanī* 140
mustache, clipping of 112–13
al-Muṣṭaliq, Banū [T] 13 n. 74; expedition against xiii, xv, 41, 51–52, 55–58
Mu'tah [P], expedition to xi, 129, 137, 152–60
Muzaynah [T] 93, 167, 168, 177, 186

N

al-Nadā [P] 11
al-Naḍīr, Banū [T] xiv, 6, 7, 32; treasure of 122
Nāfi' (*mawlā* of 'Abdallāh b. 'Umar)* 137
Nā'im (fortress at Khaybar) [P] 117
Najd [P] 14, 39; raid to 131
Nājiyah b. 'Umayr b. Ya'mar b. Dārim 74
al-Najjār (of al-Khazraj), Banū [T] 35, 56, 63
Najrān [P] 185–86
Nakhib [P] 112
Nakhlah [P] 187
Nāmūs, Great (Angel Gabriel) 145
Naq'ā' [P] 53
al-Naqī' [P] 53
Naṭāh (fortress at Khaybar) [P] 117 n. 489, 123, 128
Nawfal b. 'Abdallāh b. al-Mughīrah al-Makhzūmī 18–19
Nawfal b. Mu'āwiyah al-Dīlī 161–62
Negus (ruler of Ethiopia) xviii, 77, 98, 108–10, 143–45
Nīq al-'Uqāb [P] 169, 171
Nu'aym b. Mas'ūd b. 'Āmir b. Unayf b. Tha'labah b. Qunfudh b. Hilāl b. Khalāwah b. Ashja' b. Rayth b. Ghaṭafān 23–25
al-Nu'mān b. Muqarrin al-Muzanī 10
Numaylah b. 'Abdallāh 180

P

Palestine [P] 107
Paradise 26, 46, 125, 126
Persia/Persians xi, xiv, xviii, 100–1, 111–12, 114; *see also* Kisrā
Pharaoh 145
Pilgrimage xix, 41, 115, 137; of Fulfillment (*'umrat al-qaḍā'*) 67, 133–38;

lesser ('*umrah*) 67, 75; right of supplying water to pilgrims (*siqāyah*) 181
polytheism/polytheists 17, 40, 41, 45, 79–81, 87, 89, 92, 97, 115, 134, 137, 164, 178, 179
prayer, afternoon 28, 29; call to 125, 158; dawn 97, 125; evening 29; leading, as sign of authority 147; midafternoon 140; morning 32; peace at end of 125; for rain 95; shortened on journey 192
pulpit (*minbar*) 131, 158

Q

al-Qamūṣ (fortress at Khaybar) [P] 117, 122
al-Qa'qā' b. 'Abdallāh b. Abī Ḥadrad al-Aslamī* 151
al-Qārah [T] 13 n. 74, 16
al-Qāsim b. 'Abdallāh b. 'Umar* 83
al-Qāsim b. Bishr b. Ma'rūf* 157
Qatādah al-Sadūsī* 80, 181
Qaṭarī cloth 121
Qaynuqā', Banū [T] 33, 54
Qays 'Aylān [T] 8, 149, 187
Qays b. al-Musaḥḥar al-Ya'murī 96
Qays b. Sa'd 148
qiblah (direction of prayer) 38, 142, 190
Quḍā'ah [T] 143, 146, 175
Qudayd [P] 41, 51, 140, 141, 170
Qur'ān xi, xiii, xvi, xviii, 62–64; *see* Index of Qur'ānic Verses
Quraybah (singing girl of 'Abdallāh b. Khaṭal?) 181
Quraybah bt. Abī Umayyah b. al-Mughīrah 92
Quraysh [T] xiv, xv, xvii–xix, 7, 8, 13–15, 18, 20, 23–27, 30, 40, 52, 68, 70, 72, 73, 75, 78–82, 84–87, 90–92, 112, 120, 126, 134–36, 138, 144, 161–63, 165–68, 170–71, 174–75, 179, 181–82, 187
Qurayẓah, Banū [T] xi, xiii, xiv, 14, 20, 22–26, 42; expedition against xiv–xv, 27–41
Qurḥ [P] 154
Quṭbah b. Qatādah al-'Udhrī 156, 159

R

Rabāḥ (slave of Muḥammad) 44
Rāfi' (*mawlā* of Khuzā'ah) 162
al-Raḥmān (the Merciful, name of God) 85
rajaz (poetic meter) 9, 45, 46, 118, 119, 120, 121, 141, 155, 178
al-Rajī' [P] 16, 42
al-Rajī' (near Khaybar) [P] 116
Ramaḍān, fasting in 168
Rāshid (*mawlā* of Ibn Abī Aws)* 143
Rayḥānah bt. 'Amr b. Khunāfah xiii, 39
al-Riḍwān (Good Pleasure), pledge of xvii, 82, 83
Rifā'ah b. Qays 149–50
Rifā'ah b. Shamwīl al-Quraẓī 38
Rifā'ah b. Zayd al-Judhāmī al-Ḍubaybī 124
Rifā'ah b. Zayd b. al-Tābūt 54
Romans 100, 101, 104–7, 154, 156; *see also* Byzantines
Rome [P] 105
Rufaydah 33
Ruhāṭ [P] 188
Rūmah [P] 13, 14

S

al-Ṣa'b b. Mu'ādh 117
Sabbath (Jewish day of rest) 24, 28, 30
Sa'd b. Abī Waqqāṣ 87
Sa'd b. Bakr, Banū [T], expedition against 95
Sa'd b. Hudhaym, Banū [T] 96
Sa'd b. Manī' (father of Muḥammad b. Sa'd)* 69
Sa'd b. Mu'ādh b. al-Nu'mān b. Imru al-Qays al-Ashhalī xv, 15–22, 29–30, 33–35, 39–40; mother of (Umm Sa'd) 19, 20

Sa'd b. 'Ubādah b. Dulaym al-Sā'idī 15–17, 61, 133, 176; mother of 5
Sa'd b. Zayd al-Ashhalī al-Anṣārī 39, 49, 188
ṣadāq; *see* bride gift/price
ṣadaqah (alms, poor rate) 142, 179
Sadūs al-Quḍā'ī 143
al-Safā [P] 182
Ṣafiyyah bt. 'Abd al-Muṭṭalib 22–23, 119
Ṣafiyyah bt. Ḥuyayy b. Akhṭab xiii, 117, 122, 127–28
Ṣafwān b. al-Mu'aṭṭal al-Sulamī 59–61, 64–67
Ṣafwān b. Umayyah 92, 162, 166, 177–78, 184–85
Sahm (clan of Aslam), Banū [T] 117
Sa'īd b. 'Abd al-Raḥmān b. Ḥassān b. Thābit al-Anṣārī* 186
Sa'īd b. Abī 'Arūbah* 80
Sa'īd b. Ḥurayth al-Makhzūmī 180
Sa'īd b. al-Musayyab* 58, 125
Sa'īd b. Shuraḥbīl al-Miṣrī* 69
Sa'īd b. Yaḥyā b. Sa'īd al-Umawī* 140, 191
Sā'idah b. Ka'b b. al-Khazraj, Banū [T] 15
saj' (rhymed prose) 159, 176
Ṣakhr b. 'Āmir b. Ka'b b. Sa'd b. Taym 60
Sal' [P] 14, 18, 48
Salām b. Abī al-Ḥuqayq al-Naḍarī 7
Salamah (b. 'Amr) b. al-Akwa' al-Aslamī 43–48, 49, 50, 69, 79, 80, 82–84, 96–97, 131
Salamah b. al-Faḍl xx, 6, 13, 17, 19, 20, 22, 25, 27, 31, 34, 36, 38, 40, 41, 43, 49, 50, 51, 55, 56, 57, 58, 63, 65, 66, 67, 68, 70, 72, 74, 76, 77, 78, 81, 82, 85, 89, 90, 96, 98, 99, 100, 104, 105, 106, 108, 111, 115, 116, 117, 119, 121, 122, 124, 125, 128, 129, 132, 133, 134, 135, 136, 138, 140, 142, 143, 146, 149, 151, 152, 155, 156, 158, 159, 160, 161, 166, 168, 176, 177, 178, 181, 184, 185, 186, 187, 188, 189, 191, 192
Salamah b. Hishām b. al-Mughīrah 160; wife of 160
Salamah b. al-Maylā' al-Juhanī 178
al-Salāsil [P] 146; *see also* Dhāt al-Salāsil
Sālim (*mawlā* of 'Abdallāh b. Muṭī')* 124
Salimah, Banū [T] 49, 50, 84, 129
Salīṭ b. 'Amr b. 'Abd Shams b. 'Abd Wudd al-'Āmirī 98, 99
Salīṭ b. Qays 38
Sallām b. Mishkam 123
Salmā (maidservant of the Prophet) 3
Salmā b. al-Aswad b. Razn al-Dīlī 160–61
Salmā bt. Qays (maternal aunt of the Prophet) 38
Salmān al-Fārisī xiv, 8, 10–12
Ṣan'ā' [P], palaces of 12
Sārah (*mawlāh* of 'Amr b. Hāshim b. 'Abd al-Muṭṭalib) 167, 179–81
Sarif [P] 137
Satan 186
satire (*hijā'*) 179
Sawdah bt. Zam'ah (wife of the Prophet) xii, 79 n. 340
al-Ṣawrān [P] 28
Sāyah [P] 43
al-Sha'bī*; *see* 'Āmir b. Sharāḥīl
shahādah (profession of faith) 173
al-Sha'm [P] 107; *see also* Syria
Shaybān (of Sulaym), Banū [T] 187–88
al-Shiqq (fortress at Khaybar) [P] 117 n. 489, 123, 128
Shīrawayh (son of Kisrā) 113, 114
Shu'bah* 70
Shujā' b. Wahb (of Banū Asad b. Khuzaymah) 93, 98, 107–8, 143
Shuraḥbīl b. 'Amr al-Ghassānī xviii
Sibā' b. 'Urfuṭah al-Ghifārī 5, 116
Sinān al-Juhanī 52
singing girls (*qaynah*, pl. *qiyān*) 179–80
Sīrīn the Copt 66, 131
soothsayer, woman (*kāhinah*) 159
Subay'ah bt. 'Abd Shams (mother of 'Urwah b. Mas'ūd al-Thaqafī) 76
Sufyān b. Wakī'* 20, 29, 34, 39, 88, 104
Suhām [P] 170
Suhayl b. 'Amr (Abū Yazīd) 78–81, 84–

87, 91, 162, 166, 177, 178
Ṣukhayrāt al-Yamām [P] 42
al-Sulālim (fortress at Khaybar) [P] 117, 123
Sulaym, Banū [T] 93, 168, 170, 173, 175, 186, 187, 188, 189; raid on 138
Sulaymān b. Ḥarb* 157
sunnah 39, 135
al-Suqyā [P] 171
Surdad [P] 170
Suwāʿ (pagan god) 188
Sword of God; *see* Khālid b. al-Walīd
Syria [P] xv–xviii, 91, 100, 102–4, 106–7, 137, 143, 146, 152–53, 155

T

al-Ṭabarī (Abū Jaʿfar Muḥammad b. Jarīr)* xx–xxi, 5, 34, 42, 67, 71, 114, 130, 131, 132, 138, 139, 143
Taghlamān [P] 5
al-Ṭāʾif [P] 112, 174
Ṭalḥah b. ʿUbaydallāh 21, 44; slave of 44, 48
Tamīm, Banū [T] 171 n. 710, 187
Tamīm b. Asad al-Khuzāʿī 162
al-Ṭaraf [P], raid on 94
tasbighah (neck armor) 21
Taym b. Ghālib, Banū [T] 179
Thābit b. Aqram (of Banū al-ʿAjlān) 93, 157
Thābit b. Qays b. (al-)Shammās al-Ḥārithī 36–38, 56–57, 66
al-Thaʿlab (camel of the Prophet) 81
Thaʿlabah, Banū [T] 94
Thaʿlabah (of Ḥadas), Banū [T] 159
Thaʿlabah b. Saʿyah al-Hadlī 32, 39
Thaqīf [T] 76, 170, 175, 176
Thawr b. Zayd* 124
Tihāmah [P] 13, 75, 189
Torah 7, 30
Trench, battle of the xiv, xvi, 5, 7–27, 29, 40, 41, 144
al-Ṭulaqāʾ (Those Whose Bonds Have Been Loosed) xix, 182
Tumāḍir bt. al-Aṣbagh 95
Turabah [P] 131
Turkish-style round tent (*qubbah turkiyyah*) 11; cf. 177 (*qubbah*, round tent)
Two Shaykhs, Fortress of (*Ujum al-Shaykhayn*) 10

U

ʿUbādah b. Mālik; *see* ʿAbāyah
ʿUbādah b. al-Ṣāmit, kinsman of 51, 56
ʿUbayd b. Zayd b. Ṣāmit (Abū ʿAyyāsh) 49
ʿUbaydallāh b. ʿAbd al-Raḥmān b. Mawhab* 137–38
ʿUbaydallāh b. ʿAbdallāh b. ʿUtbah b. Masʿūd* 58, 100, 104, 168, 192
ʿUbaydallāh b. Kaʿb b. Mālik al-Anṣārī* 6, 22, 43, 50
ʿUbaydallāh b. Mūsā* 79, 80, 82
ʿUbaydallāh b. ʿUmar b. al-Khaṭṭāb 92
ʿUdhrah, Banū [T] 146, 156
Uḥud [P] 14, 15, 191; battle of xiv, 18, 182
ʿUkāẓ [P] 75
ʿUkkāshah b. Miḥṣan 49, 50, 93
ʿUmān [P] 100, 142
ʿUmar b. Dharr al-Hamdānī* 67
ʿUmar b. al-Khaṭṭāb 21, 40, 51–52, 55, 71, 81–83, 85, 87, 92, 94–95, 119–20, 131, 146, 164, 165, 167, 172–73, 182–83; caliphate of 13, 181; expels Jews of Khaybar xv, 130
ʿUmar b. Mūsā b. al-Wajīh* 181
ʿUmārah b. ʿUqbah b. Abī Muʿayṭ 92
Umaymah bt. ʿAbd al-Muṭṭalib (mother of Zaynab bt. Jaḥsh) 1 n. 1, 4
ʿUmayr b. Wahb 184–85
Umayyah b. ʿAbd Shams (clan of Quraysh), Banū [T] 82 n. 354
Umm Ayyūb (wife of Abū Ayyūb Khālid b. Zayd) 63–64
Umm Ḥabībah bt. Abī Sufyān (wife of the Prophet) xiii, 109–10, 164

Umm Ḥakīm bt. al-Ḥārith b. Hishām (wife of 'Ikrimah b. Abī Jahl) 179–80, 185
Umm Hāni' (Hind) bt. Abī Ṭālib (wife of Hubayrah b. Abī Wahb) 186
Umm Kulthūm bt. 'Amr b. Jarwal al-Khuzā'iyyah 92
Umm Kulthūm bt. 'Uqbah b. Abī Mu'ayṭ 92
Umm Misṭaḥ bt. Abī Ruhm b. al-Muṭṭalib b. 'Abd Manāf 60
Umm Mujālid (mother of 'Ikrimah b. Abī Jahl) 166
Umm Qirfah (Fāṭimah bt. Rabī'ah b. Badr) 96; daughter of 96, 97
Umm Salamah (wife of the Prophet) xii, 31–32, 89, 160, 169
Umm Shaybah bt. Abī Ṭalḥah (wife of al-Ḥajjāj b. 'Ilāṭ al-Sulamī) 126
Umm Sulaym bt. Milḥān 131
'Uraynah, Banū [T], raid on 97
'Urwah b. Mas'ūd al-Thaqafī 75–77
'Urwah b. al-Zubayr b. al-'Awwām* 6, 36, 56, 57, 58, 68, 69, 74, 88, 90, 152, 159, 161, 166, 174, 184
Usāmah b. Zayd 61, 132
Usayd b. Ḥuḍayr al-Ashhalī 53, 61
Usayd b. Sa'yah 32
Usayd b. Zuhayr al-Ḥārithī 49
'Usfān [P] 43, 70, 163, 168
'Uthmān b. 'Affān 81, 82, 84, 178–79; caliphate of 13, 181
'Uthmān b. Ṭalḥah b. Abī Ṭalḥah al-'Abdarī 143, 146
'Uyaynah b. Ḥisn b. Ḥudhayfah b. Badr al-Fazārī 5, 8, 17, 43, 45, 133, 171
al-'Uzzā (pagan goddess) 187, 188

V

vision (*ru'yā*) 87

W

al-Wadā' Pass [P] 48
Wādī al-Qurā [P], expedition to 124–25; raid on 95–96
Wā'il, Banū [T] 7
Wakī' b. al-Jarrāḥ* 88
al-Walīd b. 'Uqbah b. Abī Mu'ayṭ 92
al-Wāqidī (Muḥammad b. 'Umar) xii, xvi, xviii, xx–xxii, 1, 4, 5, 8, 40, 41, 92, 93, 94, 95, 97, 107, 109, 113, 114, 131, 132, 133, 137, 138, 139, 142, 143, 147, 150, 152, 161, 170, 181, 184, 187, 188
Ward b. 'Amr (of Banū Sa'd b. Hudhaym) 96
al-Waṭīḥ (fortress at Khaybar) [P] 117, 123
al-Watīr 160–63
whale 147–49
women, as emigrants 92; gifts from booty to 126; swear allegiance after conquest of Mecca 182–84; *see also* allegiance, oath of; *ḥijāb*

Y

Ya'fūr (donkey) 131
Yaḥyā b. 'Abbād b. 'Abdallāh b. al-Zubayr* 22, 58, 156
Yaḥyā b. 'Abd al-'Azīz b. Sa'īd* 133
Yaḥyā b. 'Abdallāh b. Abī Qatādah* 139
Yaḥyā b. Ādam* 54, 104
Yaḥyā b. Sahl b. Abī Ḥathmah* 150
Yaḥyā b. Sa'īd al-Anṣārī* 149
Yaḥyā b. Sa'īd al-Qaṭṭān* 68–69, 74, 88
Yaḥyā b. Sa'īd al-Umawī* 140, 191
al-Yamāmah [P] 99
Ya'qūb b. Ibrāhīm* 68, 74, 76, 78, 88, 92
Ya'qūb al-Qummī* 71
Ya'qūb b. 'Utbah b. al-Mughīrah b. al-Akhnas b. Sharīq* 95, 133, 140, 191
Yasār (*mawlā* of the Prophet) 133
Yāsir the Jew 118–19
Yathrib [P] 13; *see also* Medina
Yayn [P] 42
Yazīd b. 'Abdallāh b. Qusayṭ* 31, 151
Yazīd b. Abī Ḥabīb al-Miṣrī* 99, 111, 112, 113, 143

Yazīd b. Jāriyah 94
Yazīd b. Rūmān (*mawlā* of family of al-Zubayr)* 6
Yazīd b. Ziyād* 25
Yazīd b. Zuray'* 80
Yemen [P] 112, 159, 179–80, 184–85, 189
Yumn [P] 133
Yūnus b. 'Abd al-A'lā* xii, 4, 83
Yūnus b. Bukayr* xx, 120, 171
Yūsuf b. Mūsā al-Qaṭṭān* 69

Z

Zabbār (name for al-Zubayr b. al-'Awwām, q.v.) 119
al-Zabīr b. Bāṭā al-Quraẓī 36–38
Ẓafār [P] 59
Zaghābah [P] 13 n. 73
Zayd b. Arqam 52–54, 155
Zayd b. Ḥārithah xii–xiii, xviii, 1 n. 1, 2–4, 93–96, 152, 156–58; called Zayd b. Muḥammad xiii, 2
Zaynab bt. al-Ḥārith 123–24
Zaynab bt. Jaḥsh (wife of the Prophet) xii–xiii, 1–4, 61
Zaynab bt. Khuzaymah (wife of the Prophet) xii
Zaynab bt. Muḥammad (daughter of the Prophet) 94, 131, 139
Zoroastrians 142; *see also* Magians
al-Zubayr b. al-'Awwām 41, 119, 122–23, 167, 175–76
al-Zuhrī (Muḥammad b. Muslim b. 'Abdallāh Ibn Shihāb)* 6, 17, 27, 36, 57, 58, 68, 69, 70, 73, 74, 76, 77, 84, 88, 90, 92, 99, 100, 104, 111, 125, 129, 130, 137, 161, 168, 185, 191, 192
Zunaym 81
Zurayq, Banū [T] 49

Index of Qur'ānic Verses*

Sūra	
2:58	*73*
2:65	*28*
2:156	*50, 59*
3:154	*36*
4:51–55	*7*
4:94	*151*
5:60	*28*
7:161	*73*
7:166	*28*
8:41	*128*
12:18	*63*
17:64	*123*
19:71	*152*
20:14	*125*
24:4	*63*
24:11	*64*
24:12	*64*
24:15	*64*
24:22	*64*
24:62	*9*

Sūra	
24:63–64	*9*
33:9	*26*
33:10	*16, 23*
33:12	*13*
33:13	*16*
33:22	*12*
33:37	*3, 4*
33:53	*19*
48:18	*82, 83*
48:24	*80, 81*
48:24–25	*72*
48:29	*40*
49:13	*181–82*
59:7	*128, 129*
60:1–4	*167–68*
60:10	*92*
60:12	*183*
63	*54*
63:8	*52, 54*
105	*73*

*Page numbers for this volume appear in italics.

9 780791 431504